D0926319

STORY BY
KIM HYUNG-MIN

ART BY
YANG KYUNG-IL

MARCH STORY

4

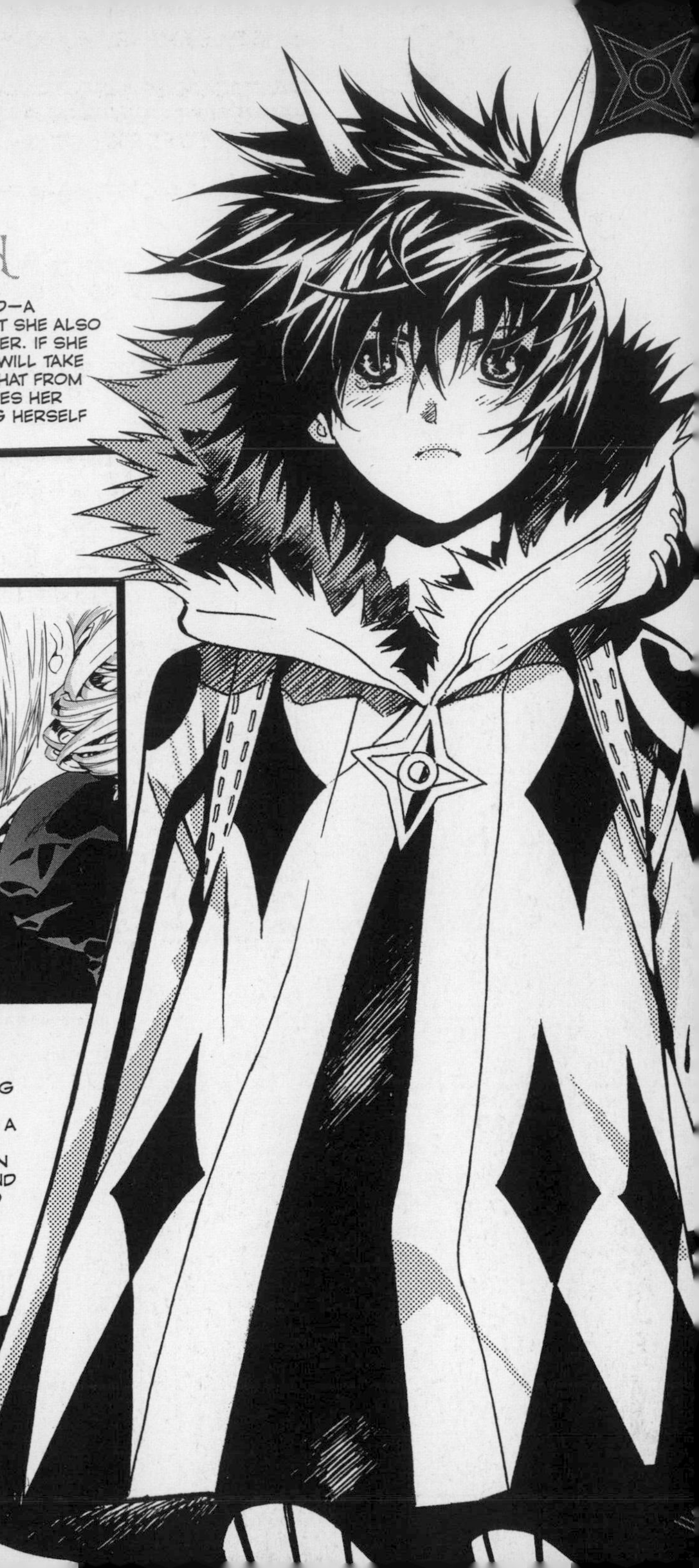

MARCH

MARCH IS A CISTE VIHAD—A HUNTER OF THE ILL—BUT SHE ALSO HARBORS ONE INSIDE HER. IF SHE FALLS IN LOVE, THE ILL WILL TAKE HER LIFE. TO PREVENT THAT FROM HAPPENING, MARCH HIDES HER TRUE GENDER, PASSING HERSELF OFF AS A BOY.

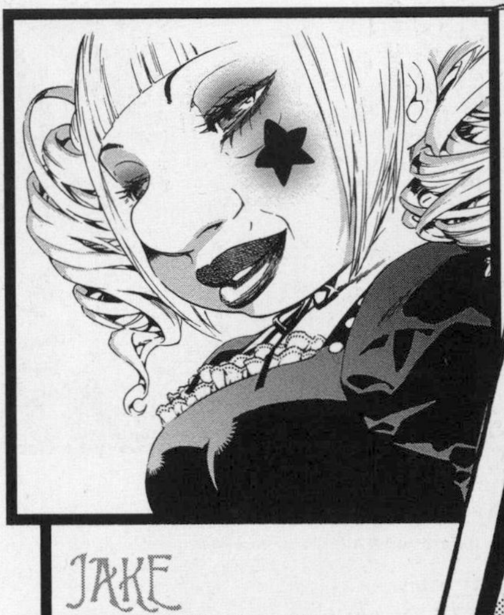

JAKE

A CISTE VIHAD, AS STRONG AS SHE IS UNIQUE, JAKE ALSO MAKES A LIVING AS A FORTUNE-TELLER. JAKE RESCUED MARCH FROM AN ILL AS A YOUNG CHILD AND IS THE ONLY PERSON WHO KNOWS MARCH'S SECRET.

STORY

IN 18TH CENTURY EUROPE...

MALICIOUS BEINGS CALLED ILL LURK SECRETLY IN CERTAIN OBJECTS, POISED TO TAKE POSSESSION OF HUMAN SOULS.

MARCH IS A CISTE VIHAD—A HUNTER OF THE ILL.

SHE BRAVES UNTOLD PERILS TO HUNT DOWN ILL AND PROTECT THEIR WOULD-BE VICTIMS.

BUT THE ILL THAT SLUMBERS WITHIN MARCH THREATENS TO REAR ITS HEAD...!!

BELMA

HIS WEAPON, THE VEILED SCARECROW, CAUSES HALLUCINATIONS. BELMA IS ALSO THE CHEF AT AN ITALIAN RESTAURANT. THE STRONG, STUPID(?!) TYPE.

RODIN

THE PROPRIETOR OF AN ANTIQUE SHOP, RODIN IS THE SECRET OBJECT OF MARCH'S AFFECTIONS. BENEATH HIS LOVELY FAÇADE LIES THE CALCULATING MIND OF A SHREWD BUSINESSMAN.

CONTENTS

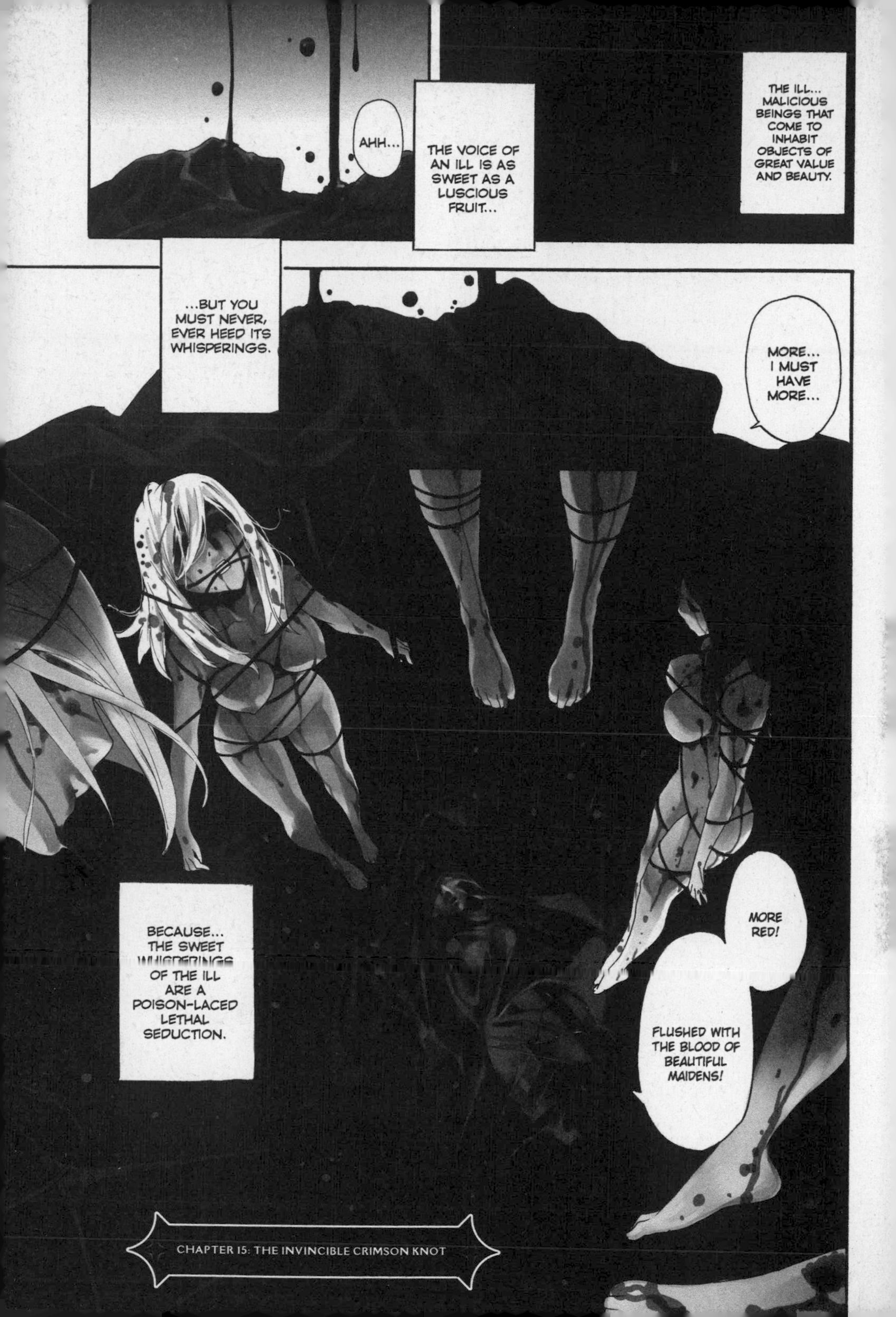
THE ILL... MALICIOUS BEINGS THAT COME TO INHABIT OBJECTS OF GREAT VALUE AND BEAUTY.
THE VOICE OF AN ILL IS AS SWEET AS A LUSCIOUS FRUIT...
AHH...
...BUT YOU MUST NEVER, EVER HEED ITS WHISPERINGS.
MORE... I MUST HAVE MORE...
MORE RED!
FLUSHED WITH THE BLOOD OF BEAUTIFUL MAIDENS!
BECAUSE... THE SWEET WHISPERINGS OF THE ILL ARE A POISON-LACED LETHAL SEDUCTION.
CHAPTER 15: THE INVINCIBLE CRIMSON KNOT

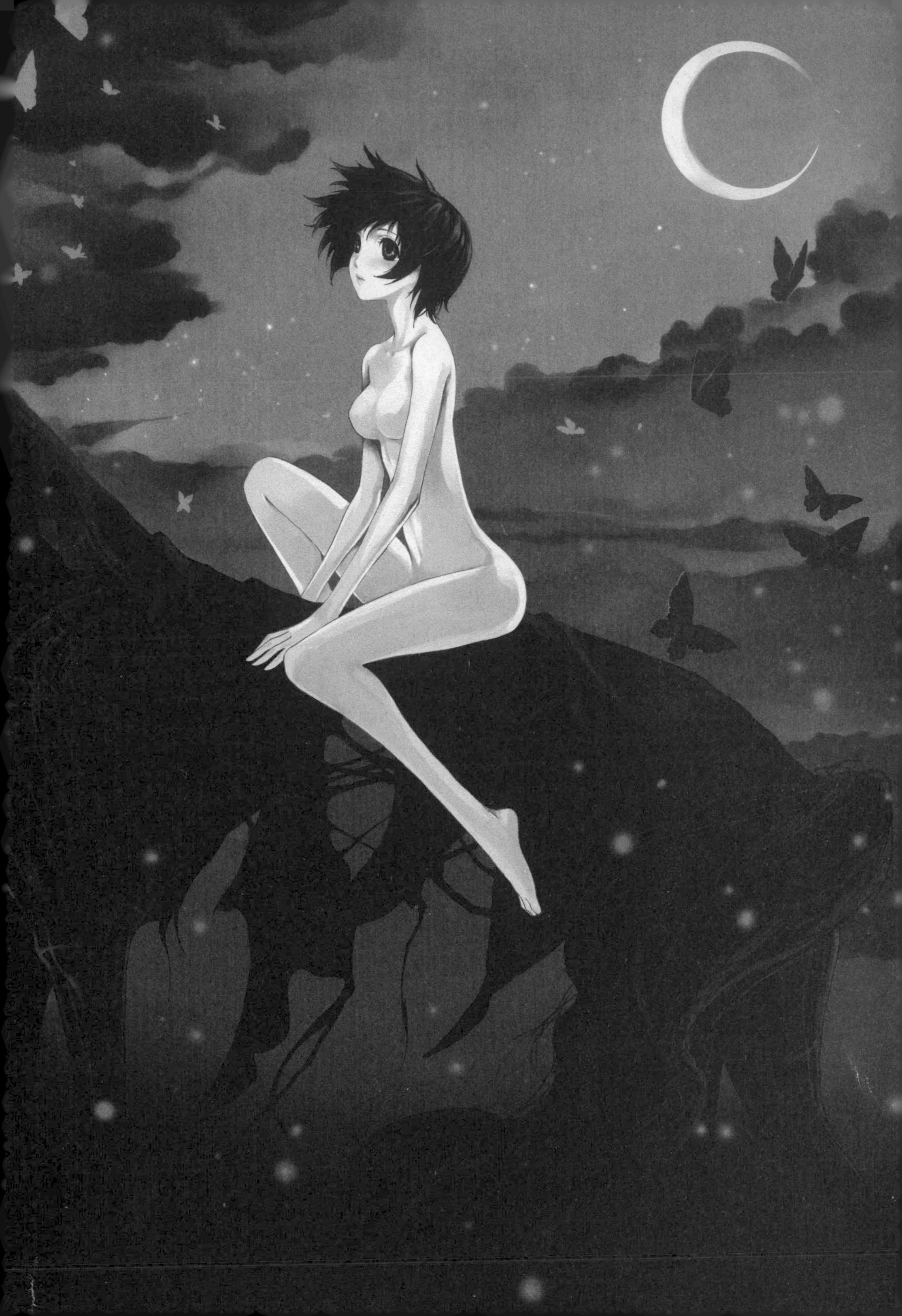

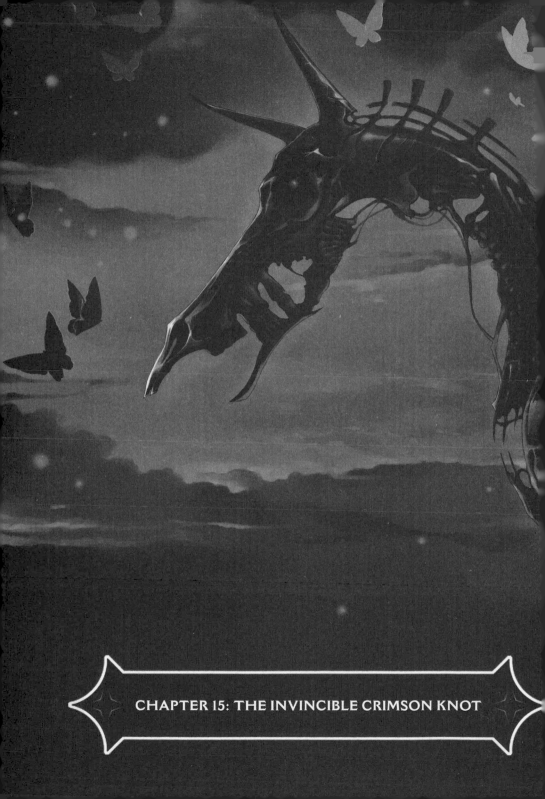

CHAPTER 15: THE INVINCIBLE CRIMSON KNOT

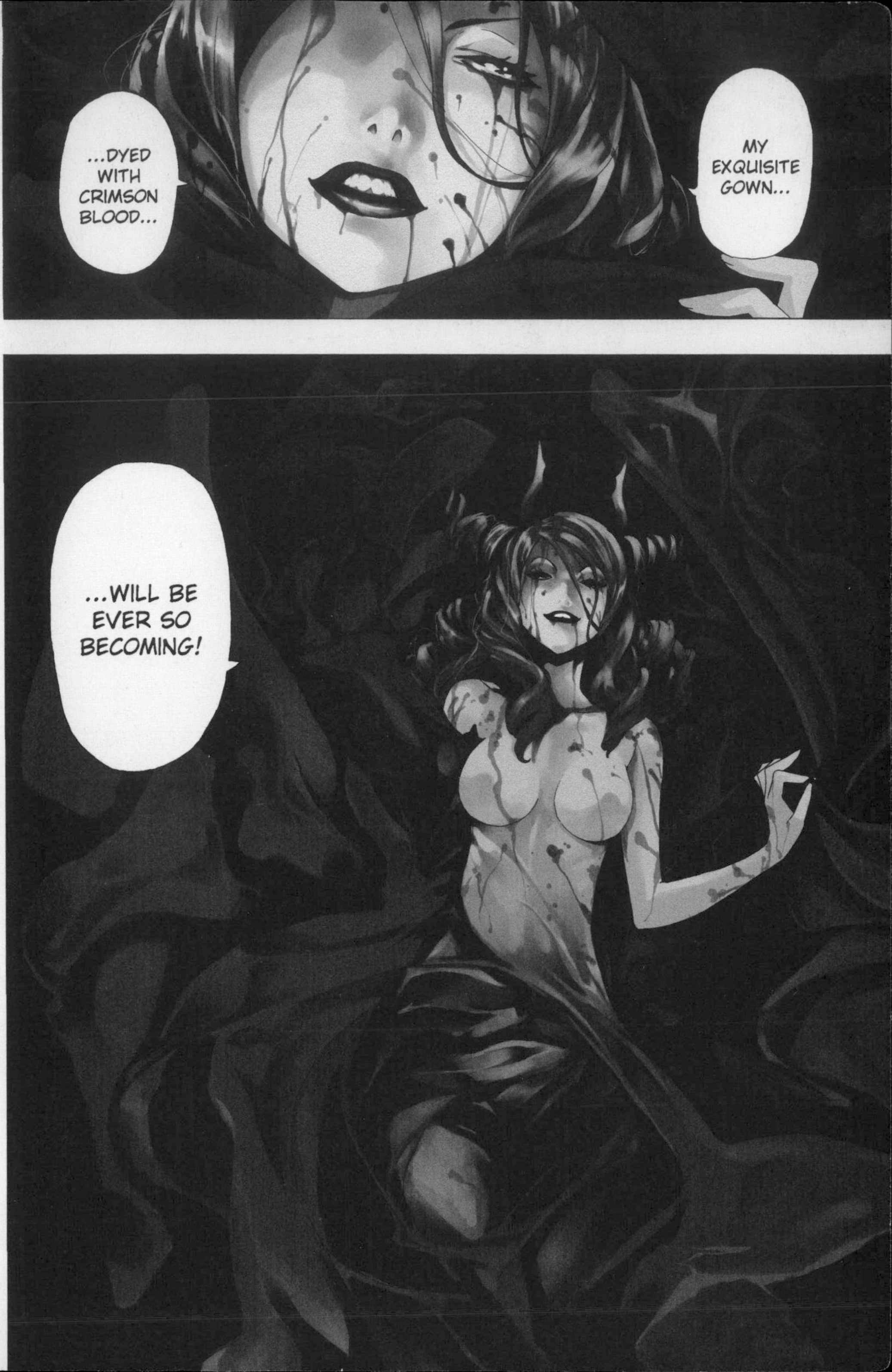
MY EXQUISITE GOWN...
...DYED WITH CRIMSON BLOOD...
...WILL BE EVER SO BECOMING!

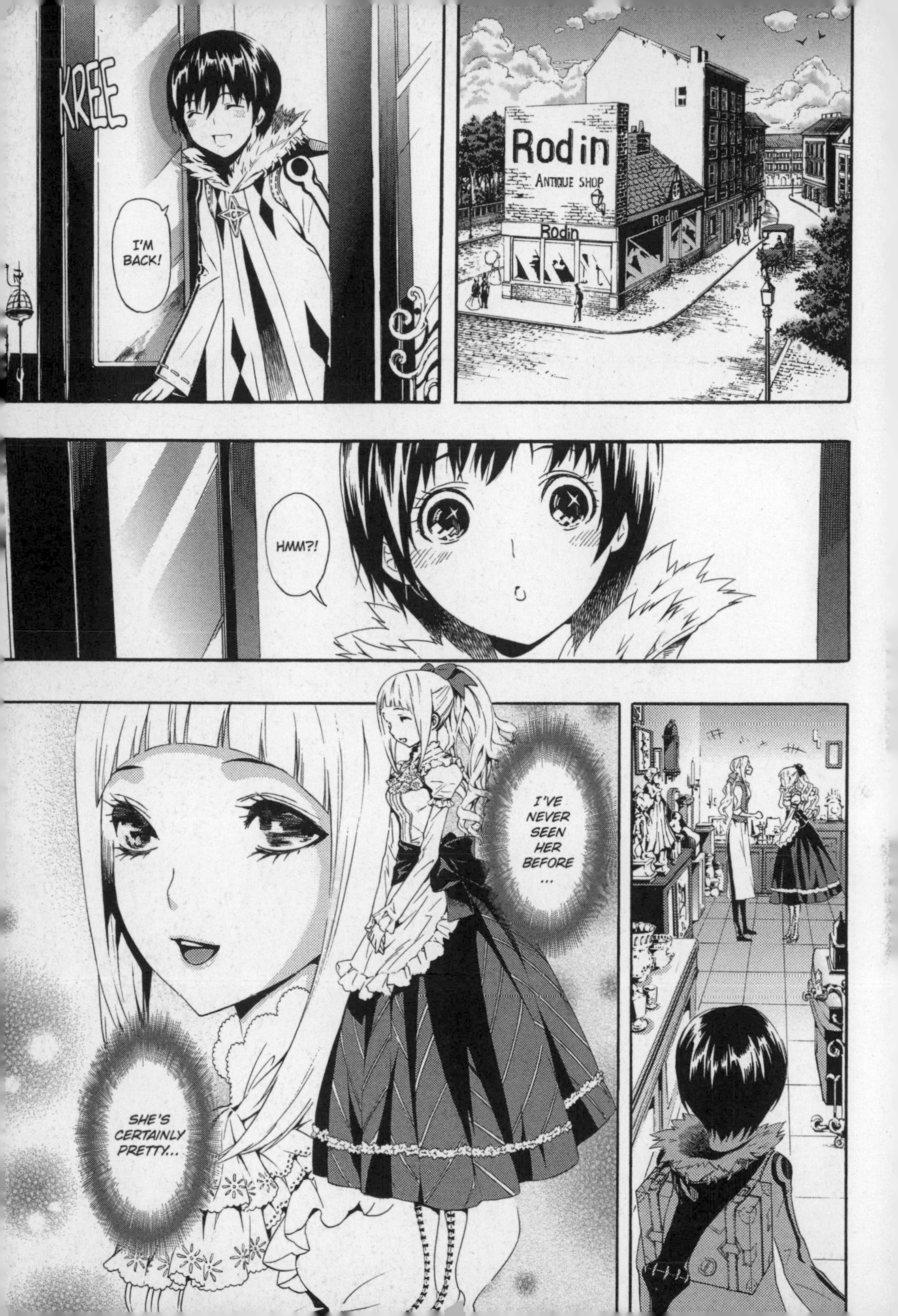
Rodin
ANTIQUE SHOP
Rodin
Rodin
KREE
I'M BACK!
HMM?!
I'VE NEVER SEEN HER BEFORE ...
SHE'S CERTAINLY PRETTY...

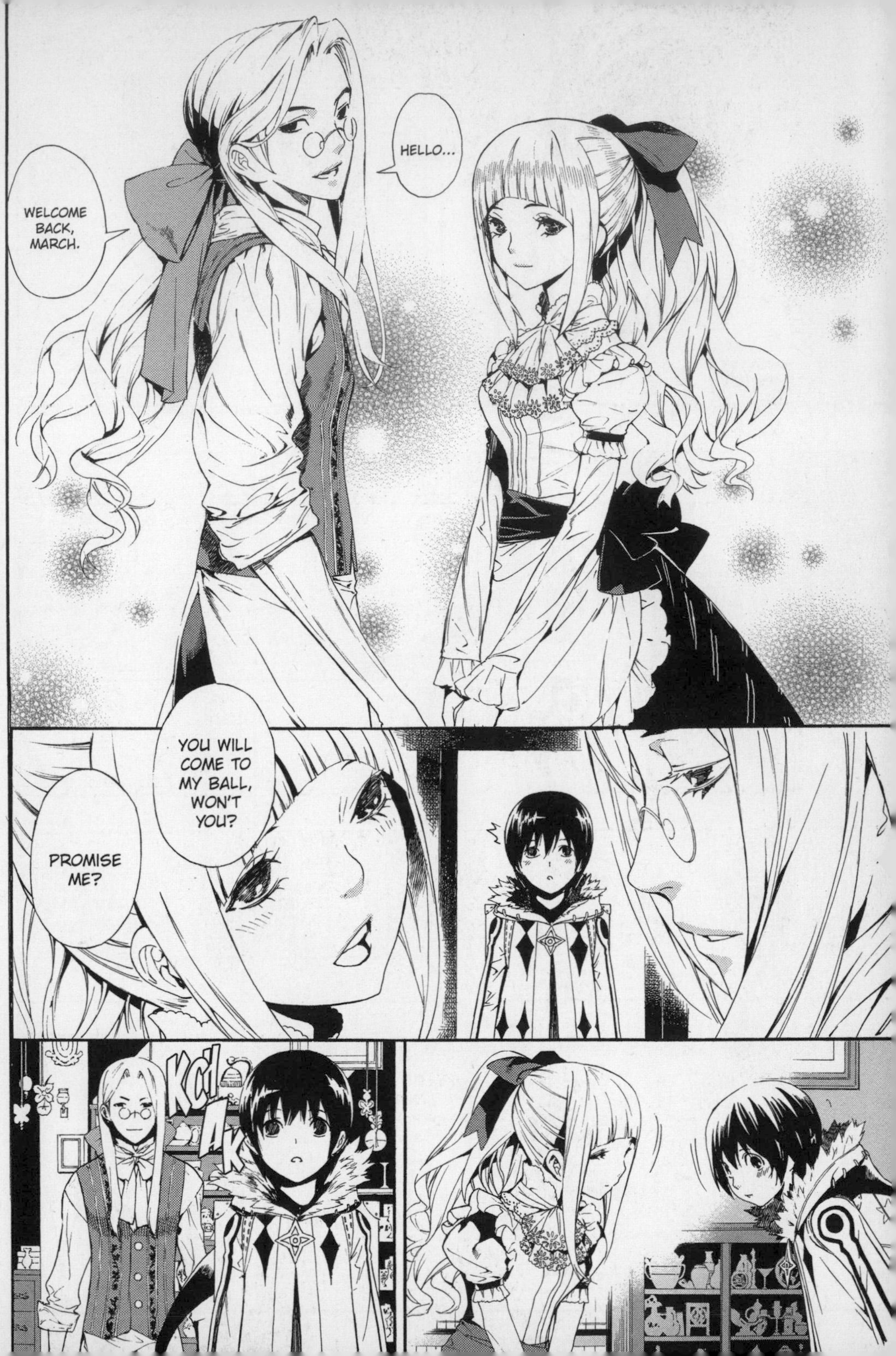
HELLO...
WELCOME BACK, MARCH.
YOU WILL COME TO MY BALL, WON'T YOU?
PROMISE ME?

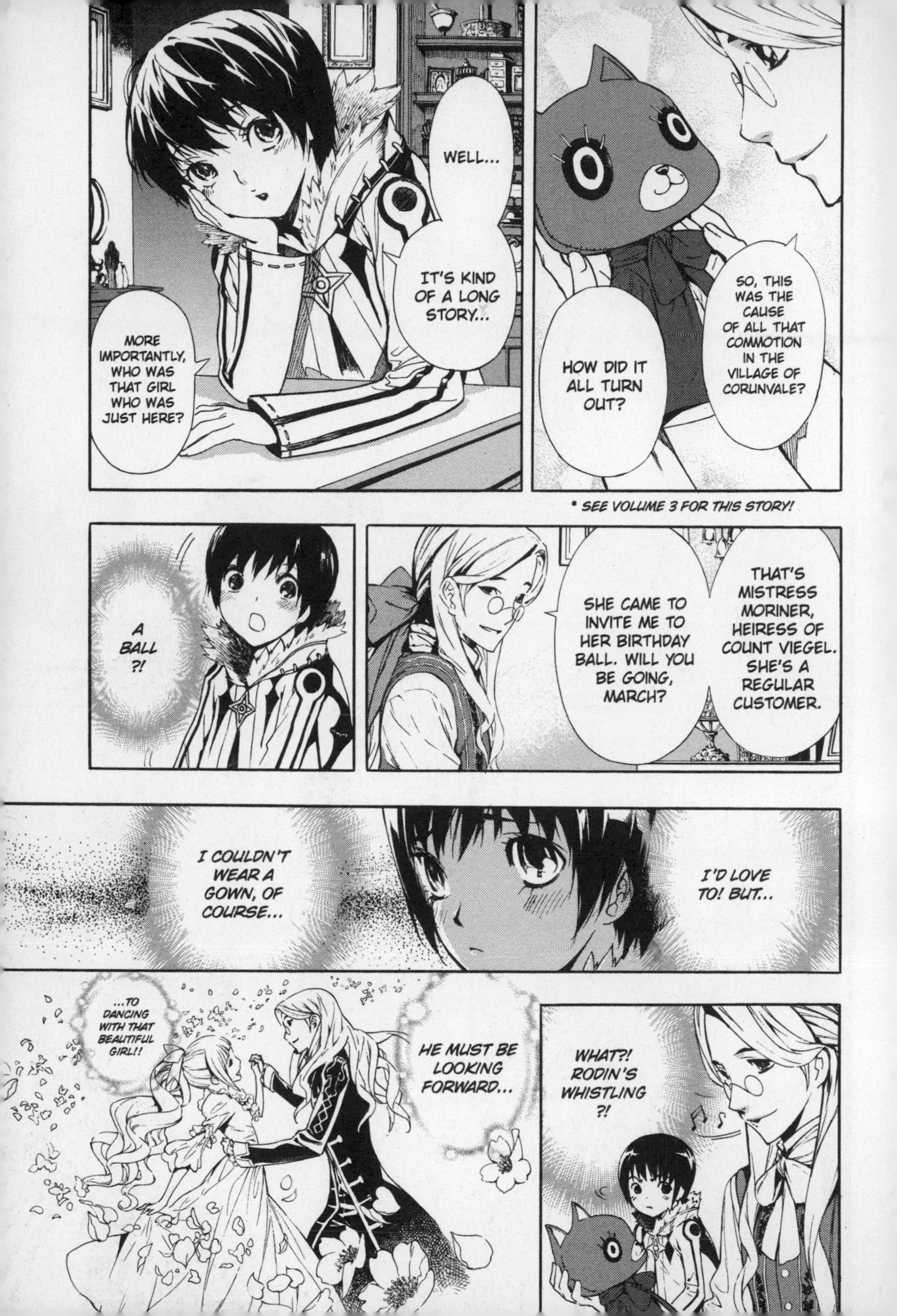
SO, THIS WAS THE CAUSE OF ALL THAT COMMOTION IN THE VILLAGE OF CORUNVALE?
HOW DID IT ALL TURN OUT?
WELL...
IT'S KIND OF A LONG STORY...
MORE IMPORTANTLY, WHO WAS THAT GIRL WHO WAS JUST HERE?
THAT'S MISTRESS MORINER, HEIRESS OF COUNT VIEGEL. SHE'S A REGULAR CUSTOMER.
SHE CAME TO INVITE ME TO HER BIRTHDAY BALL. WILL YOU BE GOING, MARCH?
A BALL?!
I'D LOVE TO! BUT...
I COULDN'T WEAR A GOWN, OF COURSE...
WHAT?! RODIN'S WHISTLING?!
HE MUST BE LOOKING FORWARD...
...TO DANCING WITH THAT BEAUTIFUL GIRL!!

* SEE VOLUME 3 FOR THIS STORY!

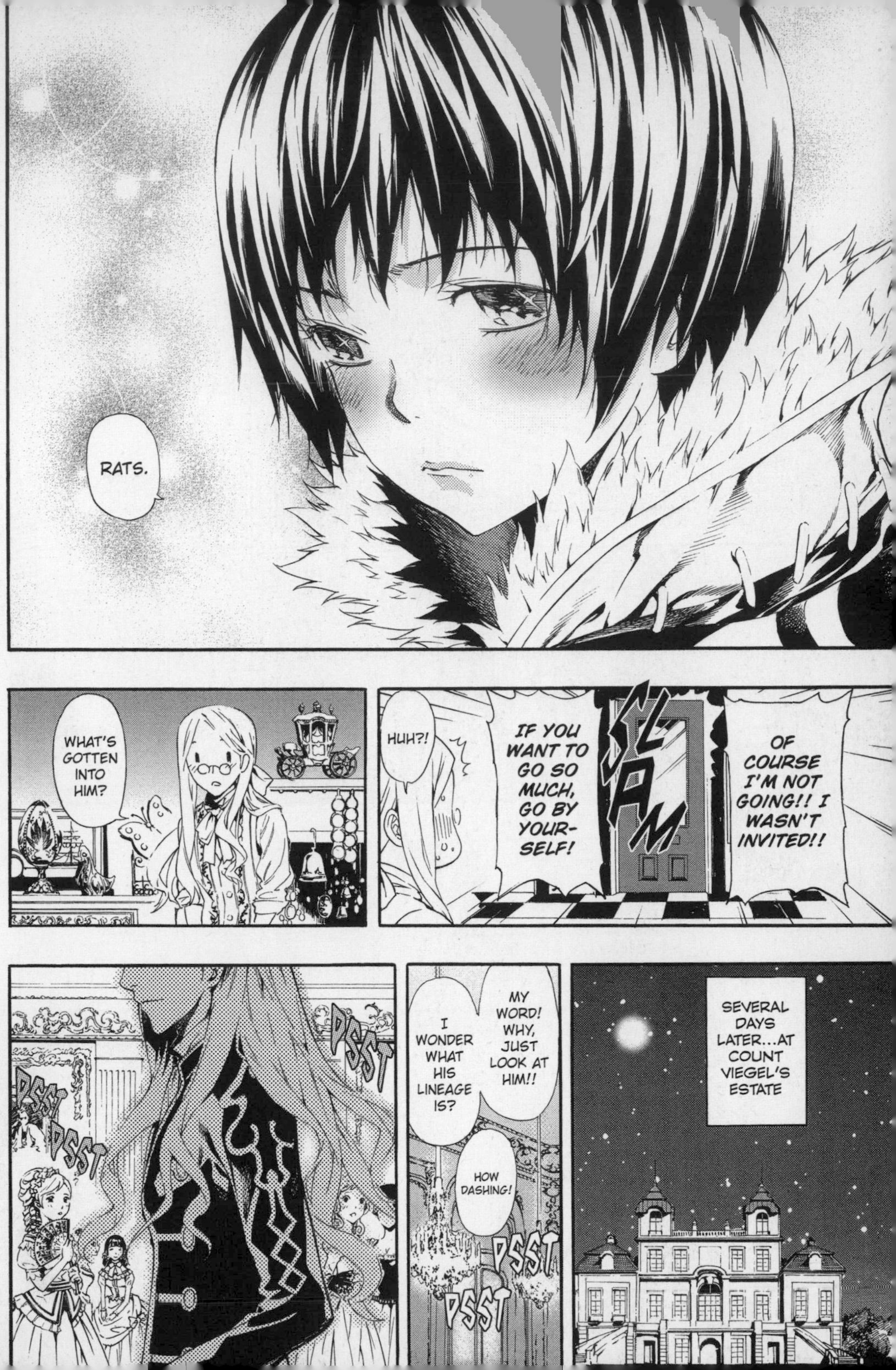
RATS.
OF COURSE I'M NOT GOING!! I WASN'T INVITED!!
SLAM
IF YOU WANT TO GO SO MUCH, GO BY YOUR-SELF!
HUH?!
WHAT'S GOTTEN INTO HIM?
SEVERAL DAYS LATER...AT COUNT VIEGEL'S ESTATE
MY WORD! WHY, JUST LOOK AT HIM!!
I WONDER WHAT HIS LINEAGE IS?
HOW DASHING!
PSST
PSST
PSST
PSST
PSST

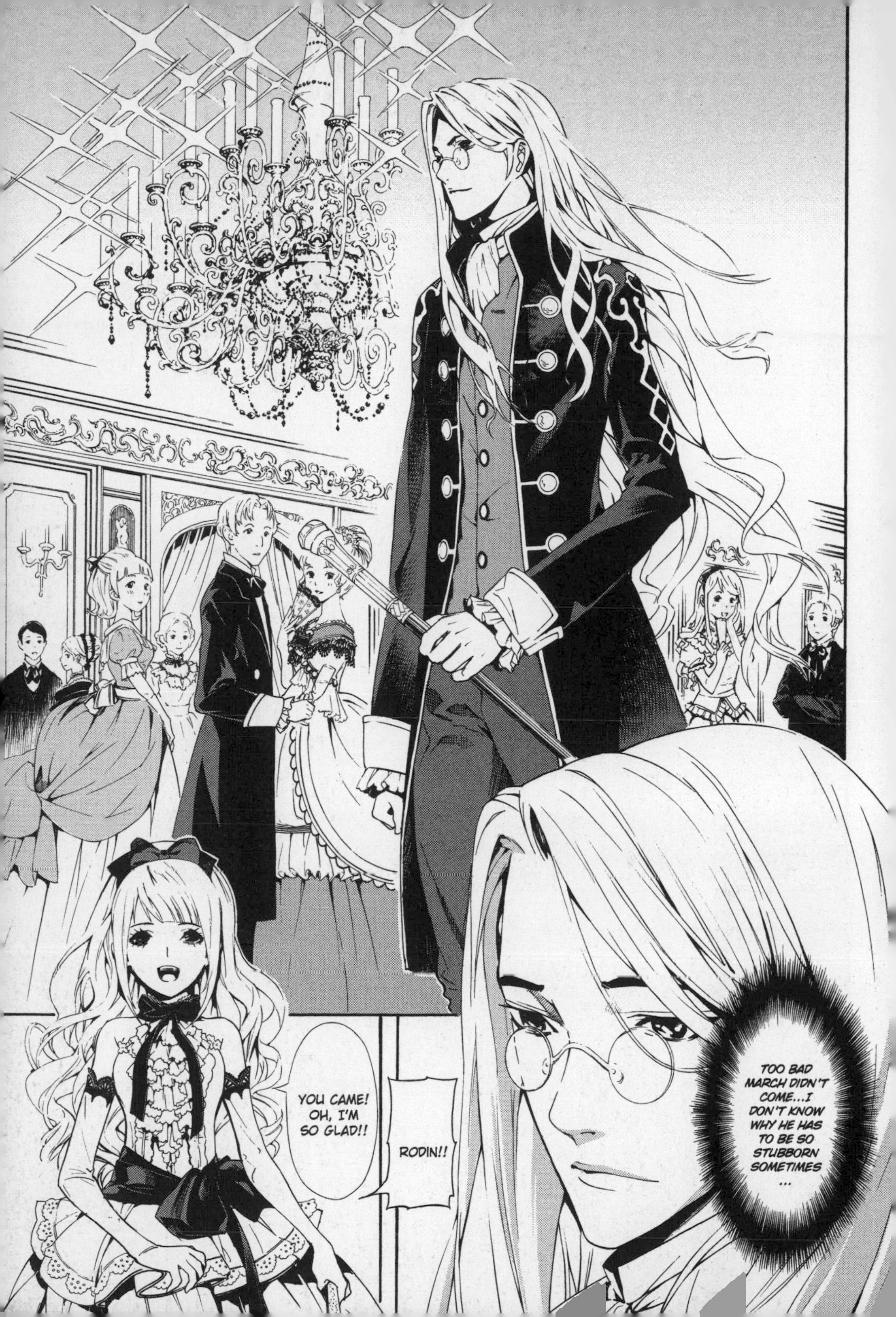
TOO BAD MARCH DIDN'T COME...I DON'T KNOW WHY HE HAS TO BE SO STUBBORN SOMETIMES ...
RODIN!!
YOU CAME! OH, I'M SO GLAD!!

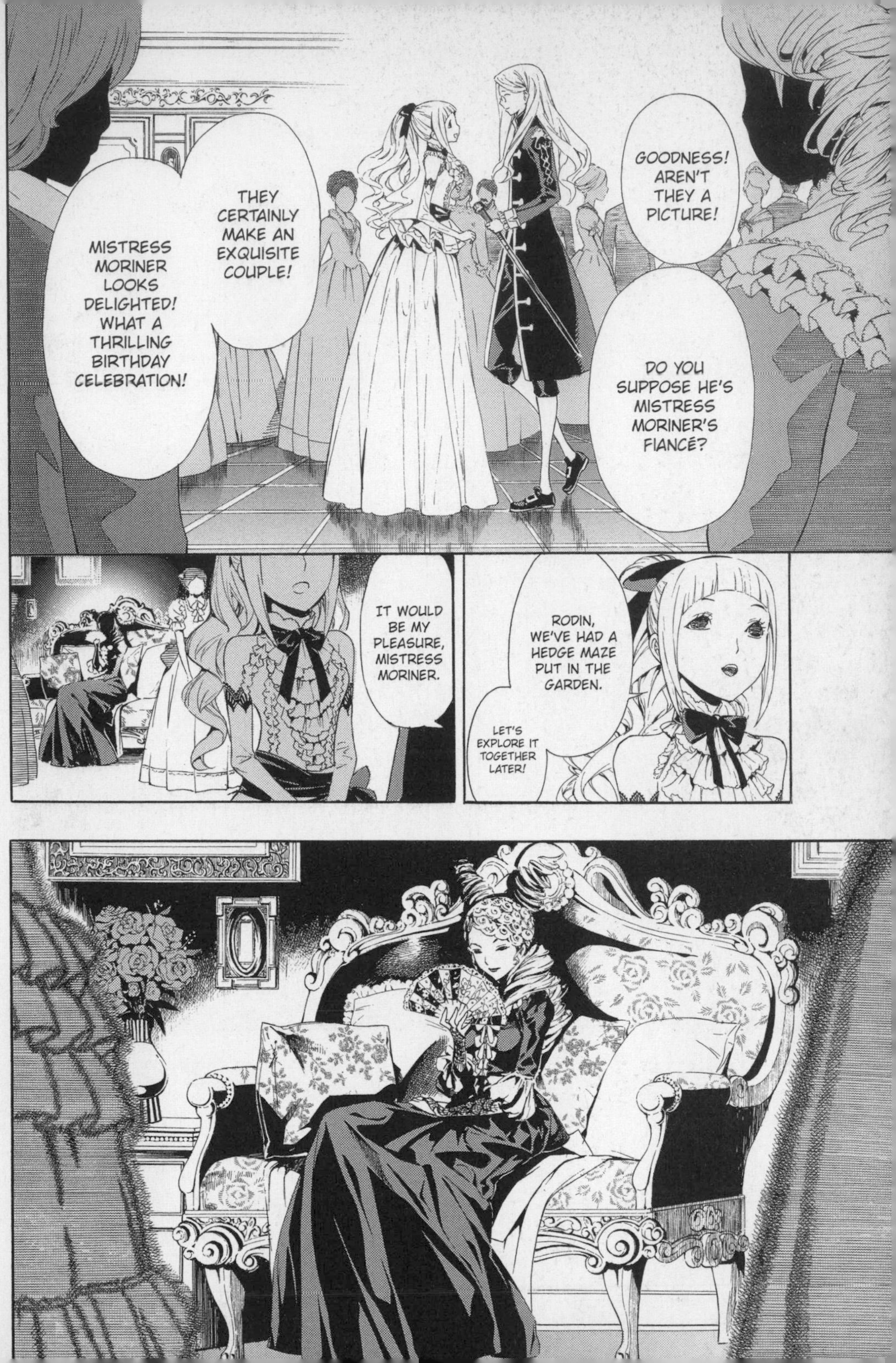
GOODNESS! AREN'T THEY A PICTURE!
DO YOU SUPPOSE HE'S MISTRESS MORINER'S FIANCÉ?
THEY CERTAINLY MAKE AN EXQUISITE COUPLE!
MISTRESS MORINER LOOKS DELIGHTED! WHAT A THRILLING BIRTHDAY CELEBRATION!
RODIN, WE'VE HAD A HEDGE MAZE PUT IN THE GARDEN.
LET'S EXPLORE IT TOGETHER LATER!
IT WOULD BE MY PLEASURE, MISTRESS MORINER.

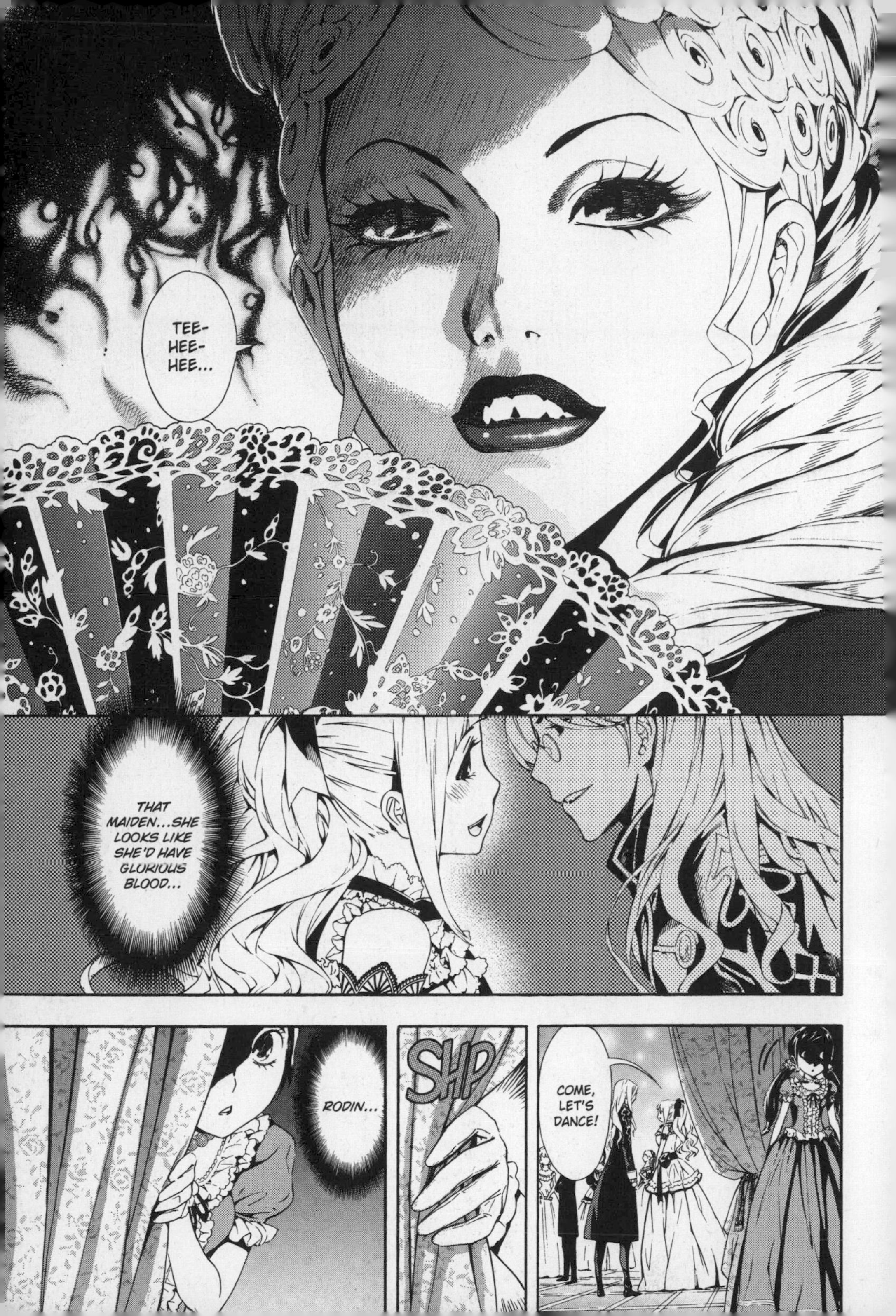
TEE-HEE-HEE...
THAT MAIDEN...SHE LOOKS LIKE SHE'D HAVE GLORIOUS BLOOD...
COME, LET'S DANCE!
SHP
RODIN...

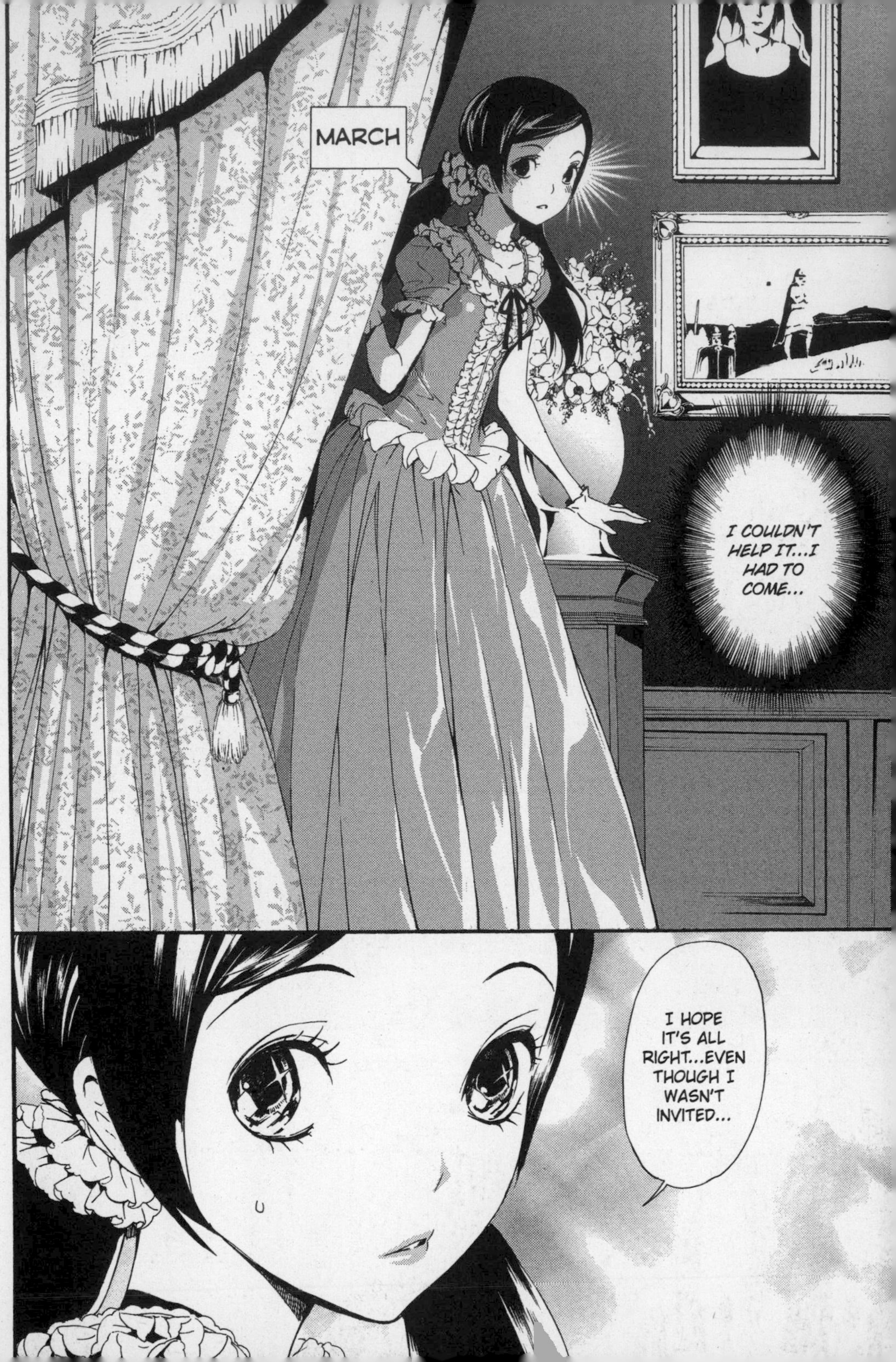
MARCH
I COULDN'T HELP IT...I HAD TO COME...
I HOPE IT'S ALL RIGHT...EVEN THOUGH I WASN'T INVITED...

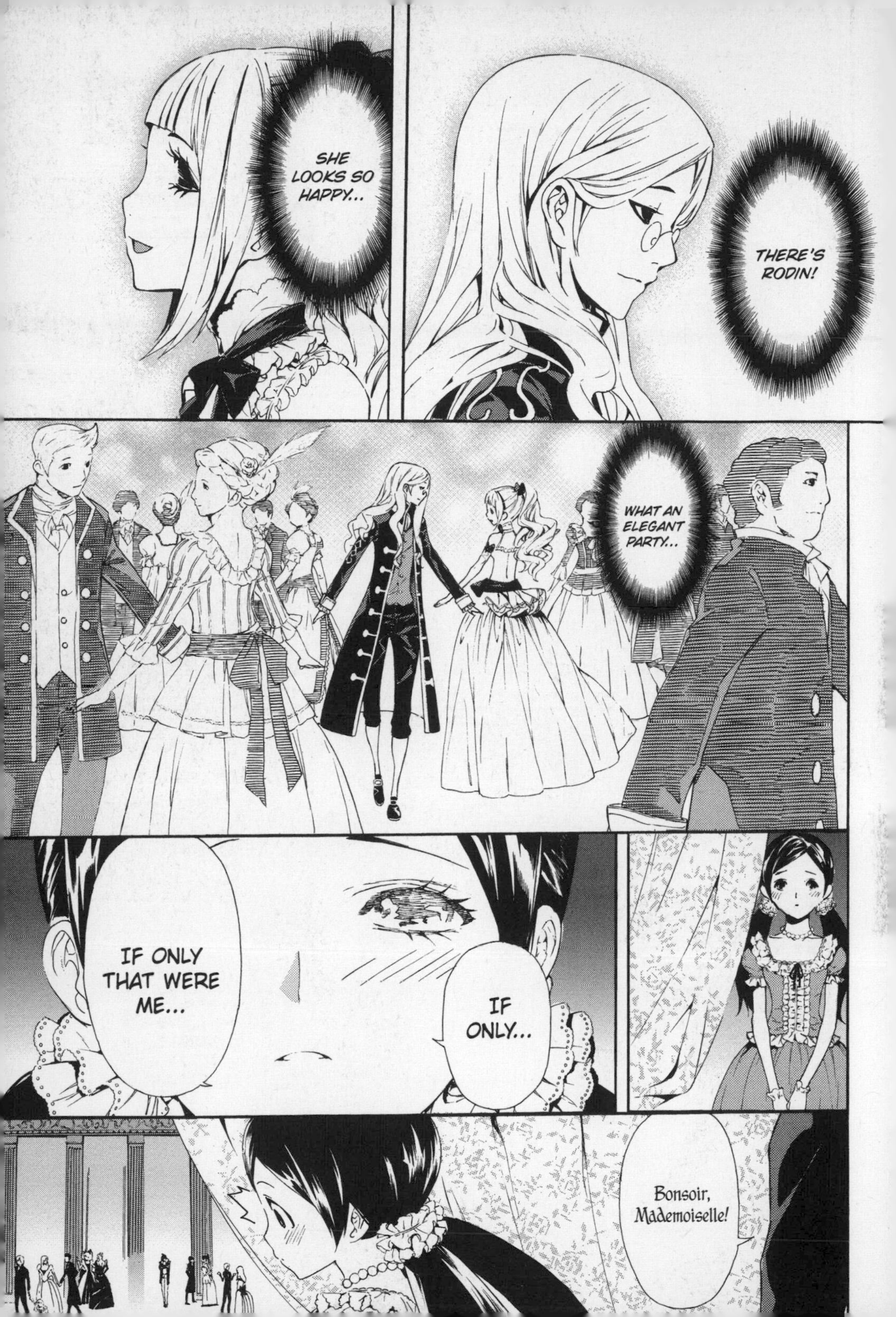
THERE'S RODIN!
SHE LOOKS SO HAPPY...
WHAT AN ELEGANT PARTY...
IF ONLY...
IF ONLY THAT WERE ME...
Bonsoir, Mademoiselle!

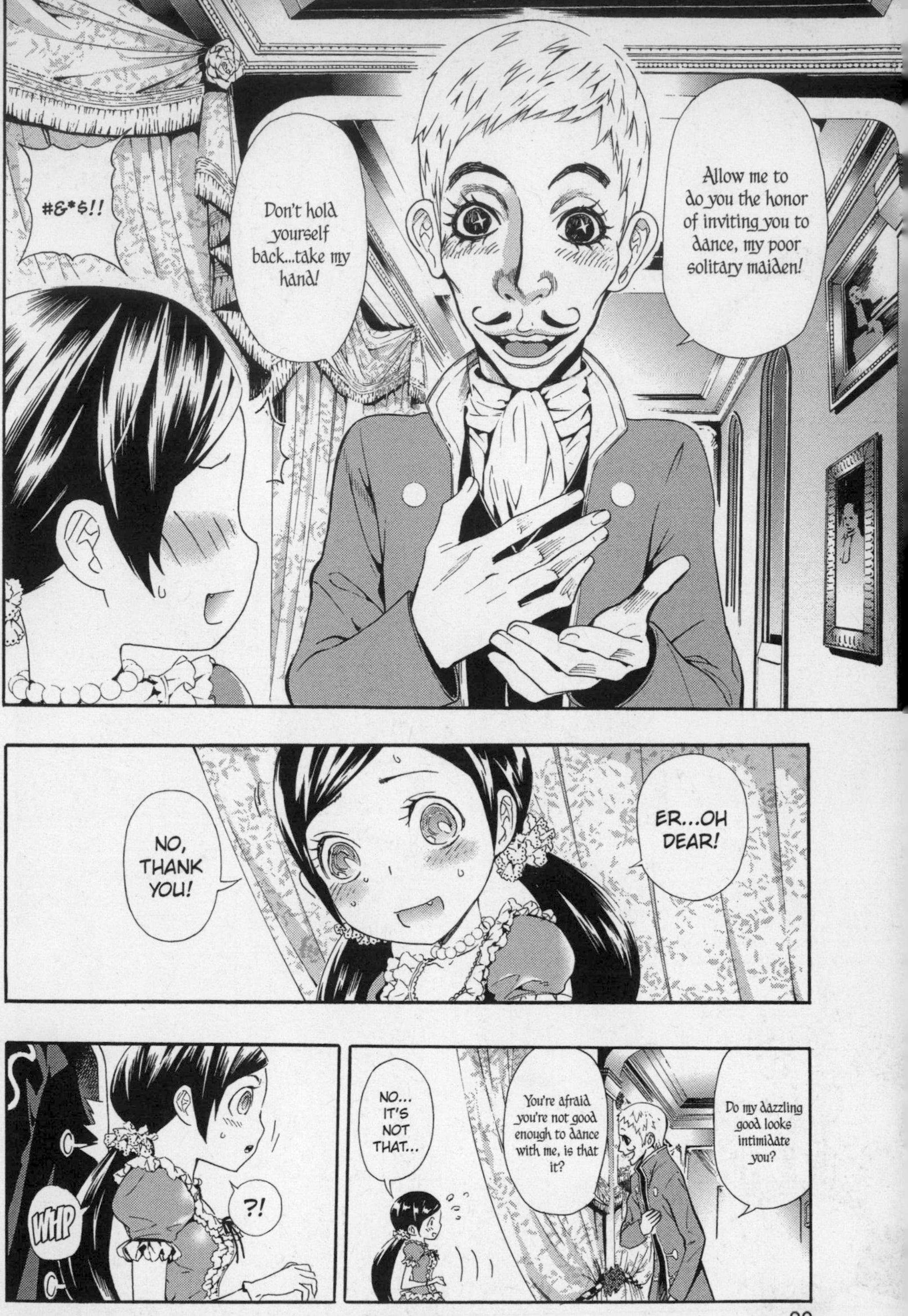
Allow me to do you the honor of inviting you to dance, my poor solitary maiden!
Don't hold yourself back...take my hand!
#&*$!!
ER...OH DEAR!
NO, THANK YOU!
Do my dazzling good looks intimidate you?
You're afraid you're not good enough to dance with me, is that it?
NO... IT'S NOT THAT...
?!
WHP

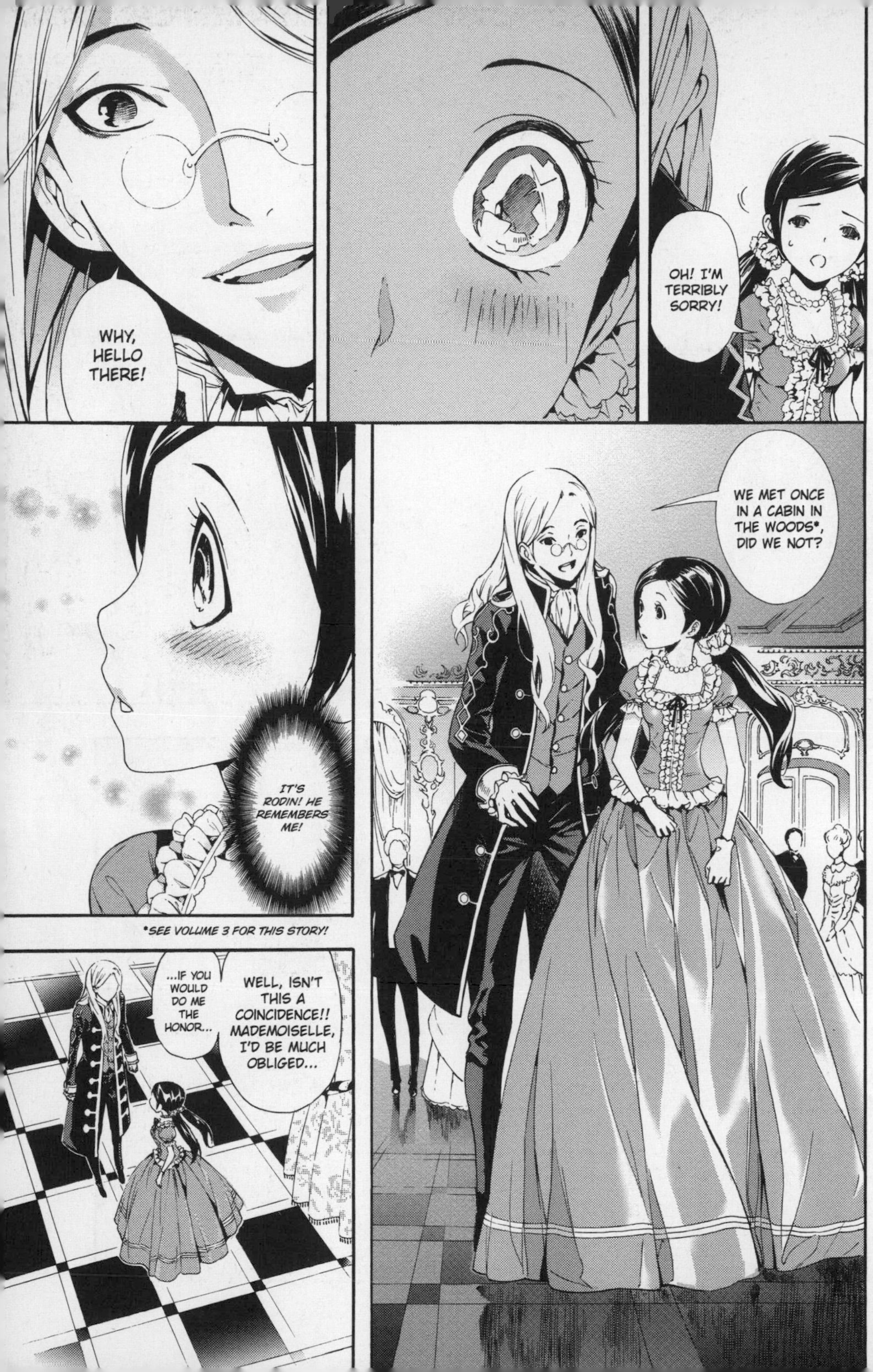
OH! I'M TERRIBLY SORRY!
WHY, HELLO THERE!
WE MET ONCE IN A CABIN IN THE WOODS*, DID WE NOT?
IT'S RODIN! HE REMEMBERS ME!
WELL, ISN'T THIS A COINCIDENCE!! MADEMOISELLE, I'D BE MUCH OBLIGED...
...IF YOU WOULD DO ME THE HONOR...
*SEE VOLUME 3 FOR THIS STORY!

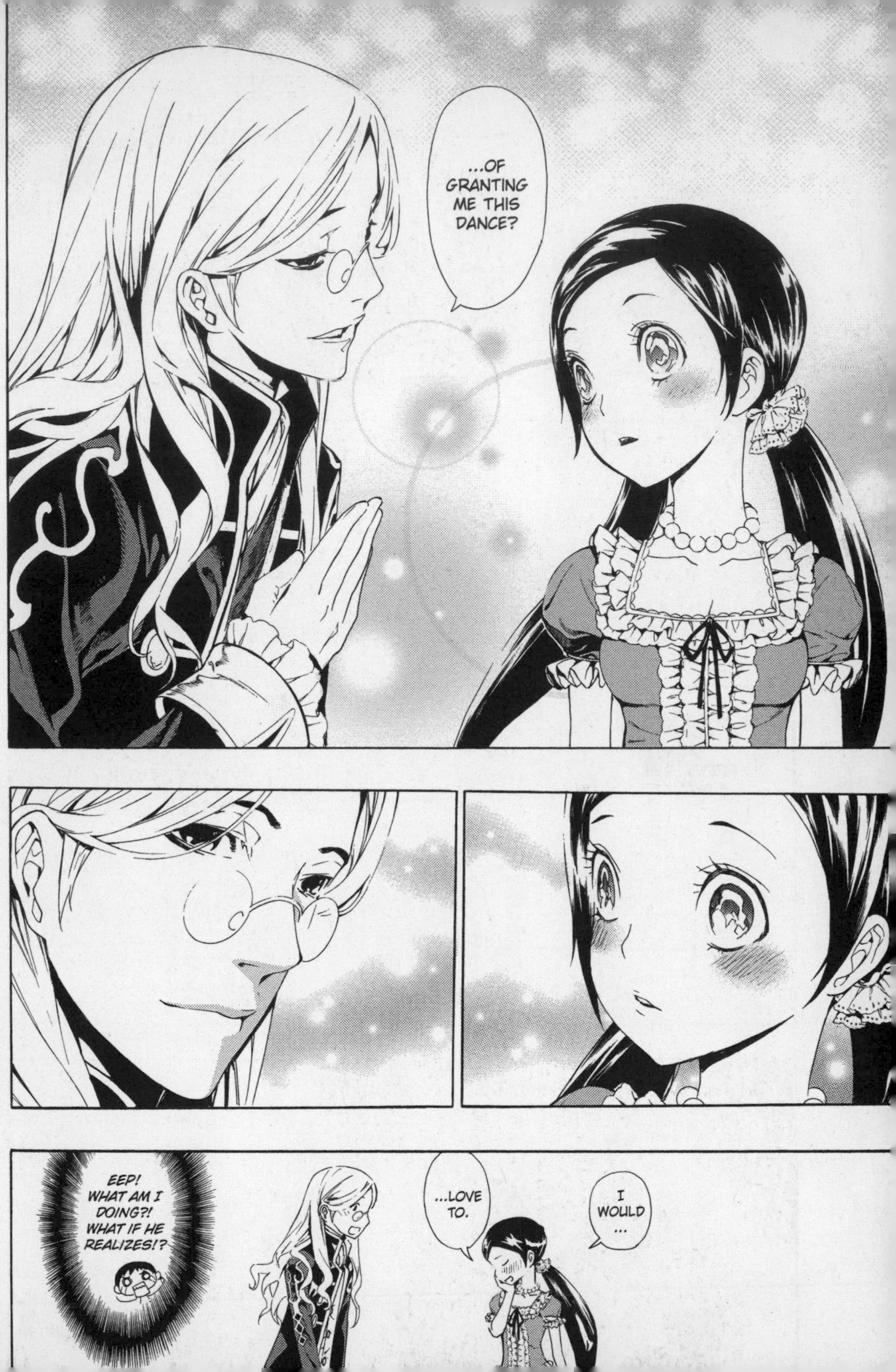
...OF GRANTING ME THIS DANCE?
I WOULD ...
...LOVE TO.
EEP! WHAT AM I DOING?! WHAT IF HE REALIZES!?

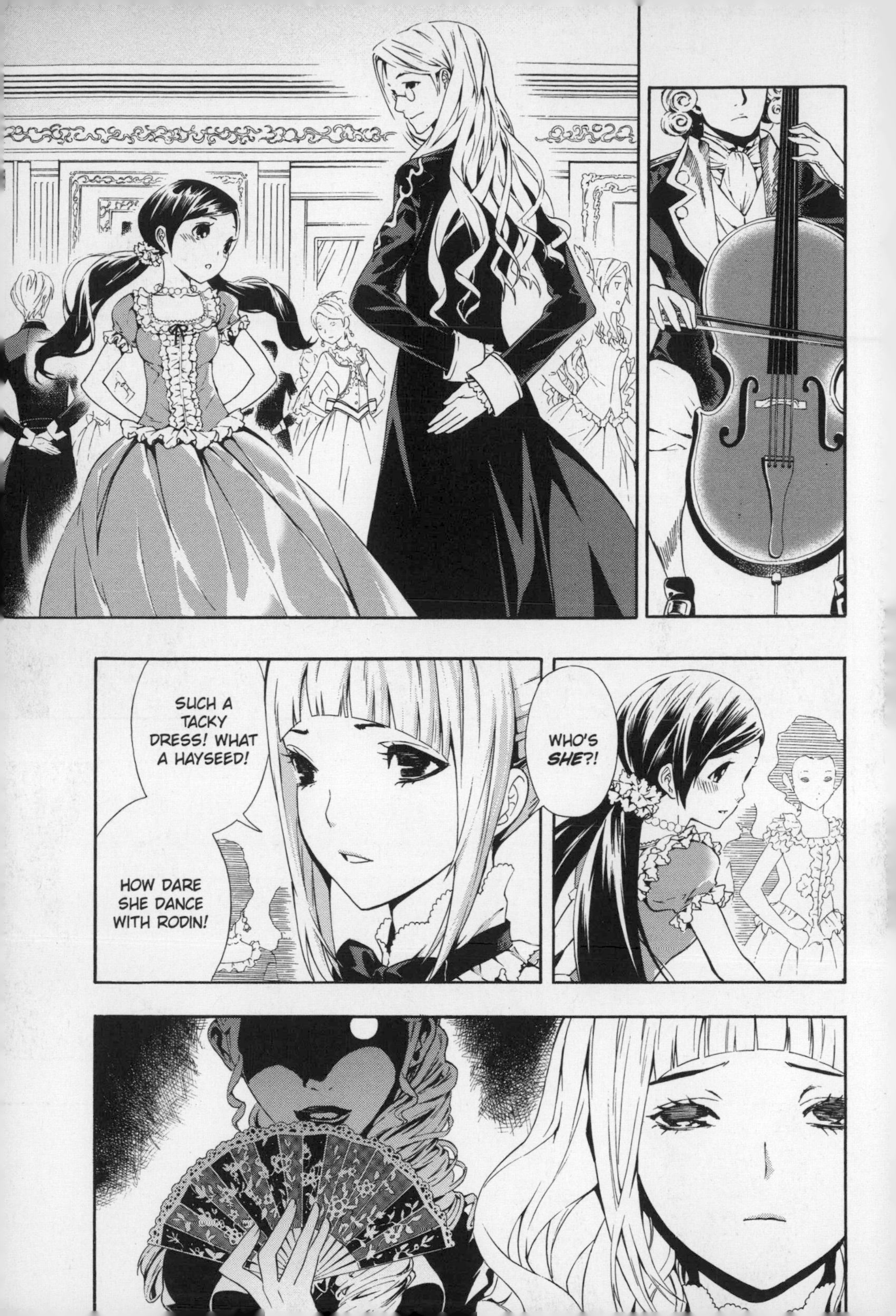
WHO'S *SHE*?!
SUCH A TACKY DRESS! WHAT A HAYSEED!
HOW DARE SHE DANCE WITH RODIN!

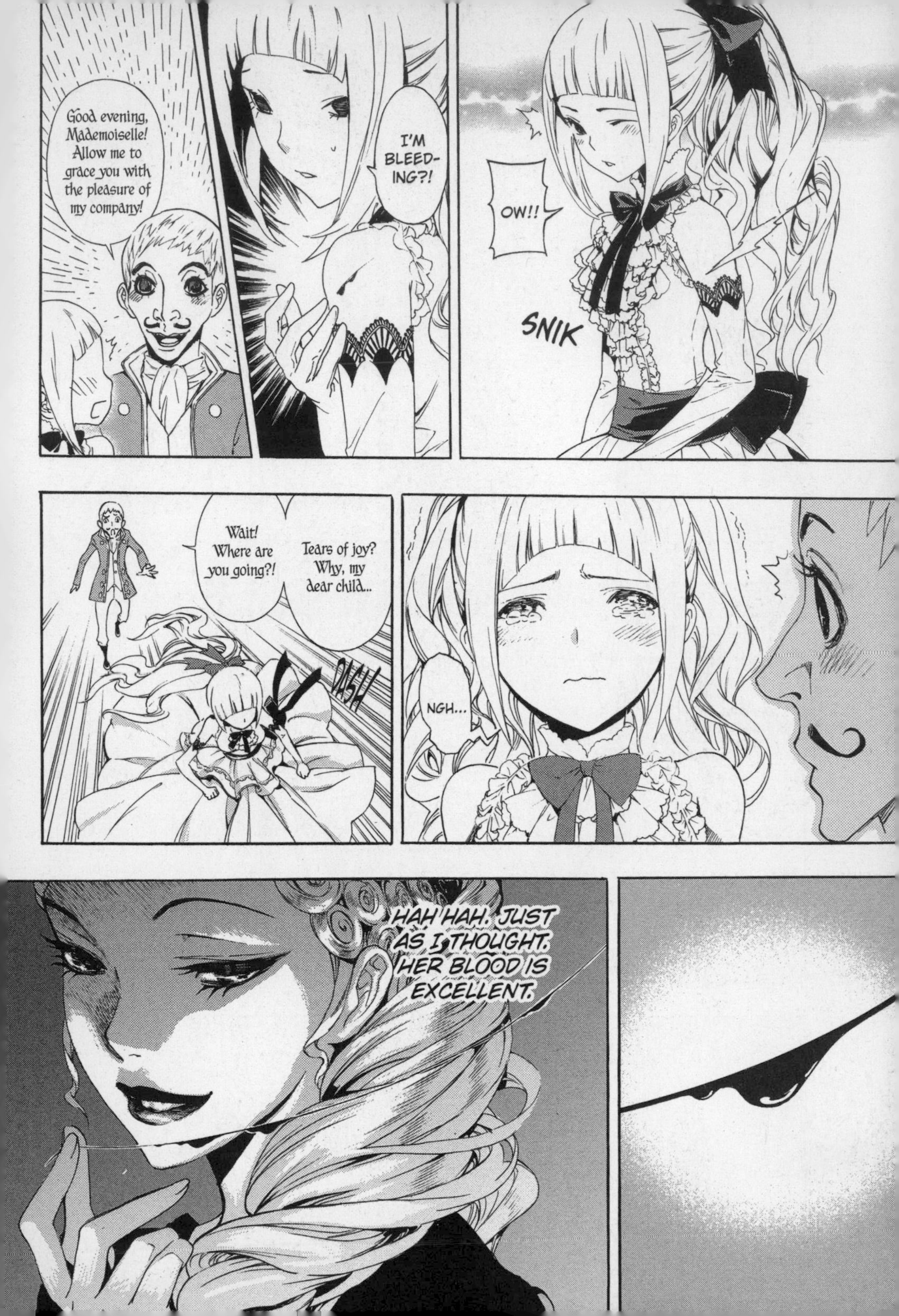
OW!!
SNIK
I'M BLEED-ING?!
Good evening, Mademoiselle! Allow me to grace you with the pleasure of my company!
NGH...
Tears of joy? Why, my dear child...
Wait! Where are you going?!
DASH
HAH HAH. JUST AS I THOUGHT. HER BLOOD IS EXCELLENT.

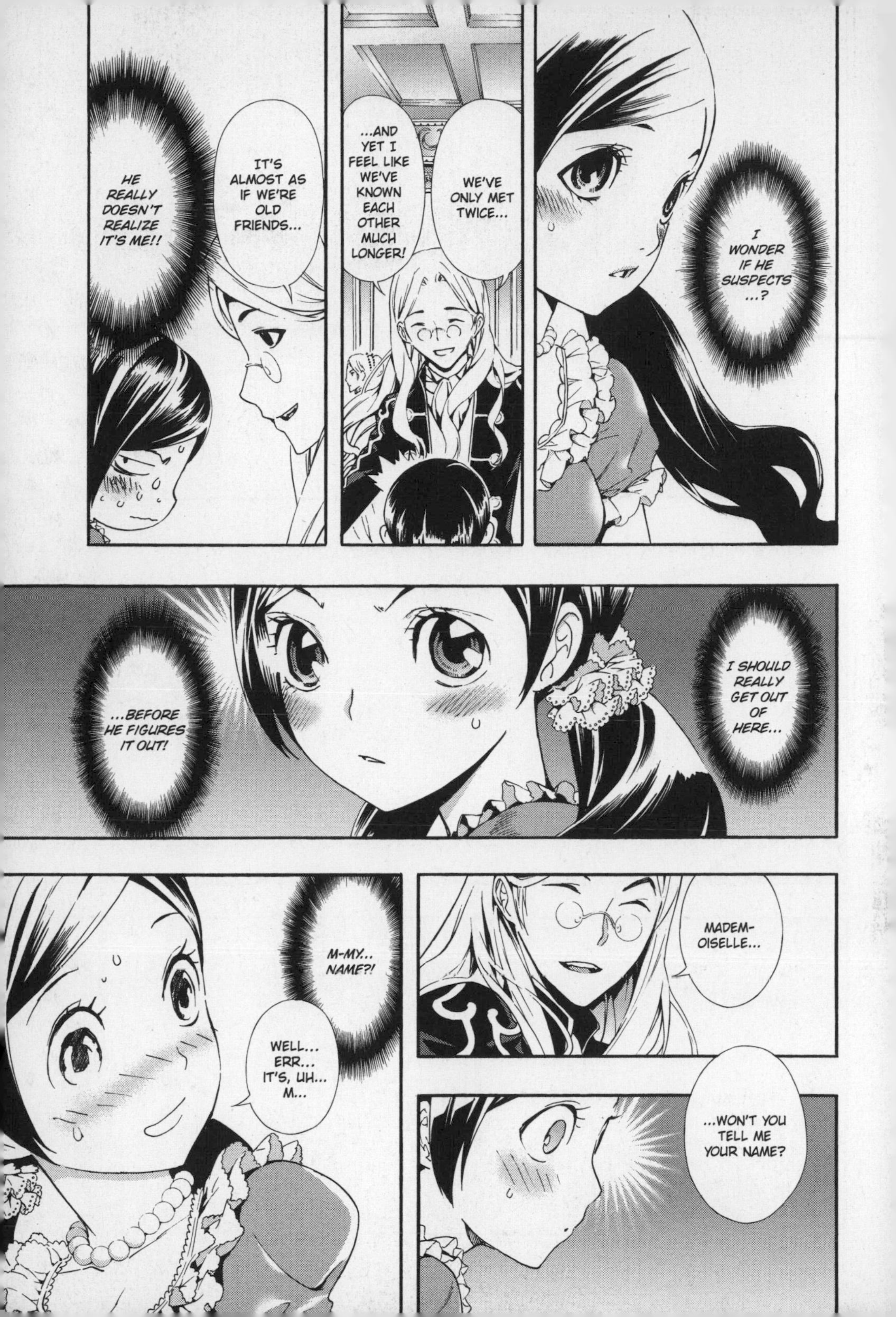
I WONDER IF HE SUSPECTS ...?
WE'VE ONLY MET TWICE...
...AND YET I FEEL LIKE WE'VE KNOWN EACH OTHER MUCH LONGER!
IT'S ALMOST AS IF WE'RE OLD FRIENDS...
HE REALLY DOESN'T REALIZE IT'S ME!!
I SHOULD REALLY GET OUT OF HERE...
...BEFORE HE FIGURES IT OUT!
MADEM-OISELLE...
...WON'T YOU TELL ME YOUR NAME?
M-MY... NAME?!
WELL... ERR... IT'S, UH... M...

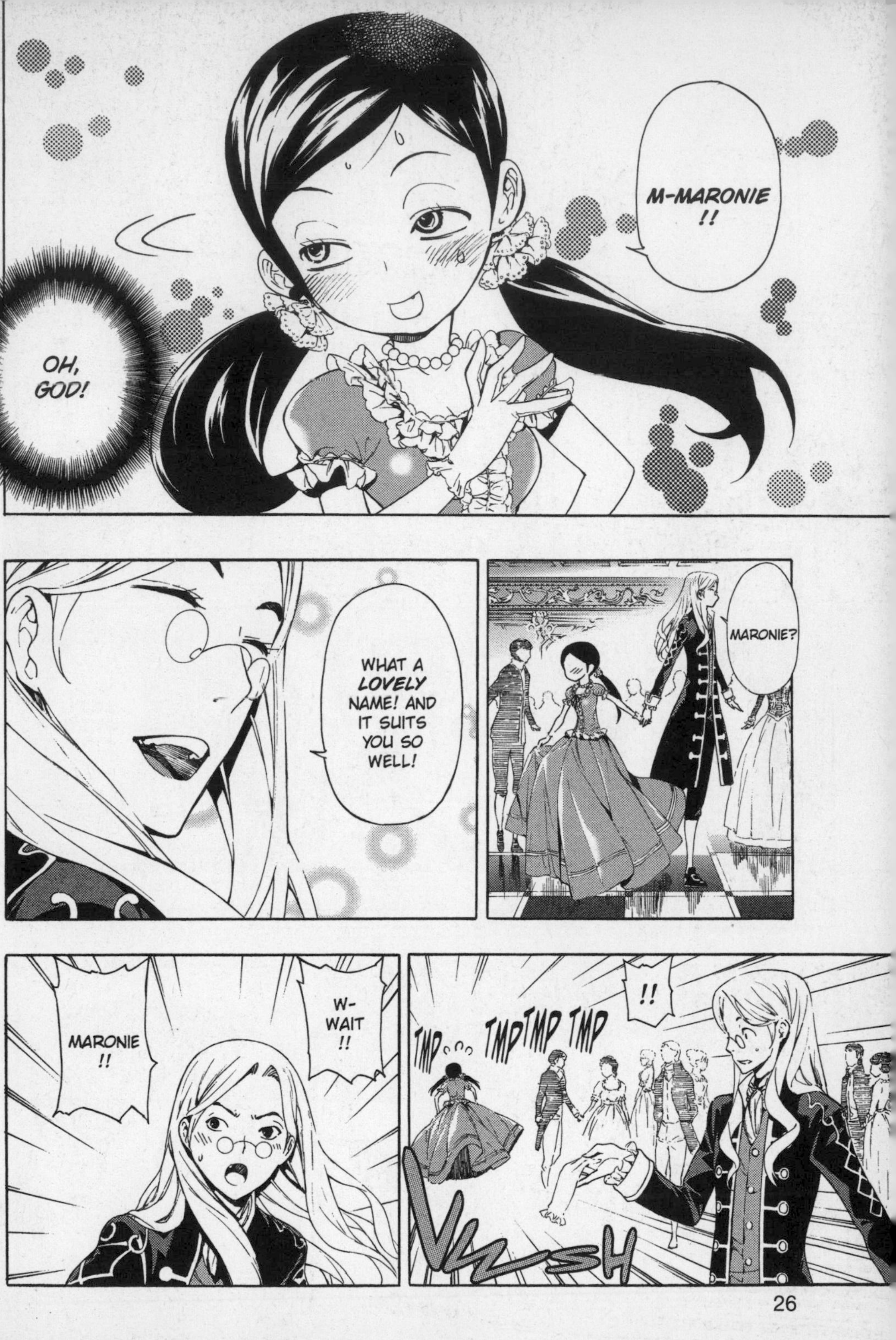
M-MARONIE !!
OH, GOD!
MARONIE?
WHAT A *LOVELY* NAME! AND IT SUITS YOU SO WELL!
!!
TMP
TMP TMP TMP
VWSH
W-WAIT !!
MARONIE !!

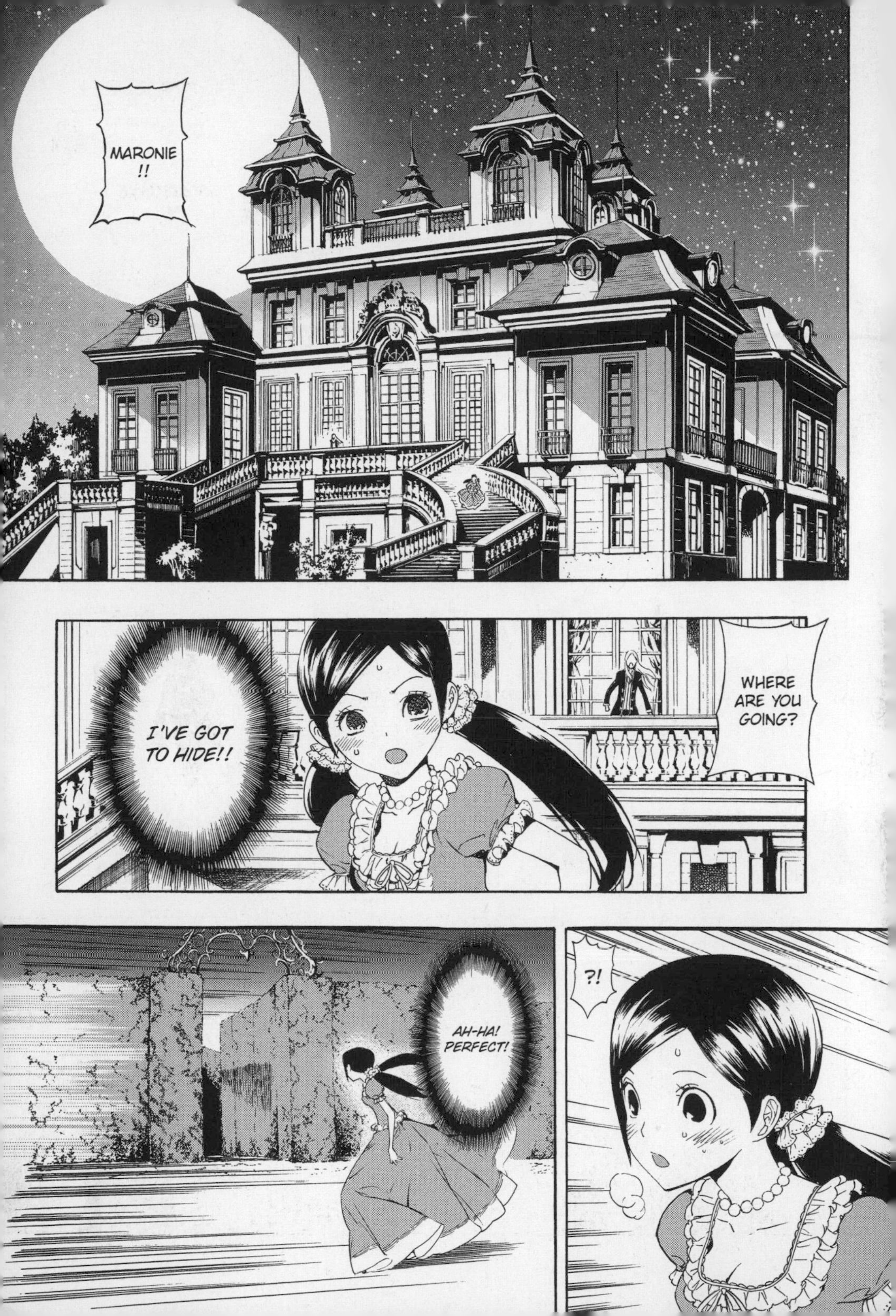
MARONIE !!
WHERE ARE YOU GOING?
I'VE GOT TO HIDE!!
?!
AH-HA! PERFECT!

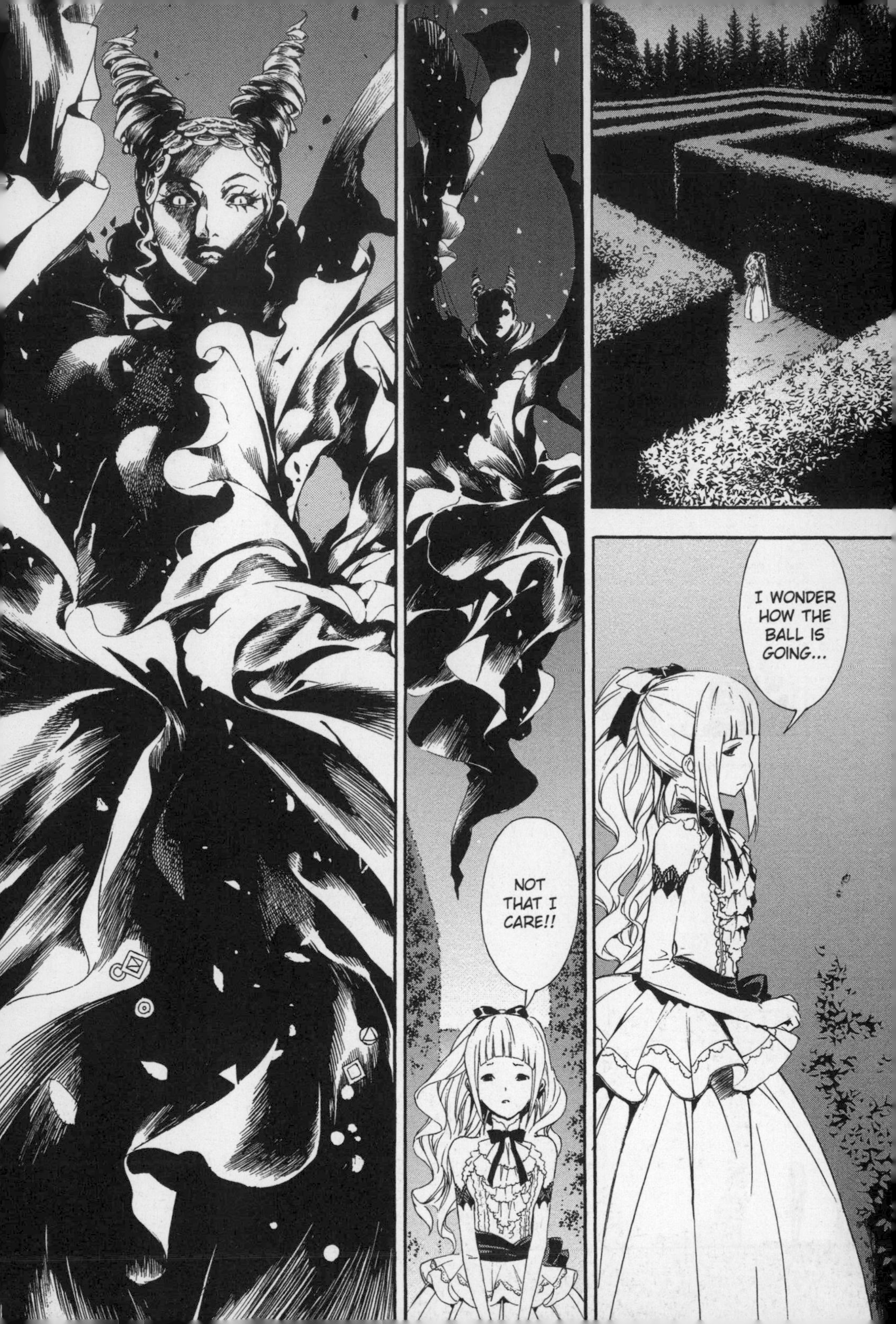
I WONDER HOW THE BALL IS GOING...
NOT THAT I CARE!!

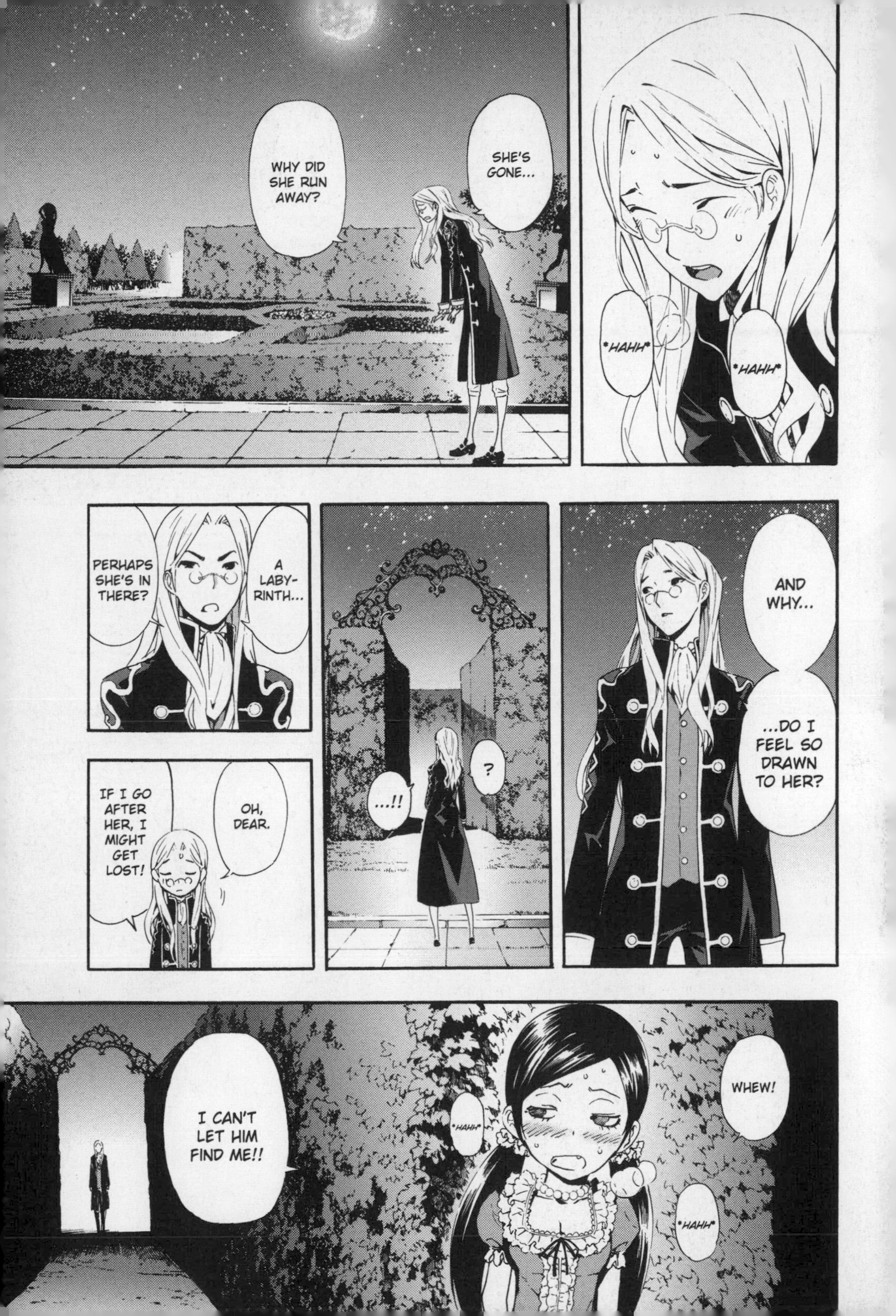
HAHH
HAHH
SHE'S GONE...
WHY DID SHE RUN AWAY?
AND WHY...
...DO I FEEL SO DRAWN TO HER?
?
...!!
A LABY-RINTH...
PERHAPS SHE'S IN THERE?
OH, DEAR.
IF I GO AFTER HER, I MIGHT GET LOST!
WHEW!
HAHH
I CAN'T LET HIM FIND ME!!
HAHH

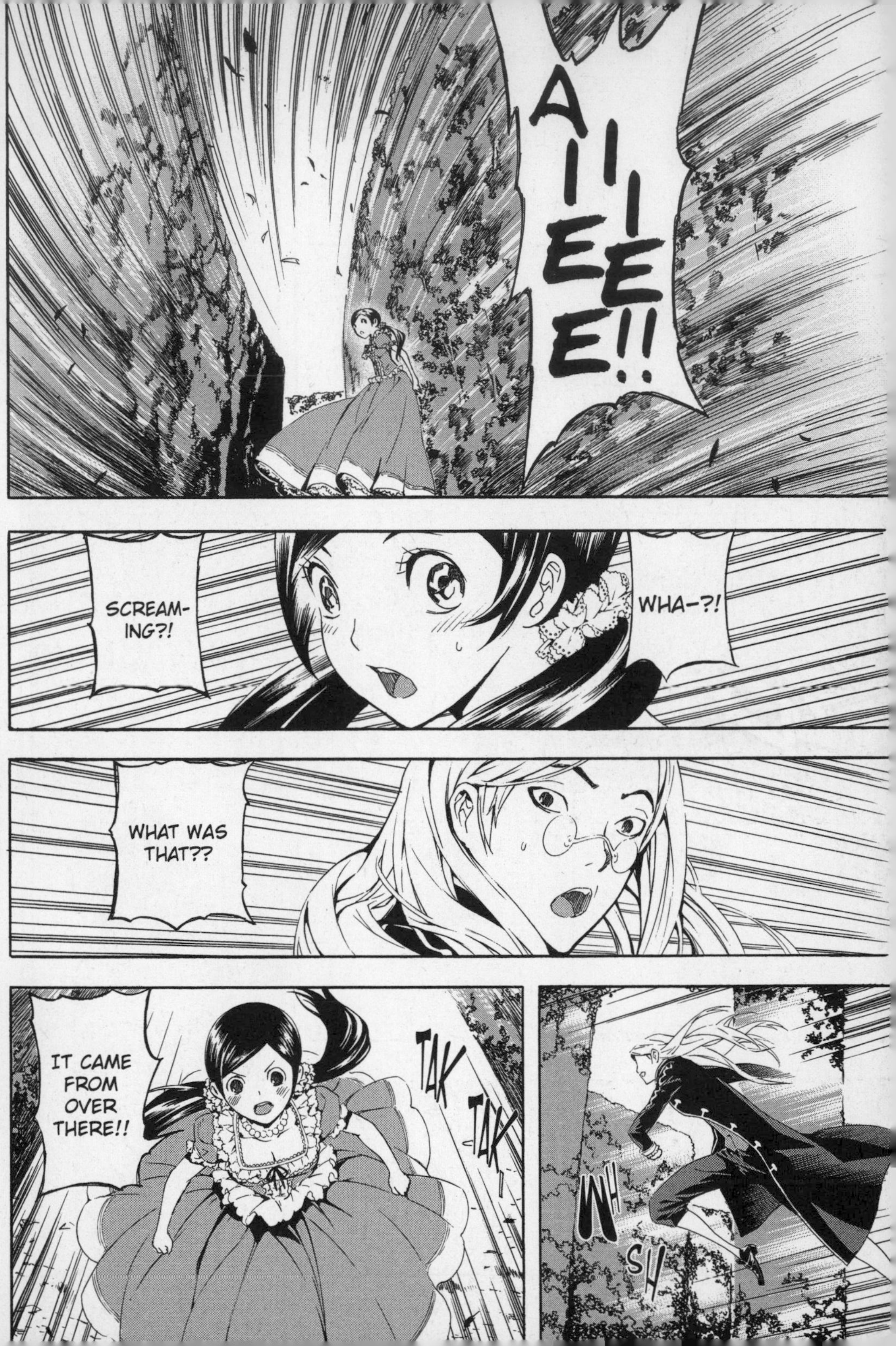
AIIIEEE!!
WHA-?!
SCREAM-ING?!
WHAT WAS THAT??
IT CAME FROM OVER THERE!!
TAK TAK
WHSH

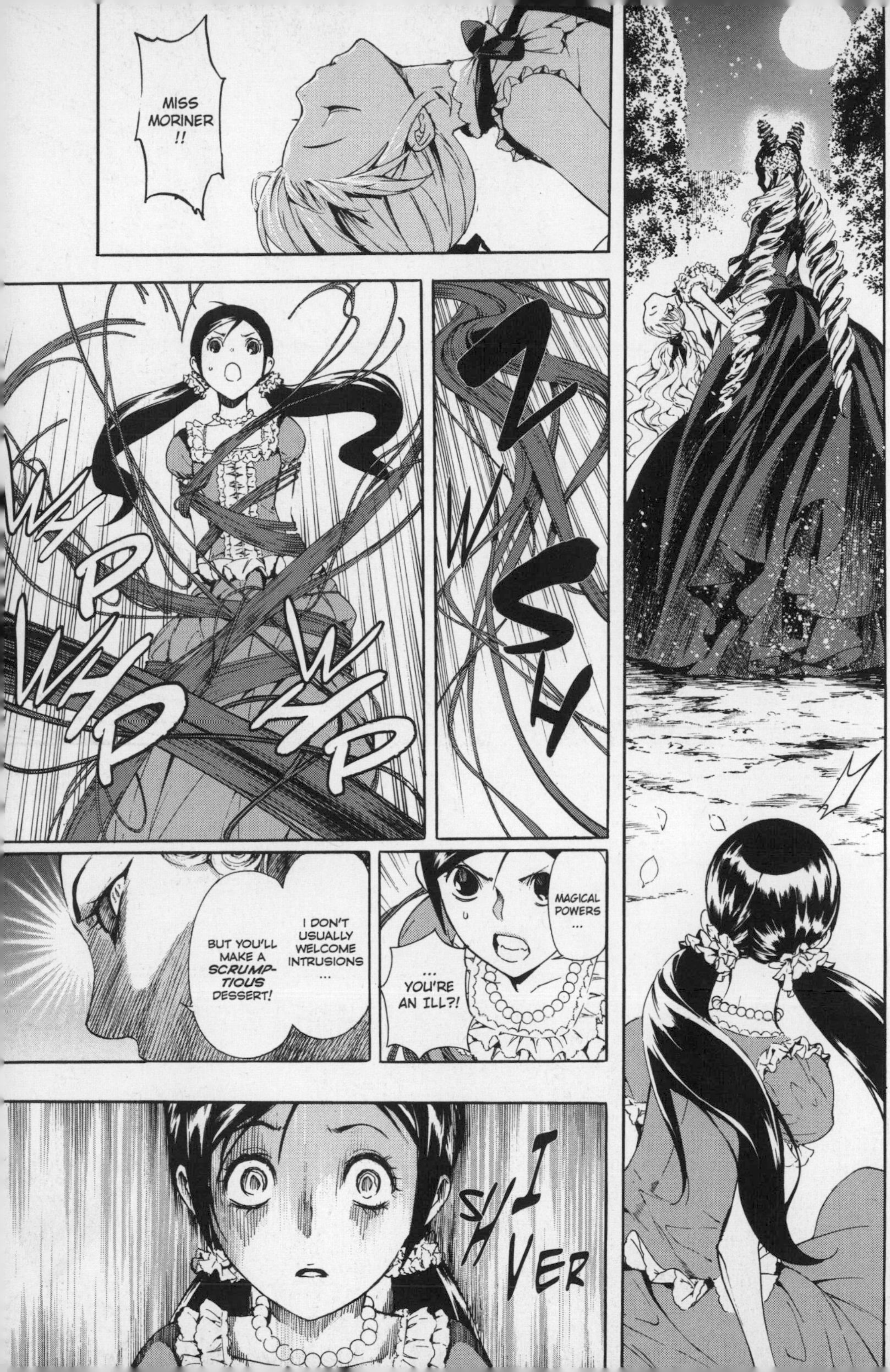

MISS MORINER !!
SWISH
WHIP
WHIP
WHIP
MAGICAL POWERS ...
... YOU'RE AN ILL?!
I DON'T USUALLY WELCOME INTRUSIONS ...
BUT YOU'LL MAKE A *SCRUMPTIOUS* DESSERT!
SHIVER

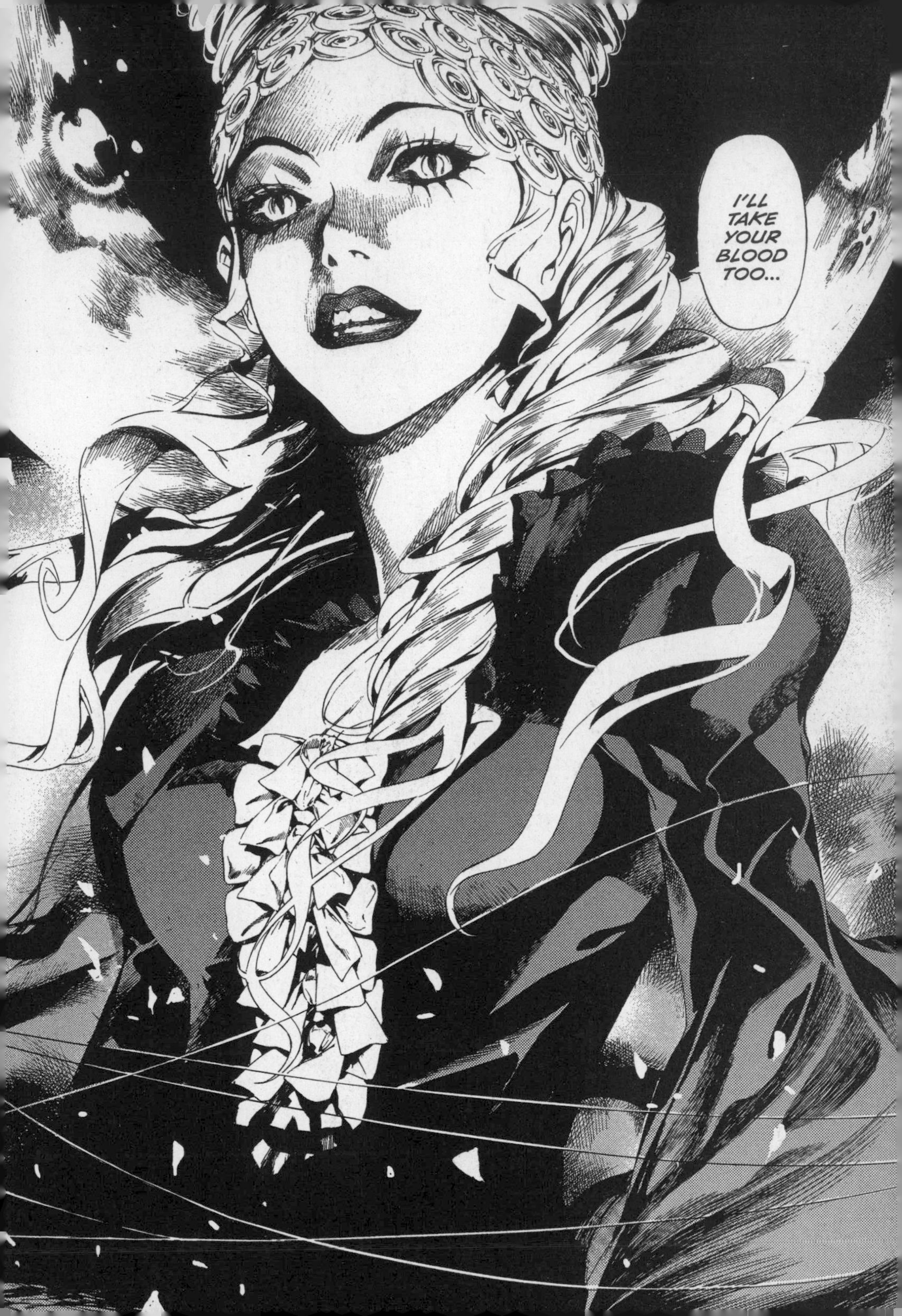
I'LL TAKE YOUR BLOOD TOO...

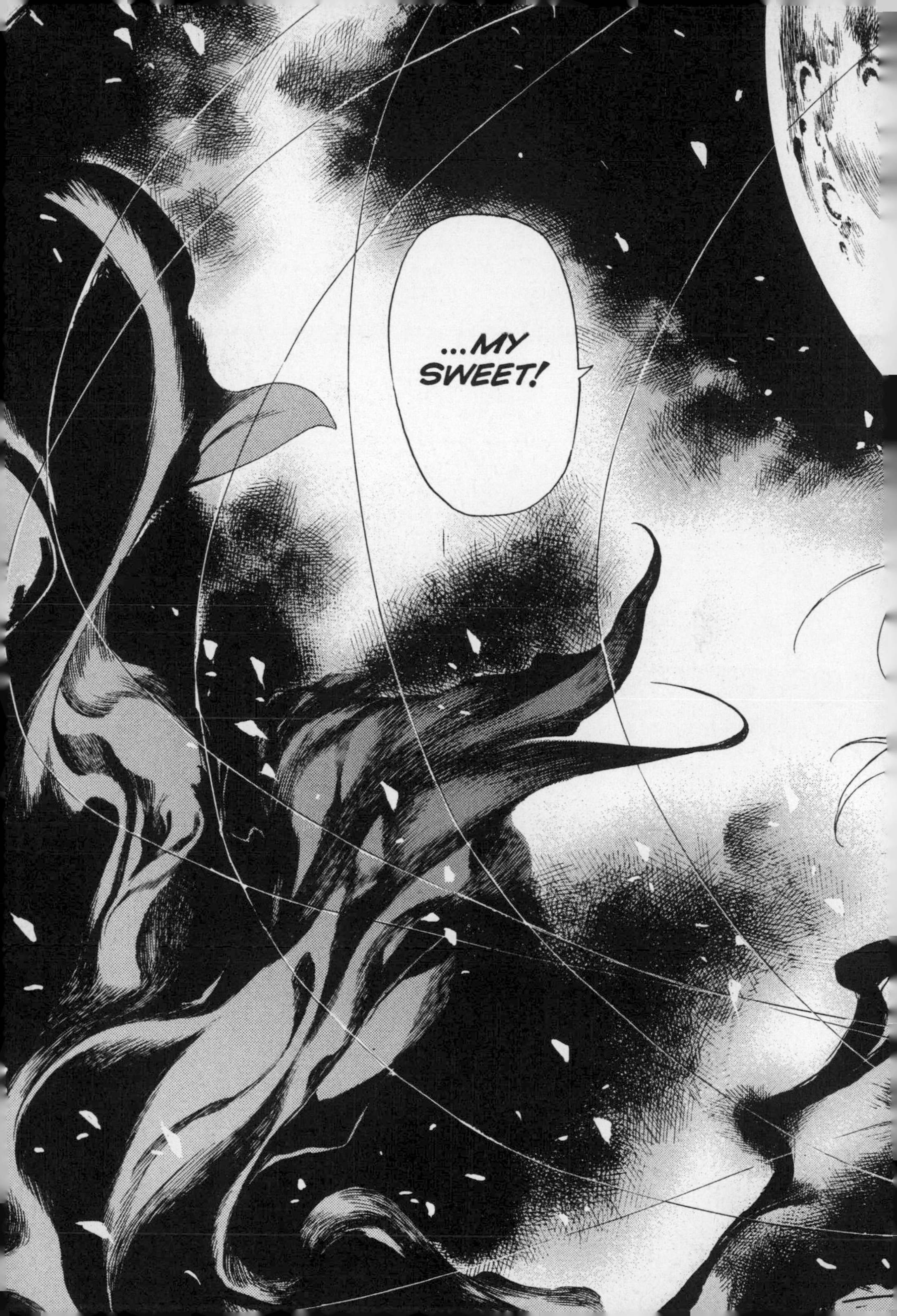
...MY SWEET!

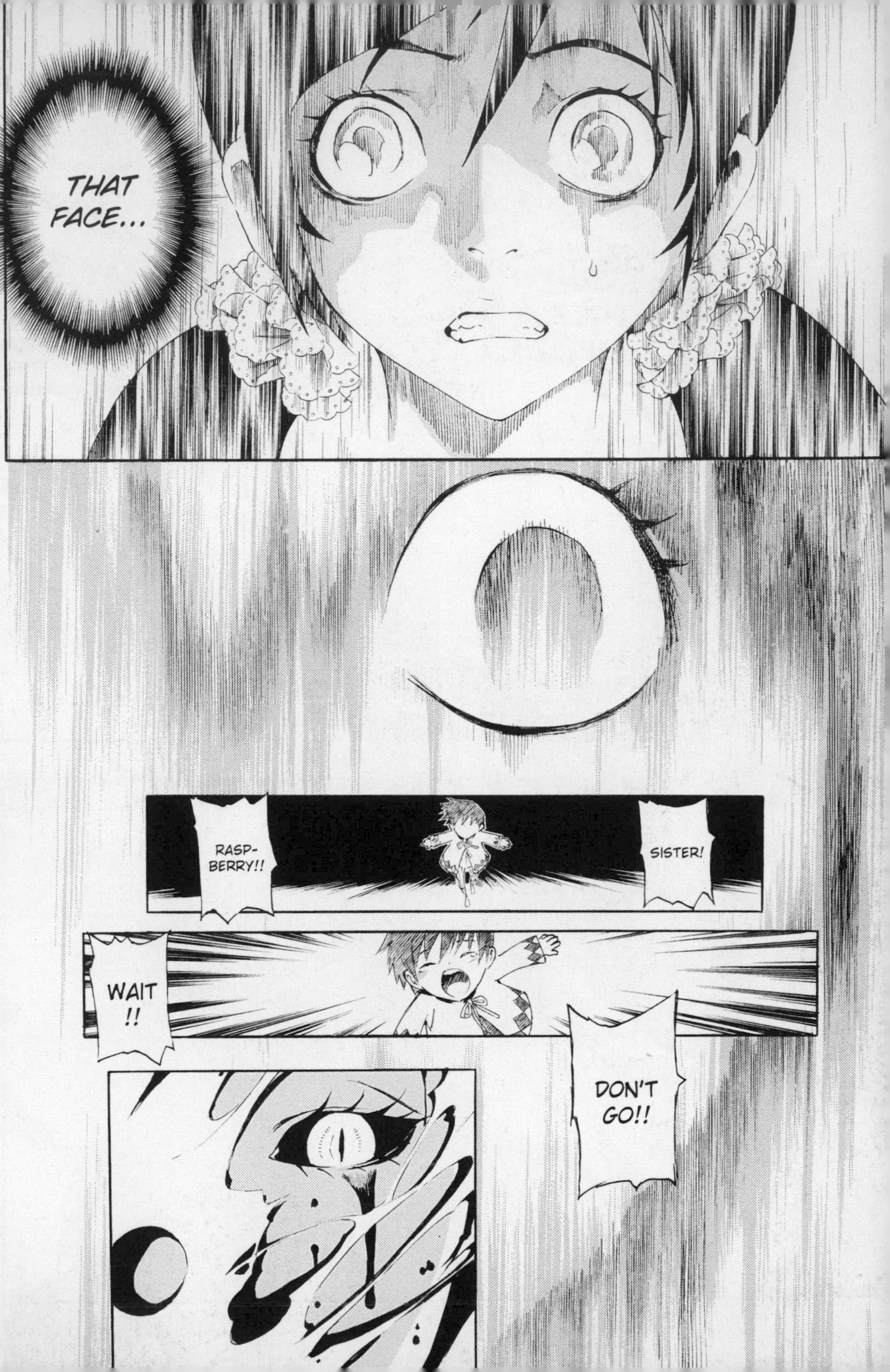
THAT FACE...
SISTER!
RASP-BERRY!!
WAIT!!
DON'T GO!!

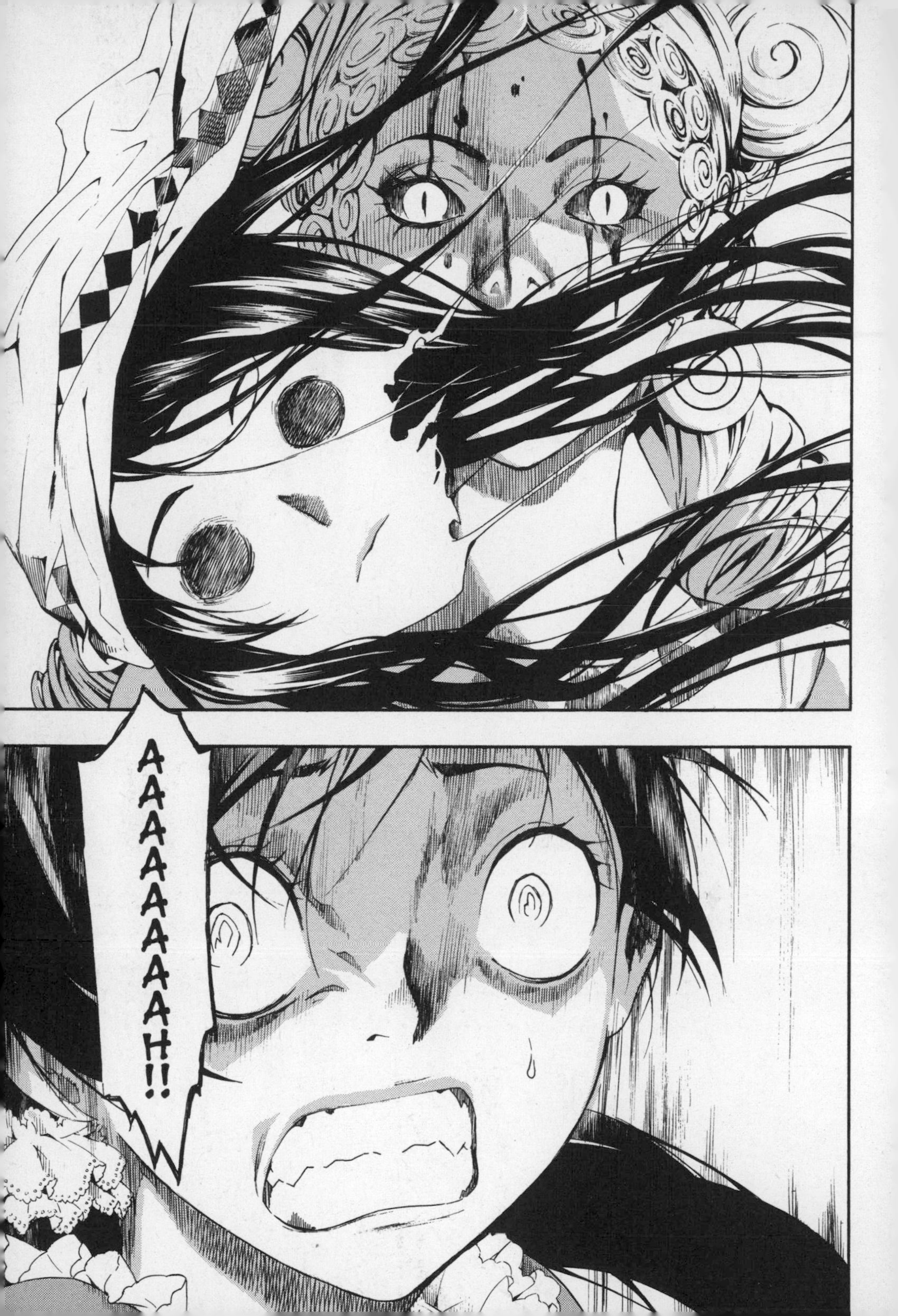
AAAAAAAAAAAH!!

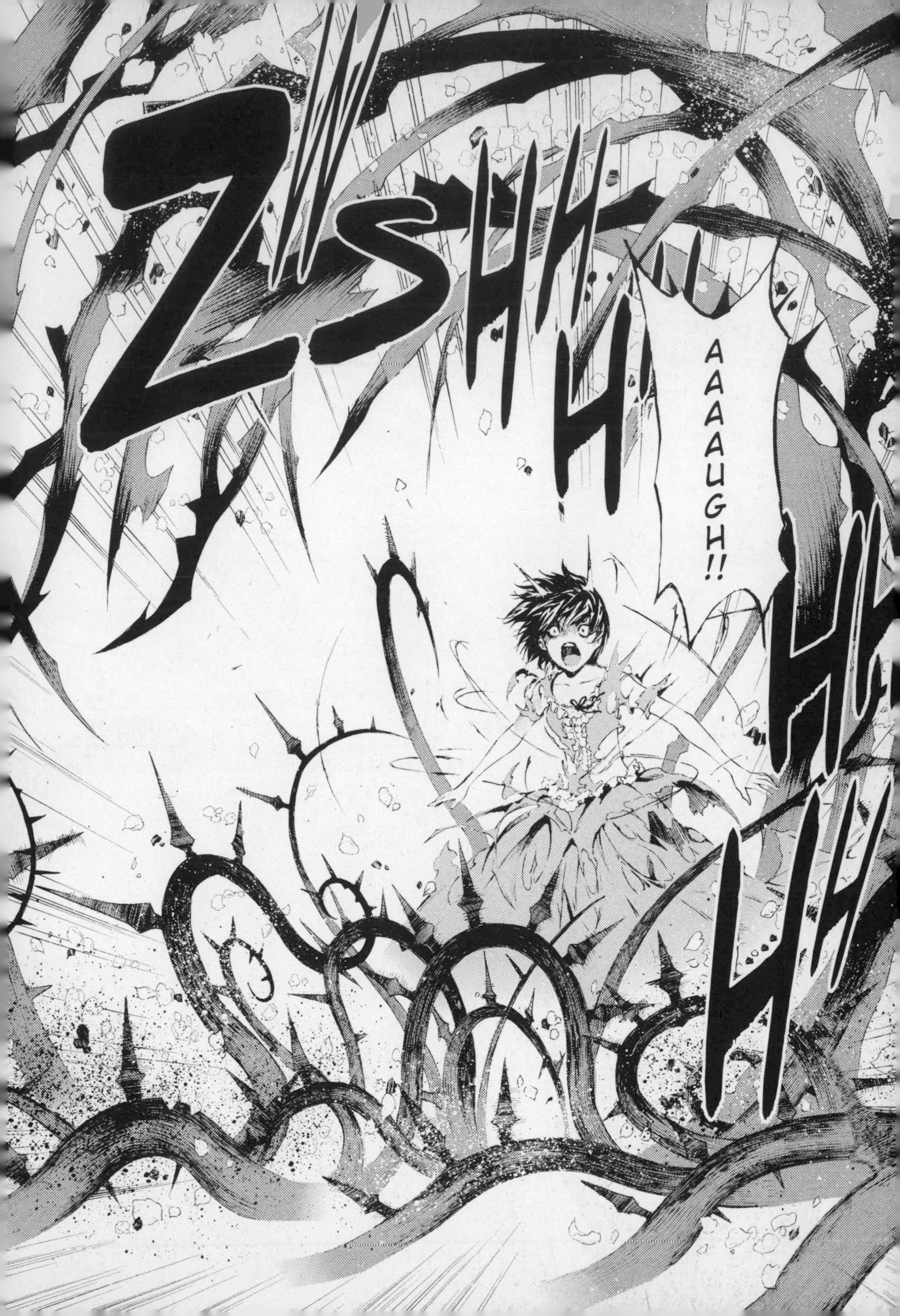
ZSHHH...
AAAAAUGH!!
HHH

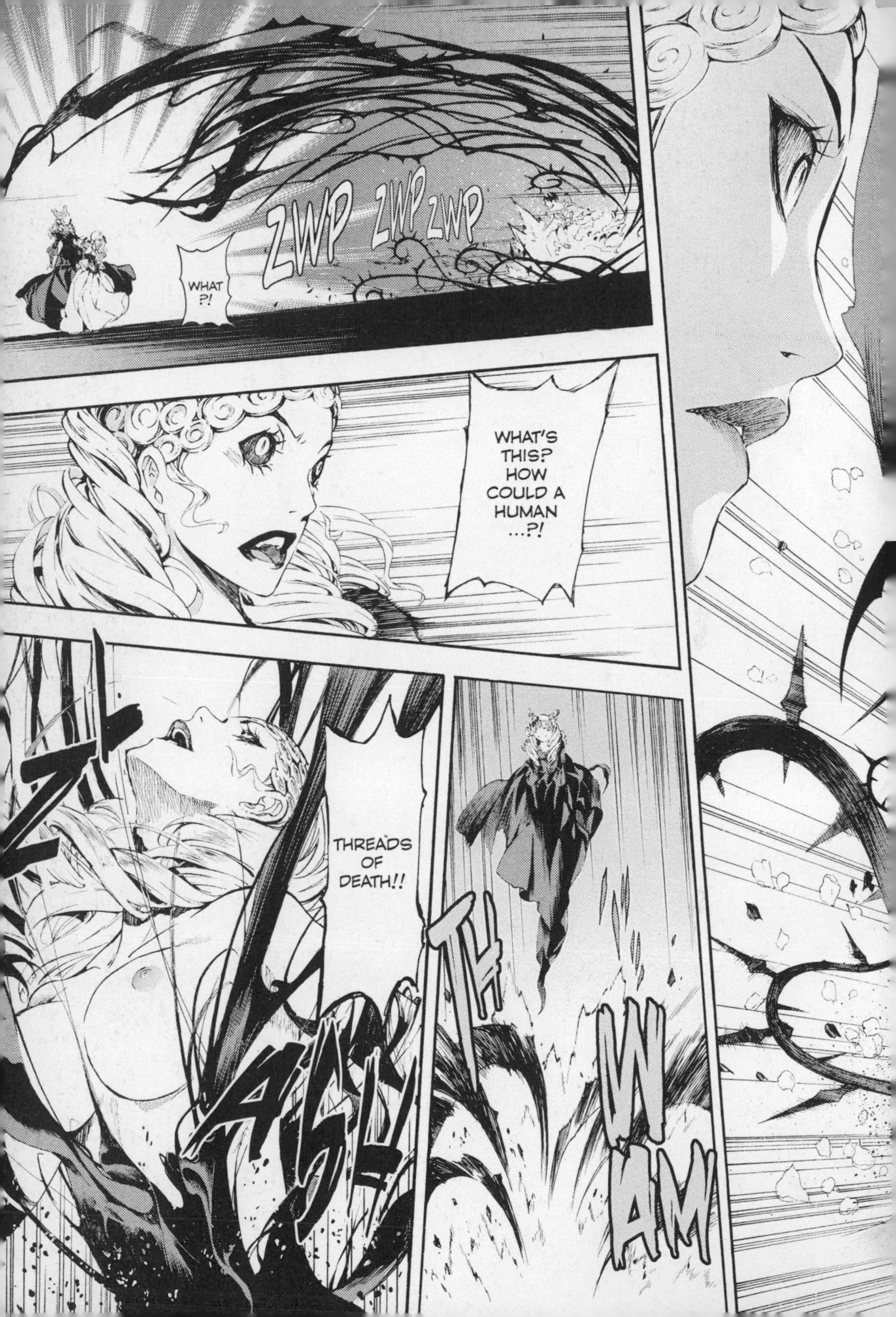
ZWP ZWP ZWP
WHAT ?!
WHAT'S THIS? HOW COULD A HUMAN ...?!
THREADS OF DEATH!!

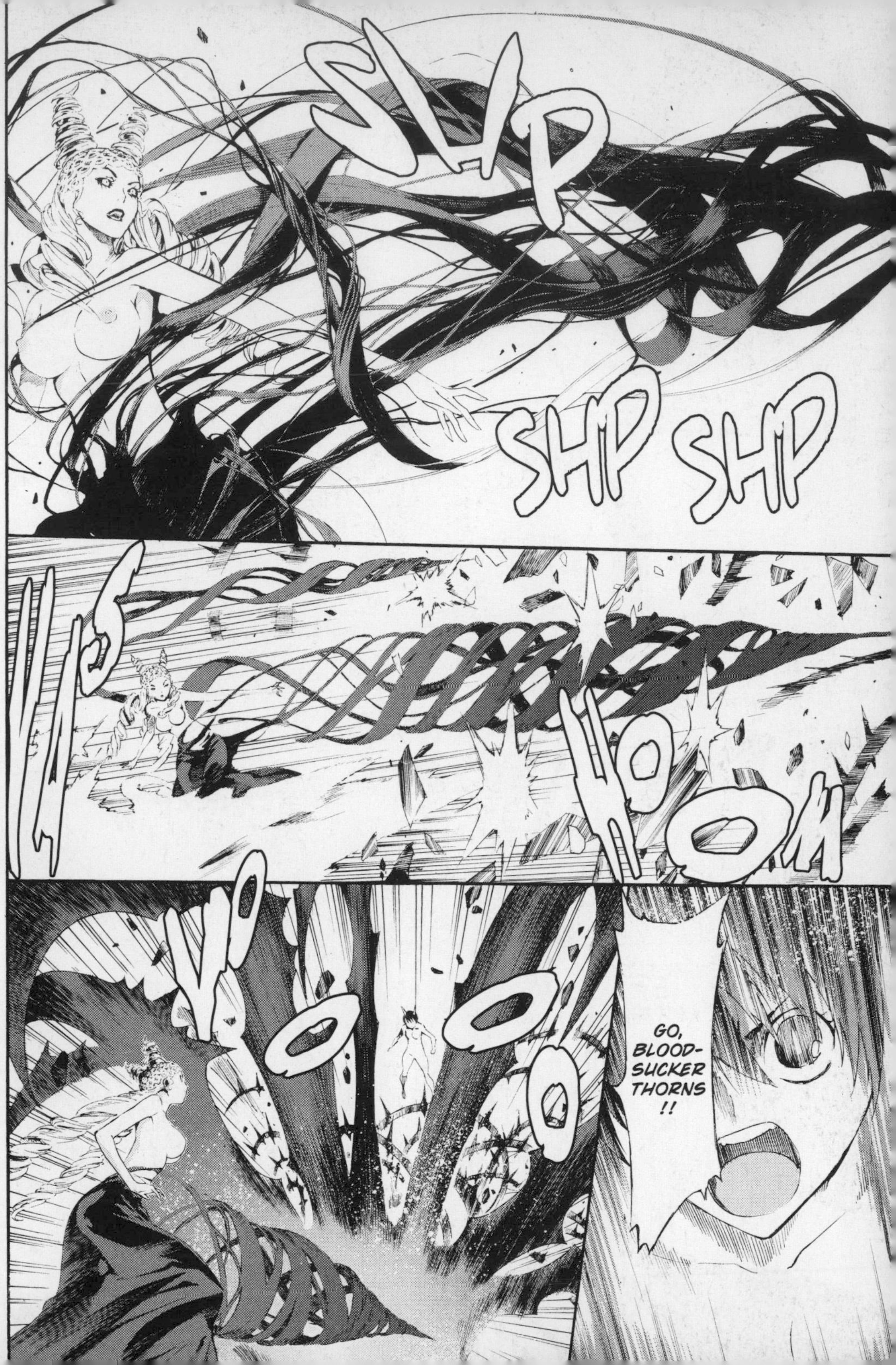
SHP
SHP SHP
GO, BLOOD-SUCKER THORNS!!

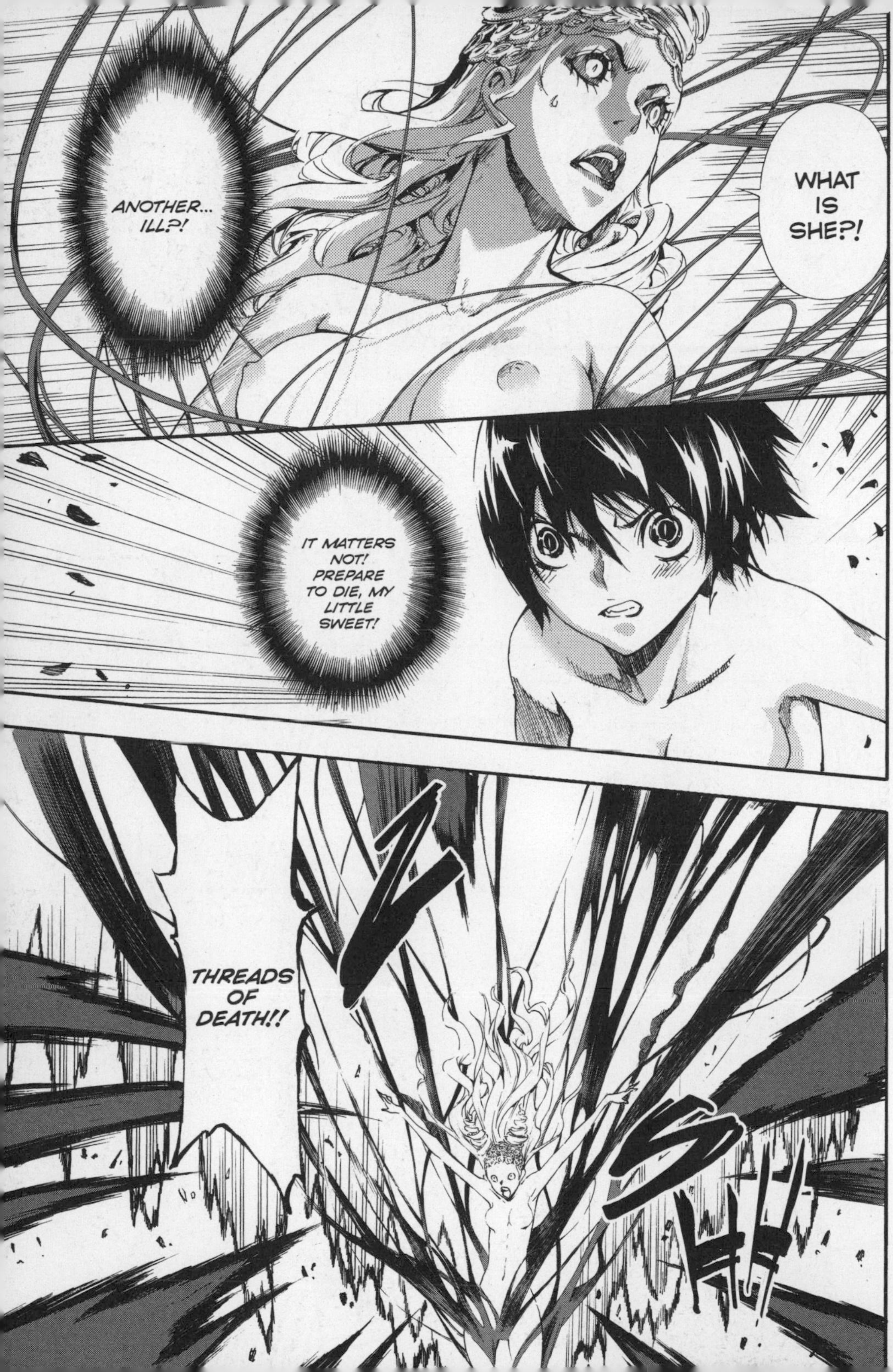
WHAT IS SHE?!
ANOTHER... ILL?!
IT MATTERS NOT! PREPARE TO DIE, MY LITTLE SWEET!
THREADS OF DEATH!!

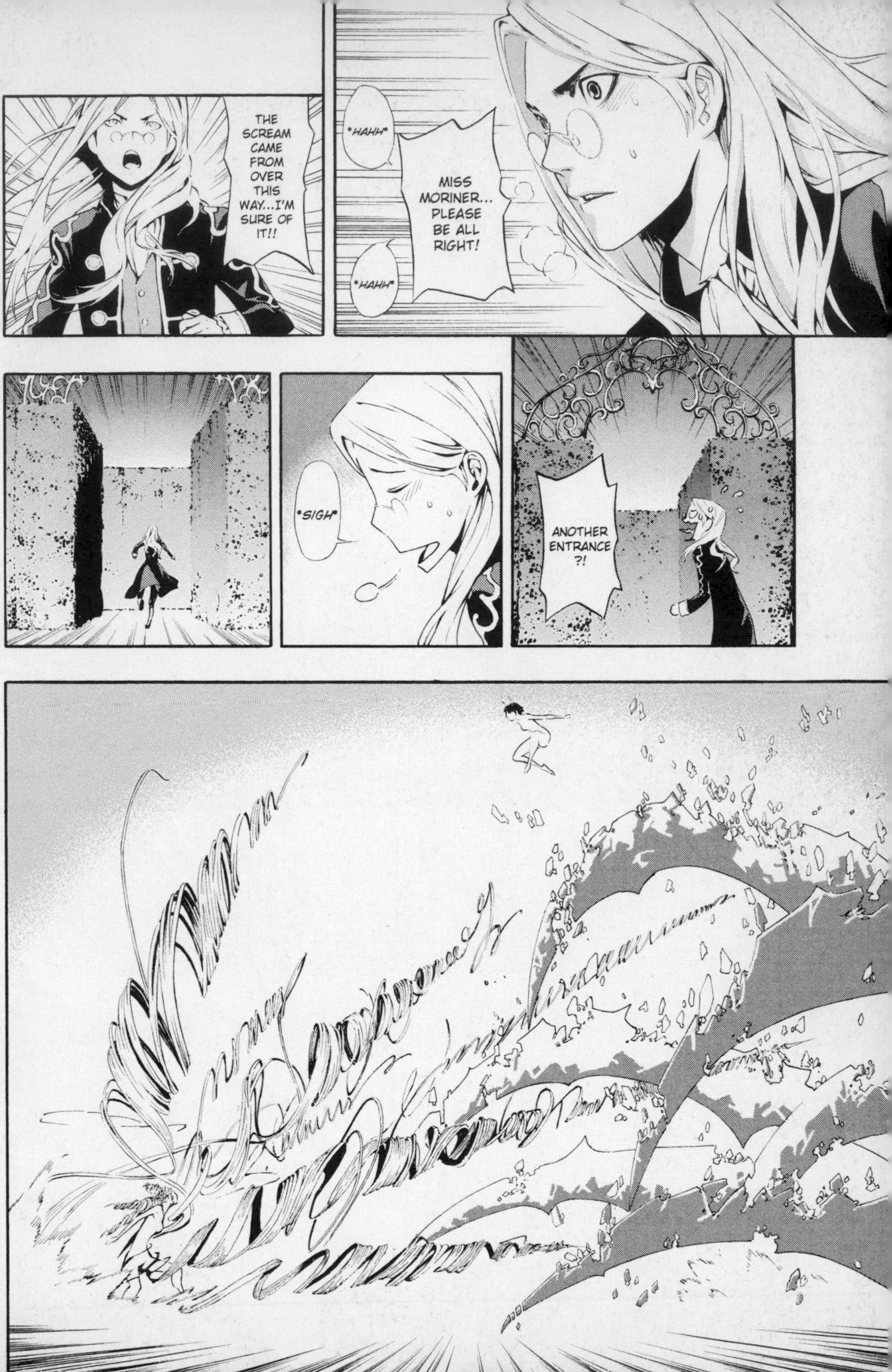
HAHH
MISS MORINER... PLEASE BE ALL RIGHT!
HAHH
THE SCREAM CAME FROM OVER THIS WAY...I'M SURE OF IT!!
ANOTHER ENTRANCE ?!
SIGH

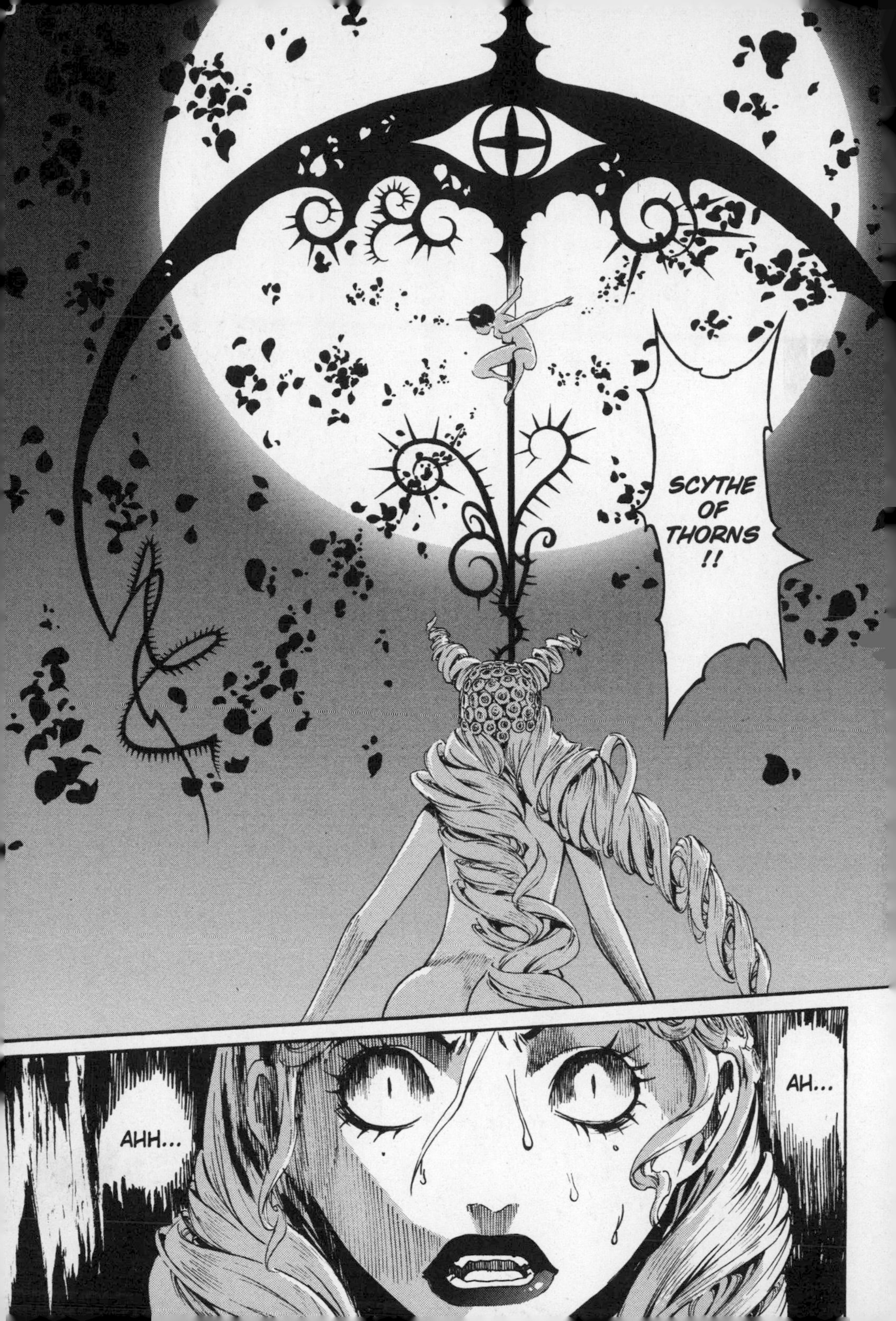
SCYTHE OF THORNS !!
AH...
AHH...

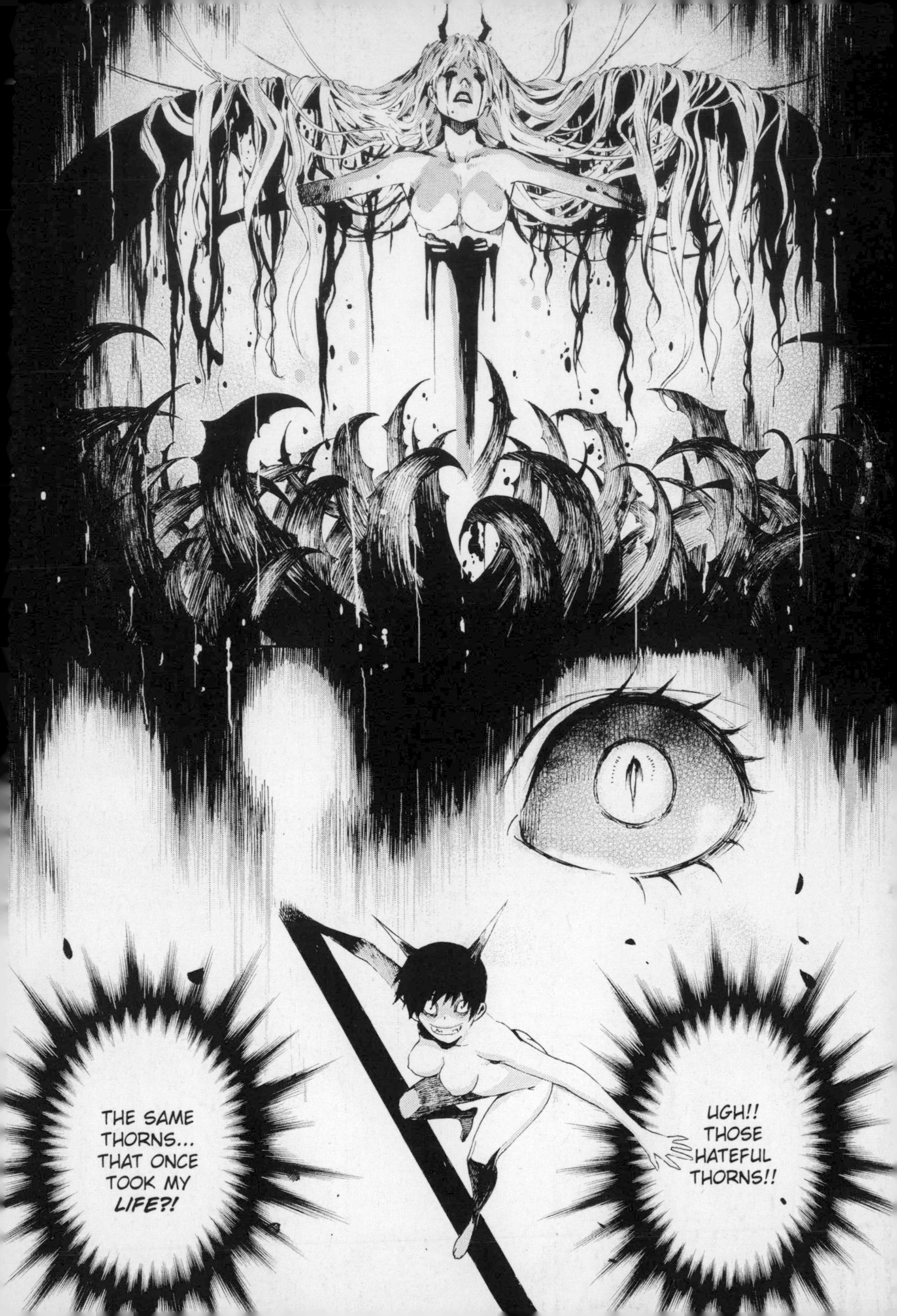
UGH!! THOSE HATEFUL THORNS!!
THE SAME THORNS... THAT ONCE TOOK MY *LIFE?!*

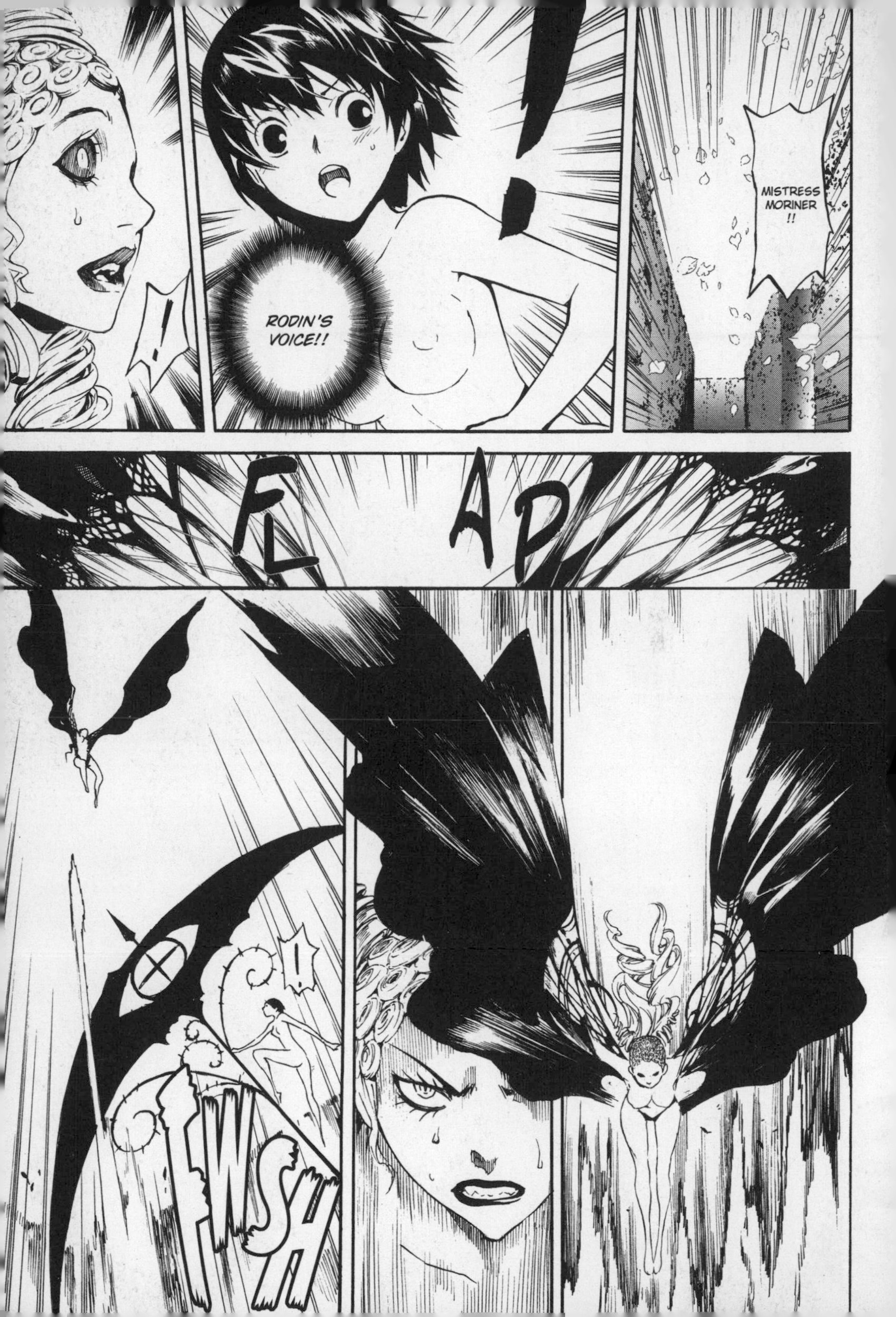
MISTRESS MORINER !!
!
RODIN'S VOICE!!
!
FLAP
!
FWSH

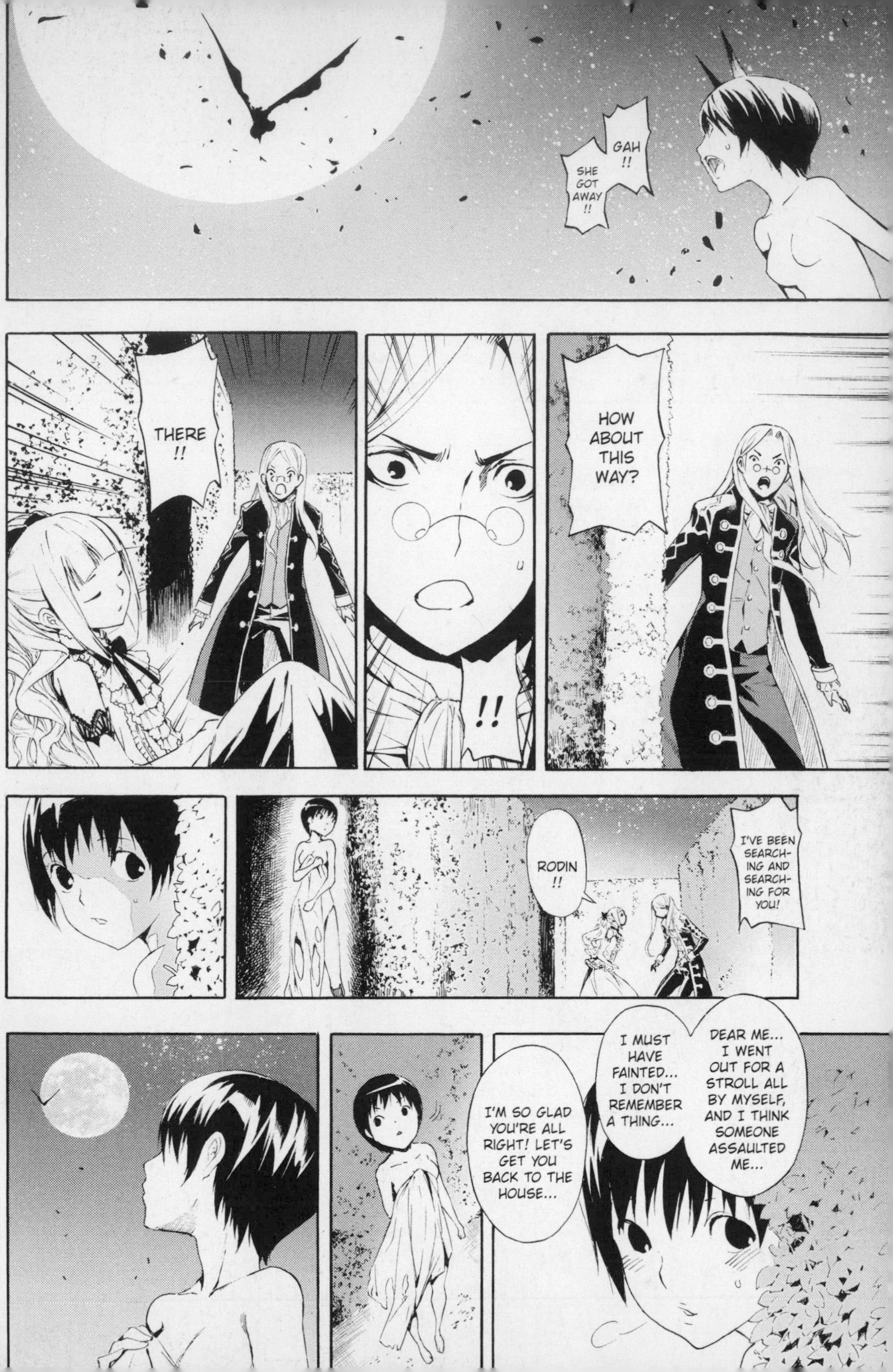
GAH !!
SHE GOT AWAY !!
HOW ABOUT THIS WAY?
!!
THERE !!
I'VE BEEN SEARCH-ING AND SEARCH-ING FOR YOU!
RODIN !!
DEAR ME... I WENT OUT FOR A STROLL ALL BY MYSELF, AND I THINK SOMEONE ASSAULTED ME...
I MUST HAVE FAINTED... I DON'T REMEMBER A THING...
I'M SO GLAD YOU'RE ALL RIGHT! LET'S GET YOU BACK TO THE HOUSE...

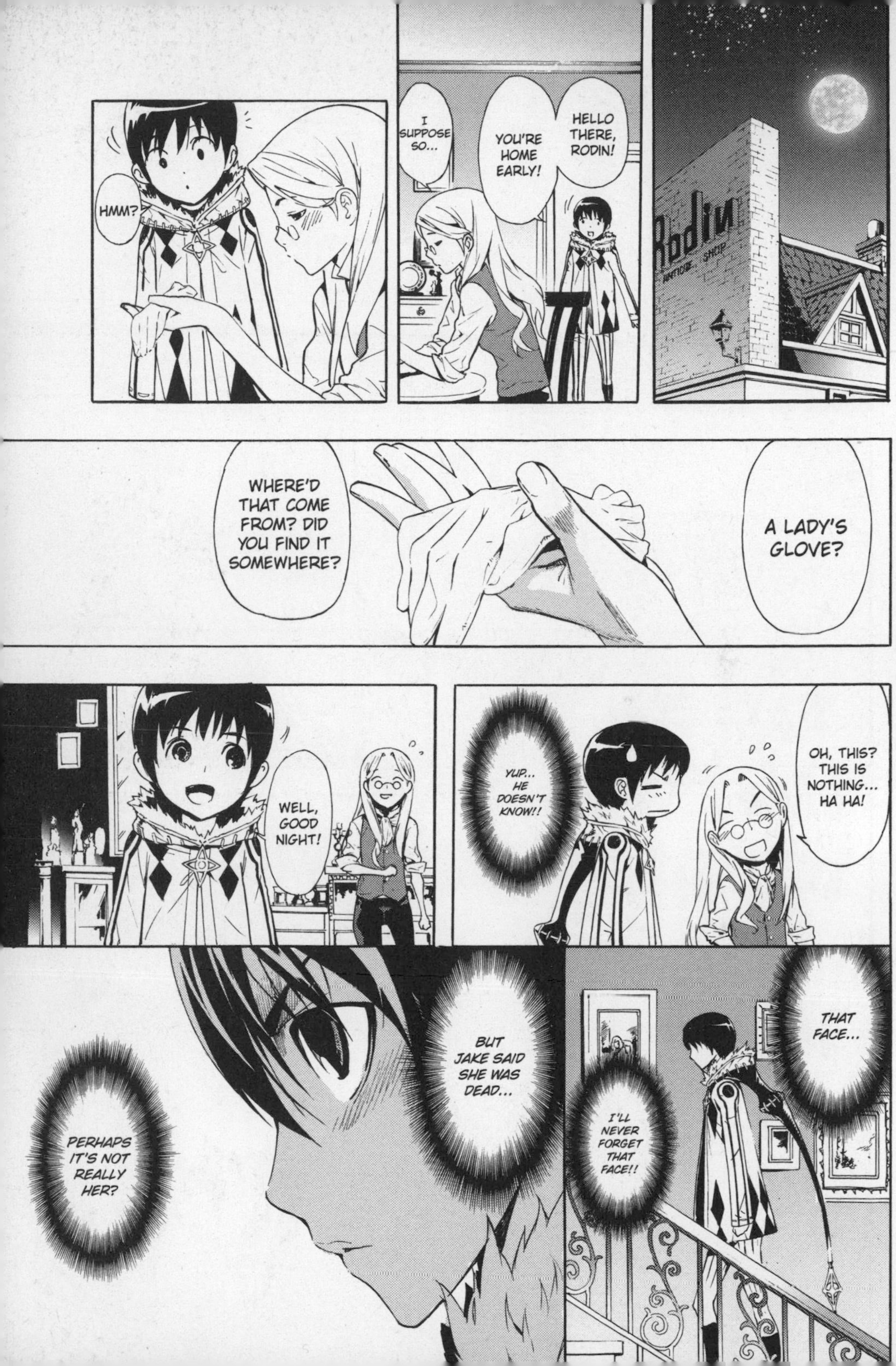
Rodin
HELLO THERE, RODIN!
YOU'RE HOME EARLY!
I SUPPOSE SO...
HMM?
A LADY'S GLOVE?
WHERE'D THAT COME FROM? DID YOU FIND IT SOMEWHERE?
OH, THIS? THIS IS NOTHING... HA HA!
YUP... HE DOESN'T KNOW!!
WELL, GOOD NIGHT!
THAT FACE...
I'LL NEVER FORGET THAT FACE!!
BUT JAKE SAID SHE WAS DEAD...
PERHAPS IT'S NOT REALLY HER?

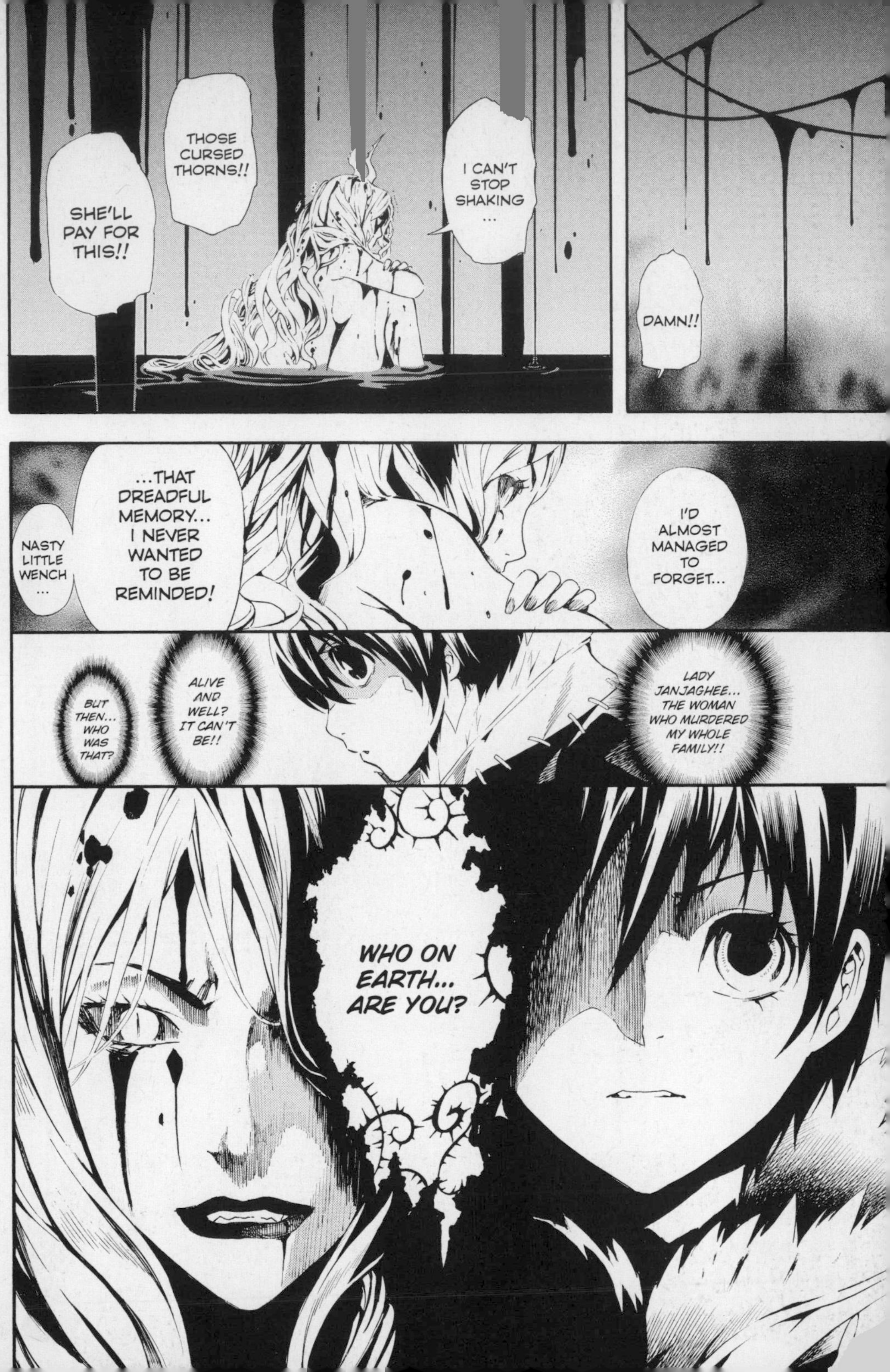
DAMN!!
I CAN'T STOP SHAKING ...
THOSE CURSED THORNS!!
SHE'LL PAY FOR THIS!!
I'D ALMOST MANAGED TO FORGET...
...THAT DREADFUL MEMORY... I NEVER WANTED TO BE REMINDED!
NASTY LITTLE WENCH ...
LADY JANJAGHEE... THE WOMAN WHO MURDERED MY WHOLE FAMILY!!
ALIVE AND WELL? IT CAN'T BE!!
BUT THEN... WHO WAS THAT?
WHO ON EARTH... ARE YOU?

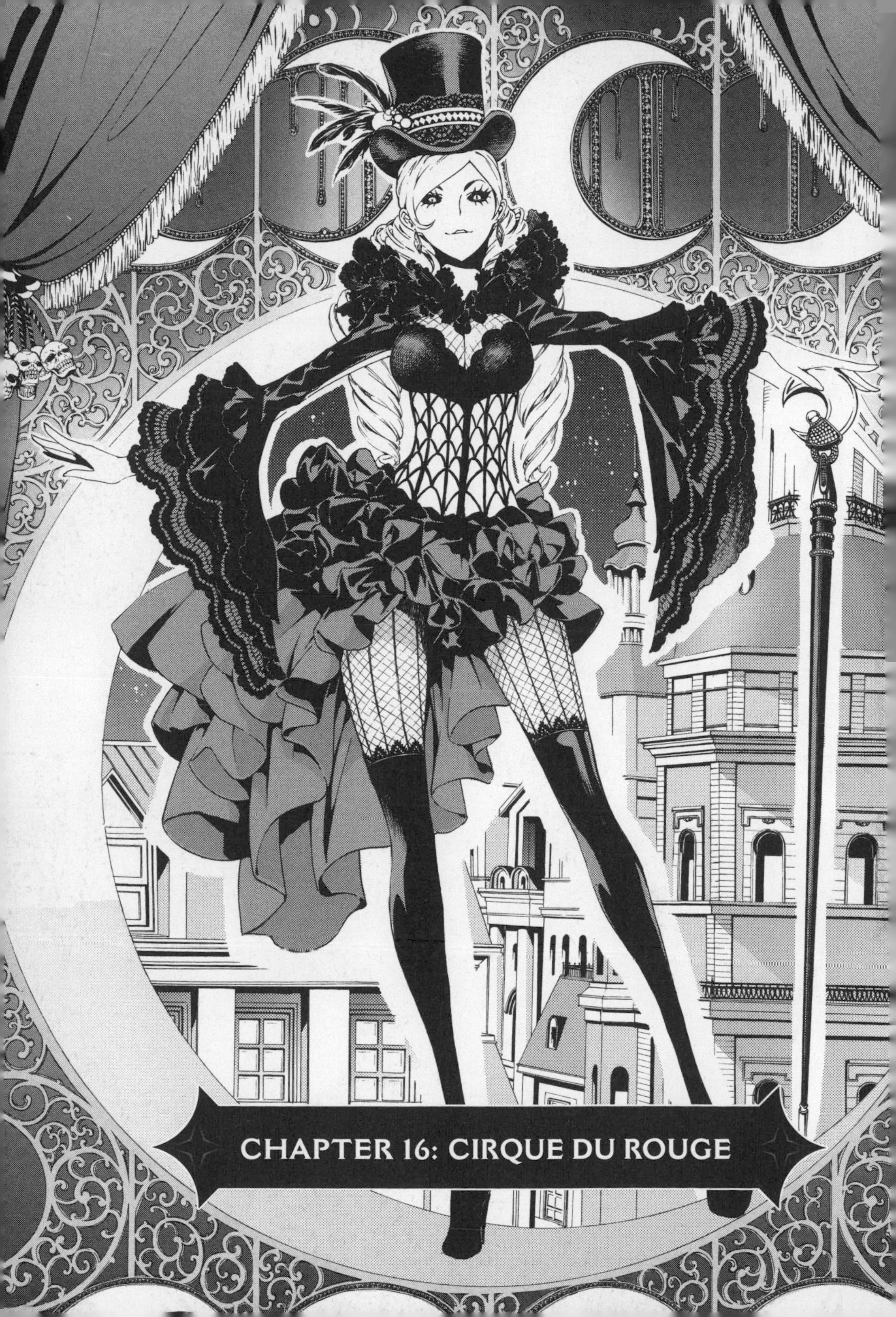
CHAPTER 16: CIRQUE DU ROUGE

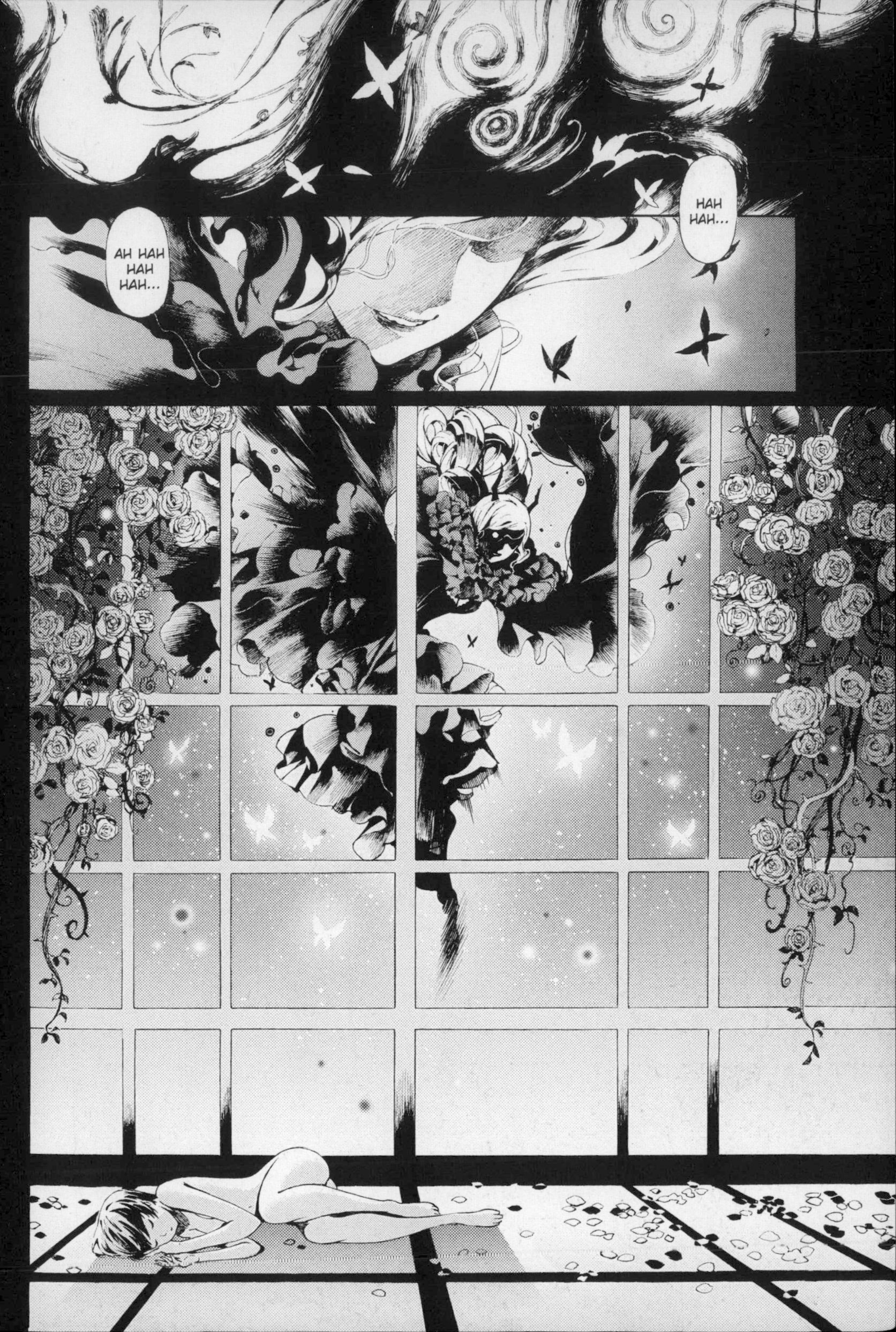
HAH HAH...
AH HAH HAH HAH...

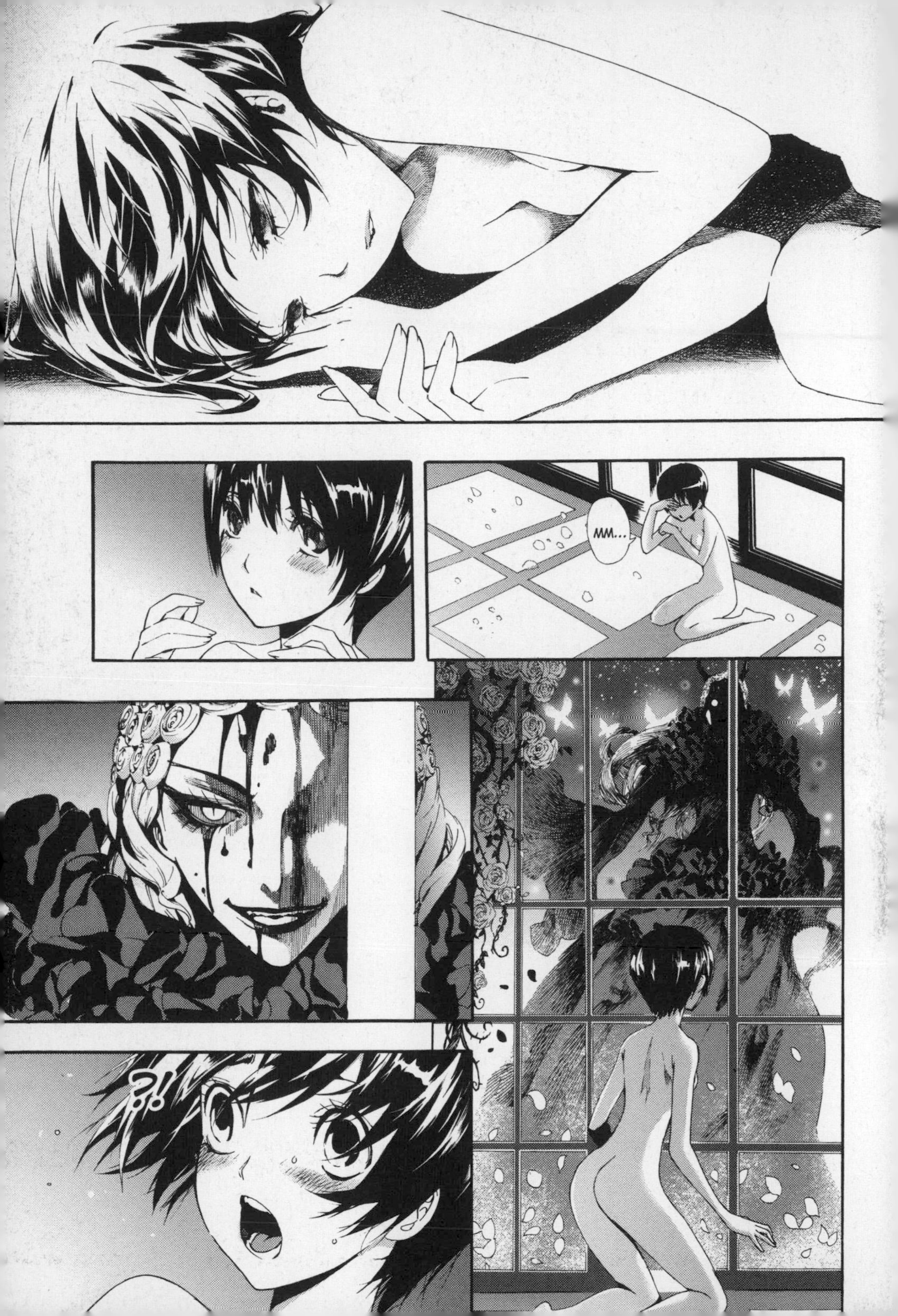
MM...
?!

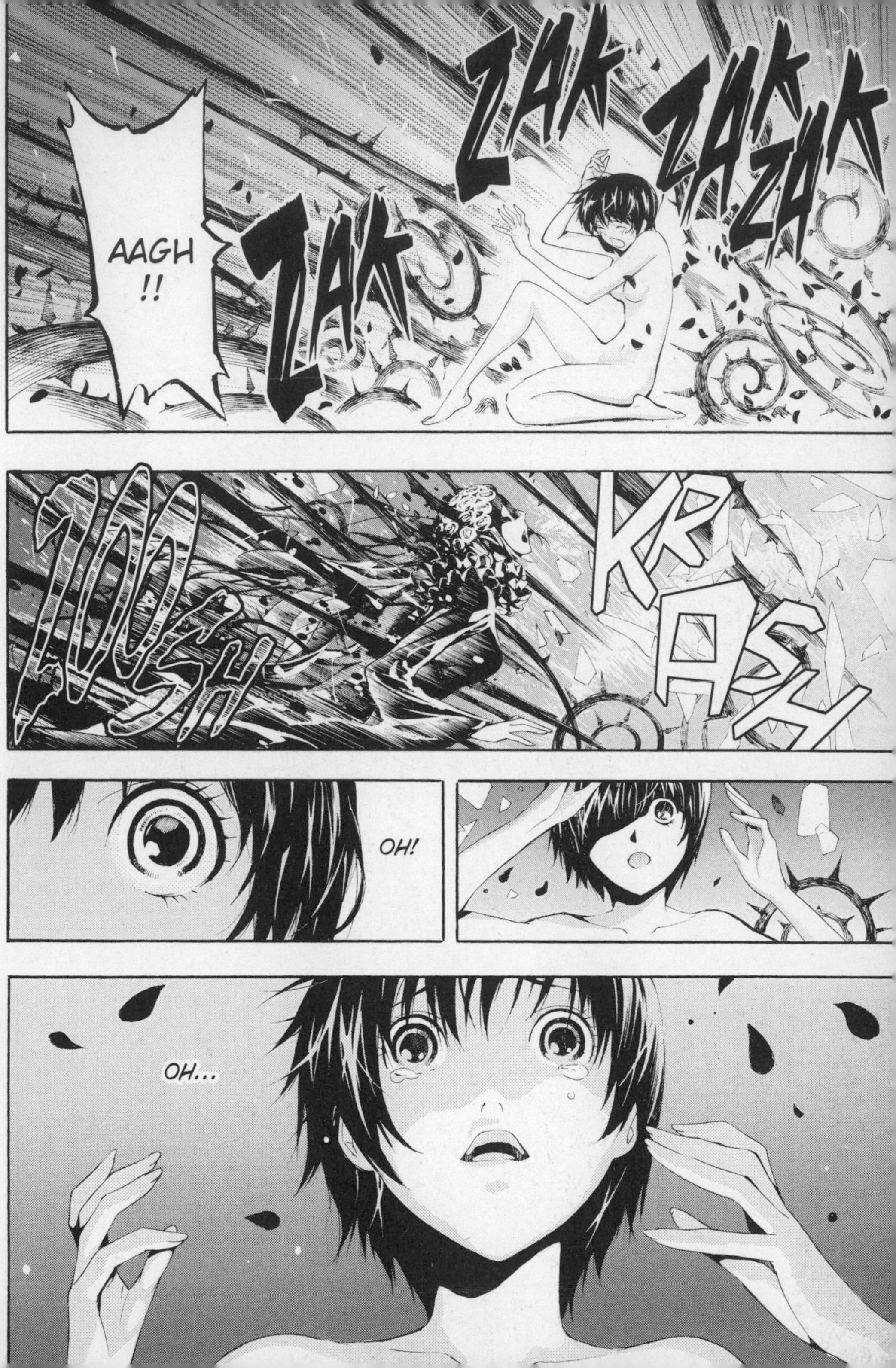
ZAZAZAK
ZAK
ZAK
AAGH !!
KRASH
WOOSH
OH!
OH...

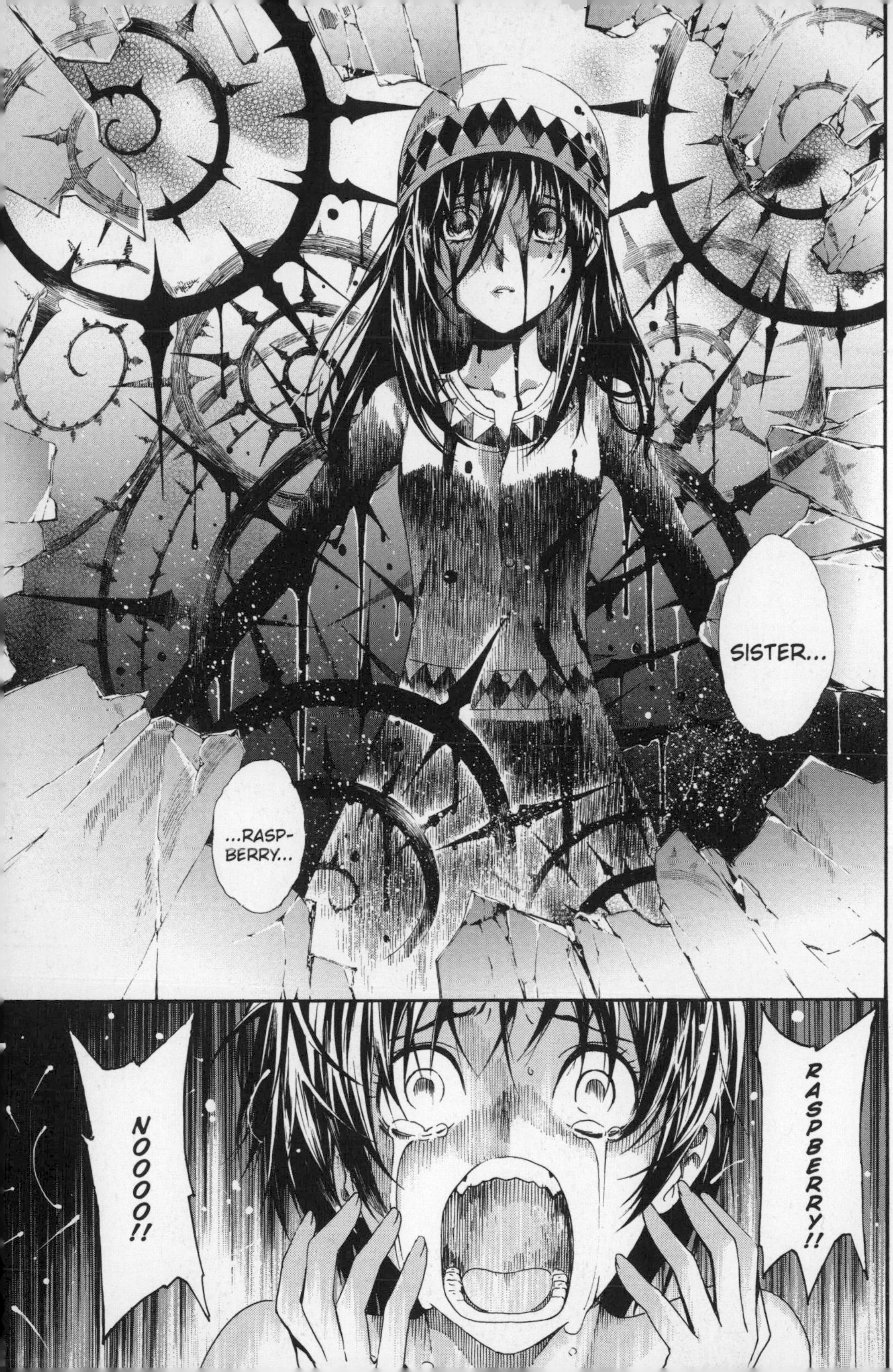
SISTER...
...RASP-BERRY...
RASPBERRY!!
NOOOOO!!

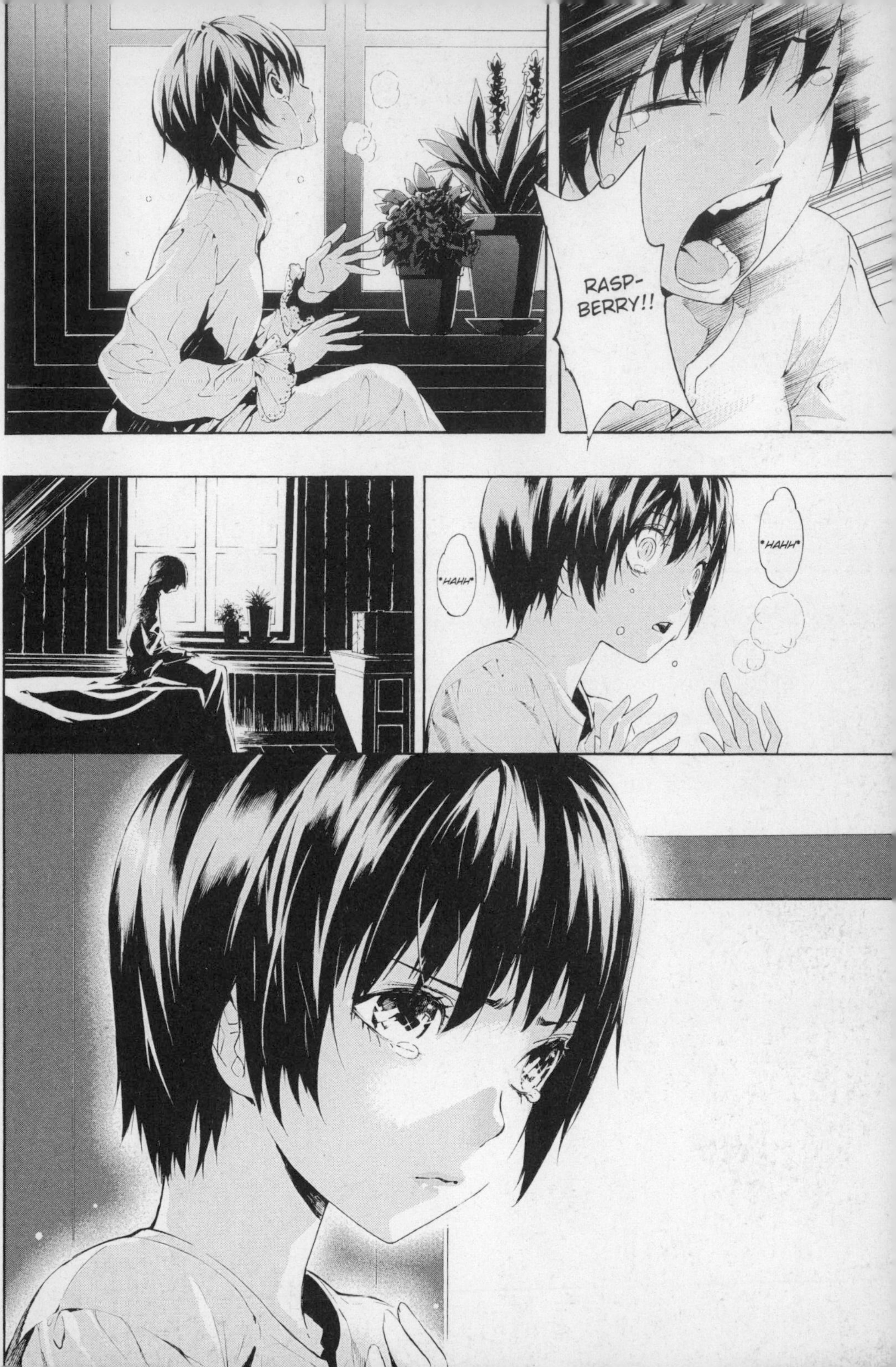
RASP-
BERRY!!
HAHH
HAHH

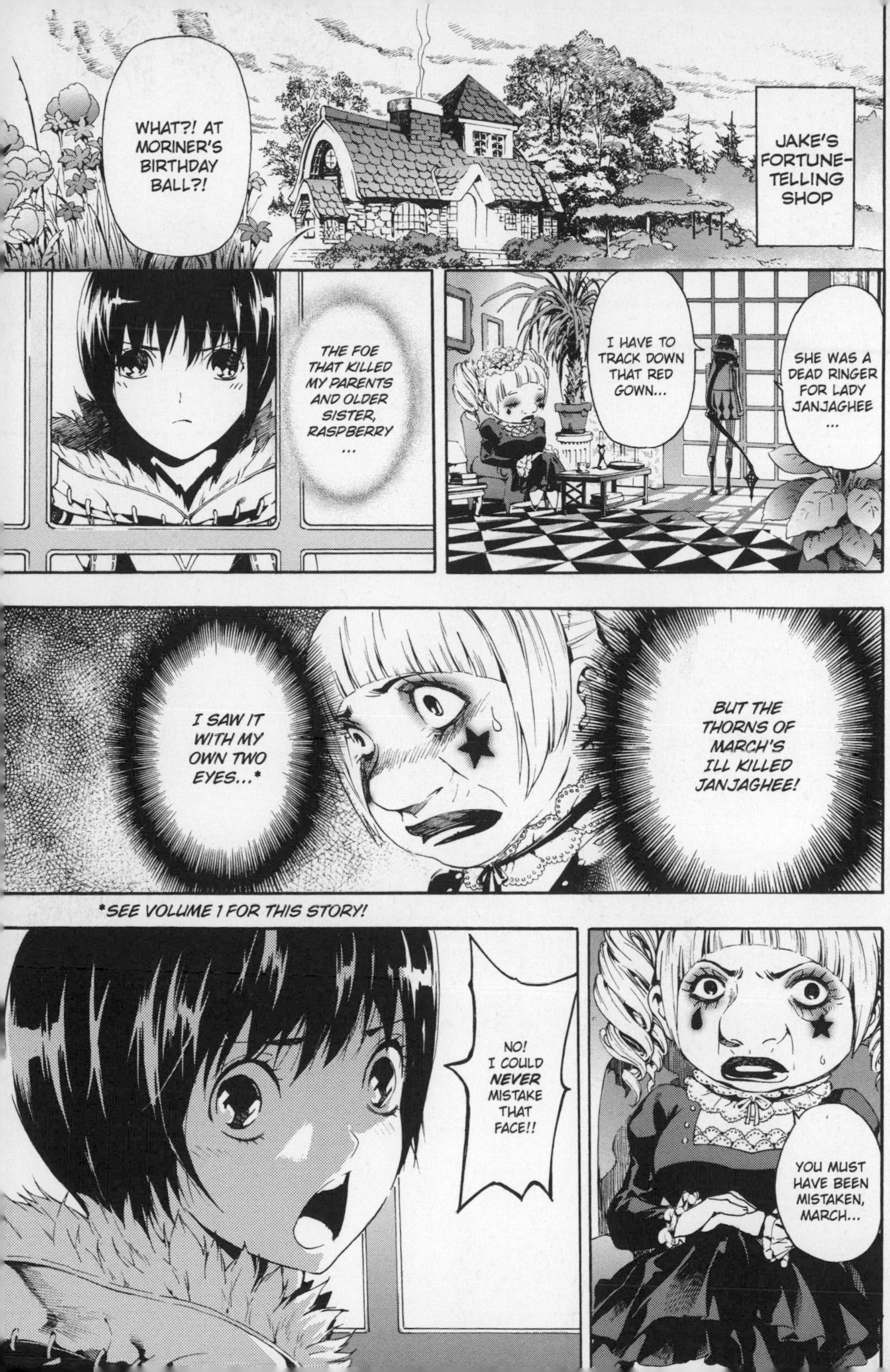
JAKE'S FORTUNE-TELLING SHOP
WHAT?! AT MORINER'S BIRTHDAY BALL?!
SHE WAS A DEAD RINGER FOR LADY JANJAGHEE...
I HAVE TO TRACK DOWN THAT RED GOWN...
THE FOE THAT KILLED MY PARENTS AND OLDER SISTER, RASPBERRY...
BUT THE THORNS OF MARCH'S ILL KILLED JANJAGHEE!
I SAW IT WITH MY OWN TWO EYES...*
*SEE VOLUME 1 FOR THIS STORY!
YOU MUST HAVE BEEN MISTAKEN, MARCH...
NO! I COULD NEVER MISTAKE THAT FACE!!

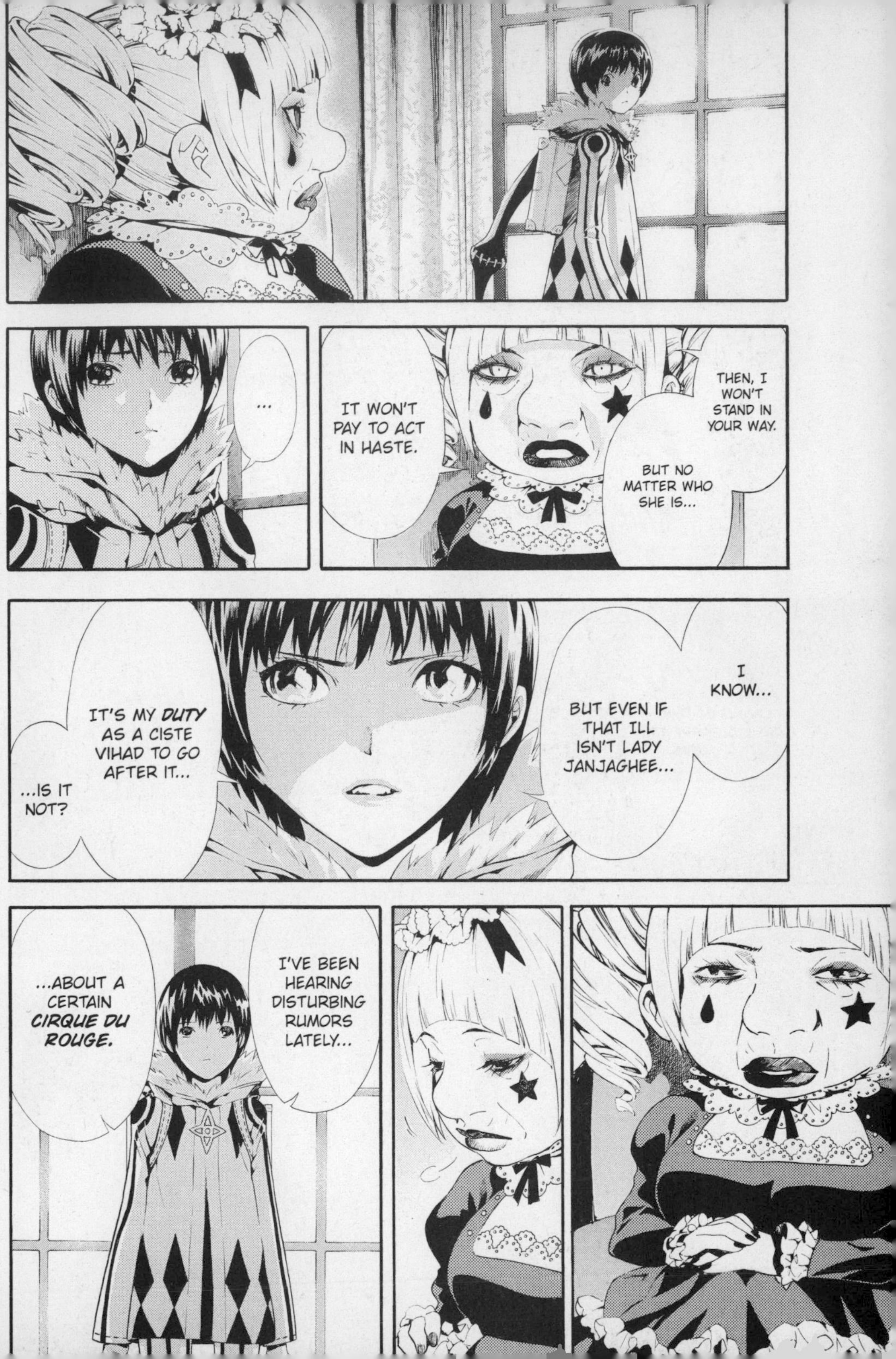
THEN, I WON'T STAND IN YOUR WAY.
BUT NO MATTER WHO SHE IS...
IT WON'T PAY TO ACT IN HASTE.
...
I KNOW...
BUT EVEN IF THAT ILL ISN'T LADY JANJAGHEE...
IT'S MY *DUTY* AS A CISTE VIHAD TO GO AFTER IT...
...IS IT NOT?
I'VE BEEN HEARING DISTURBING RUMORS LATELY...
...ABOUT A CERTAIN ***CIRQUE DU ROUGE.***

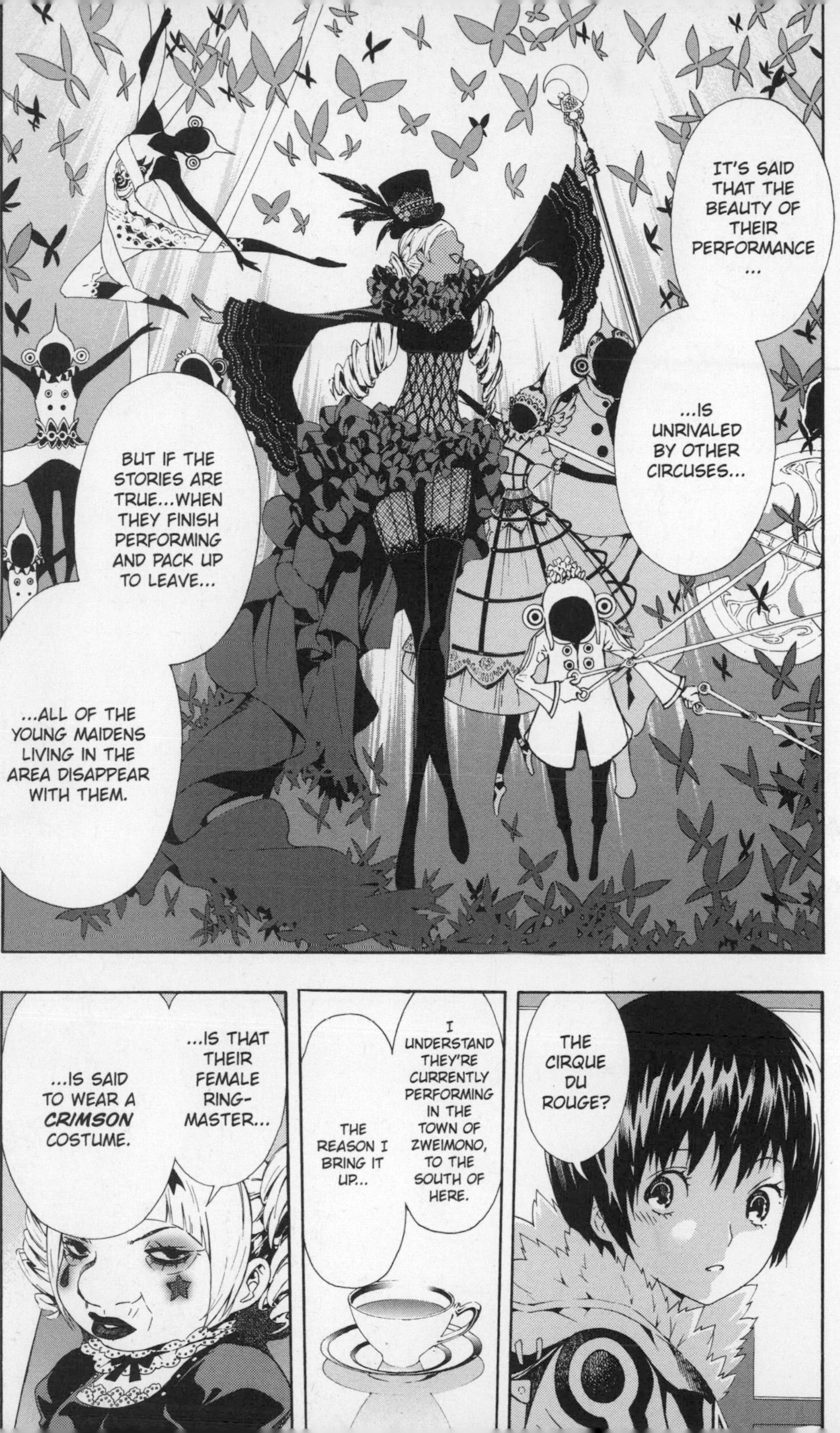
IT'S SAID THAT THE BEAUTY OF THEIR PERFORMANCE ...
...IS UNRIVALED BY OTHER CIRCUSES...
BUT IF THE STORIES ARE TRUE...WHEN THEY FINISH PERFORMING AND PACK UP TO LEAVE...
...ALL OF THE YOUNG MAIDENS LIVING IN THE AREA DISAPPEAR WITH THEM.
THE CIRQUE DU ROUGE?
I UNDERSTAND THEY'RE CURRENTLY PERFORMING IN THE TOWN OF ZWEIMONO, TO THE SOUTH OF HERE.
THE REASON I BRING IT UP...
...IS THAT THEIR FEMALE RING-MASTER...
...IS SAID TO WEAR A ***CRIMSON*** COSTUME.

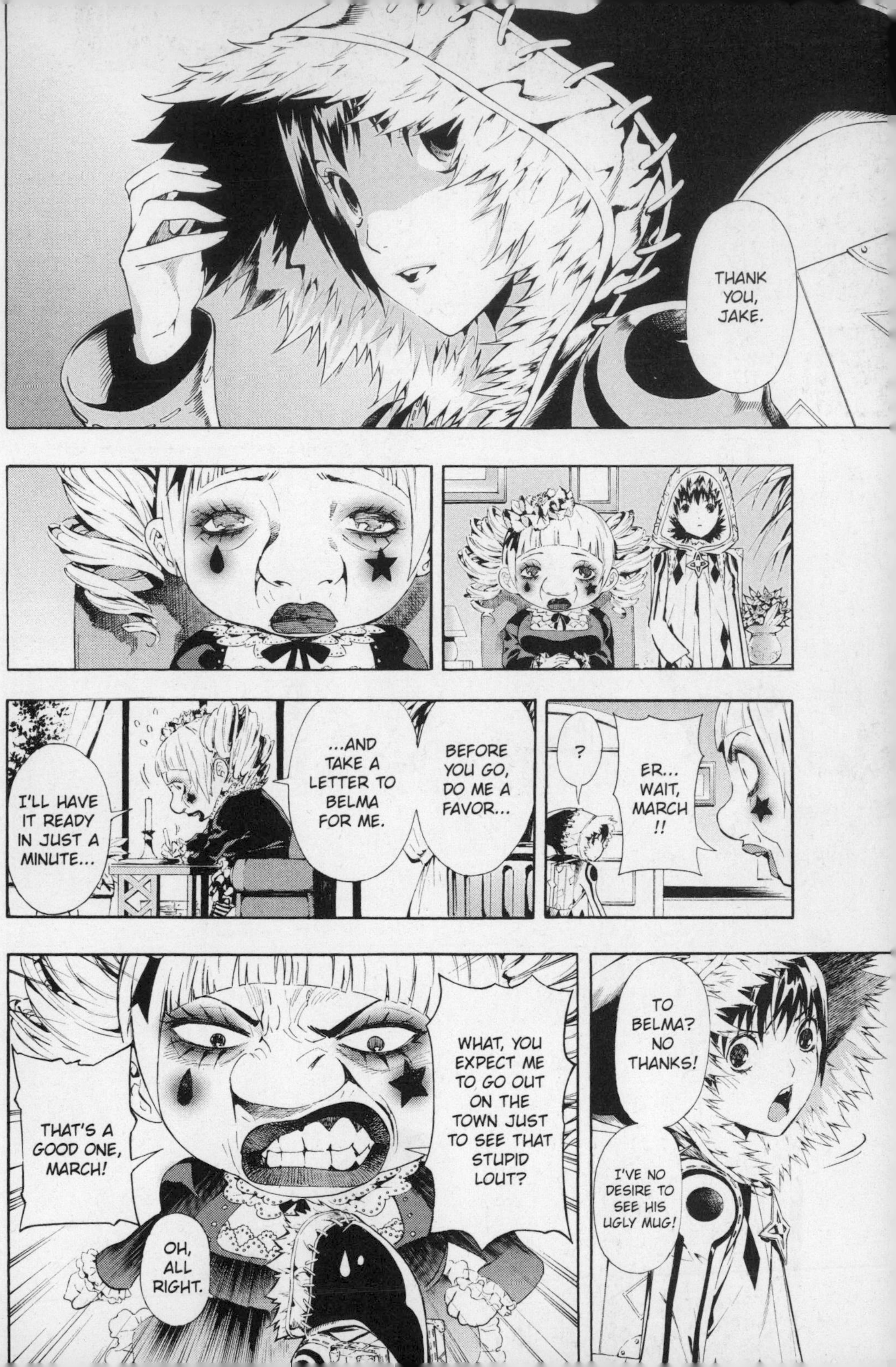
THANK YOU, JAKE.
ER... WAIT, MARCH !!
?
BEFORE YOU GO, DO ME A FAVOR...
...AND TAKE A LETTER TO BELMA FOR ME.
I'LL HAVE IT READY IN JUST A MINUTE...
TO BELMA? NO THANKS!
I'VE NO DESIRE TO SEE HIS UGLY MUG!
WHAT, YOU EXPECT ME TO GO OUT ON THE TOWN JUST TO SEE THAT STUPID LOUT?
THAT'S A GOOD ONE, MARCH!
OH, ALL RIGHT.

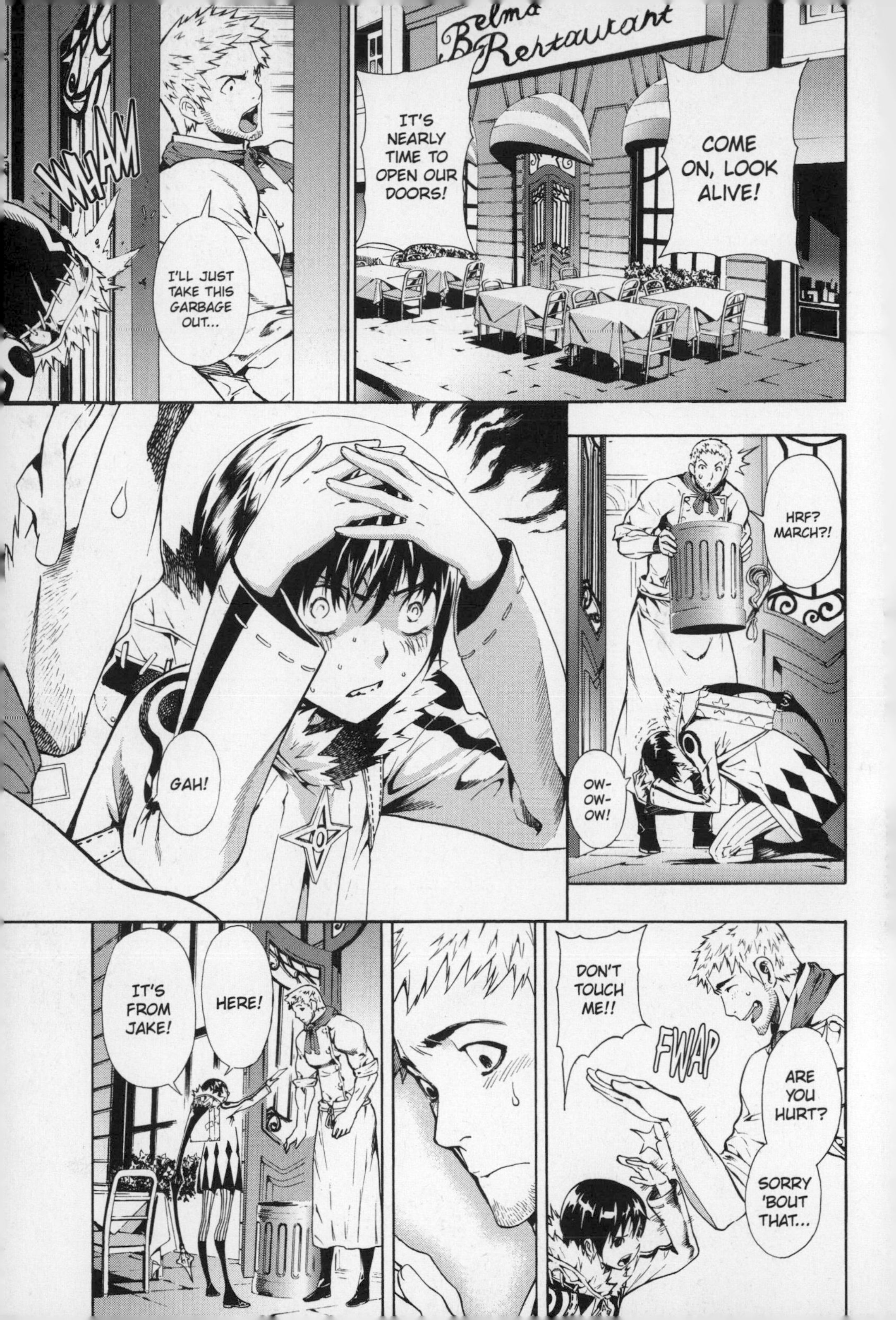
COME ON, LOOK ALIVE!
IT'S NEARLY TIME TO OPEN OUR DOORS!
WHAM
I'LL JUST TAKE THIS GARBAGE OUT...
HRF? MARCH?!
OW-OW-OW!
GAH!
ARE YOU HURT?
DON'T TOUCH ME!!
FWAP
SORRY 'BOUT THAT...
HERE!
IT'S FROM JAKE!

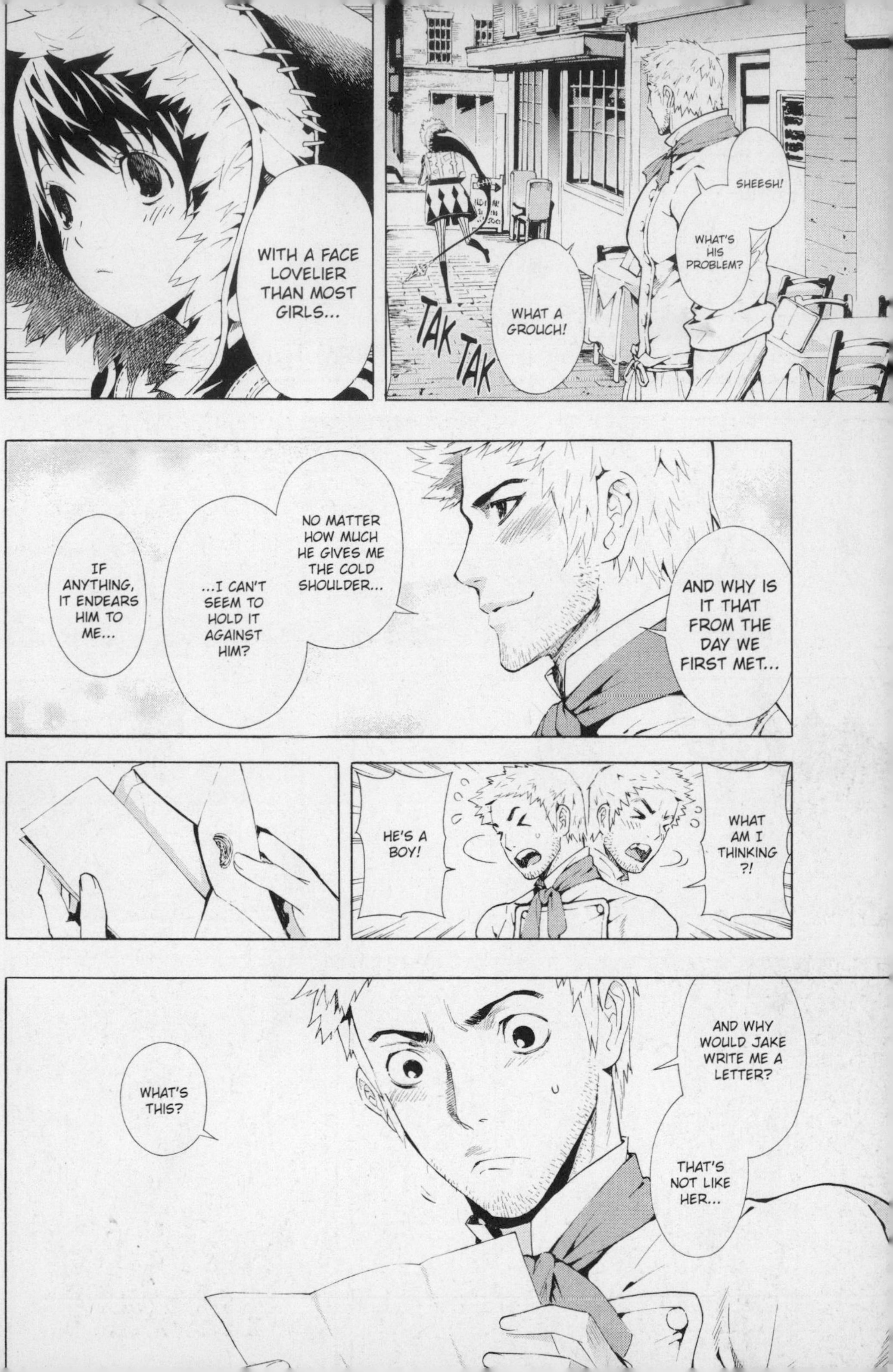
SHEESH!
WHAT'S HIS PROBLEM?
WHAT A GROUCH!
TAK TAK
WITH A FACE LOVELIER THAN MOST GIRLS...
AND WHY IS IT THAT FROM THE DAY WE FIRST MET...
NO MATTER HOW MUCH HE GIVES ME THE COLD SHOULDER...
...I CAN'T SEEM TO HOLD IT AGAINST HIM?
IF ANYTHING, IT ENDEARS HIM TO ME...
WHAT AM I THINKING ?!
HE'S A BOY!
AND WHY WOULD JAKE WRITE ME A LETTER?
THAT'S NOT LIKE HER...
WHAT'S THIS?

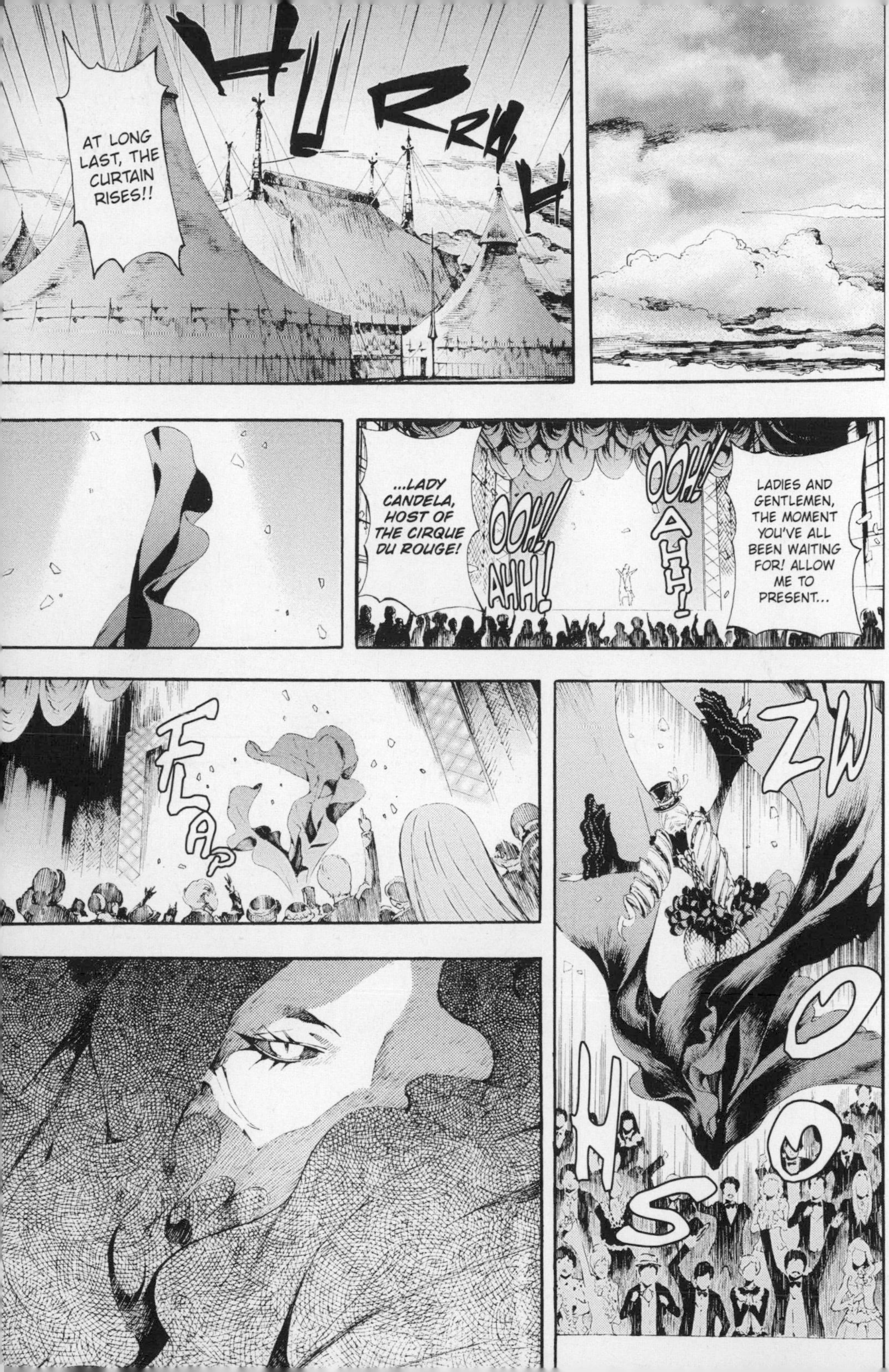
HURRAY
AT LONG LAST, THE CURTAIN RISES!!
LADIES AND GENTLEMEN, THE MOMENT YOU'VE ALL BEEN WAITING FOR! ALLOW ME TO PRESENT...
OOH! AHH!
OOH! AHH!
...LADY CANDELA, HOST OF THE CIRQUE DU ROUGE!
ZWOOSH
FLAP

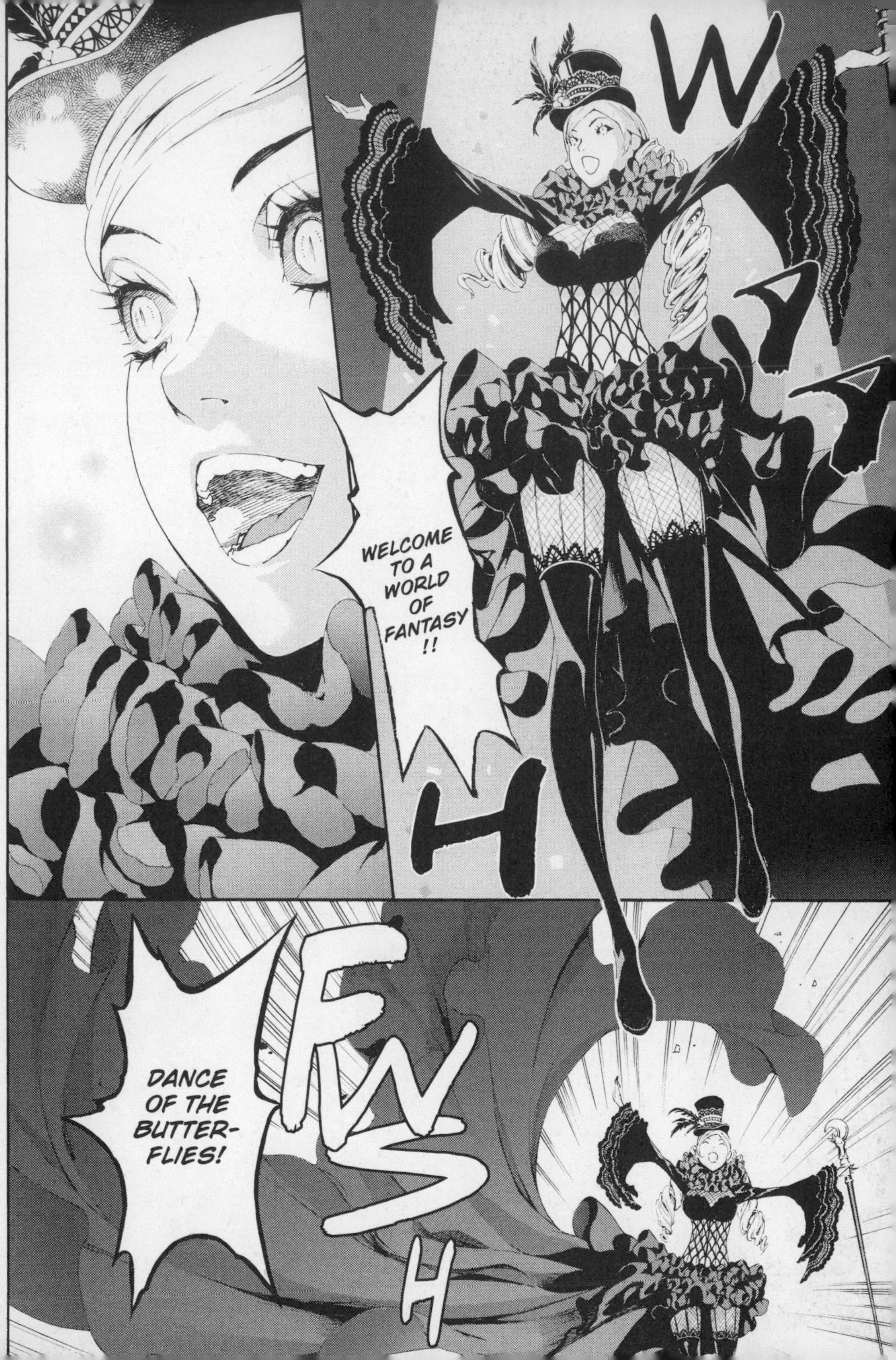
WAAH
WELCOME TO A WORLD OF FANTASY!!
DANCE OF THE BUTTER-FLIES!
FWSH

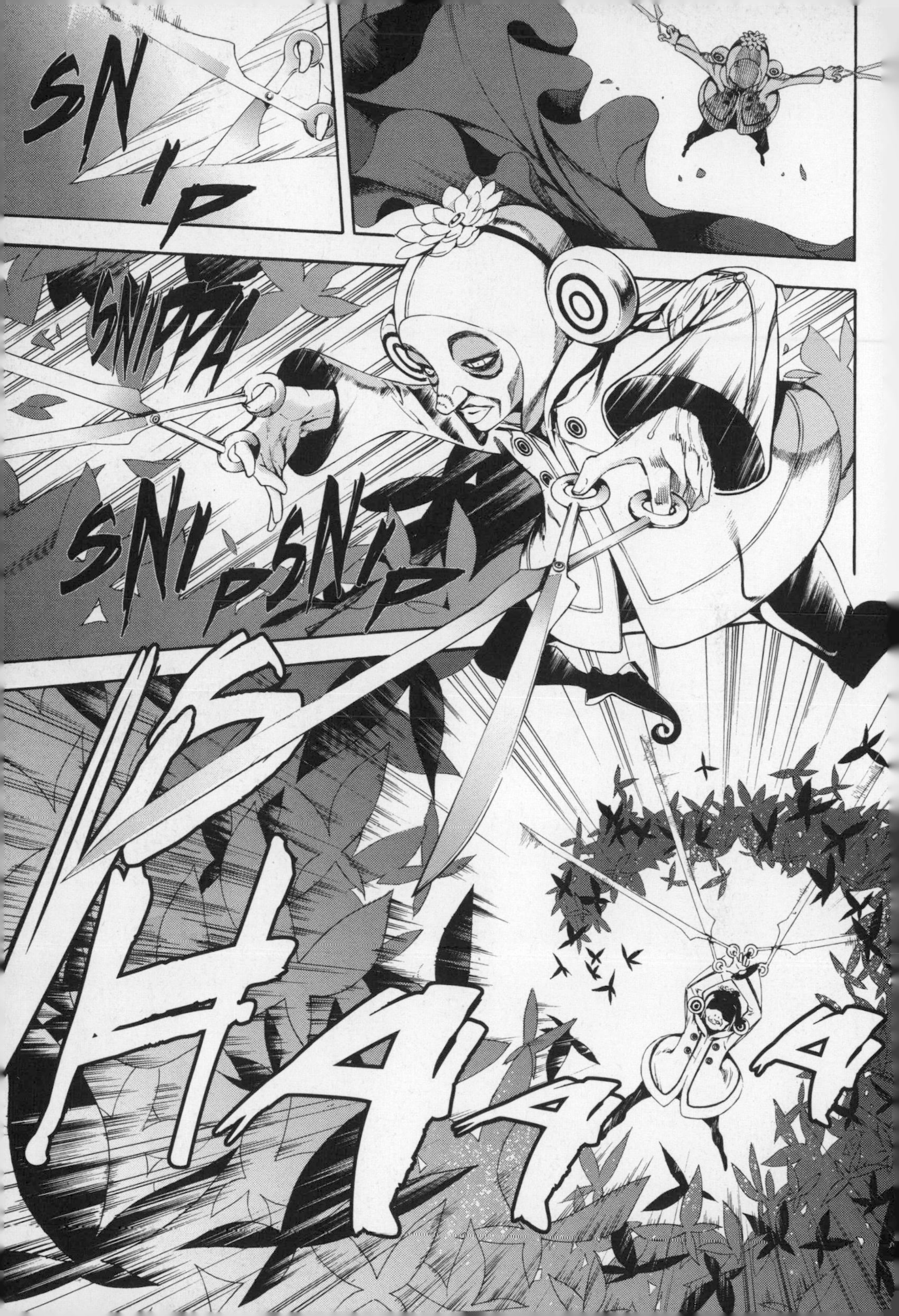
SNIP
SNIPPA
SNIPSNIP
HAAAA

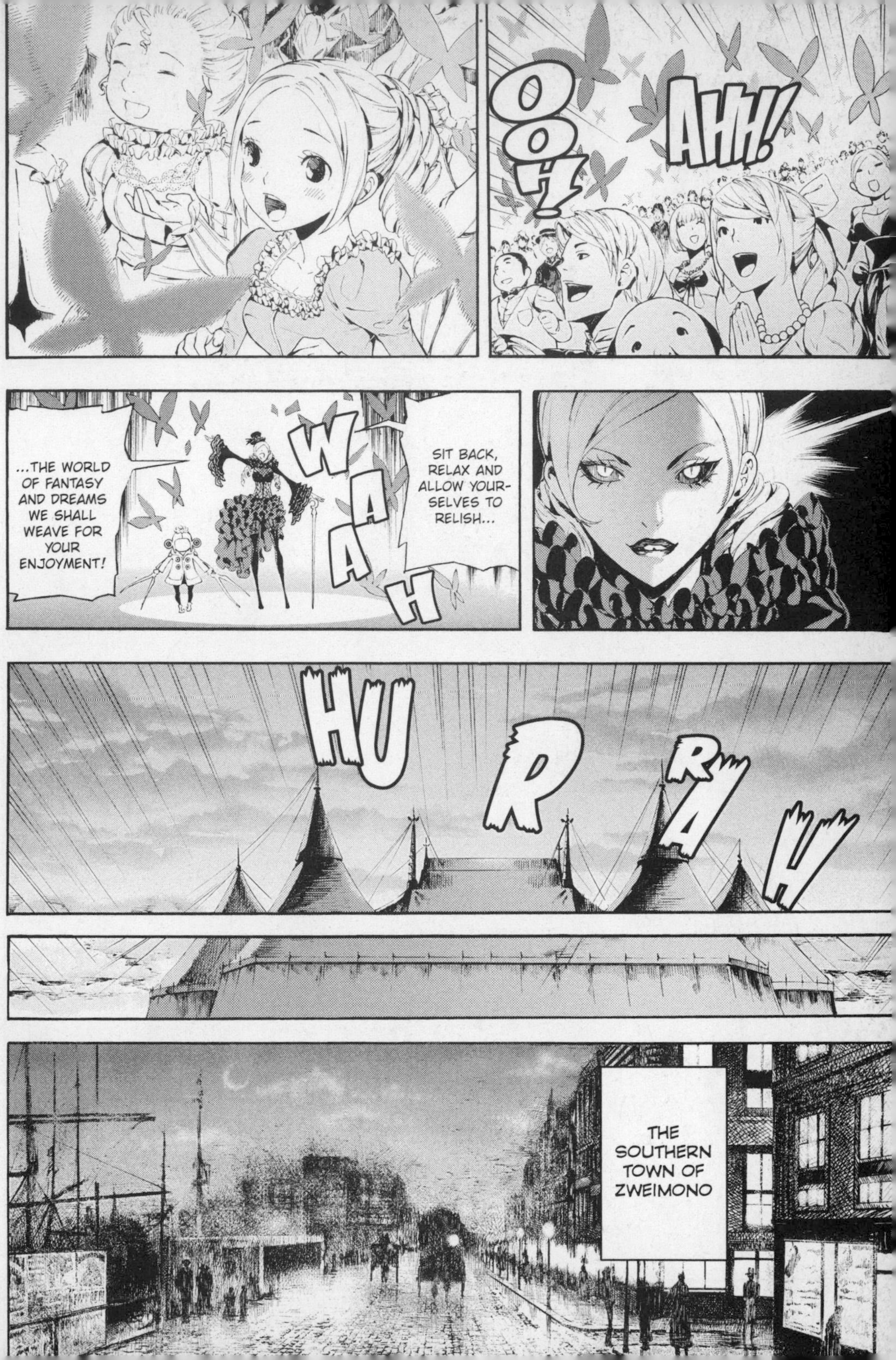
OOH!
AHH!
SIT BACK, RELAX AND ALLOW YOUR-SELVES TO RELISH...
WAAH
...THE WORLD OF FANTASY AND DREAMS WE SHALL WEAVE FOR YOUR ENJOYMENT!
HURRAH
THE SOUTHERN TOWN OF ZWEIMONO

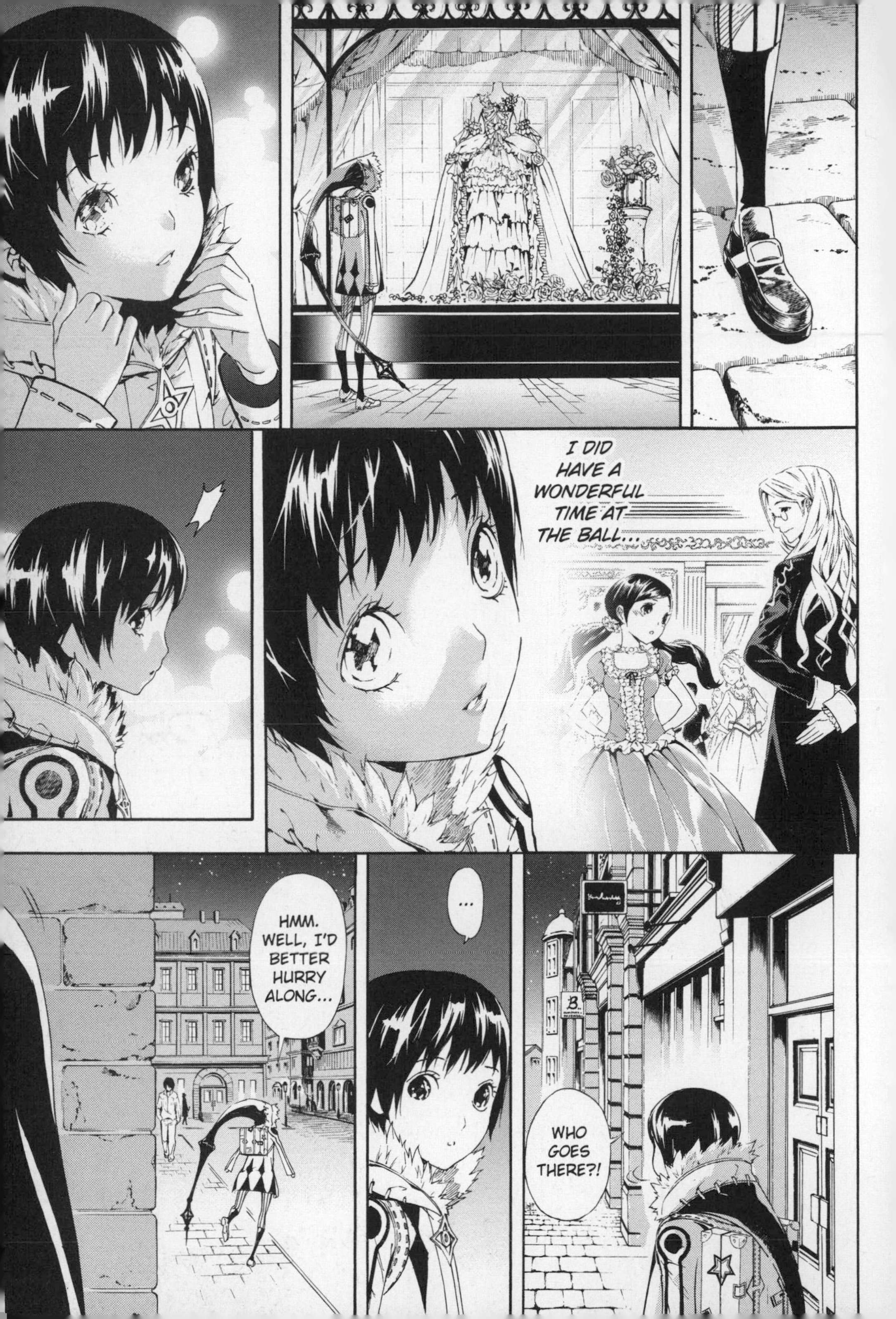
I DID HAVE A WONDERFUL TIME AT THE BALL...
WHO GOES THERE?!
...
HMM. WELL, I'D BETTER HURRY ALONG...

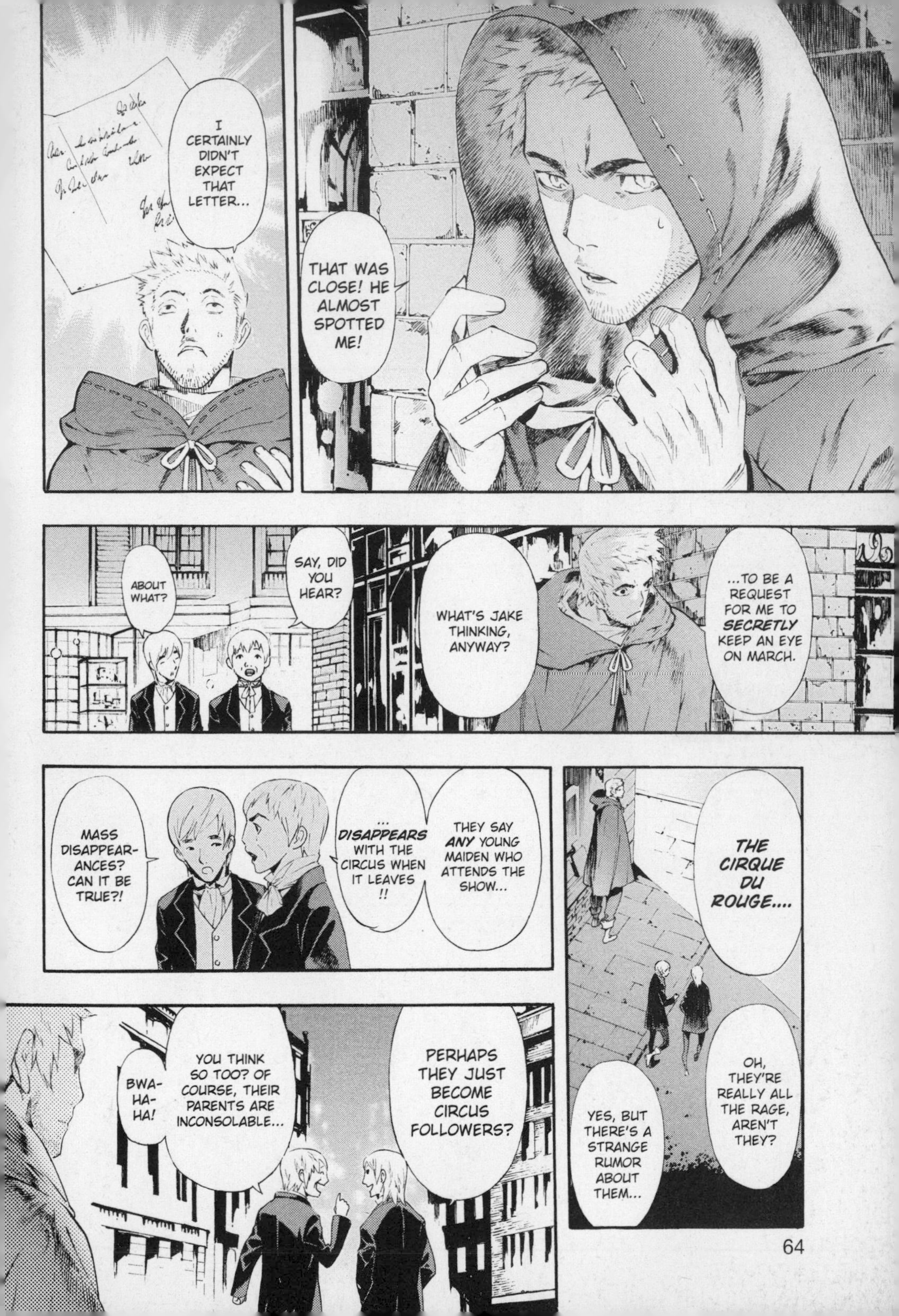

THAT WAS CLOSE! HE ALMOST SPOTTED ME!
I CERTAINLY DIDN'T EXPECT THAT LETTER...
...TO BE A REQUEST FOR ME TO SECRETLY KEEP AN EYE ON MARCH.
WHAT'S JAKE THINKING, ANYWAY?
SAY, DID YOU HEAR?
ABOUT WHAT?
THE CIRQUE DU ROUGE....
OH, THEY'RE REALLY ALL THE RAGE, AREN'T THEY?
YES, BUT THERE'S A STRANGE RUMOR ABOUT THEM...
THEY SAY ANY YOUNG MAIDEN WHO ATTENDS THE SHOW...
...DISAPPEARS WITH THE CIRCUS WHEN IT LEAVES!!
MASS DISAPPEAR-ANCES? CAN IT BE TRUE?!
PERHAPS THEY JUST BECOME CIRCUS FOLLOWERS?
YOU THINK SO TOO? OF COURSE, THEIR PARENTS ARE INCONSOLABLE...
BWA-HA-HA!

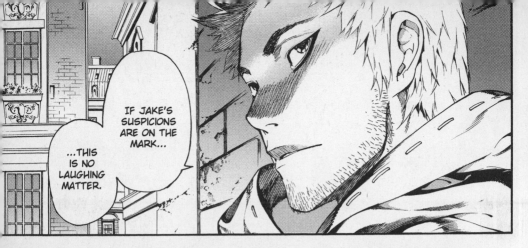

IF JAKE'S SUSPICIONS ARE ON THE MARK...
...THIS IS NO LAUGHING MATTER.
WHY, THAT WAS RAPTUROUS!
WASN'T SHE AMAZING?
THE RING-MASTER, YOU MEAN?
OH, YES!
I THINK I MAY BE IN LOVE!

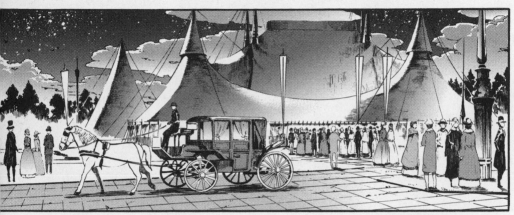

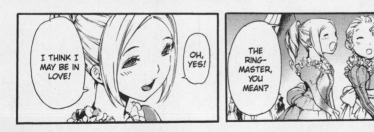

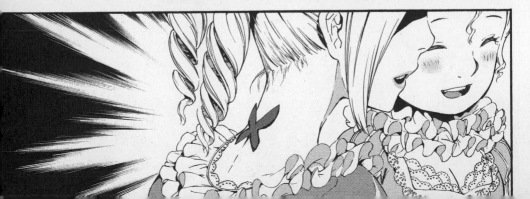

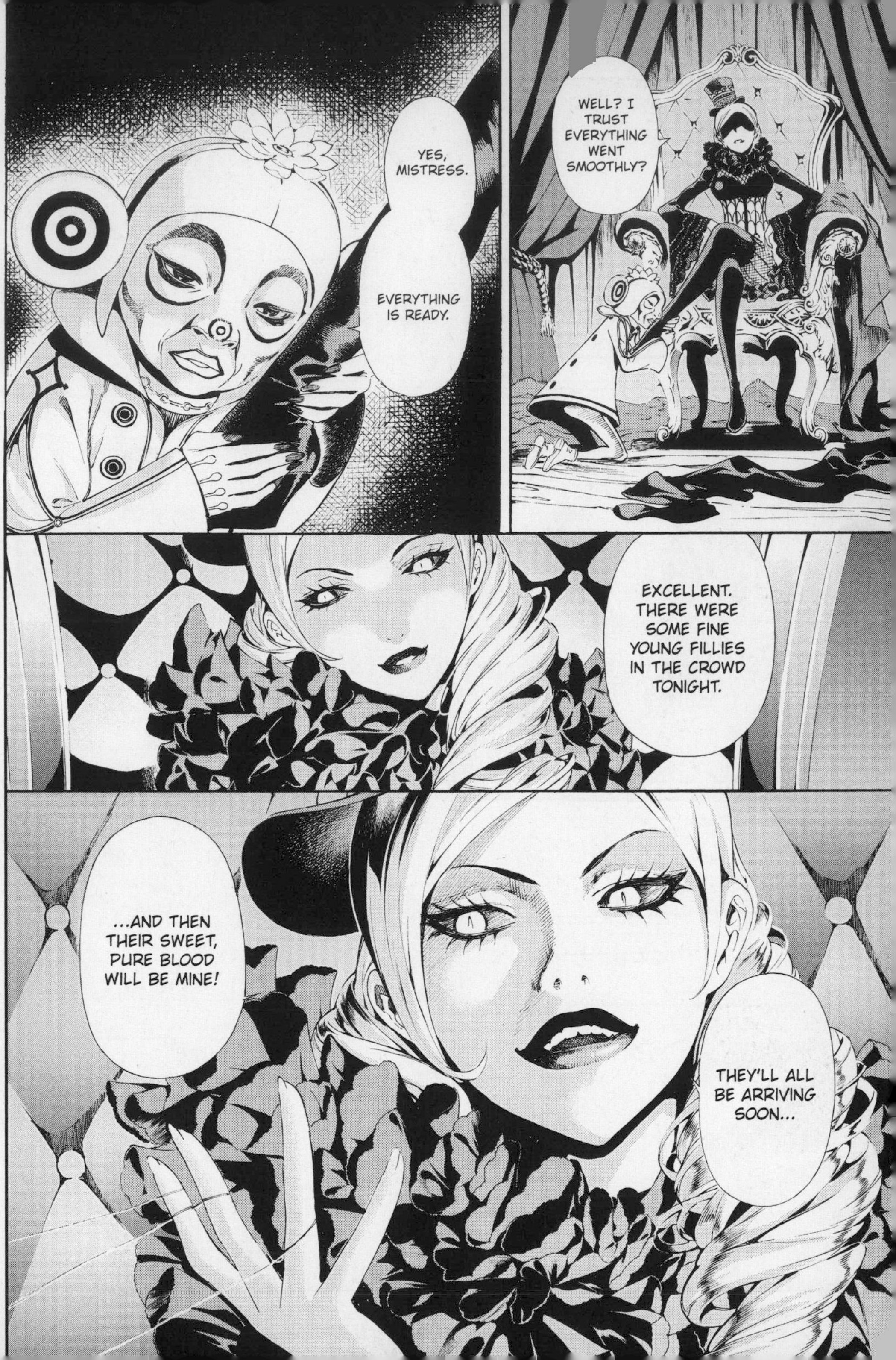
WELL? I TRUST EVERYTHING WENT SMOOTHLY?
YES, MISTRESS.
EVERYTHING IS READY.
EXCELLENT. THERE WERE SOME FINE YOUNG FILLIES IN THE CROWD TONIGHT.
THEY'LL ALL BE ARRIVING SOON...
...AND THEN THEIR SWEET, PURE BLOOD WILL BE MINE!

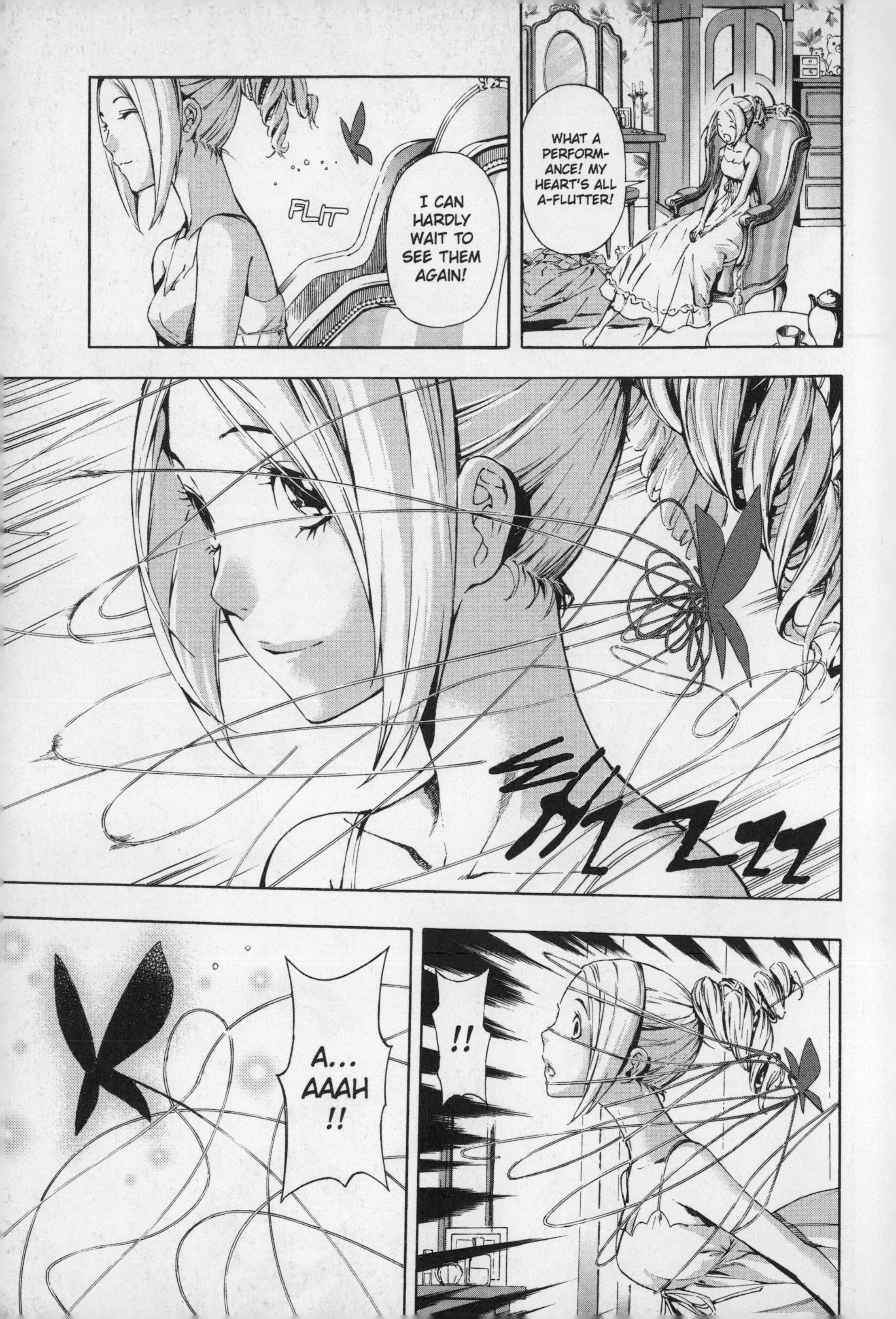
WHAT A PERFORMANCE! MY HEART'S ALL A-FLUTTER!
I CAN HARDLY WAIT TO SEE THEM AGAIN!
FLIT
SHHZZZ
!!
A... AAAH !!

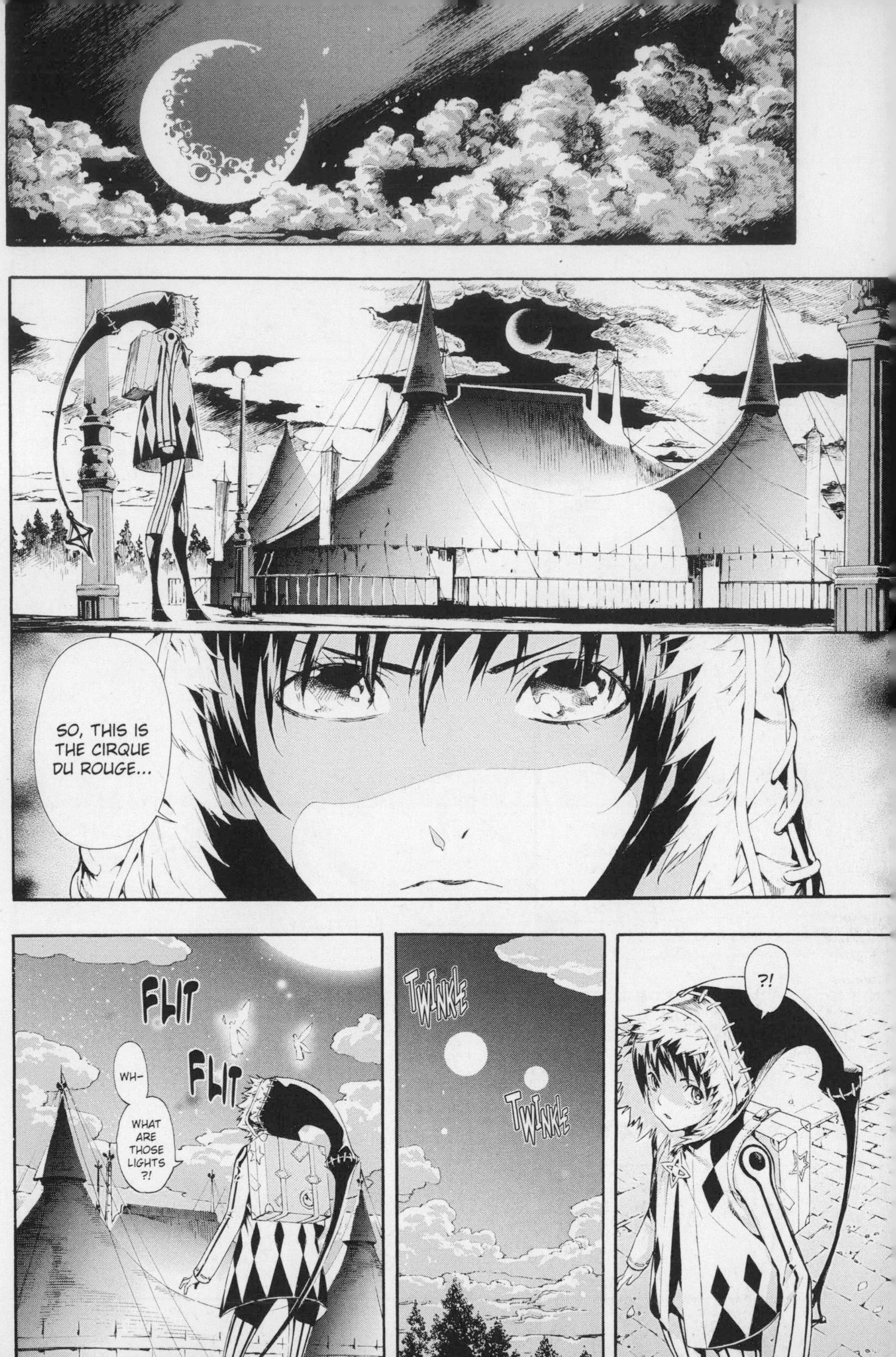
SO, THIS IS THE CIRQUE DU ROUGE...
?!
TWINKLE
TWINKLE
FLIT
FLIT
WH-
WHAT ARE THOSE LIGHTS?!

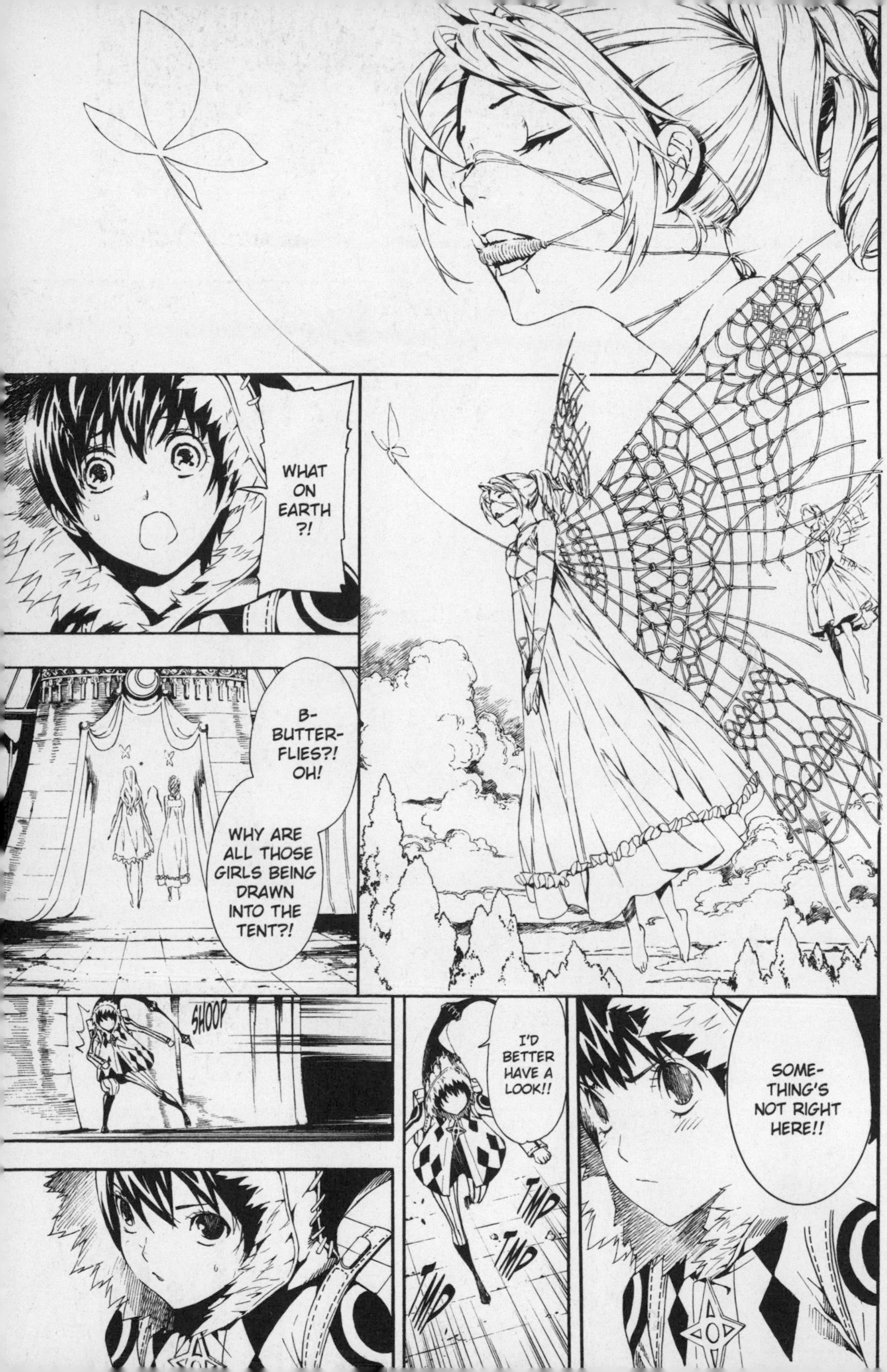
WHAT ON EARTH?!
B-BUTTERFLIES?! OH!
WHY ARE ALL THOSE GIRLS BEING DRAWN INTO THE TENT?!
SOME-THING'S NOT RIGHT HERE!!
I'D BETTER HAVE A LOOK!!
TMP
TMP
TMP
SHOOP

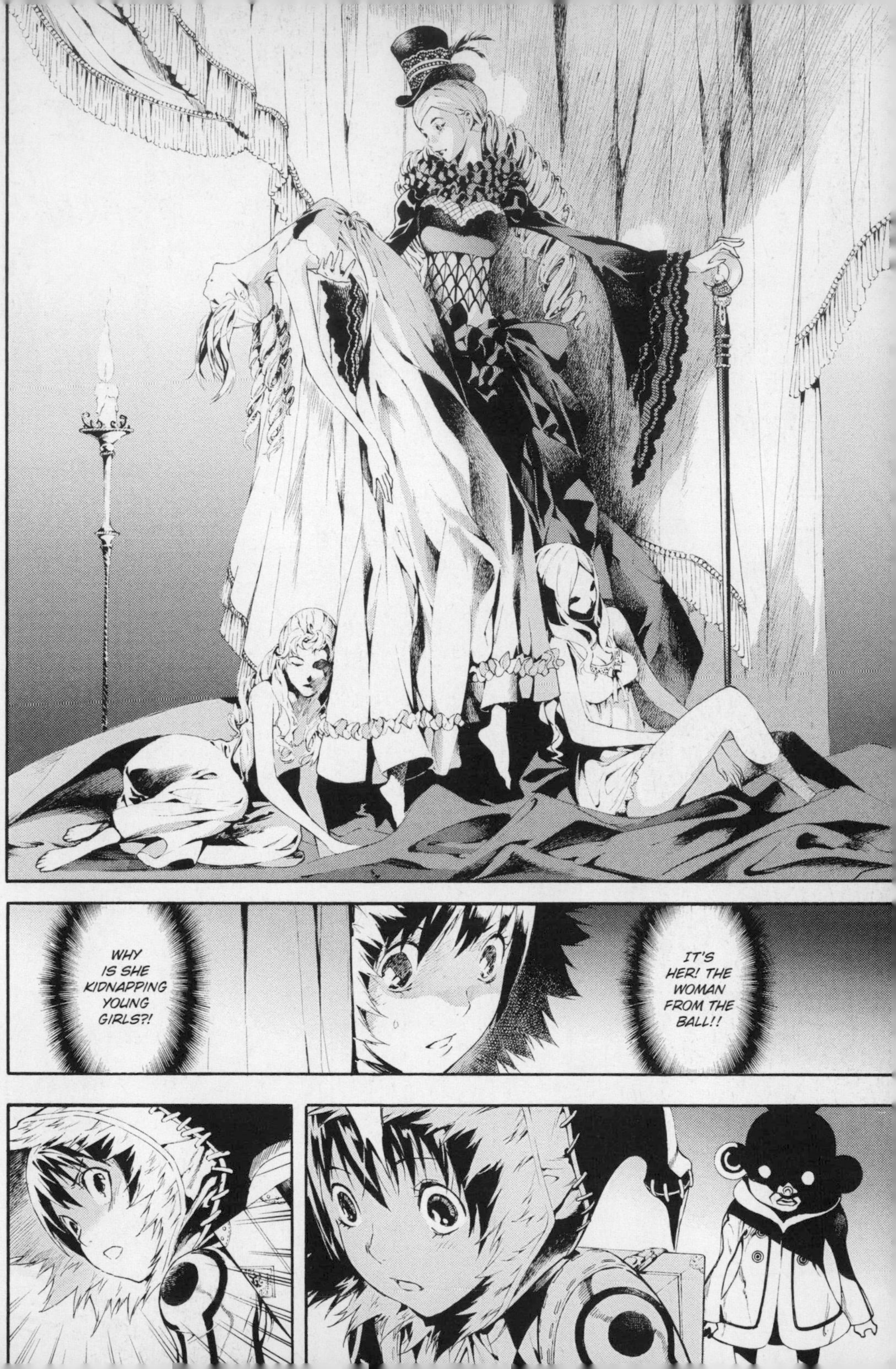
IT'S HER! THE WOMAN FROM THE BALL!!
WHY IS SHE KIDNAPPING YOUNG GIRLS?!

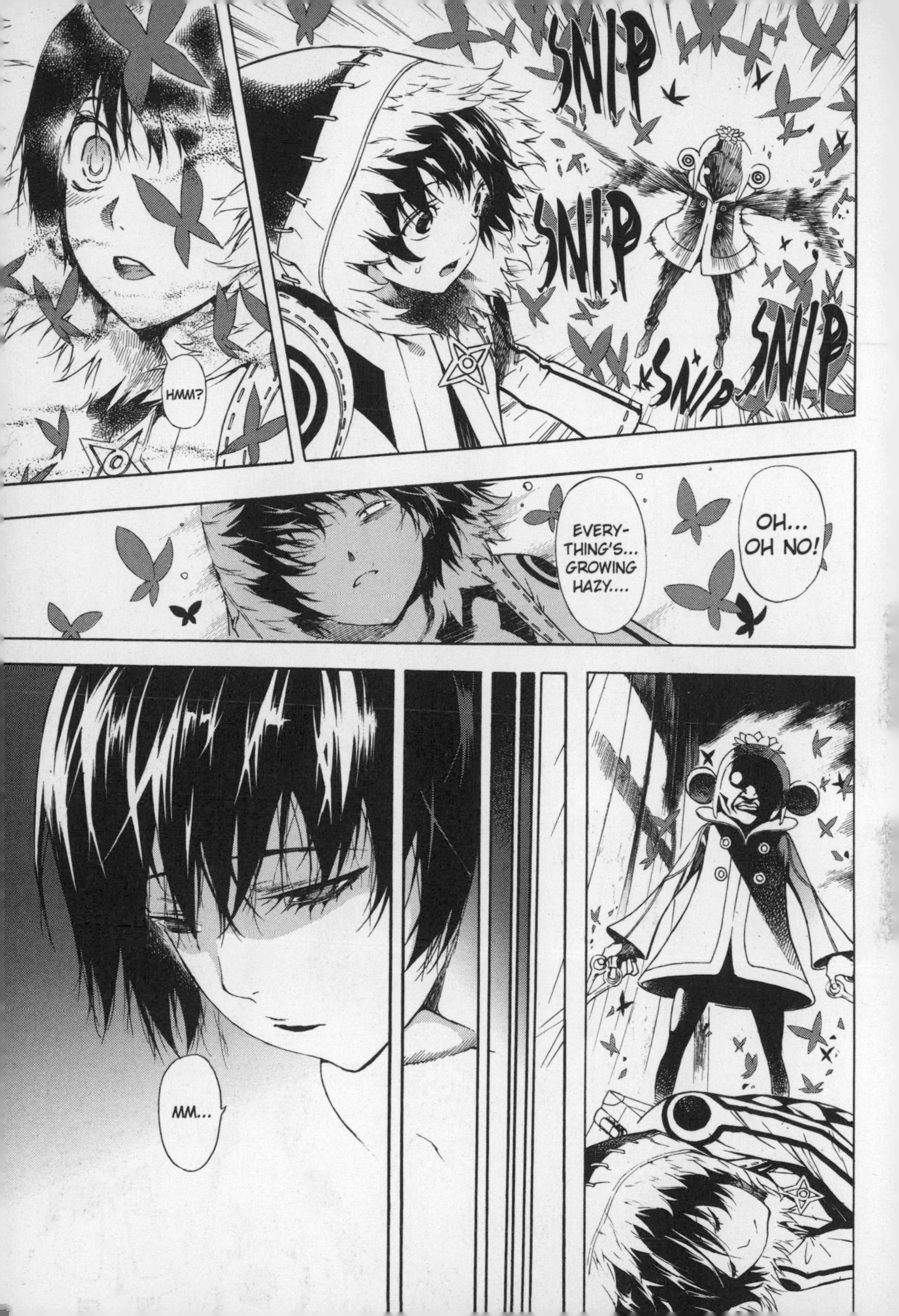
SNIP
SNIP
SNIP
SNIP
HMM?
OH... OH NO!
EVERY-THING'S... GROWING HAZY....
MM...

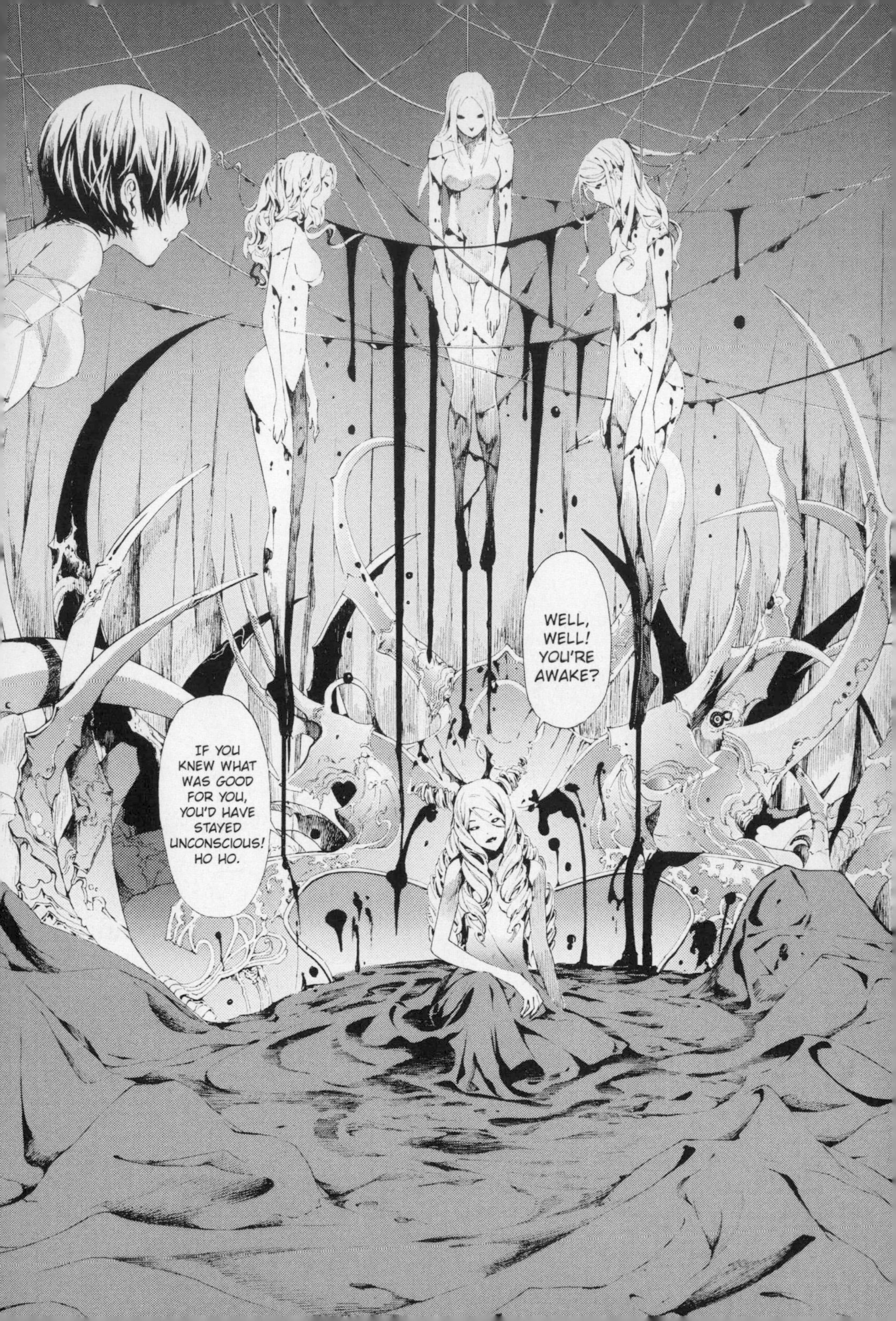
WELL, WELL! YOU'RE AWAKE?
IF YOU KNEW WHAT WAS GOOD FOR YOU, YOU'D HAVE STAYED UNCONSCIOUS! HO HO.

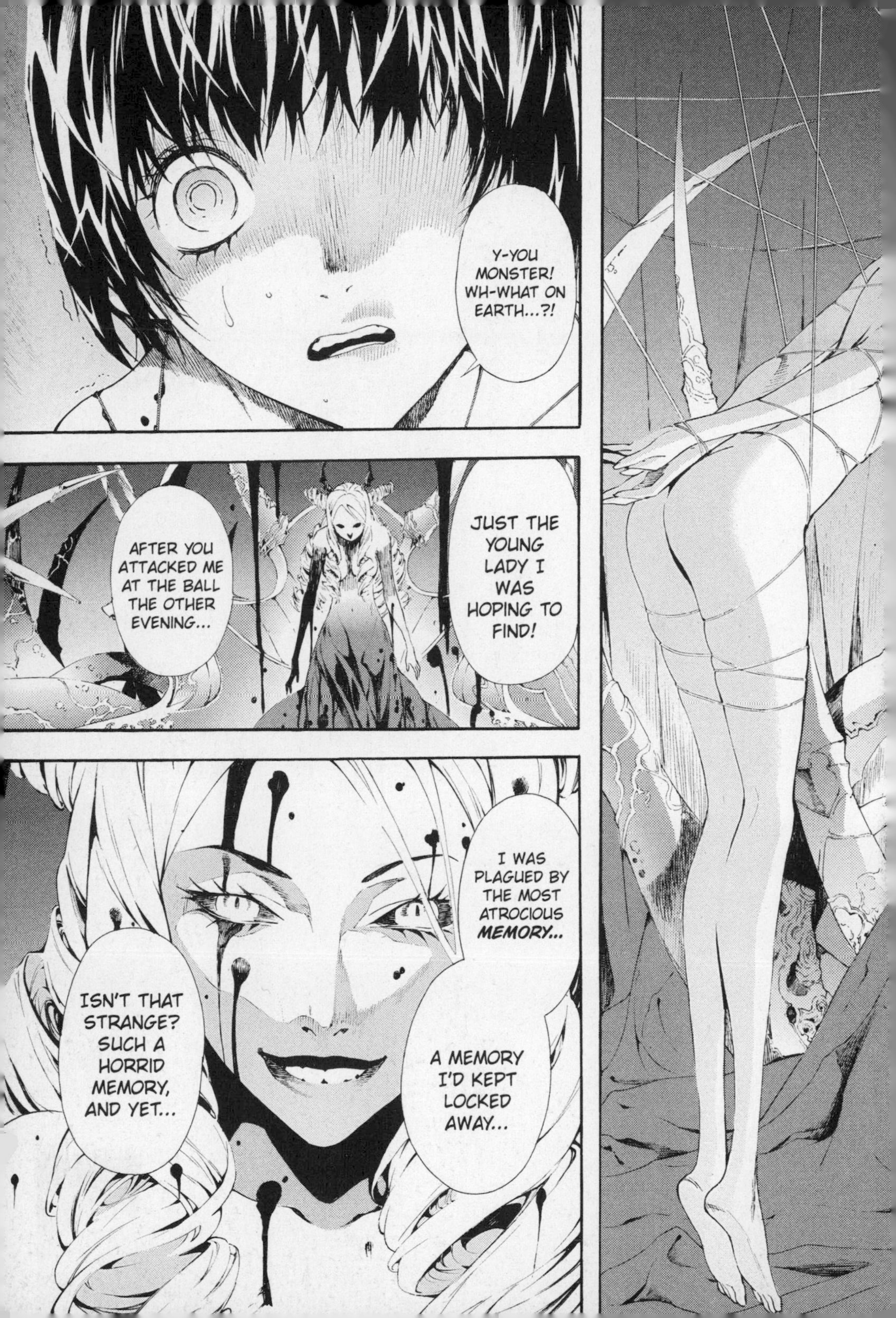
Y-YOU MONSTER! WH-WHAT ON EARTH...?!
JUST THE YOUNG LADY I WAS HOPING TO FIND!
AFTER YOU ATTACKED ME AT THE BALL THE OTHER EVENING...
I WAS PLAGUED BY THE MOST ATROCIOUS ***MEMORY...***
A MEMORY I'D KEPT LOCKED AWAY...
ISN'T THAT STRANGE? SUCH A HORRID MEMORY, AND YET...

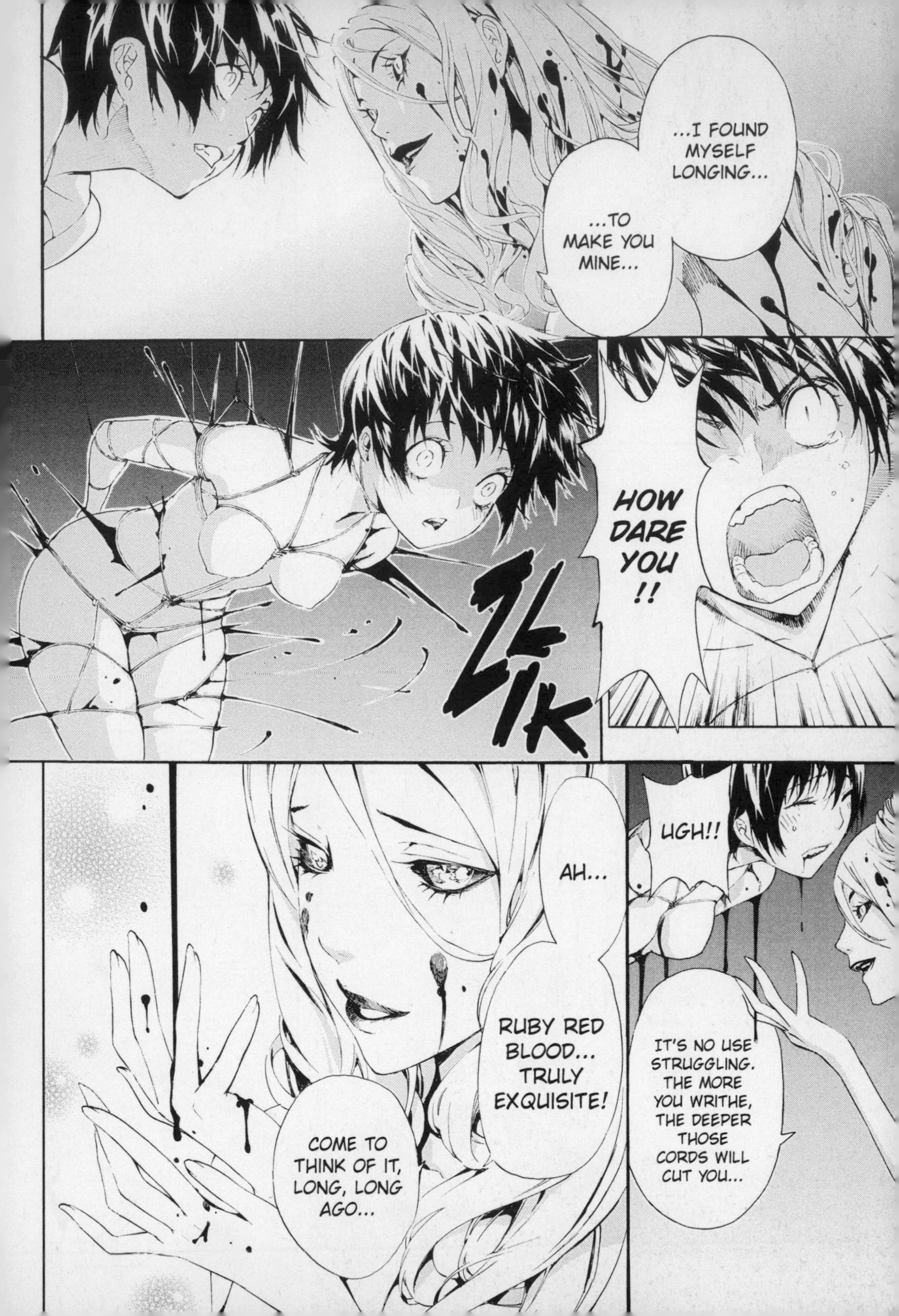
...I FOUND MYSELF LONGING...
...TO MAKE YOU MINE...
HOW DARE YOU!!
ZLIK
UGH!!
IT'S NO USE STRUGGLING. THE MORE YOU WRITHE, THE DEEPER THOSE CORDS WILL CUT YOU...
AH...
RUBY RED BLOOD... TRULY EXQUISITE!
COME TO THINK OF IT, LONG, LONG AGO...

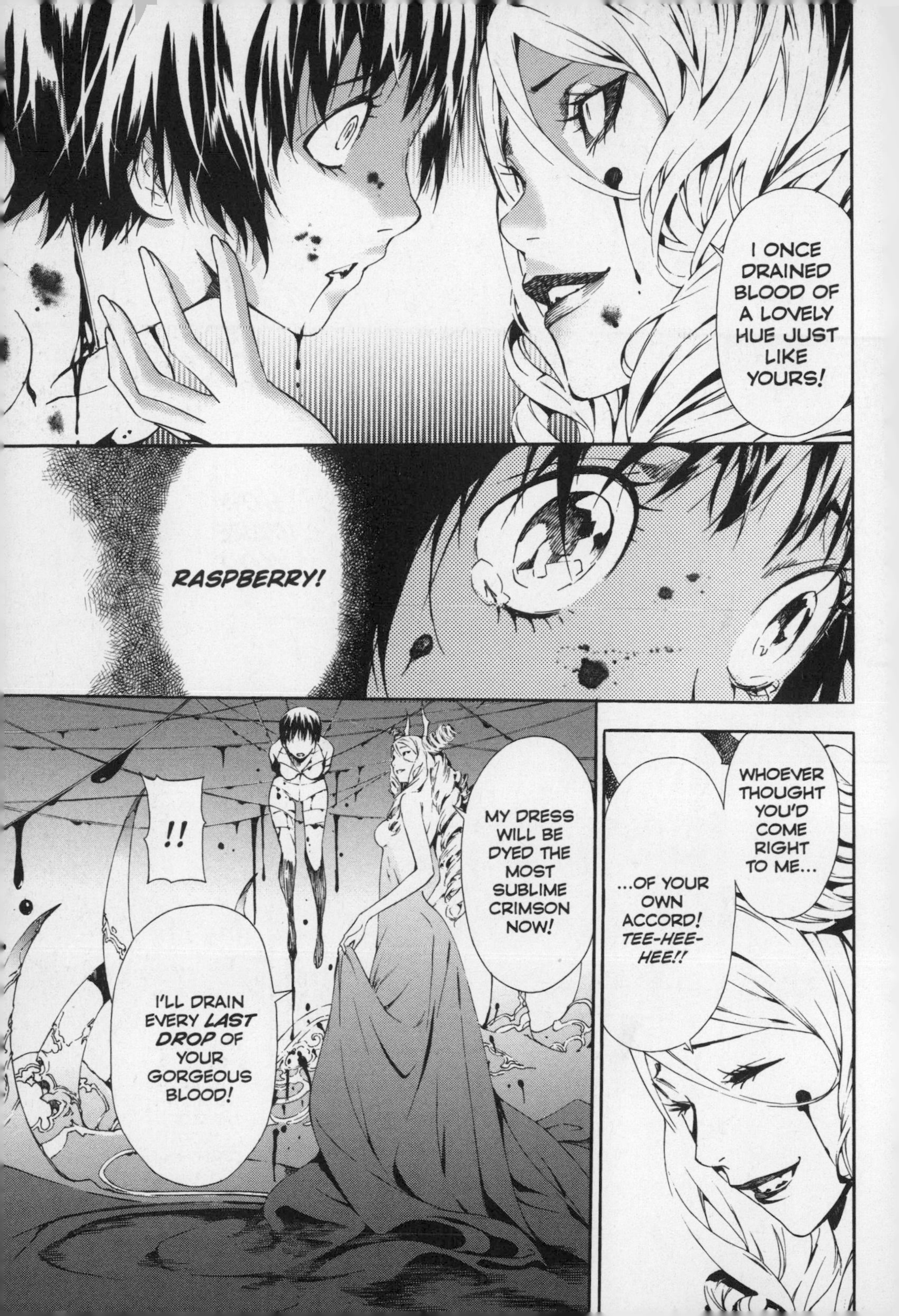
I ONCE DRAINED BLOOD OF A LOVELY HUE JUST LIKE YOURS!
RASPBERRY!
WHOEVER THOUGHT YOU'D COME RIGHT TO ME...
...OF YOUR OWN ACCORD! *TEE-HEE-HEE!!*
MY DRESS WILL BE DYED THE MOST SUBLIME CRIMSON NOW!
!!
I'LL DRAIN EVERY *LAST DROP* OF YOUR GORGEOUS BLOOD!

THE PAIN!!

NGNH...

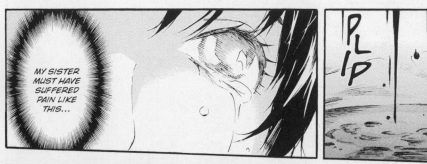

MY SISTER MUST HAVE SUFFERED PAIN LIKE THIS...

PL IP

PL IP

...

R-RASP-BERRY...

AH-HA-HA! YES, MY DEAR...

...IT WILL HURT LESS IF YOU GO TO SLEEP!

MARCH !!

ARE YOU IN THERE?!

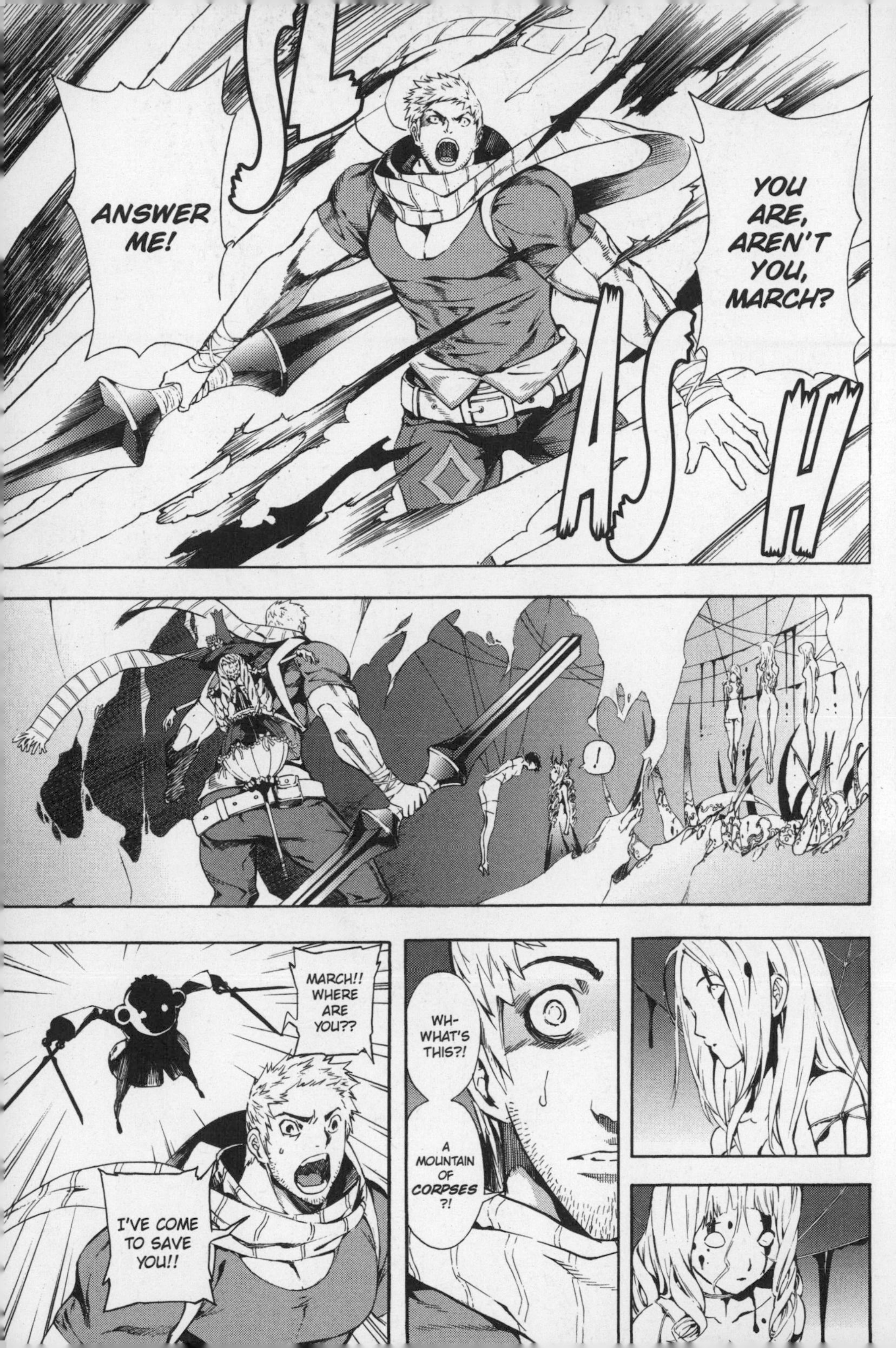
YOU ARE, AREN'T YOU, MARCH?
ANSWER ME!
SLASH
!
WH- WHAT'S THIS?!
A MOUNTAIN OF CORPSES ?!
MARCH!! WHERE ARE YOU??
I'VE COME TO SAVE YOU!!

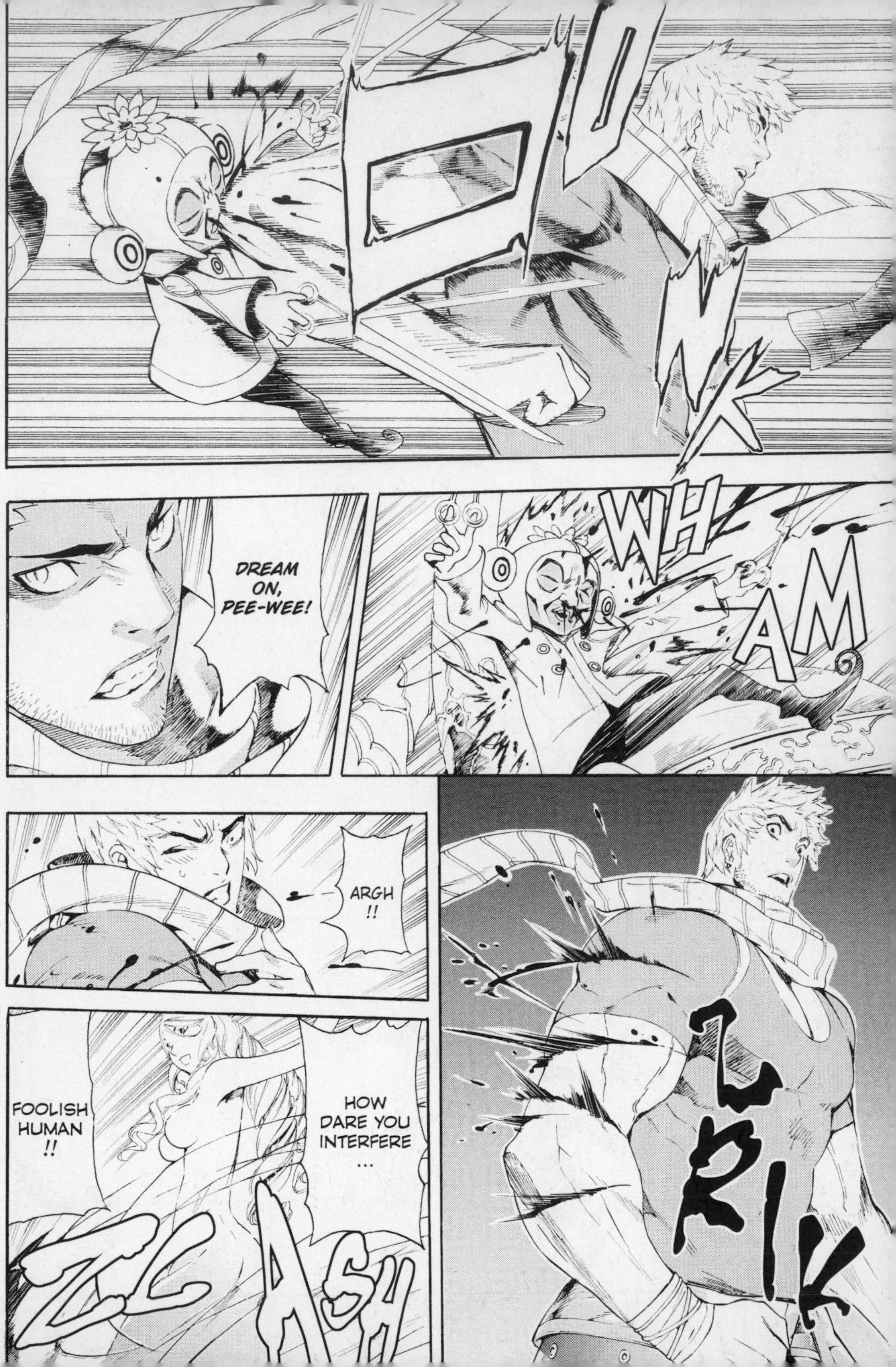

WHAM
DREAM ON, PEE-WEE!
ARGH !!
HOW DARE YOU INTERFERE ...
FOOLISH HUMAN !!

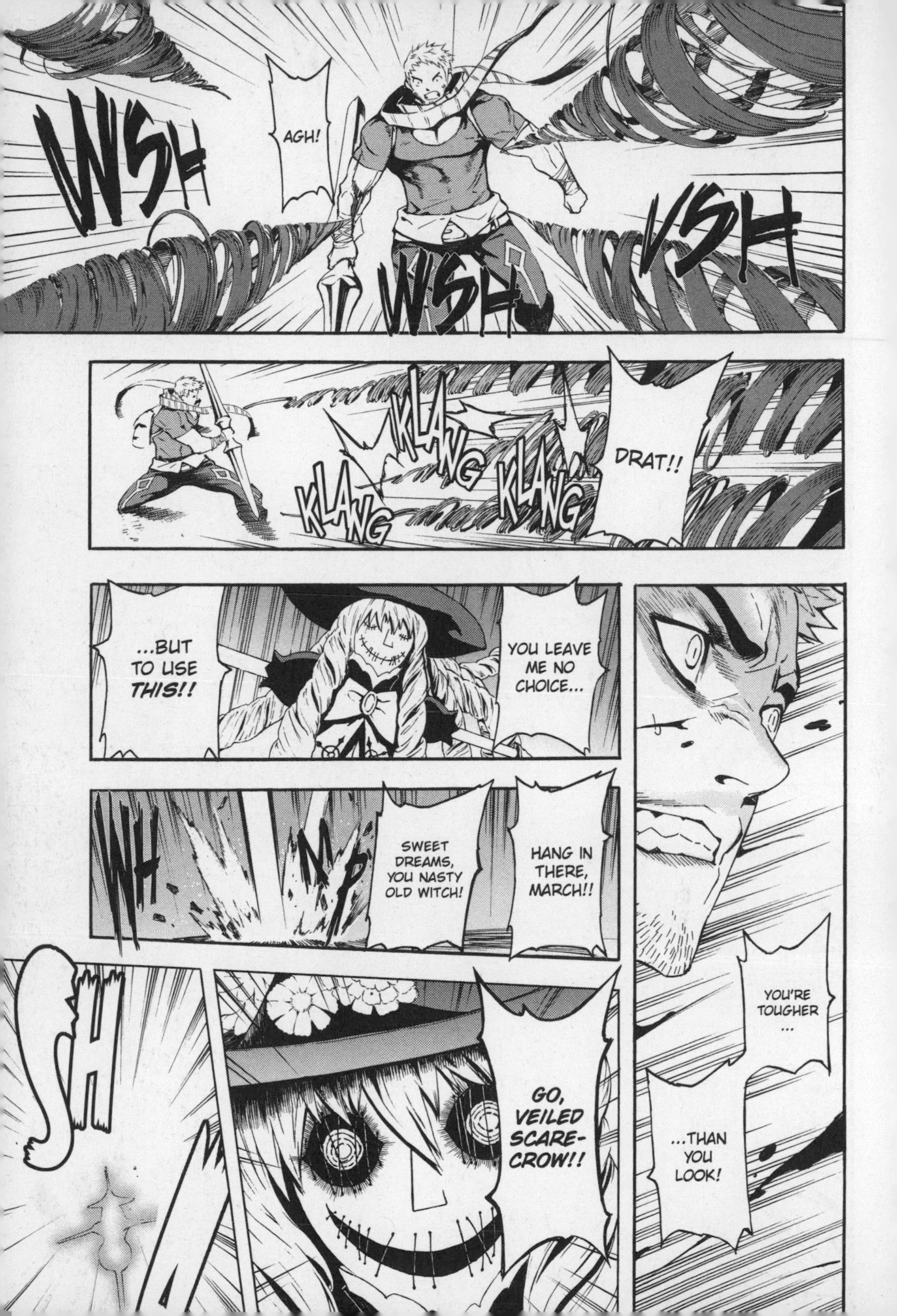
VSH
AGH!
WSH
WSH
DRAT!!
KLANG
KLANG
KLANG
YOU LEAVE ME NO CHOICE...
...BUT TO USE *THIS!!*
HANG IN THERE, MARCH!!
SWEET DREAMS, YOU NASTY OLD WITCH!
WHMP
YOU'RE TOUGHER ...
...THAN YOU LOOK!
GO, VEILED SCARE-CROW!!
SH

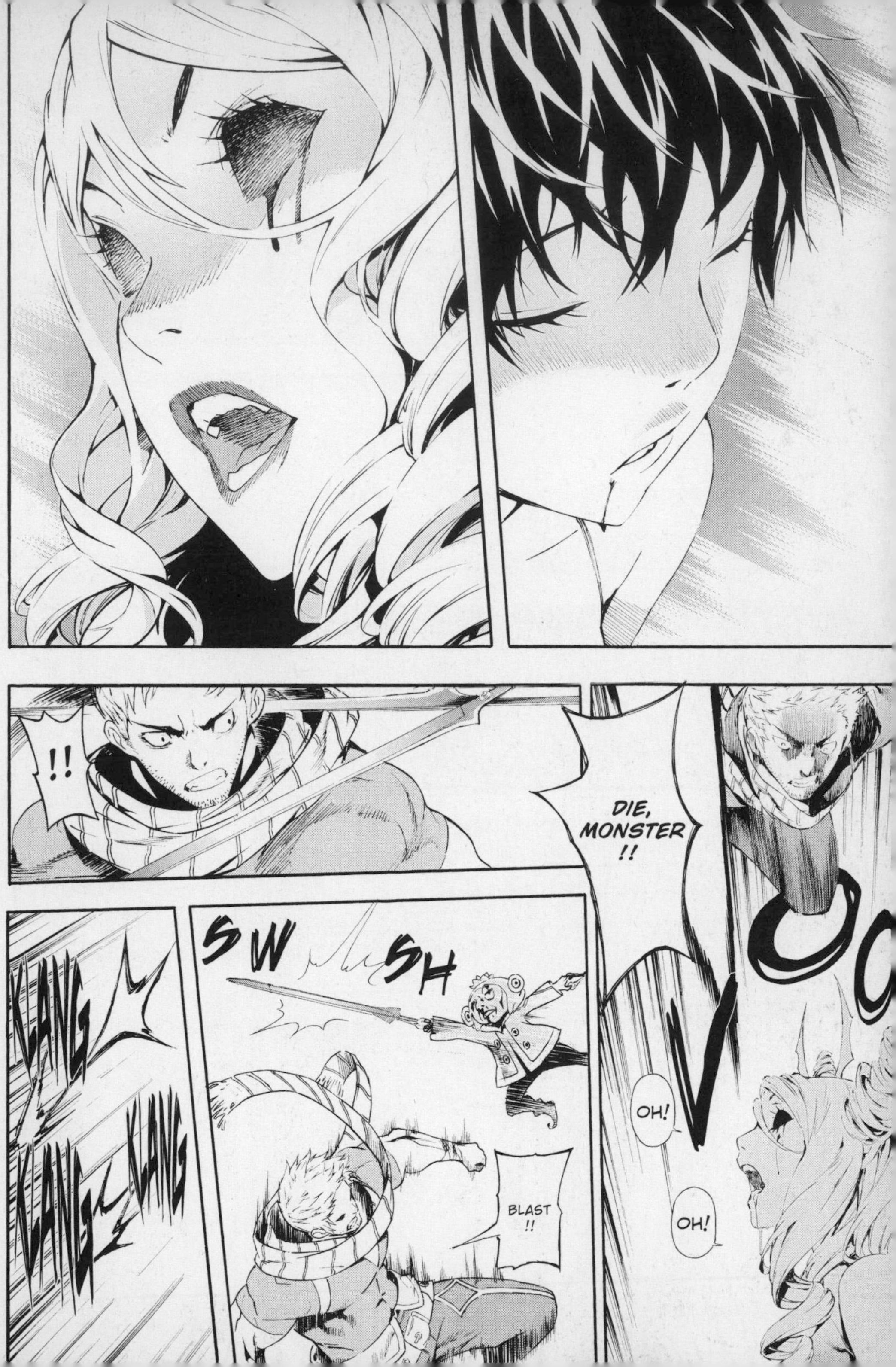
DIE, MONSTER !!
OH!
OH!
!!
SW SH
BLAST !!
KLANG
KLANG
KLANG

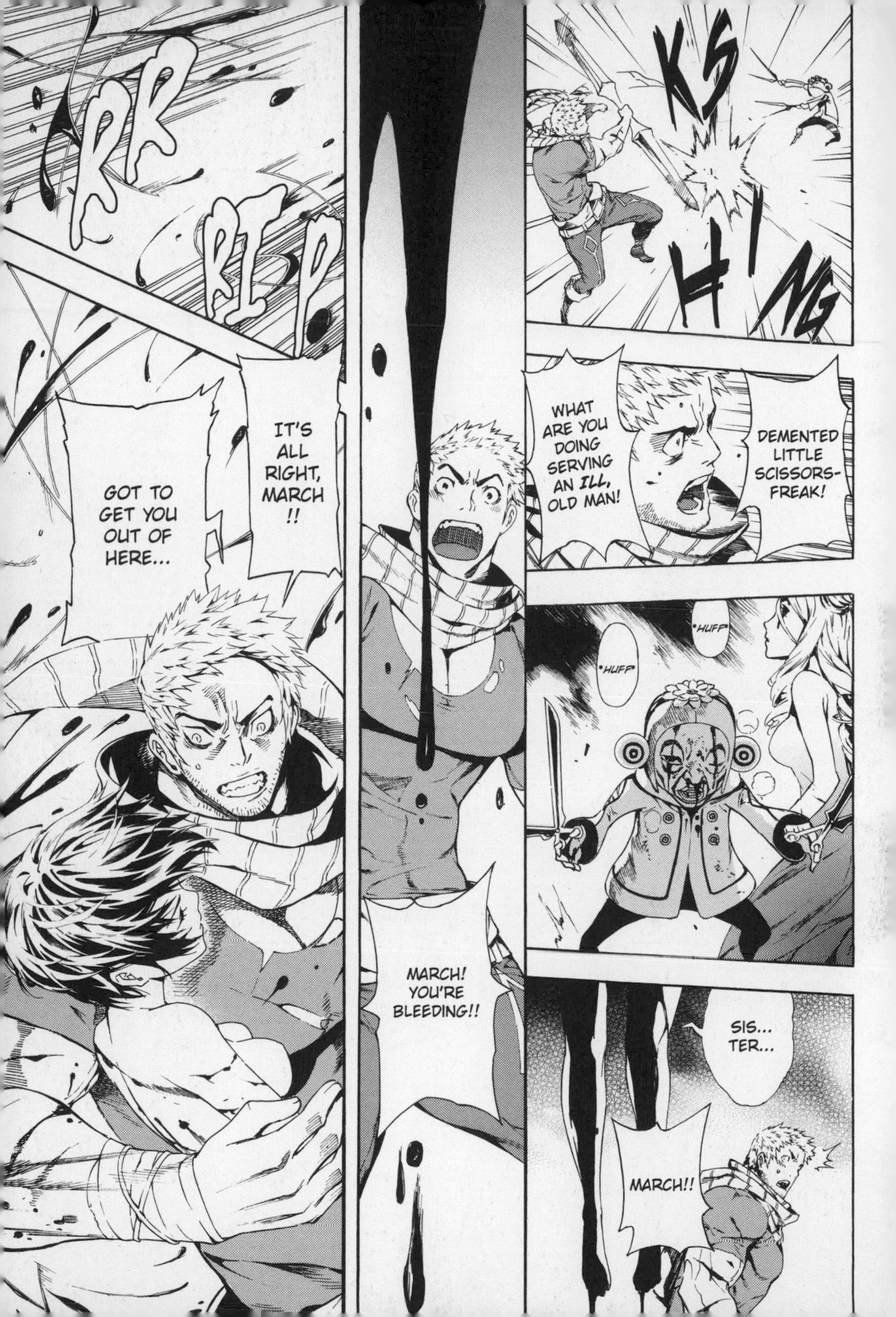
KS
HING
DEMENTED LITTLE SCISSORS-FREAK!
WHAT ARE YOU DOING SERVING AN ILL, OLD MAN!
HUFF
HUFF
SIS... TER...
MARCH!!
MARCH! YOU'RE BLEEDING!!
RR
RIP
IT'S ALL RIGHT, MARCH!!
GOT TO GET YOU OUT OF HERE...

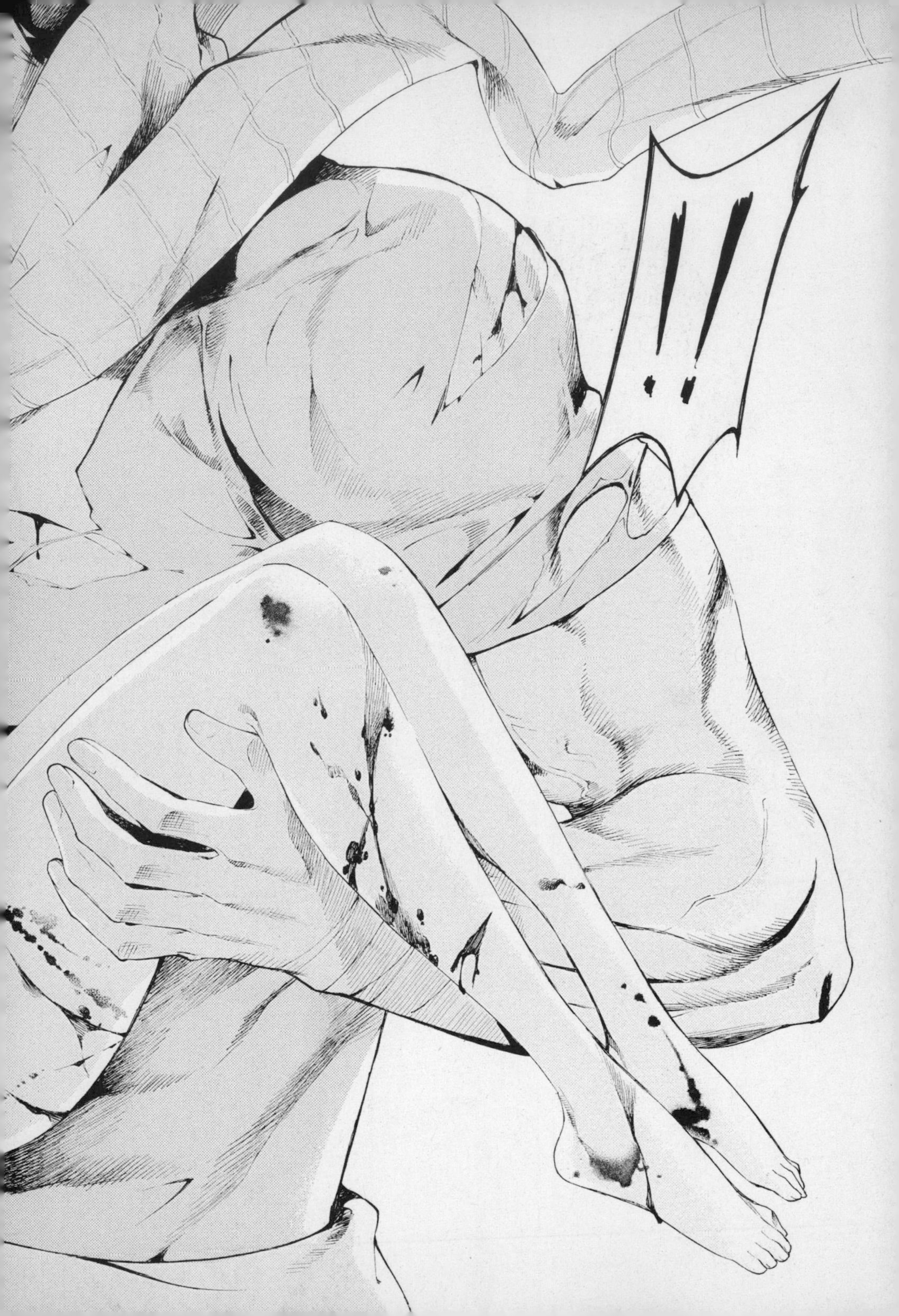
!!

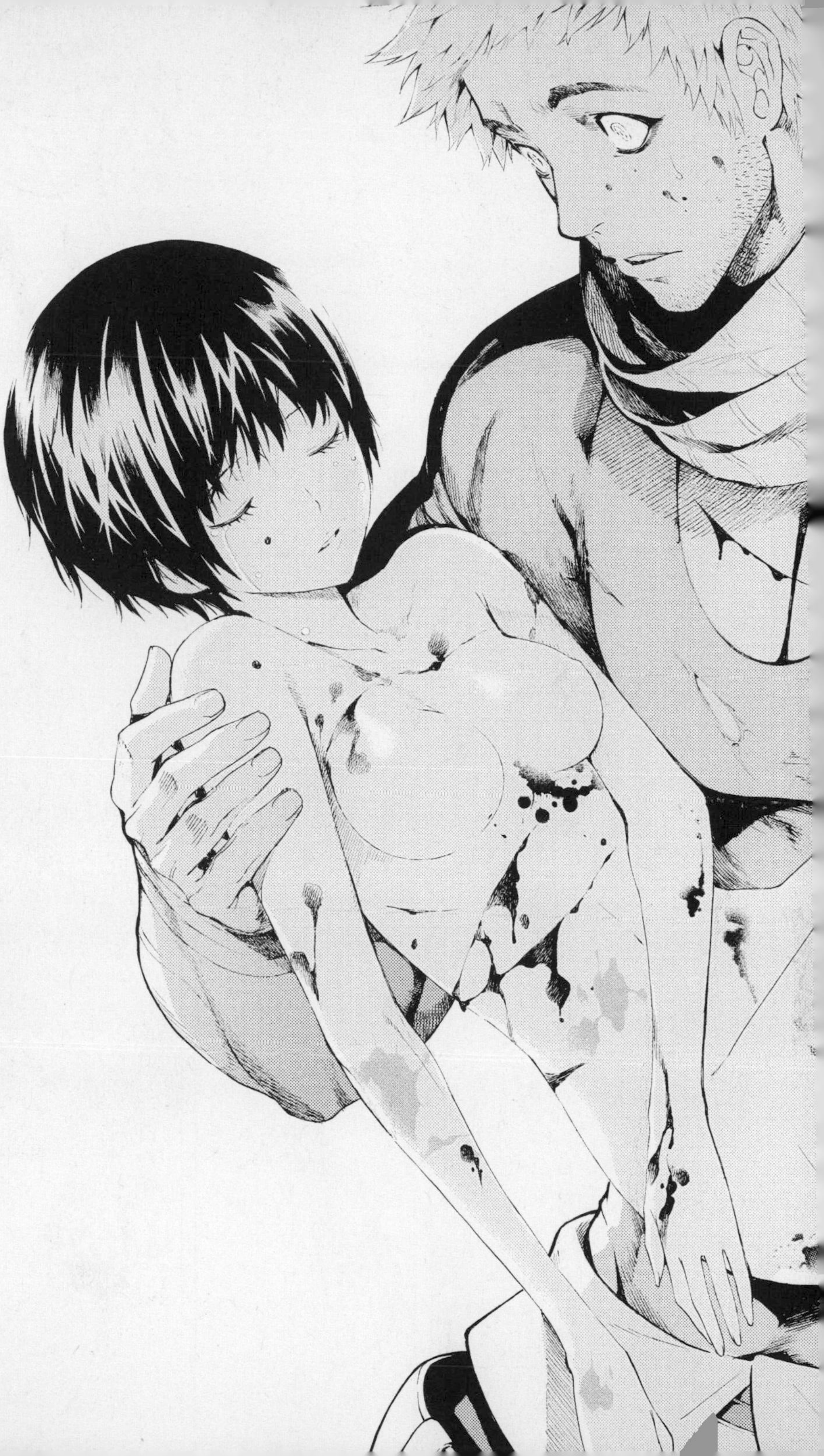

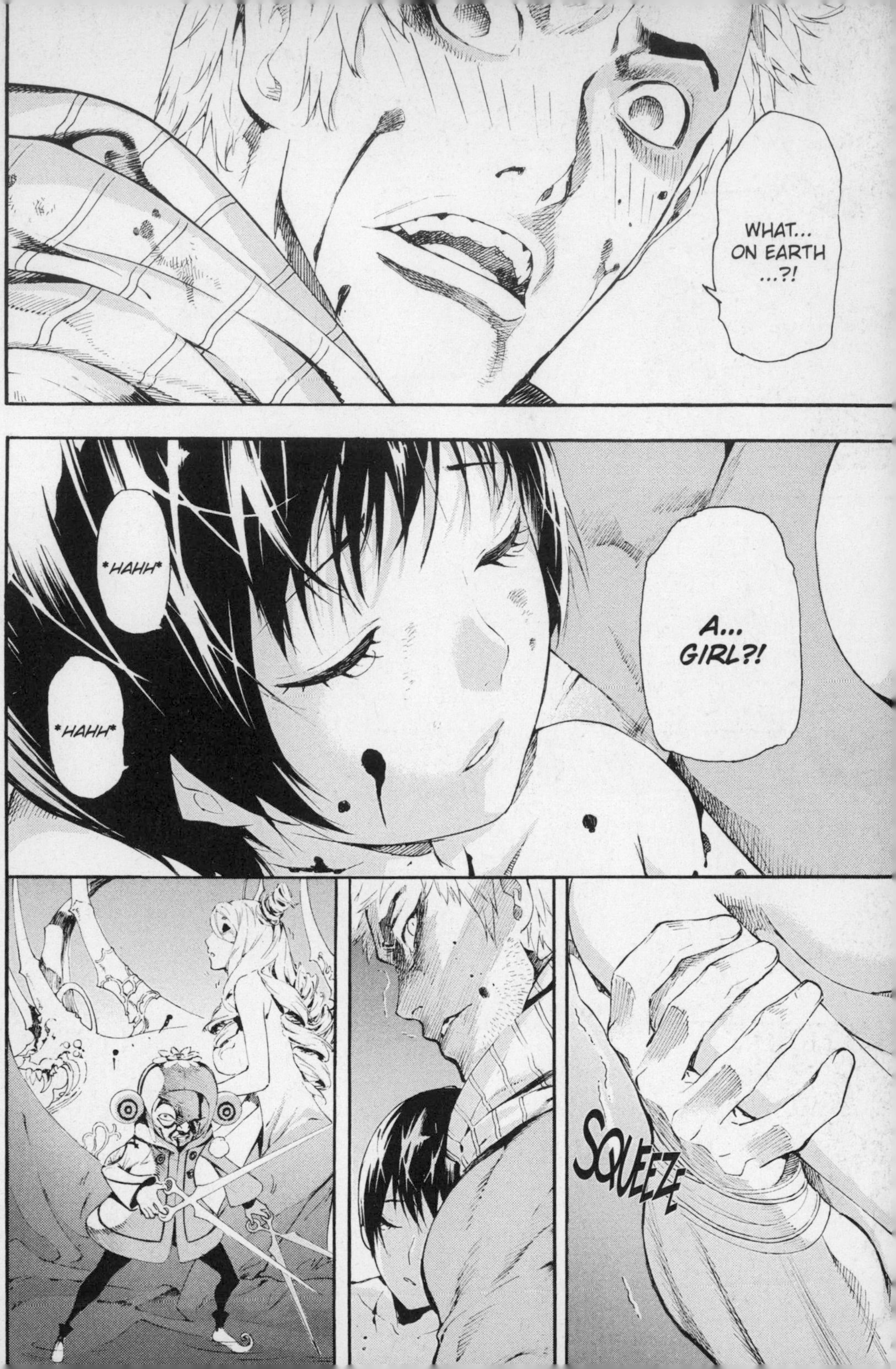
WHAT... ON EARTH ...?!
A... GIRL?!
HAHH
HAHH
SQUEEZE

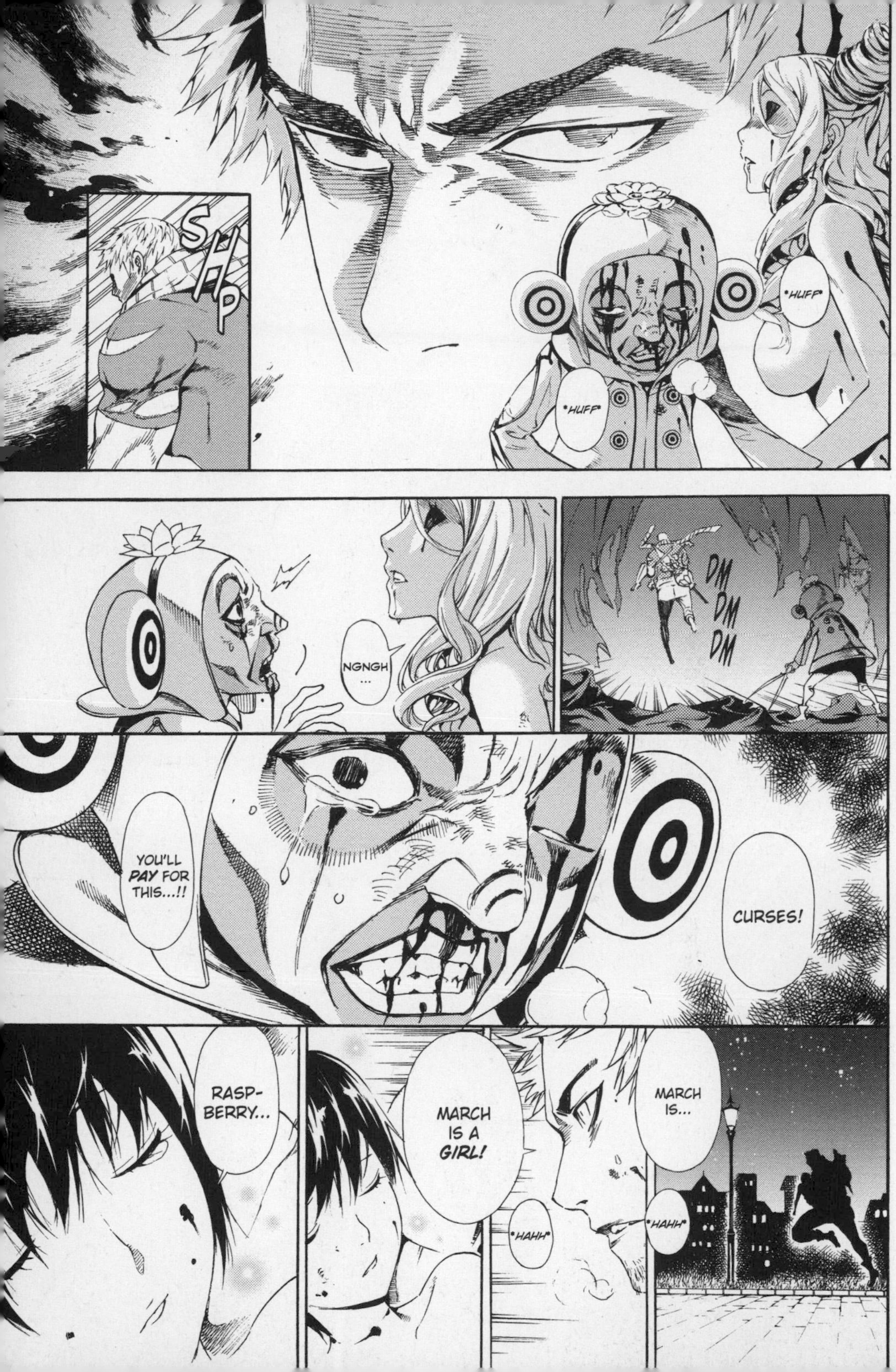
HUFF
HUFF
SHP
DM DM DM
NGNGH...
CURSES!
YOU'LL PAY FOR THIS...!!
MARCH IS...
HAHH
MARCH IS A GIRL!
HAHH
RASP-BERRY...

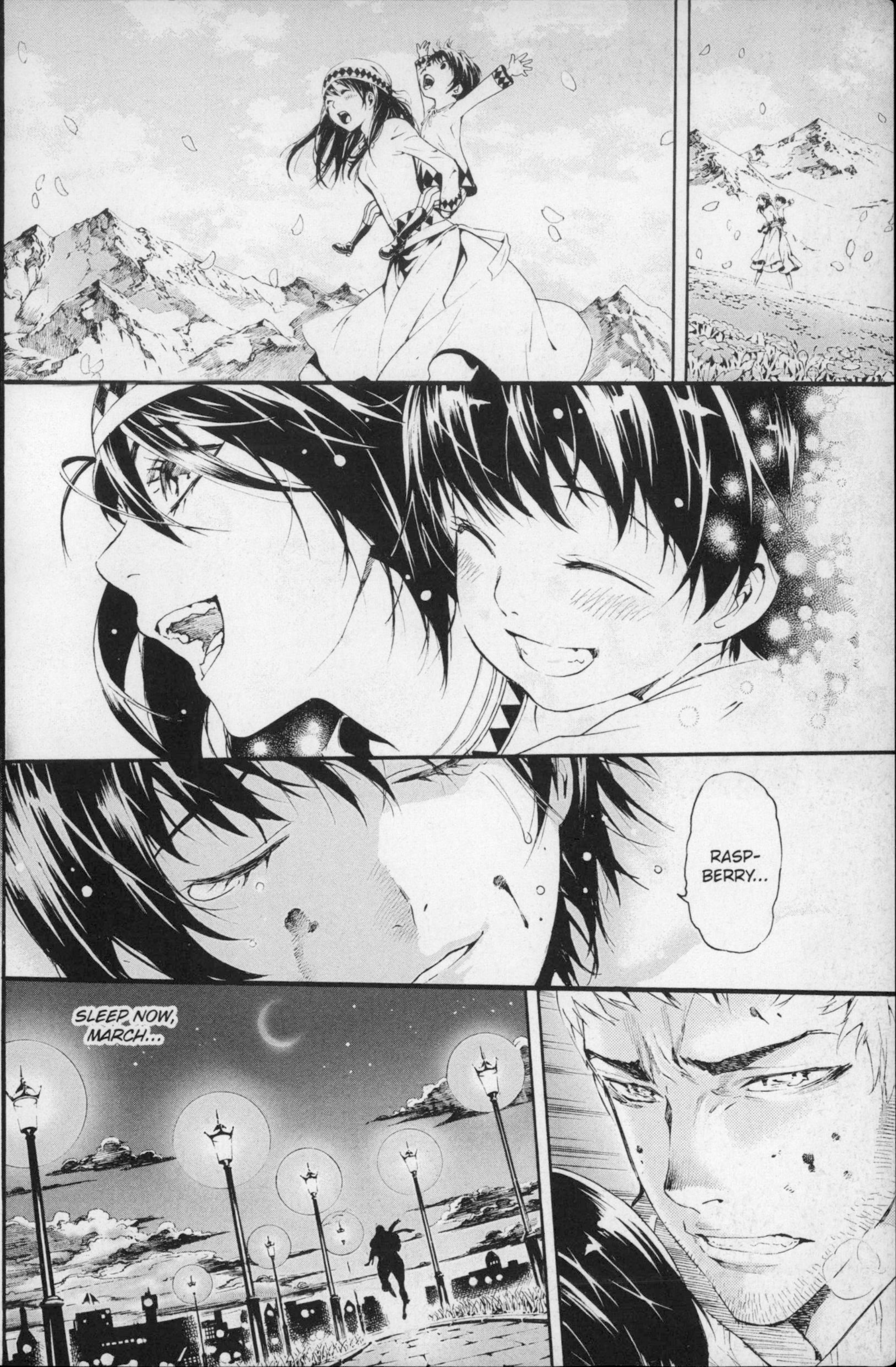
RASP-
BERRY...
SLEEP NOW,
MARCH...

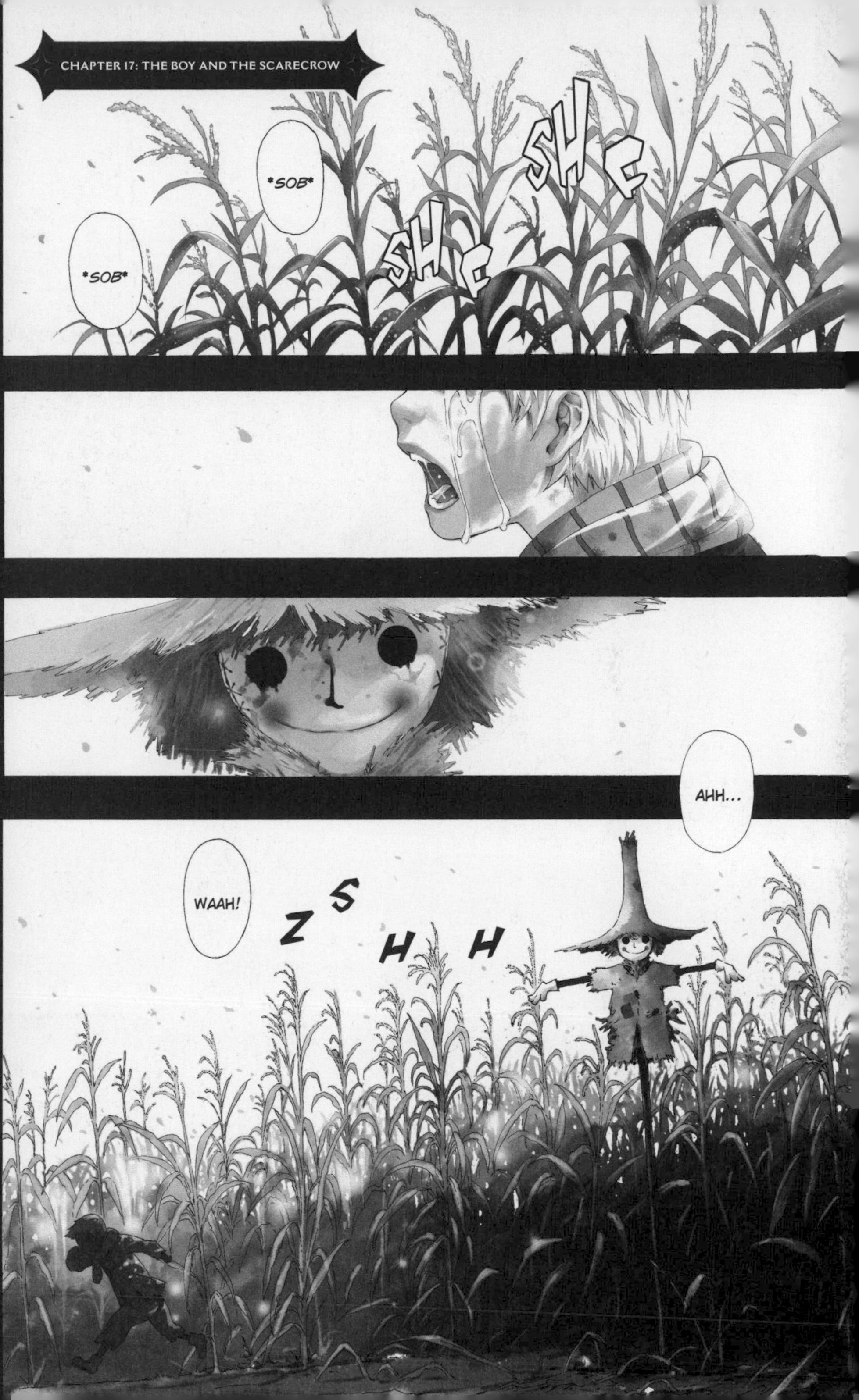
CHAPTER 17: THE BOY AND THE SCARECROW
SHF
SOB
SHF
SOB
AHH...
ZSHH
WAAH!

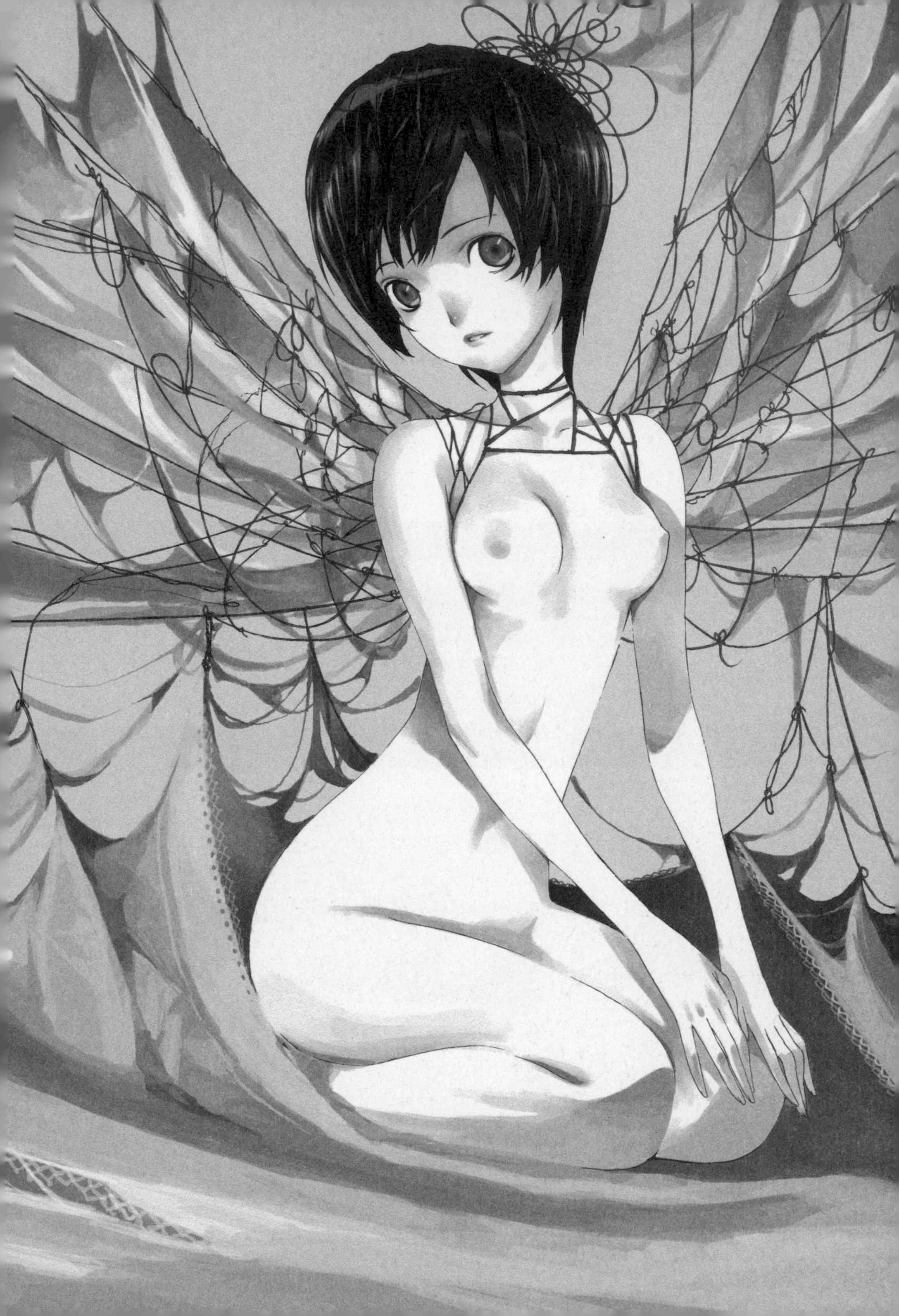

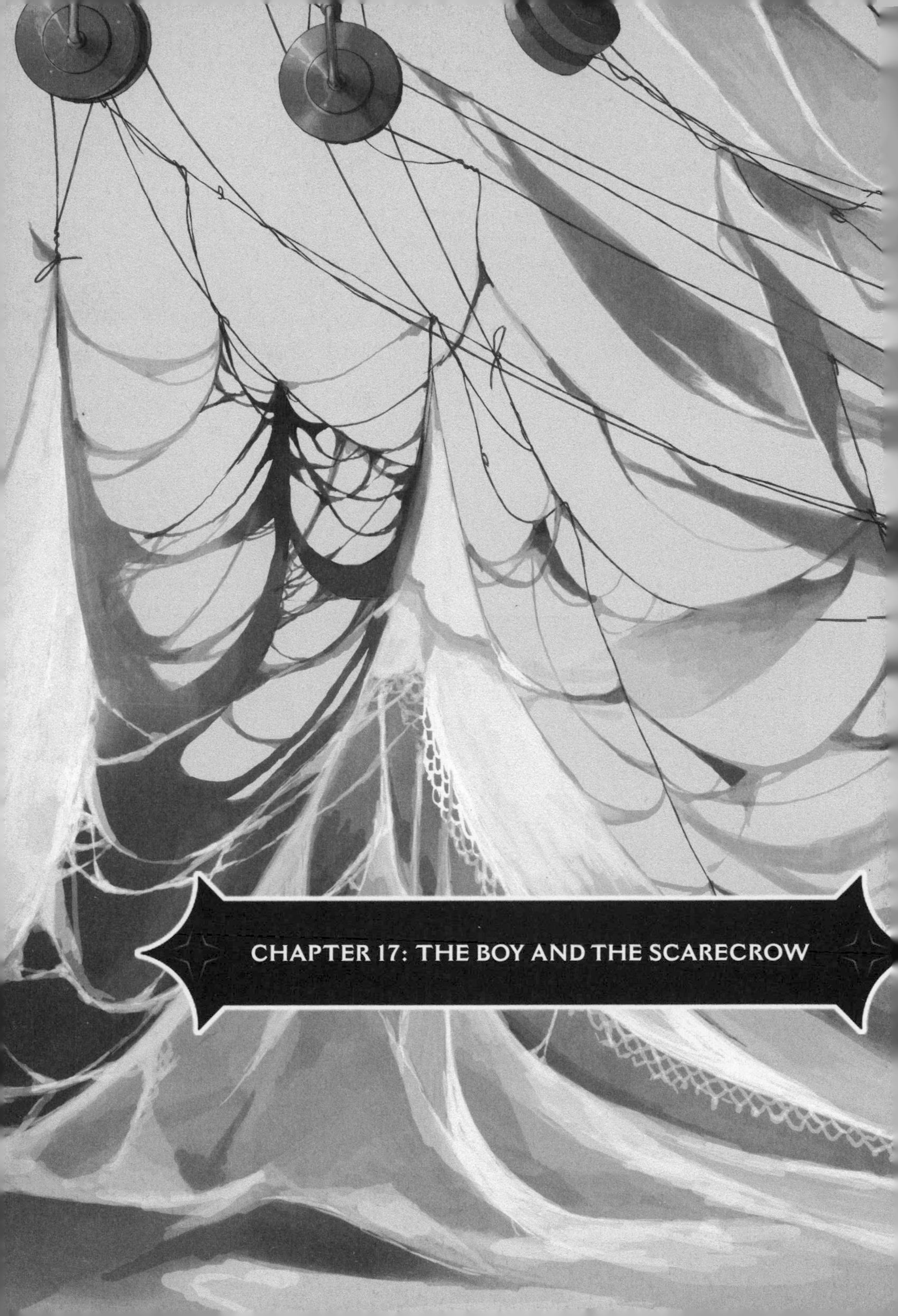

CHAPTER 17: THE BOY AND THE SCARECROW

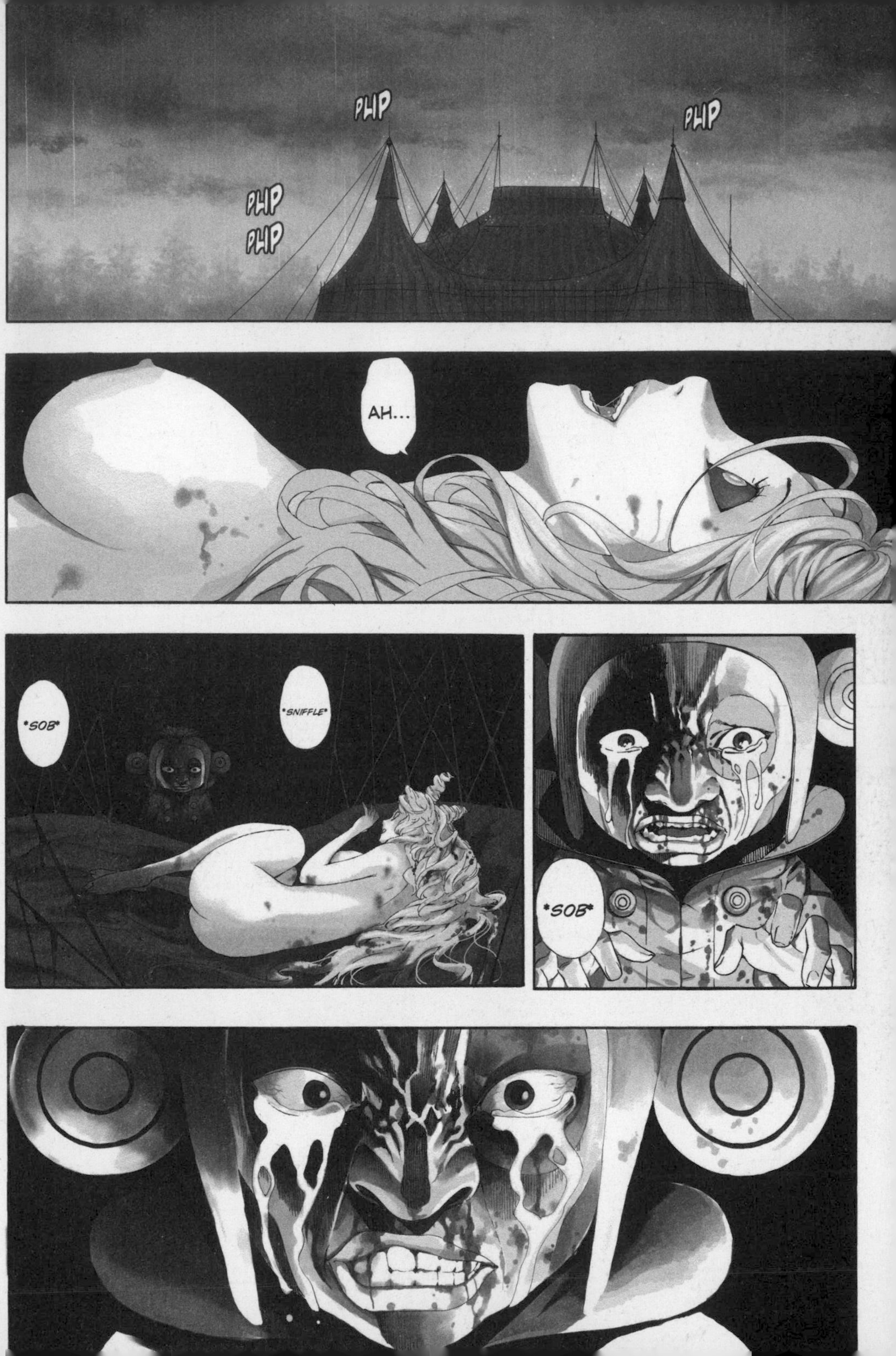
PLIP
PLIP
PLIP
PLIP
AH...
SOB
SNIFFLE
SOB

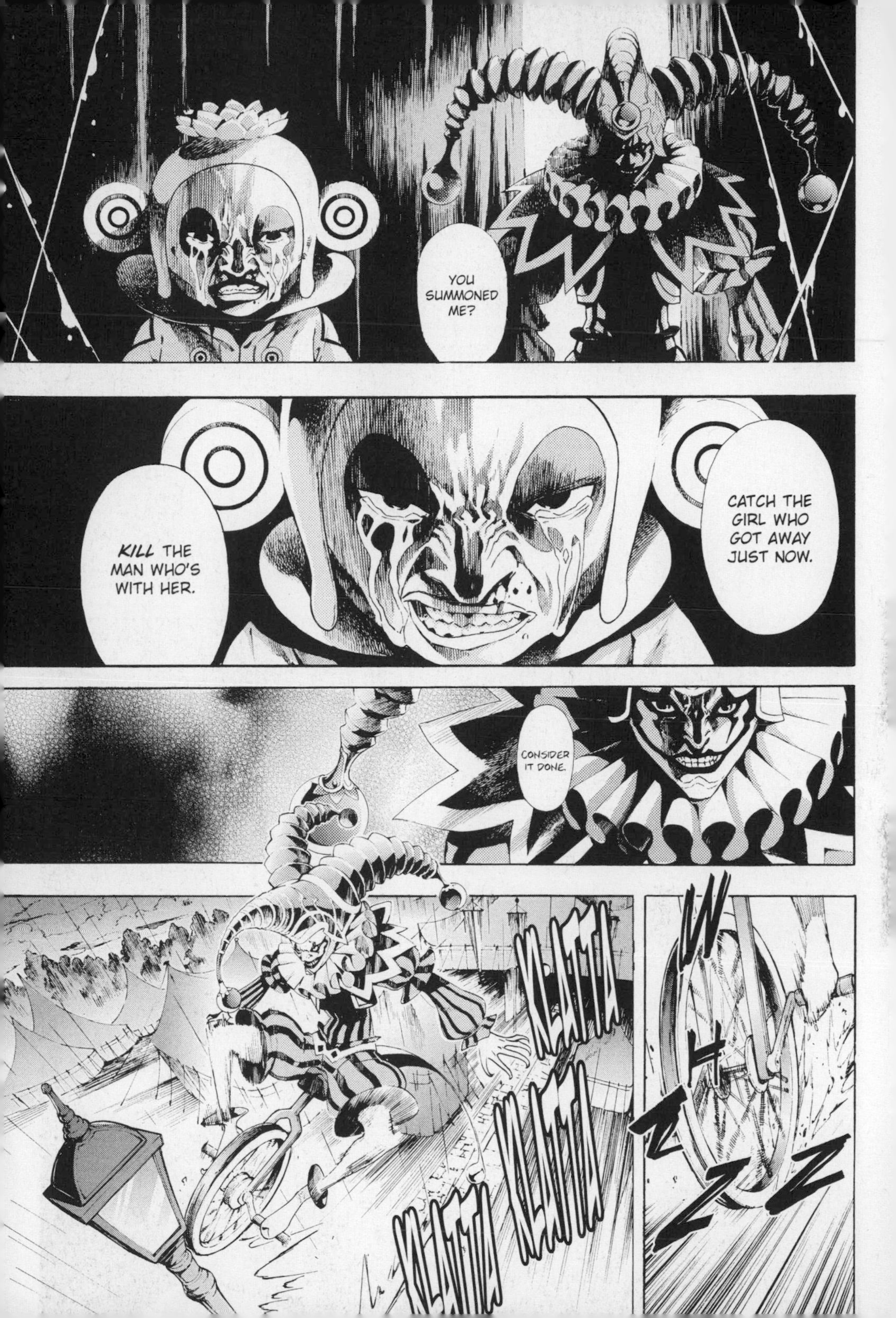
YOU SUMMONED ME?
CATCH THE GIRL WHO GOT AWAY JUST NOW.
KILL THE MAN WHO'S WITH HER.
CONSIDER IT DONE.
WHZZZ
KLATTA
KLATTA
KLATTA

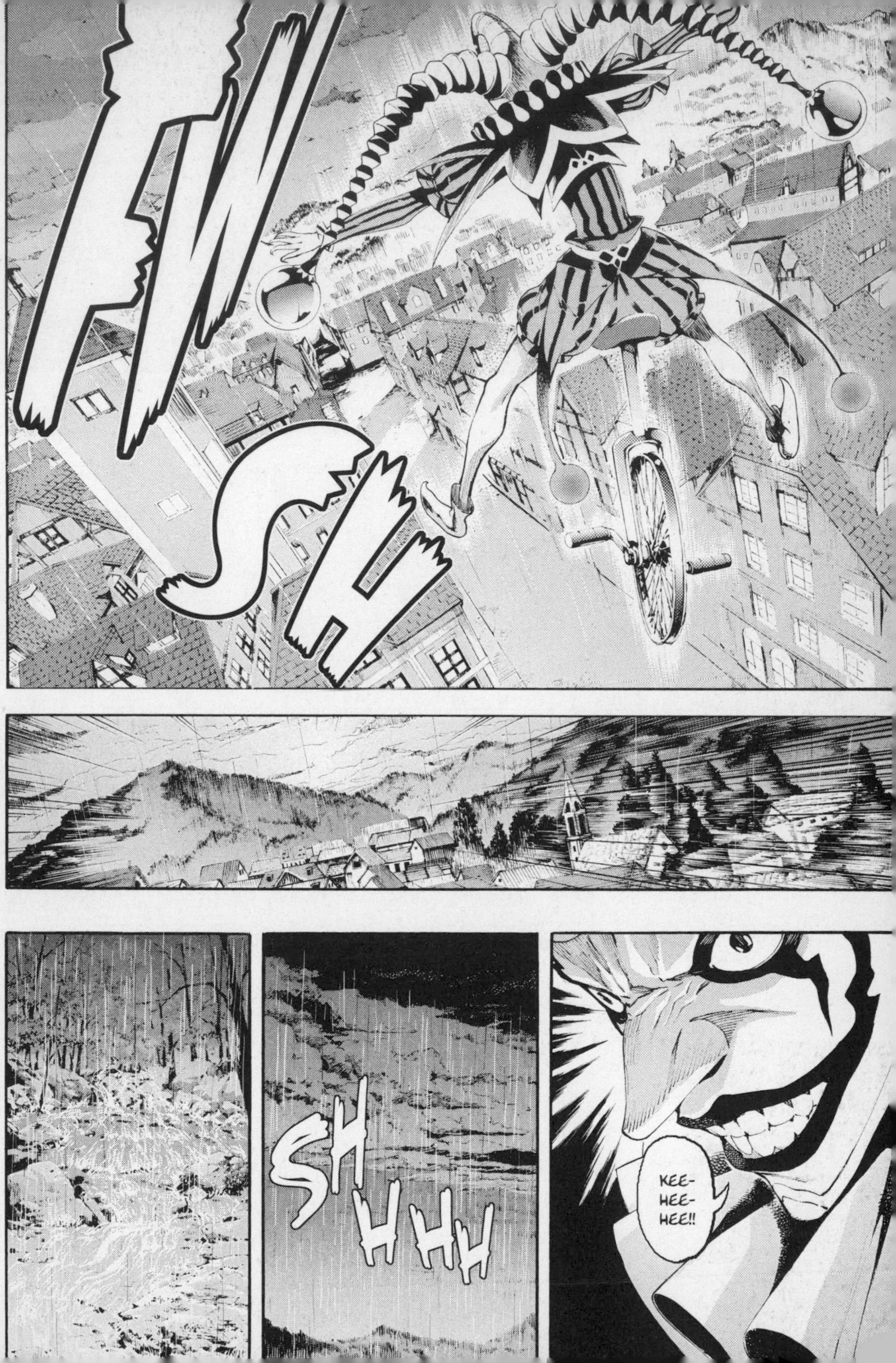
FWSH
KEE-HEE-HEE!!
SHHHH

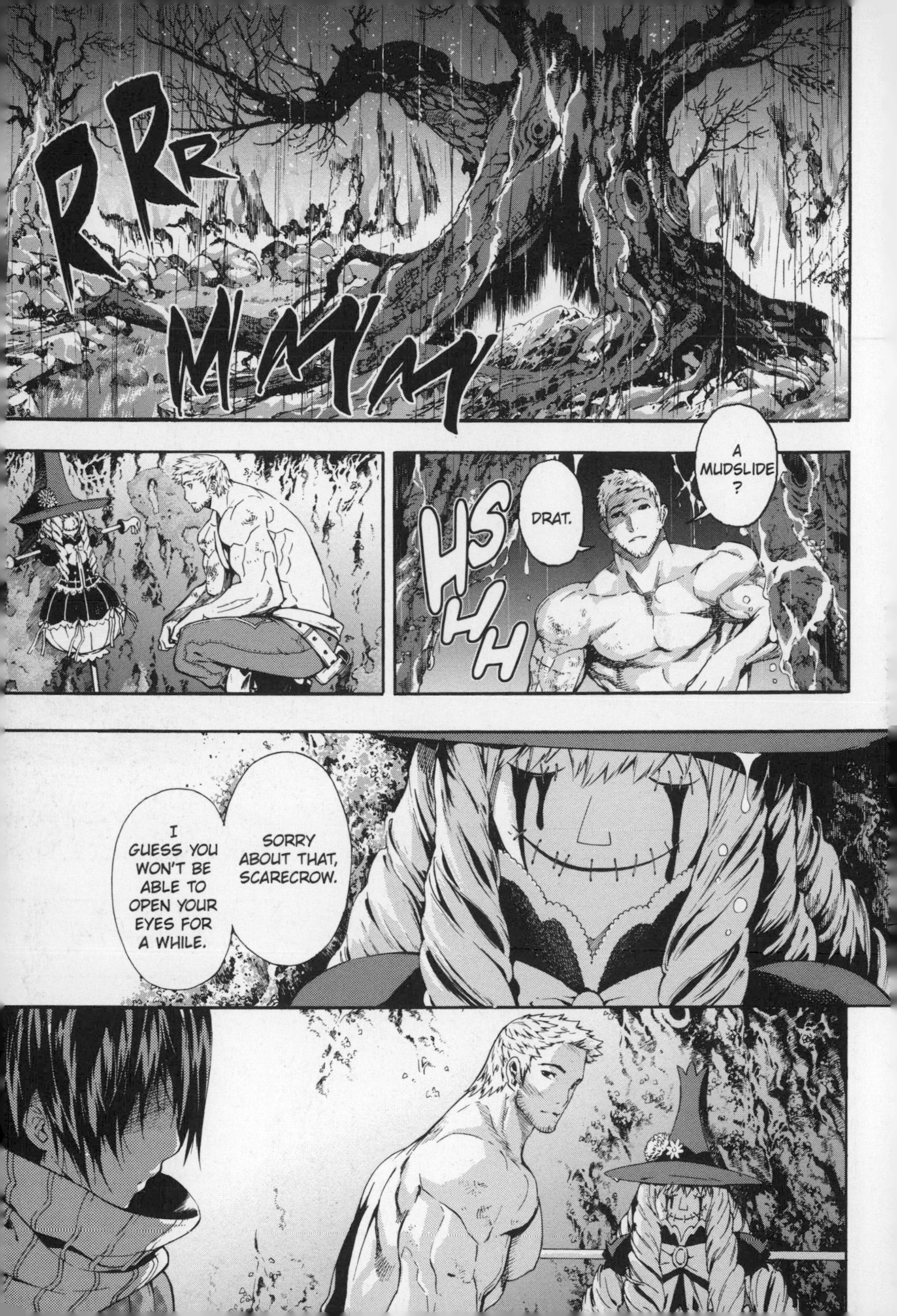
RRRMMMM
A MUDSLIDE?
DRAT.
HSHHH
SORRY ABOUT THAT, SCARECROW.
I GUESS YOU WON'T BE ABLE TO OPEN YOUR EYES FOR A WHILE.

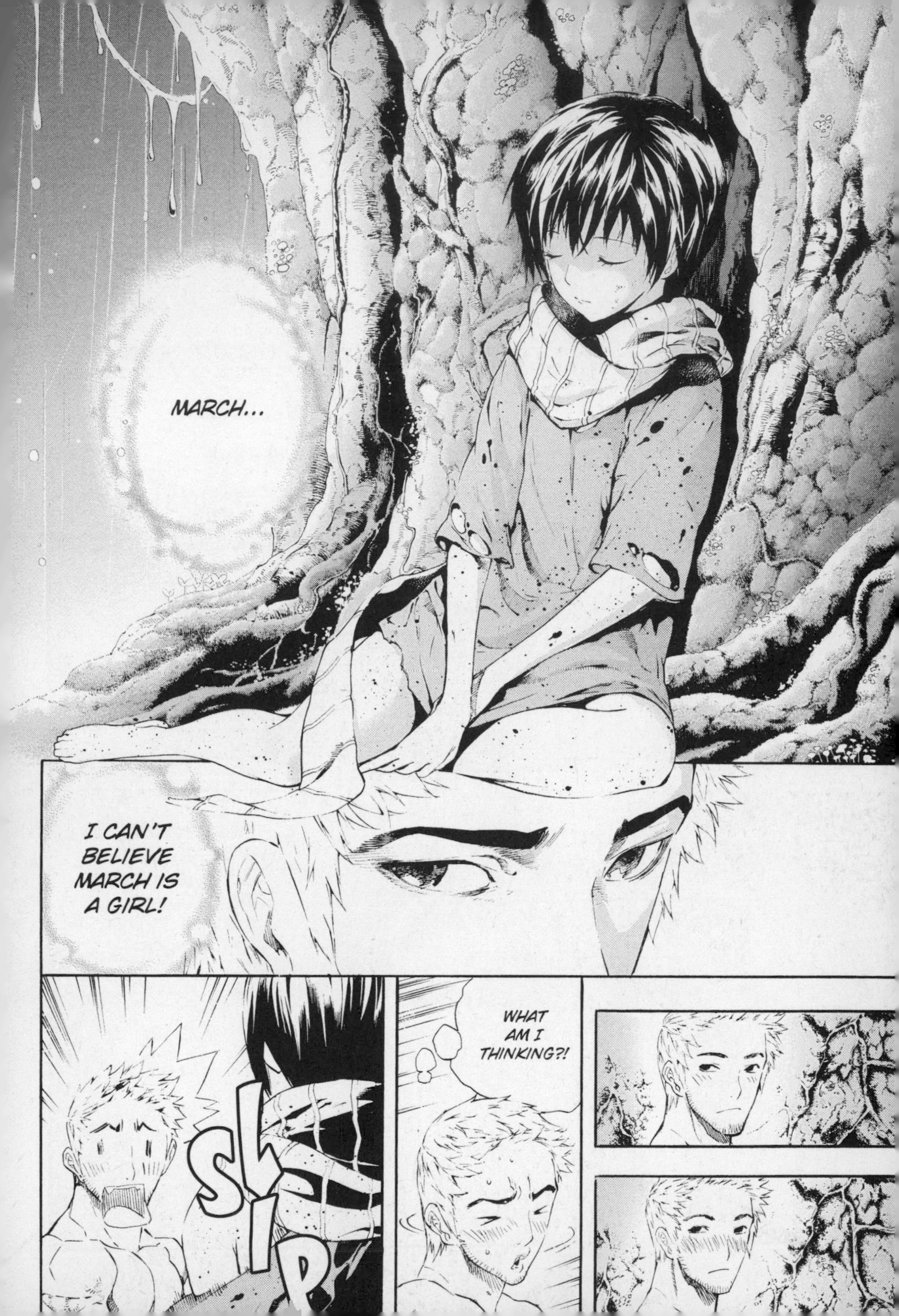
MARCH...
I CAN'T BELIEVE MARCH IS A GIRL!
WHAT AM I THINKING?!
SLIP

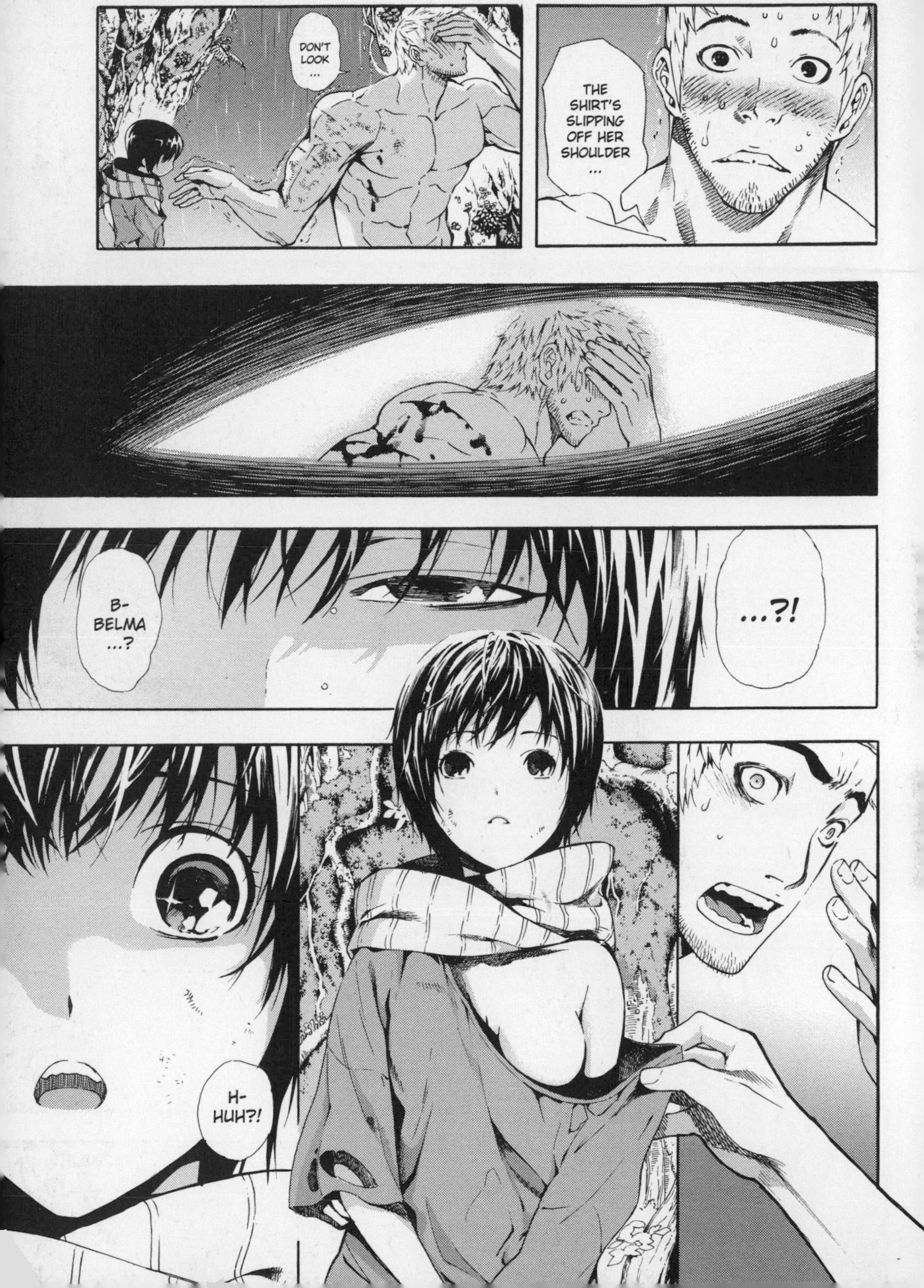
THE SHIRT'S SLIPPING OFF HER SHOULDER ...
DON'T LOOK ...
...?!
B- BELMA ...?
H- HUH?!

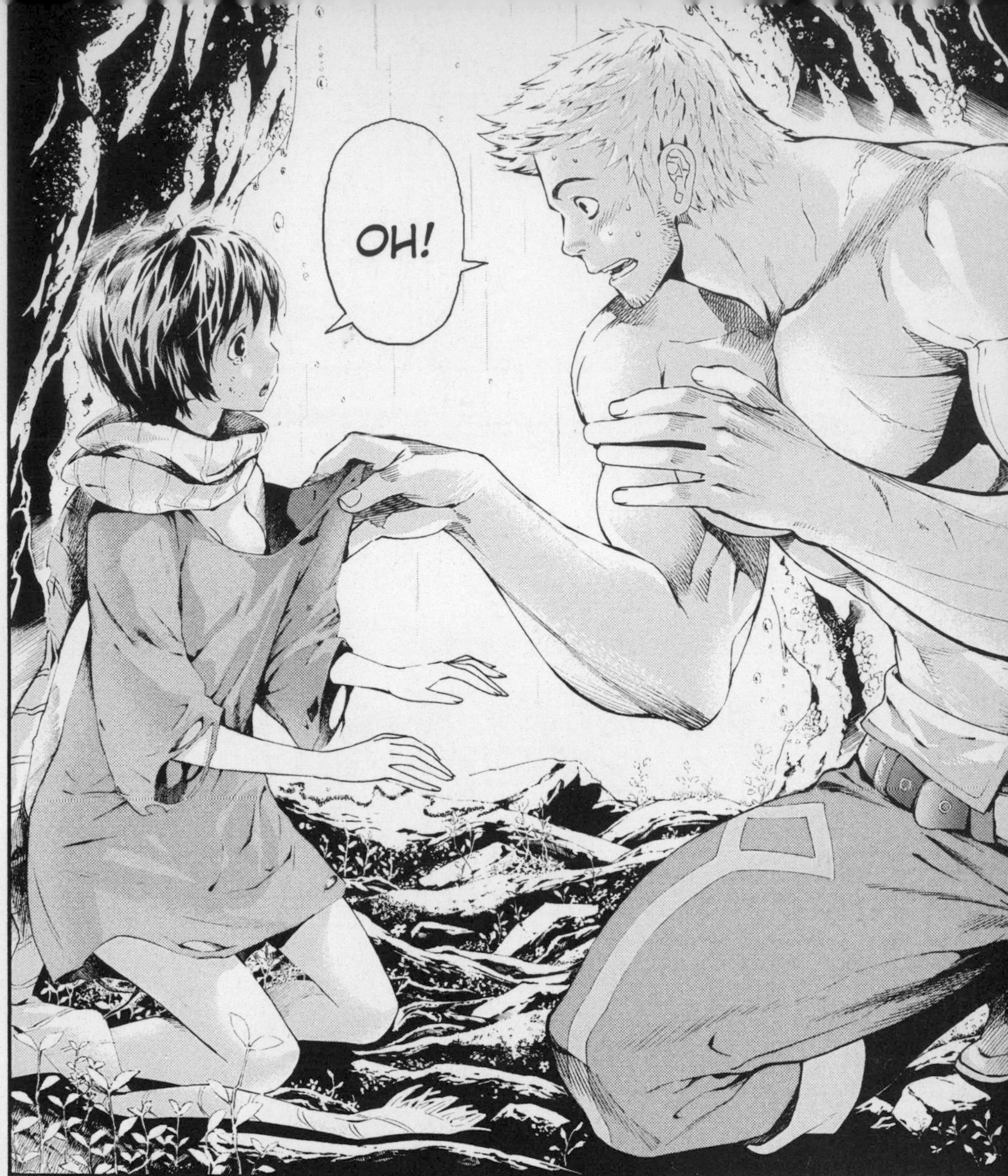
OH!

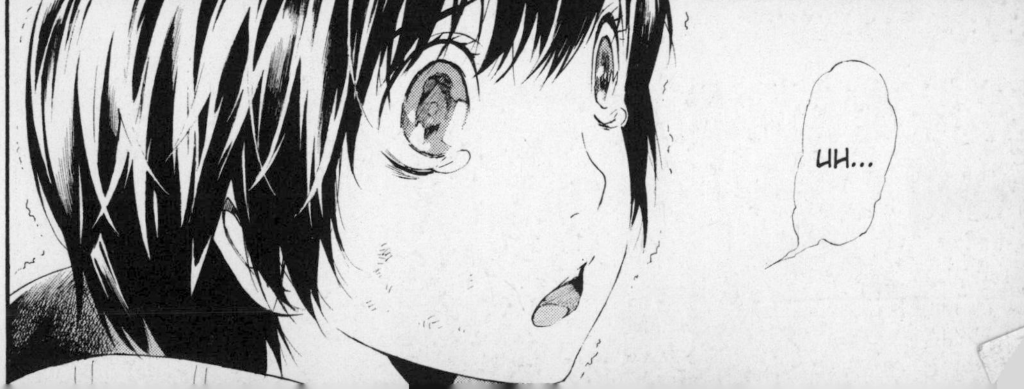
UH...

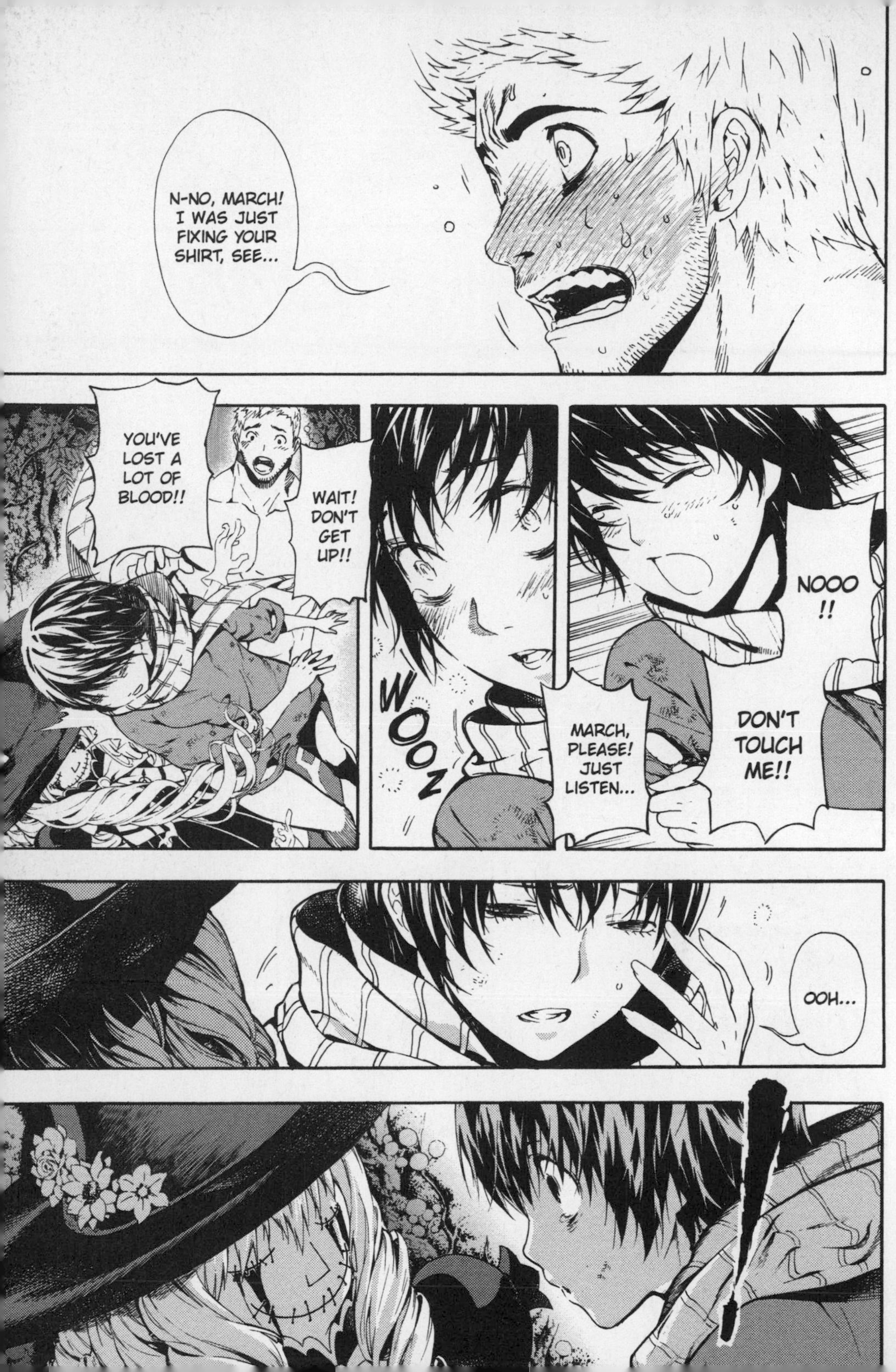
N-NO, MARCH! I WAS JUST FIXING YOUR SHIRT, SEE...
NOOO!!
DON'T TOUCH ME!!
MARCH, PLEASE! JUST LISTEN...
WOON
WAIT! DON'T GET UP!!
YOU'VE LOST A LOT OF BLOOD!!
OOH...

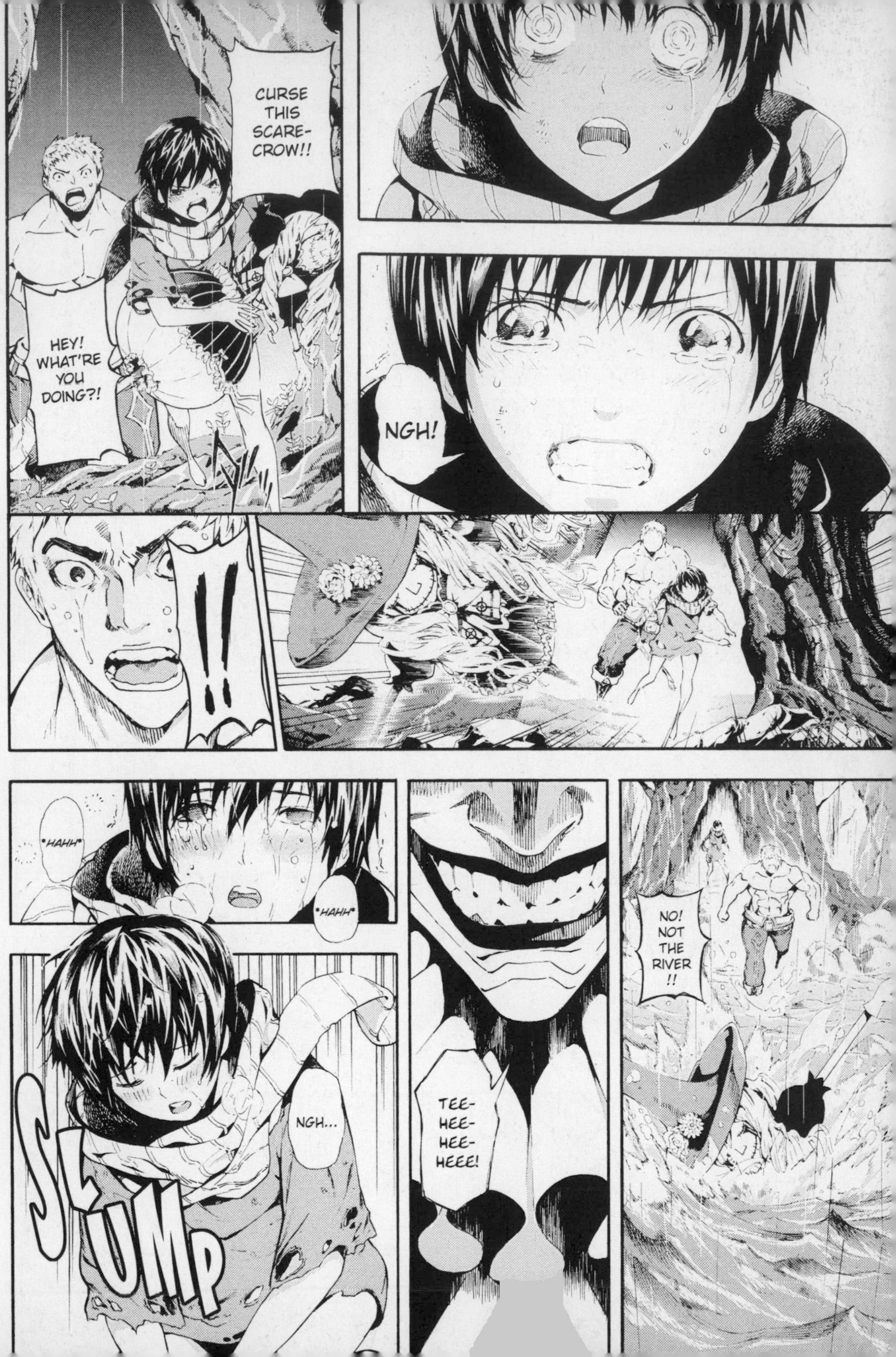
NGH!
CURSE THIS SCARE-CROW!!
HEY! WHAT'RE YOU DOING?!
!!
NO! NOT THE RIVER !!
TEE-HEE-HEE-HEEE!
HAHH
HAHH
NGH...
SLUMP

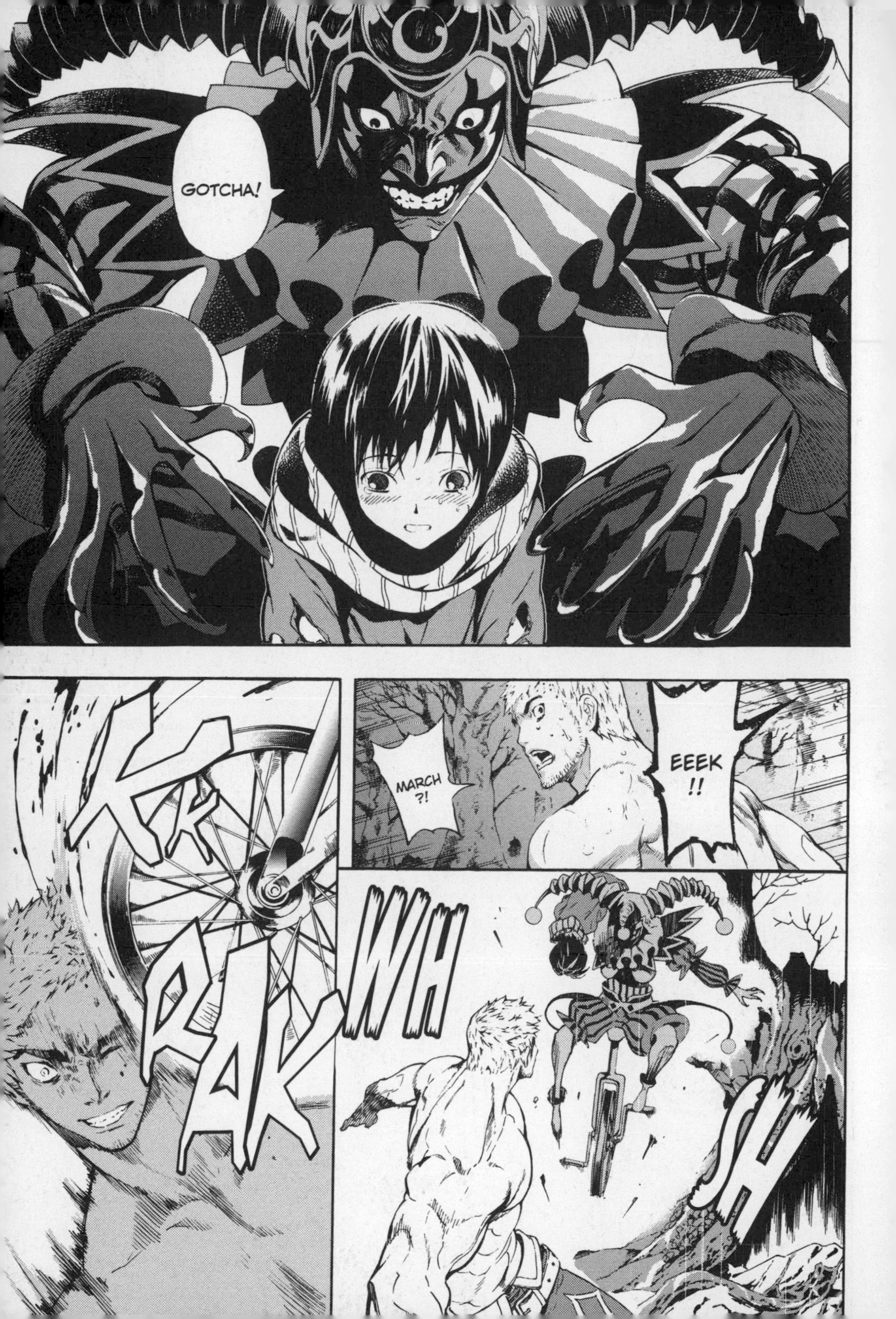
GOTCHA!
EEEK !!
MARCH ?!
WH
SH
KR
RAK

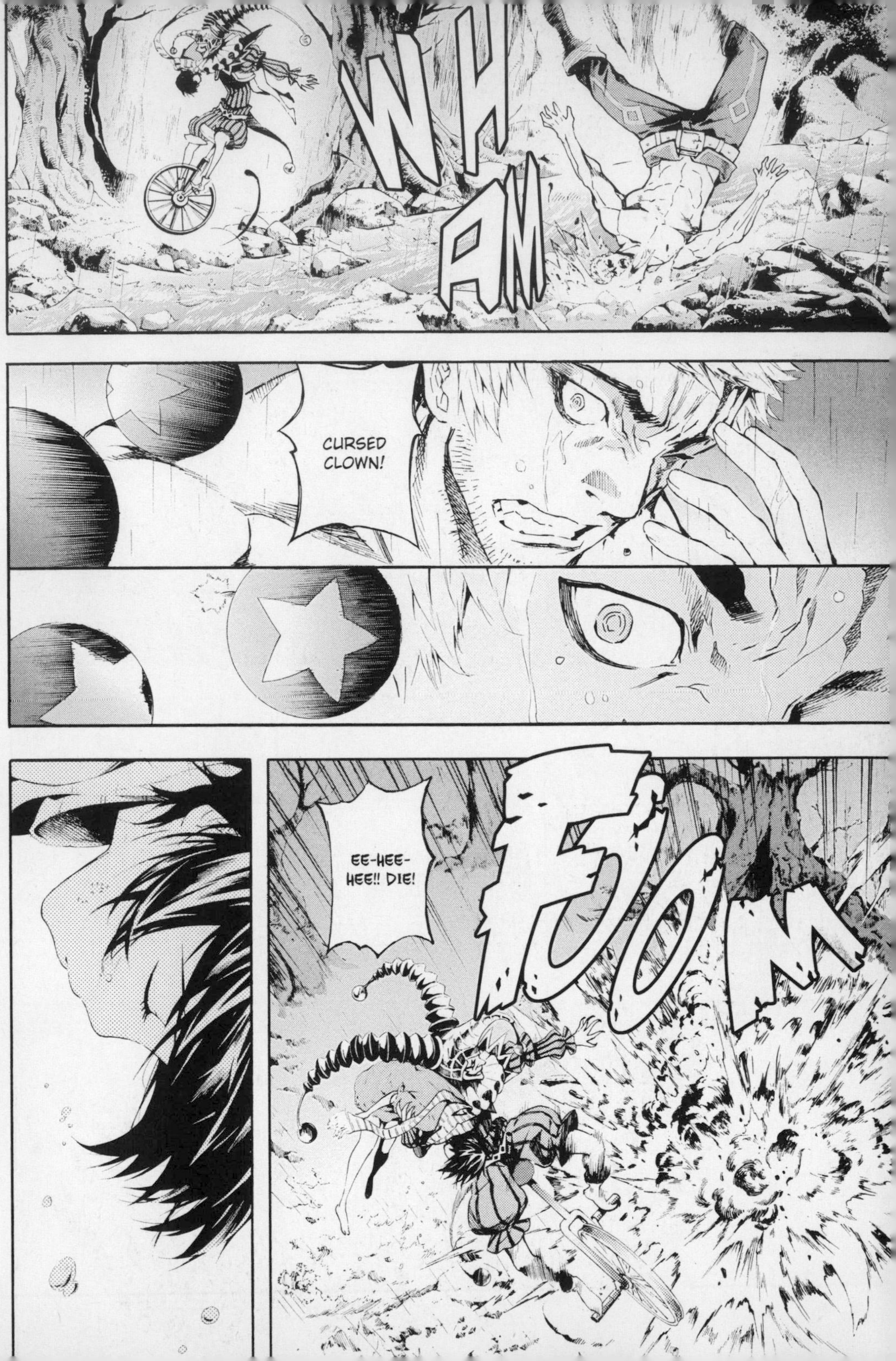
WHAM
CURSED CLOWN!
FOOM
EE-HEE-HEE!! DIE!

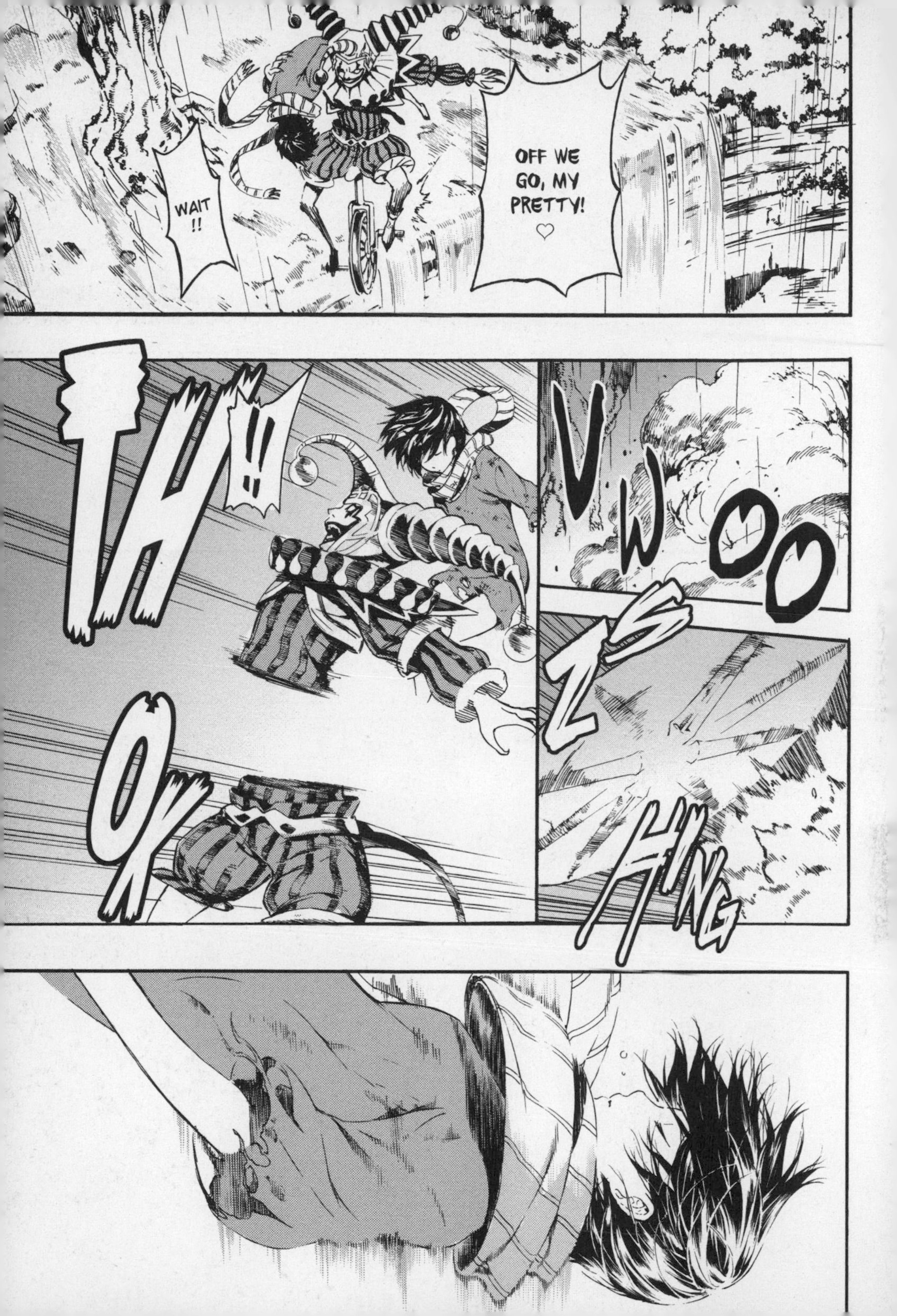
OFF WE GO, MY PRETTY! ♡
WAIT !!
VWOO
THOK
!!

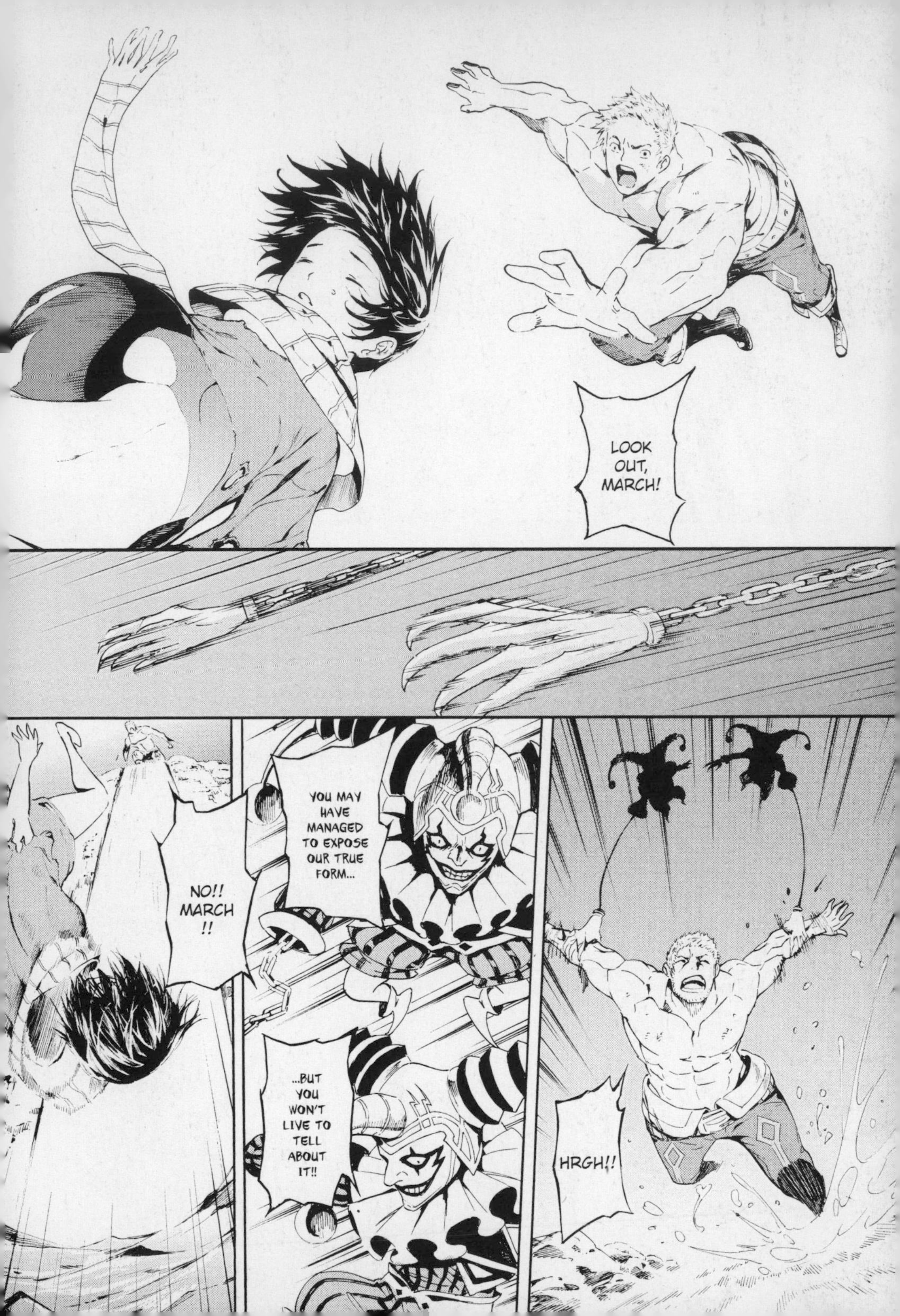
LOOK OUT, MARCH!
HRGH!!
YOU MAY HAVE MANAGED TO EXPOSE OUR TRUE FORM...
...BUT YOU WON'T LIVE TO TELL ABOUT IT!!
NO!! MARCH!!

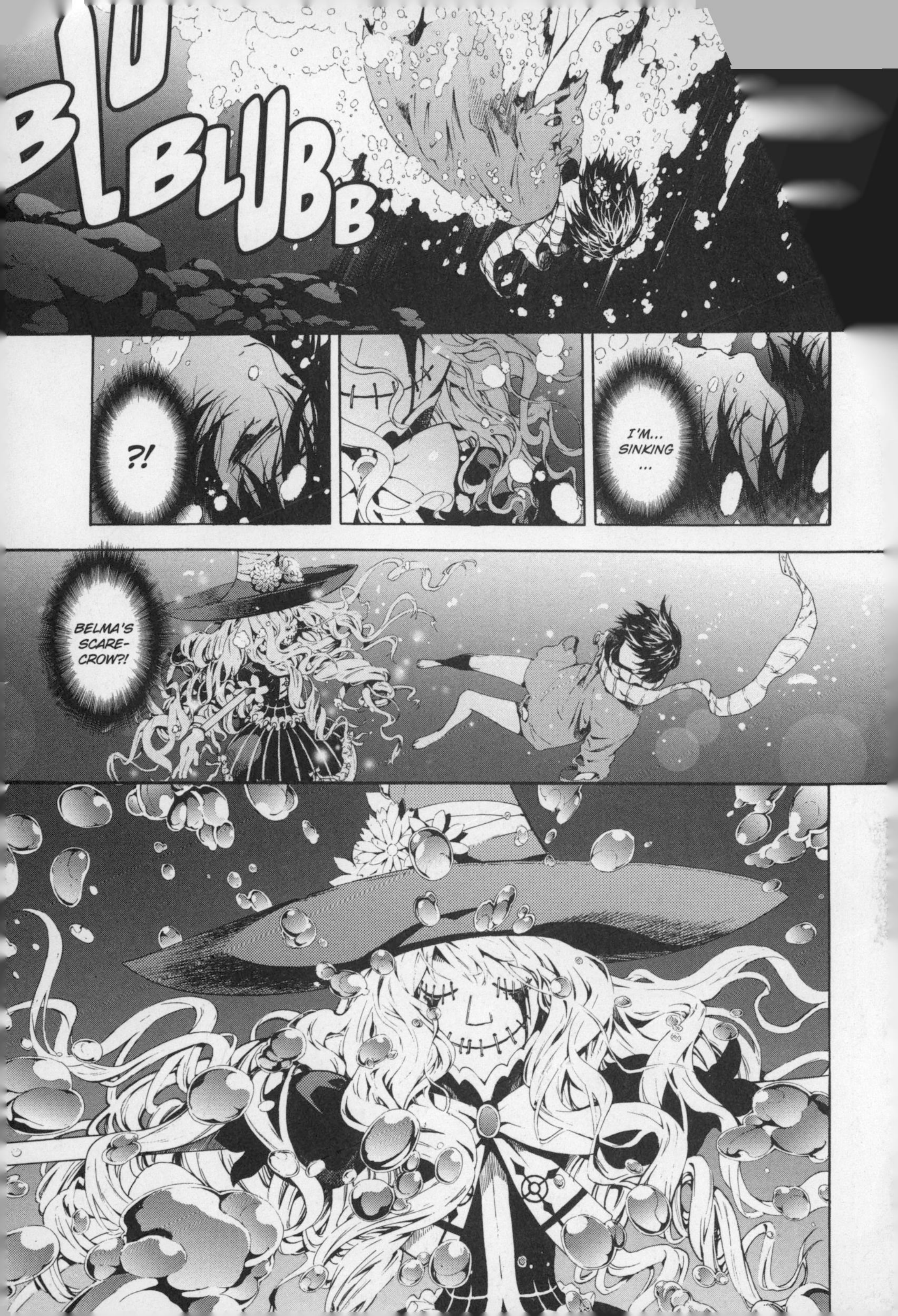
BLUBLUBB
I'M... SINKING ...
?!
BELMA'S SCARE-CROW?!

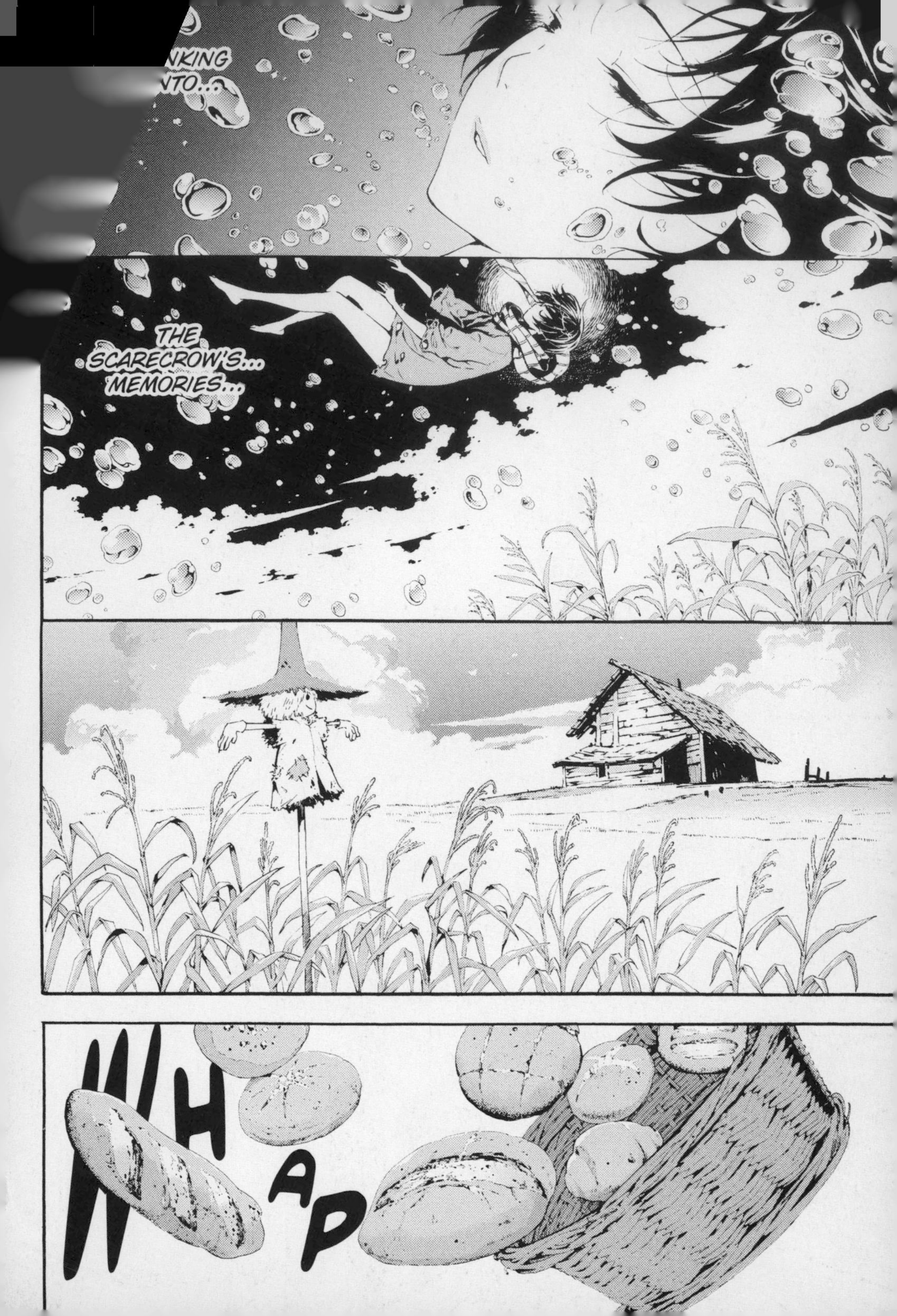
[redacted]NKING
NTO...
THE SCARECROW'S... MEMORIES...
WHAP

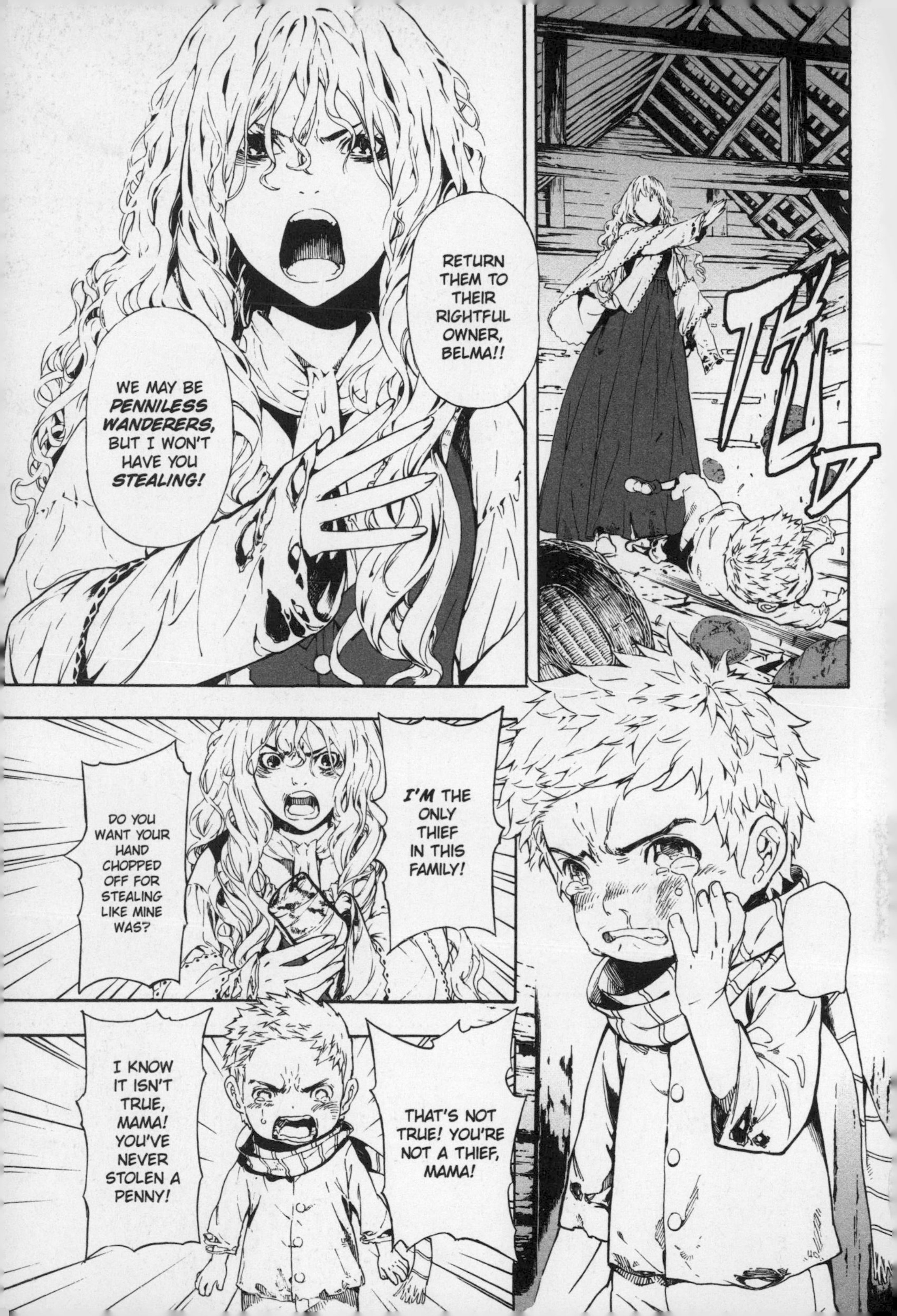
RETURN THEM TO THEIR RIGHTFUL OWNER, BELMA!!
WE MAY BE *PENNILESS WANDERERS*, BUT I WON'T HAVE YOU *STEALING!*
I'M THE ONLY THIEF IN THIS FAMILY!
DO YOU WANT YOUR HAND CHOPPED OFF FOR STEALING LIKE MINE WAS?
THAT'S NOT TRUE! YOU'RE NOT A THIEF, MAMA!
I KNOW IT ISN'T TRUE, MAMA! YOU'VE NEVER STOLEN A PENNY!

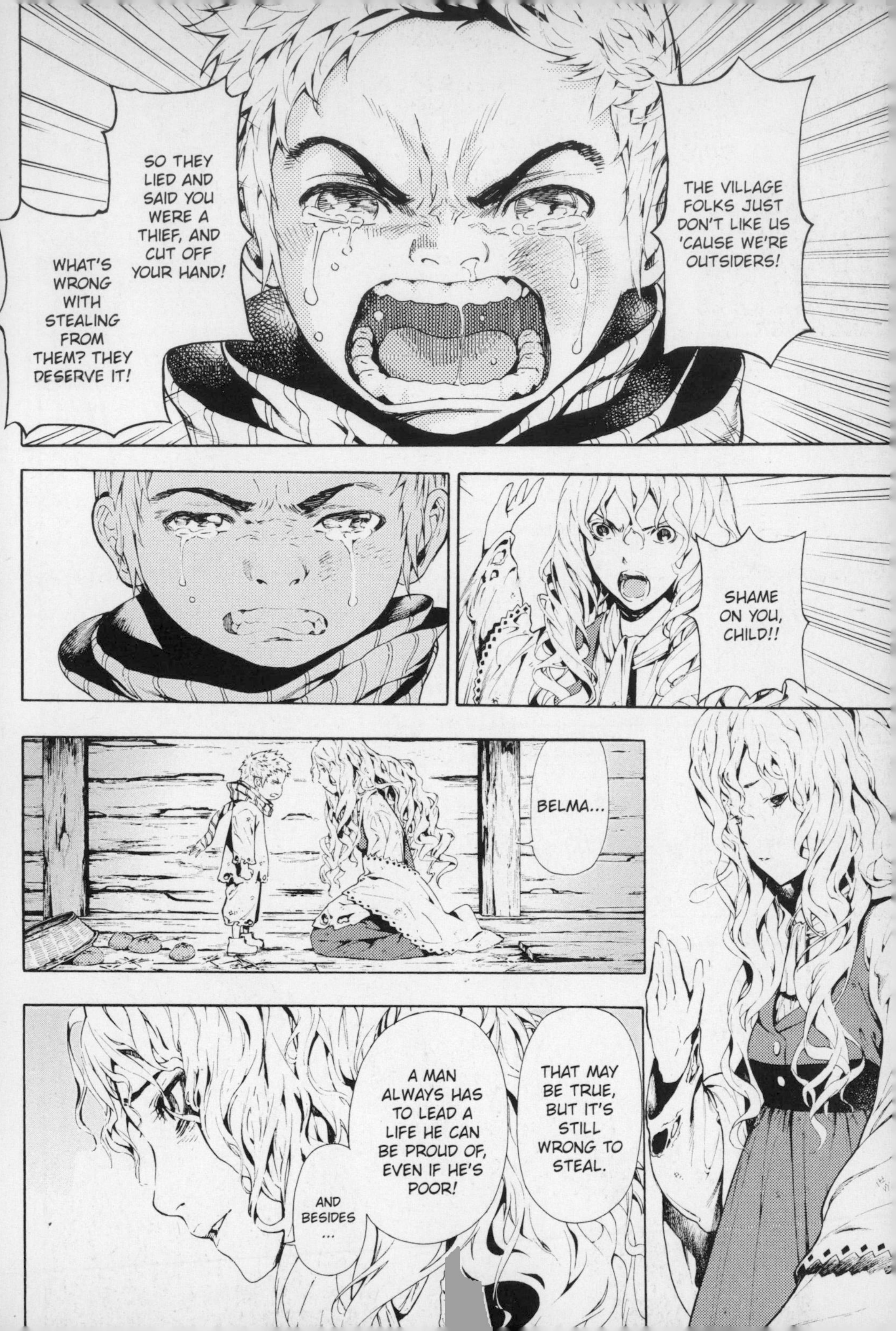
THE VILLAGE FOLKS JUST DON'T LIKE US 'CAUSE WE'RE OUTSIDERS!
SO THEY LIED AND SAID YOU WERE A THIEF, AND CUT OFF YOUR HAND!
WHAT'S WRONG WITH STEALING FROM THEM? THEY DESERVE IT!
SHAME ON YOU, CHILD!!
BELMA...
THAT MAY BE TRUE, BUT IT'S STILL WRONG TO STEAL.
A MAN ALWAYS HAS TO LEAD A LIFE HE CAN BE PROUD OF, EVEN IF HE'S POOR!
AND BESIDES ...

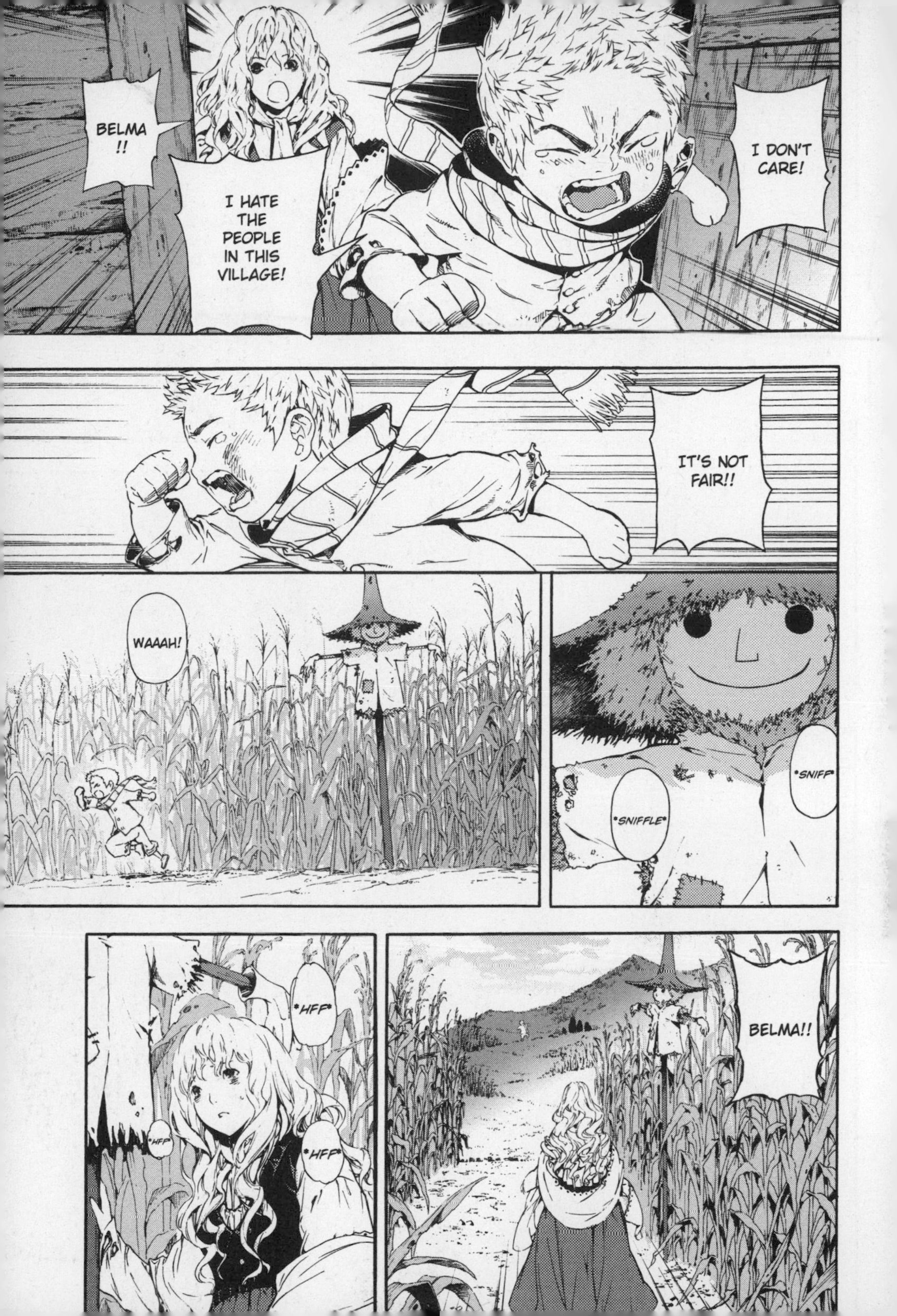
I DON'T CARE!
I HATE THE PEOPLE IN THIS VILLAGE!
BELMA !!
IT'S NOT FAIR!!
SNIFF
SNIFFLE
WAAAH!
BELMA!!
HFF
HFF
HFF

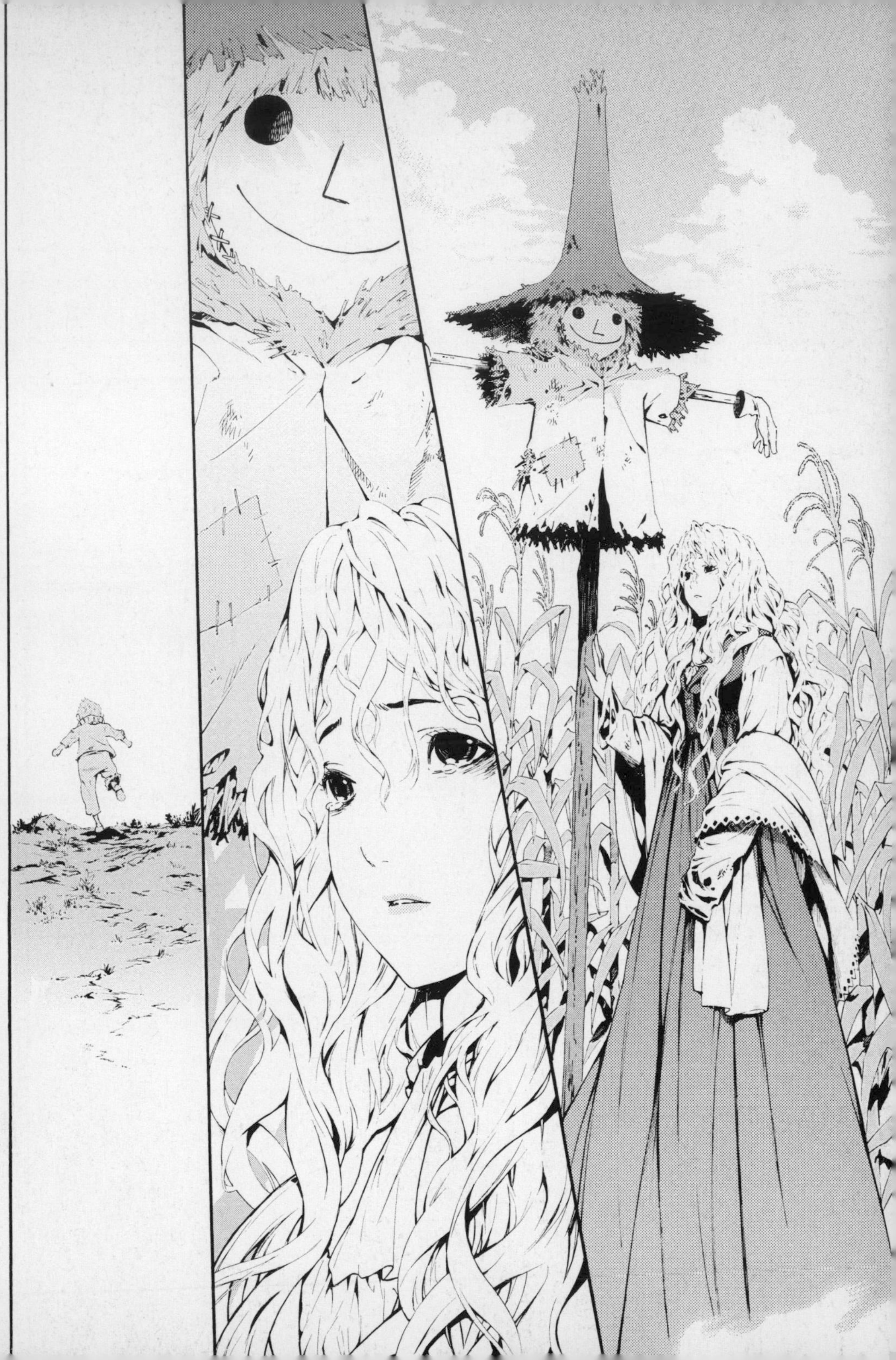

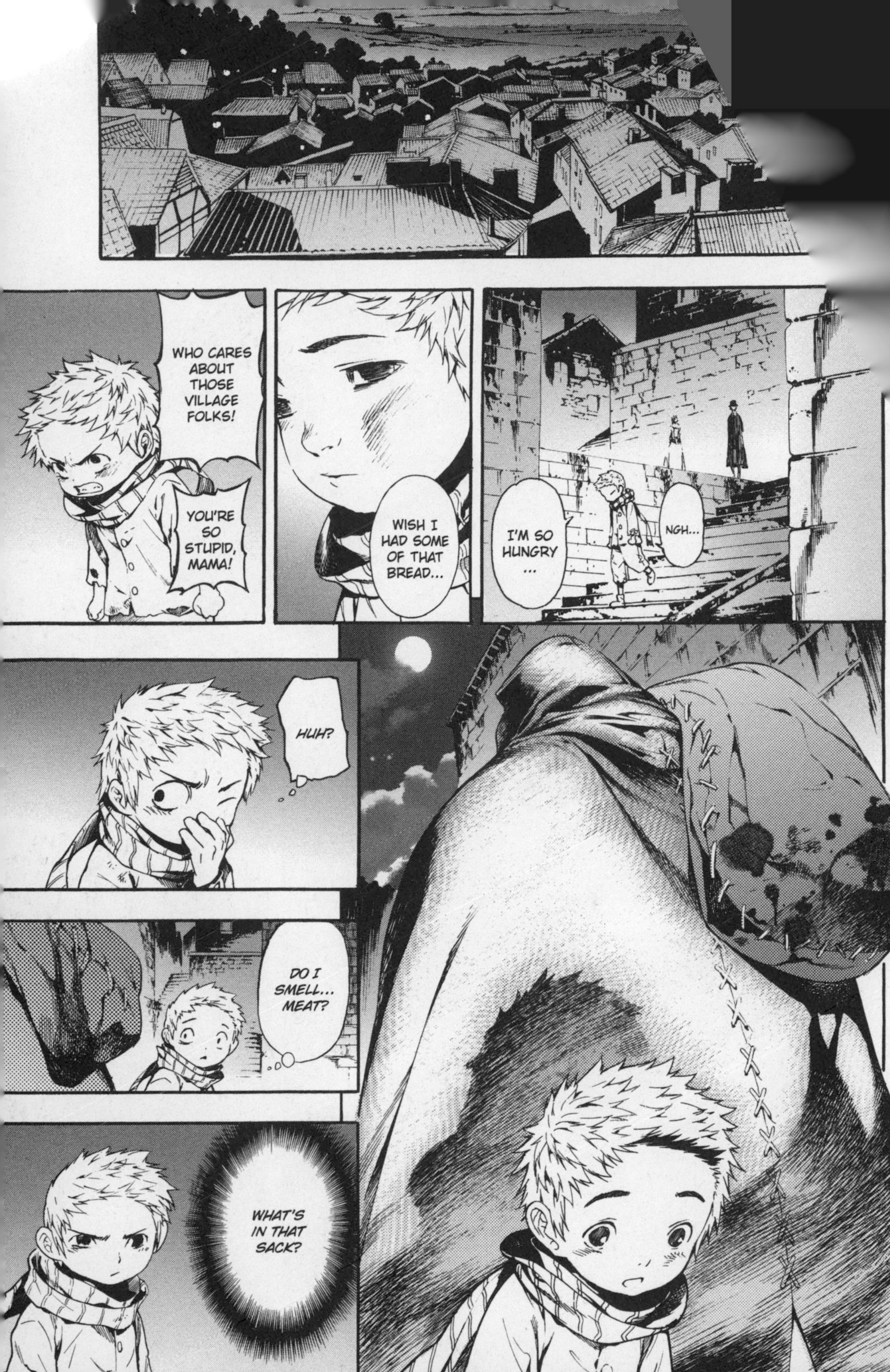
NGH...
I'M SO HUNGRY ...
WISH I HAD SOME OF THAT BREAD...
WHO CARES ABOUT THOSE VILLAGE FOLKS!
YOU'RE SO STUPID, MAMA!
HUH?
DO I SMELL... MEAT?
WHAT'S IN THAT SACK?

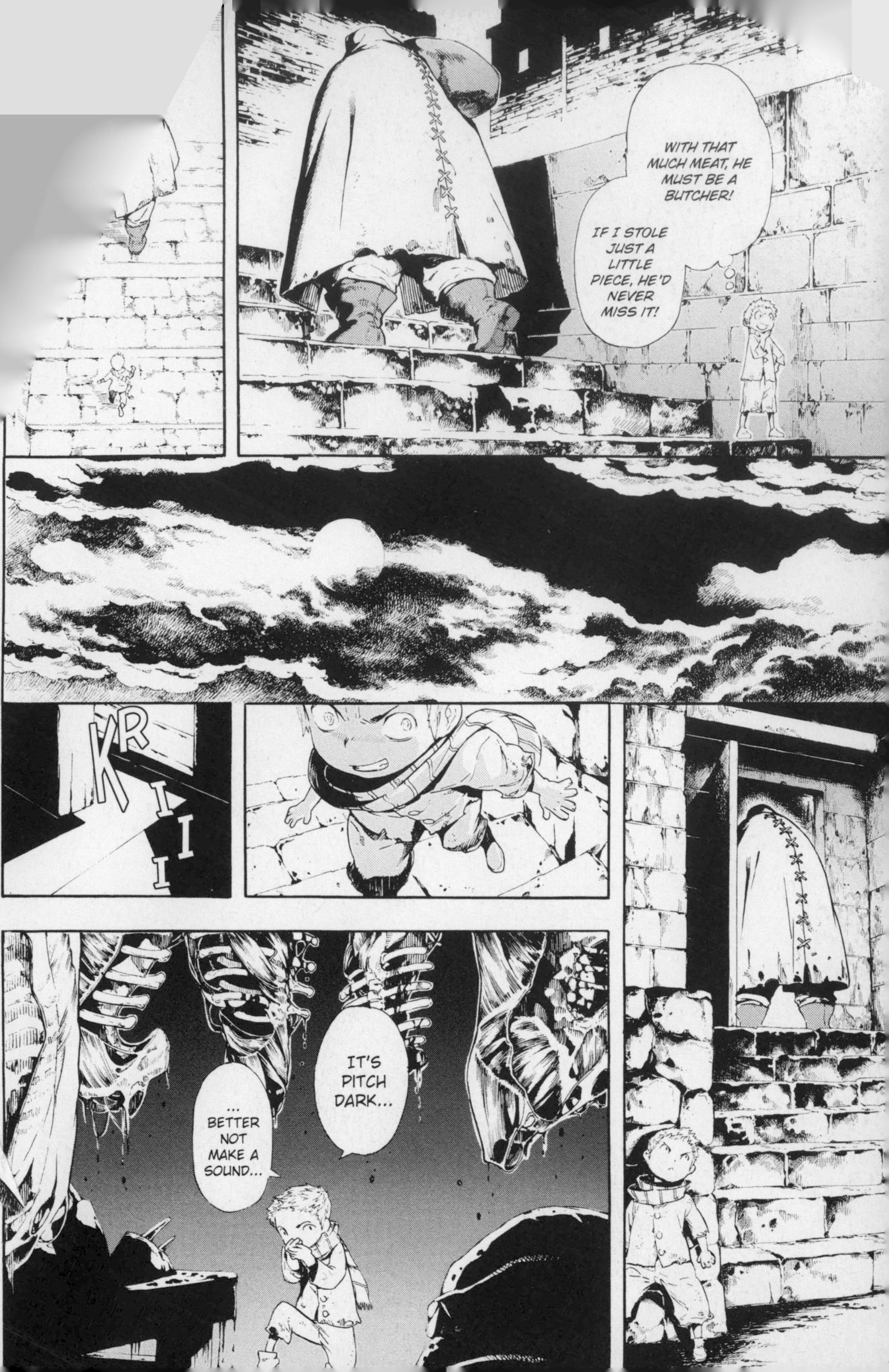
WITH THAT MUCH MEAT, HE MUST BE A BUTCHER!
IF I STOLE JUST A LITTLE PIECE, HE'D NEVER MISS IT!
KRIII
IT'S PITCH DARK...
...BETTER NOT MAKE A SOUND...

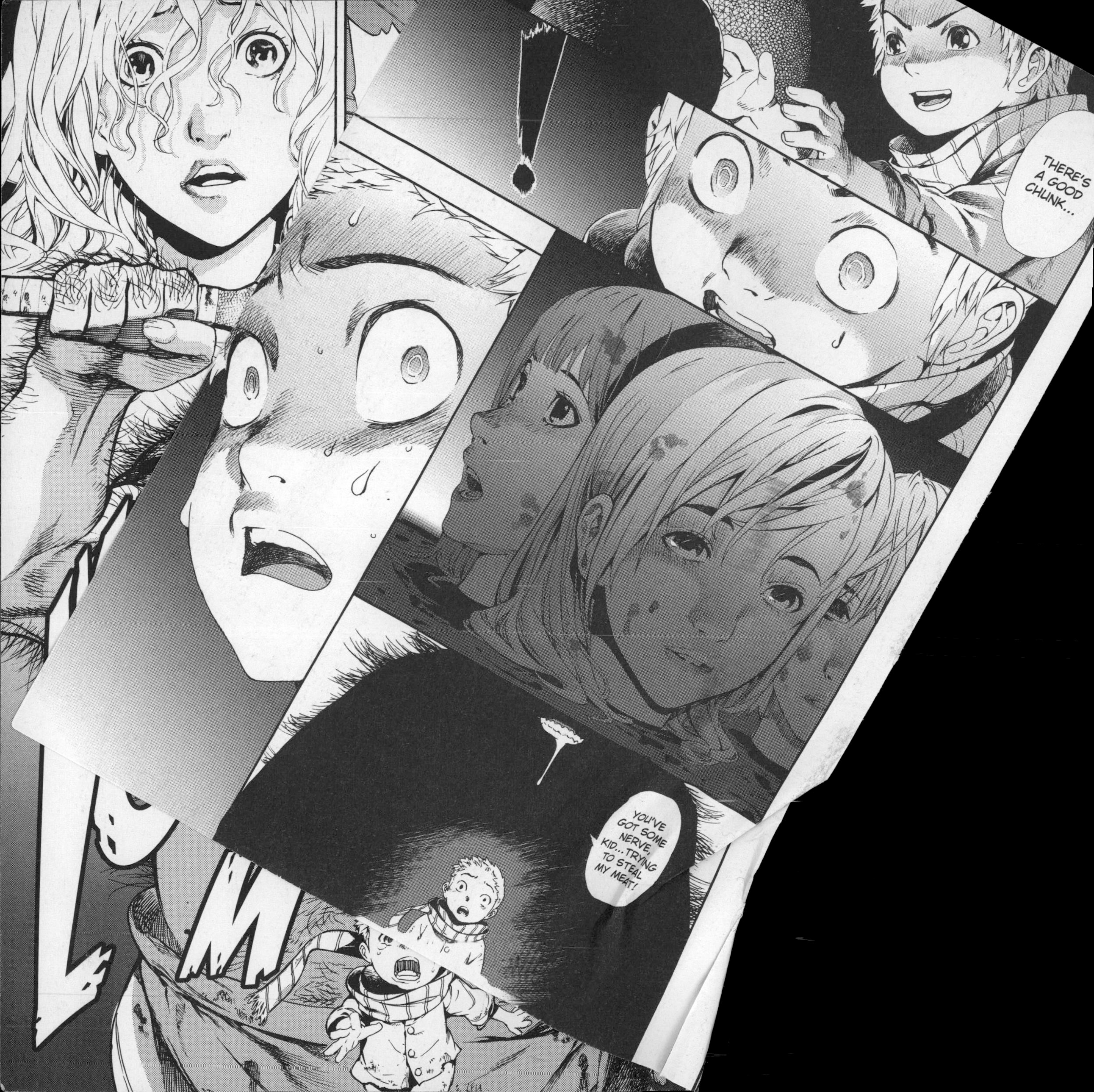
THERE'S A GOOD CHUNK...
YOU'VE GOT SOME NERVE, KID...TRYING TO STEAL MY MEAT!

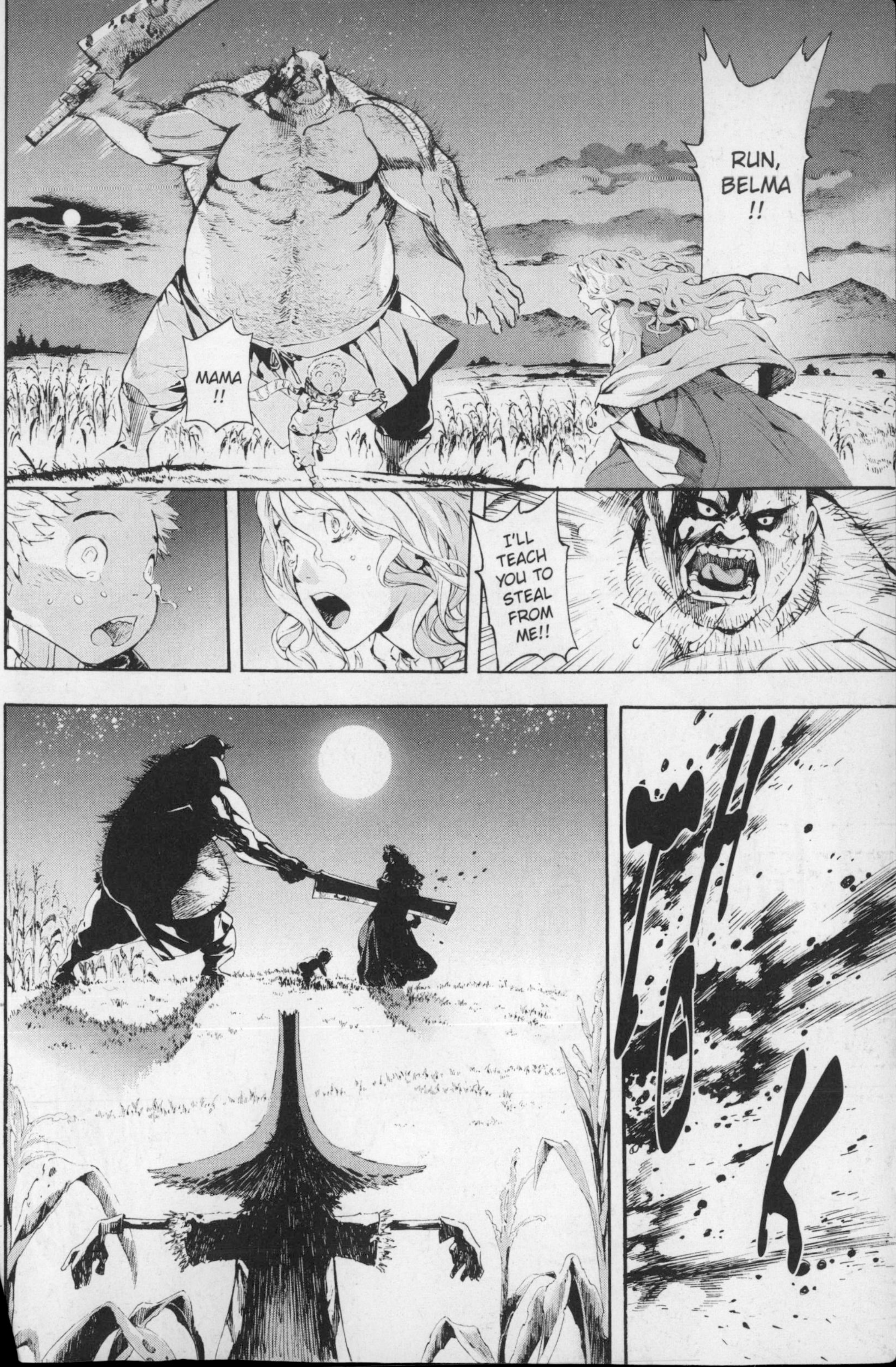
RUN, BELMA !!
MAMA !!
I'LL TEACH YOU TO STEAL FROM ME!!

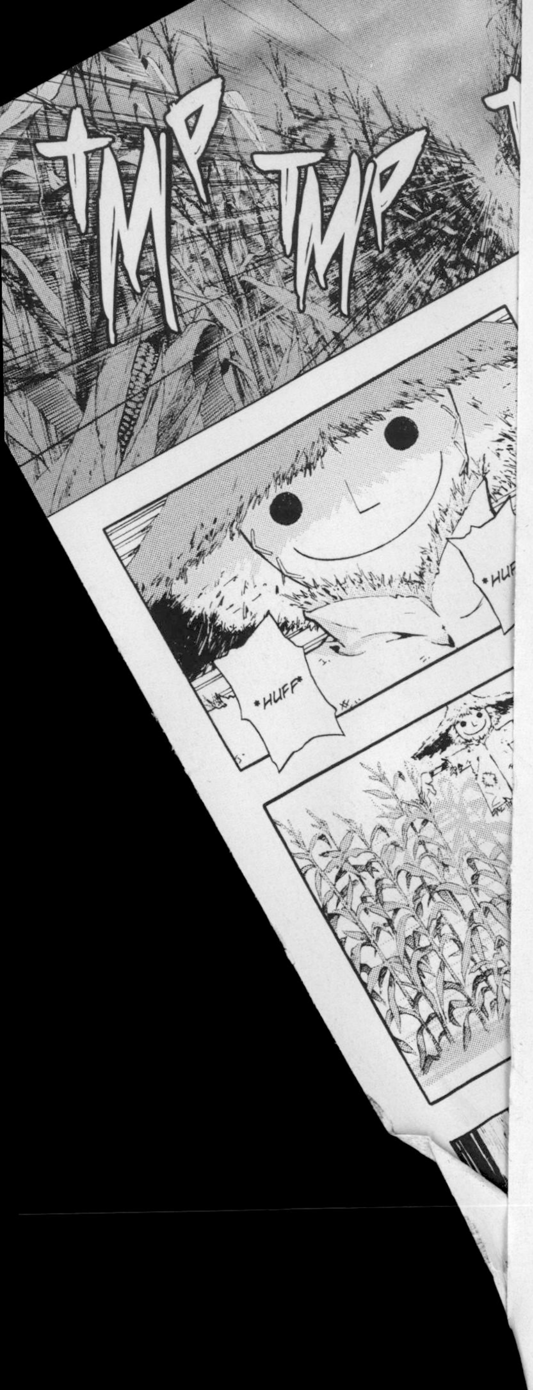
TMP TMP
HUFF

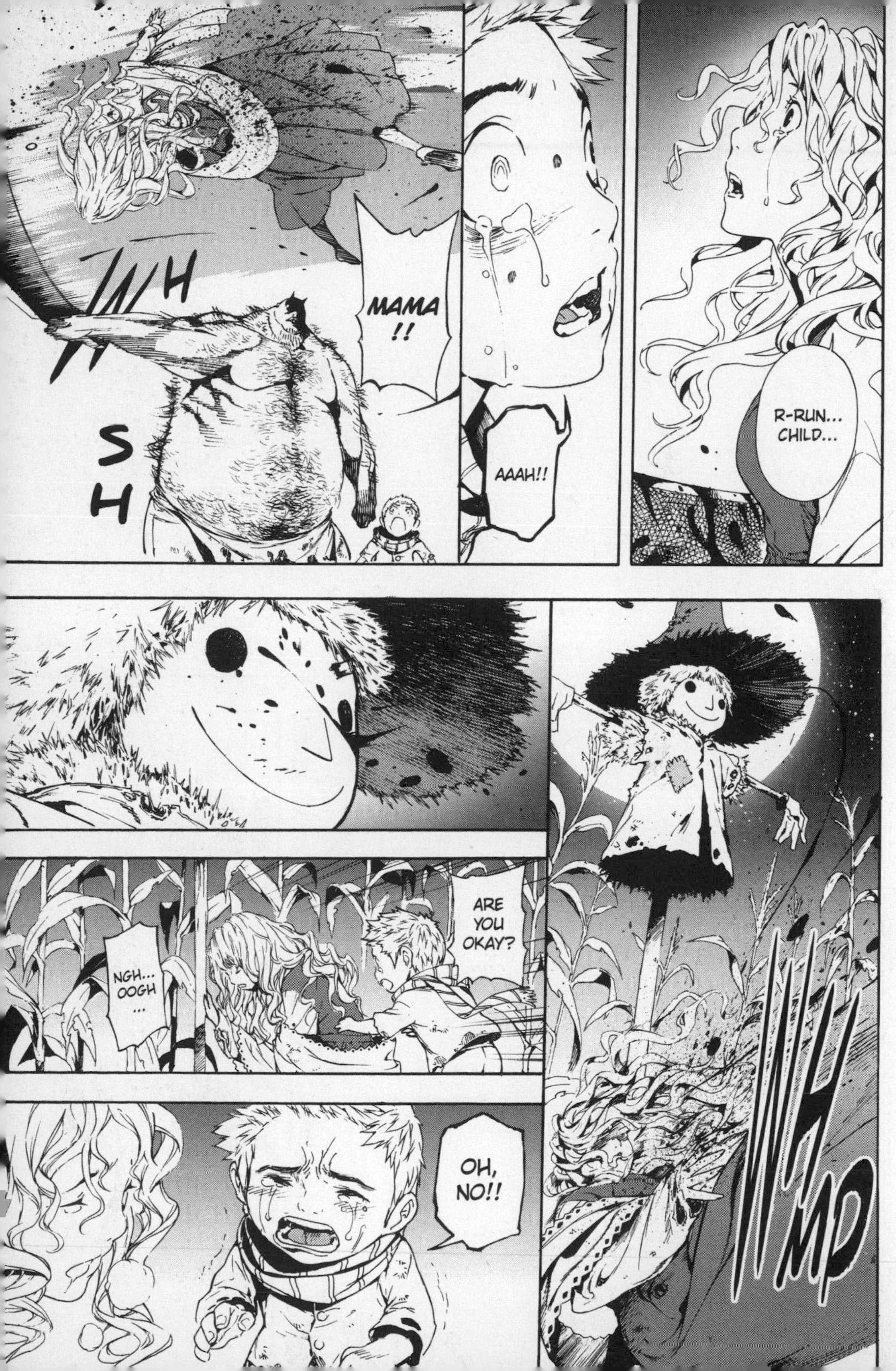
R-RUN... CHILD...
AAAH!!
MAMA !!
ARE YOU OKAY?
NGH... OOGH ...
OH, NO!!

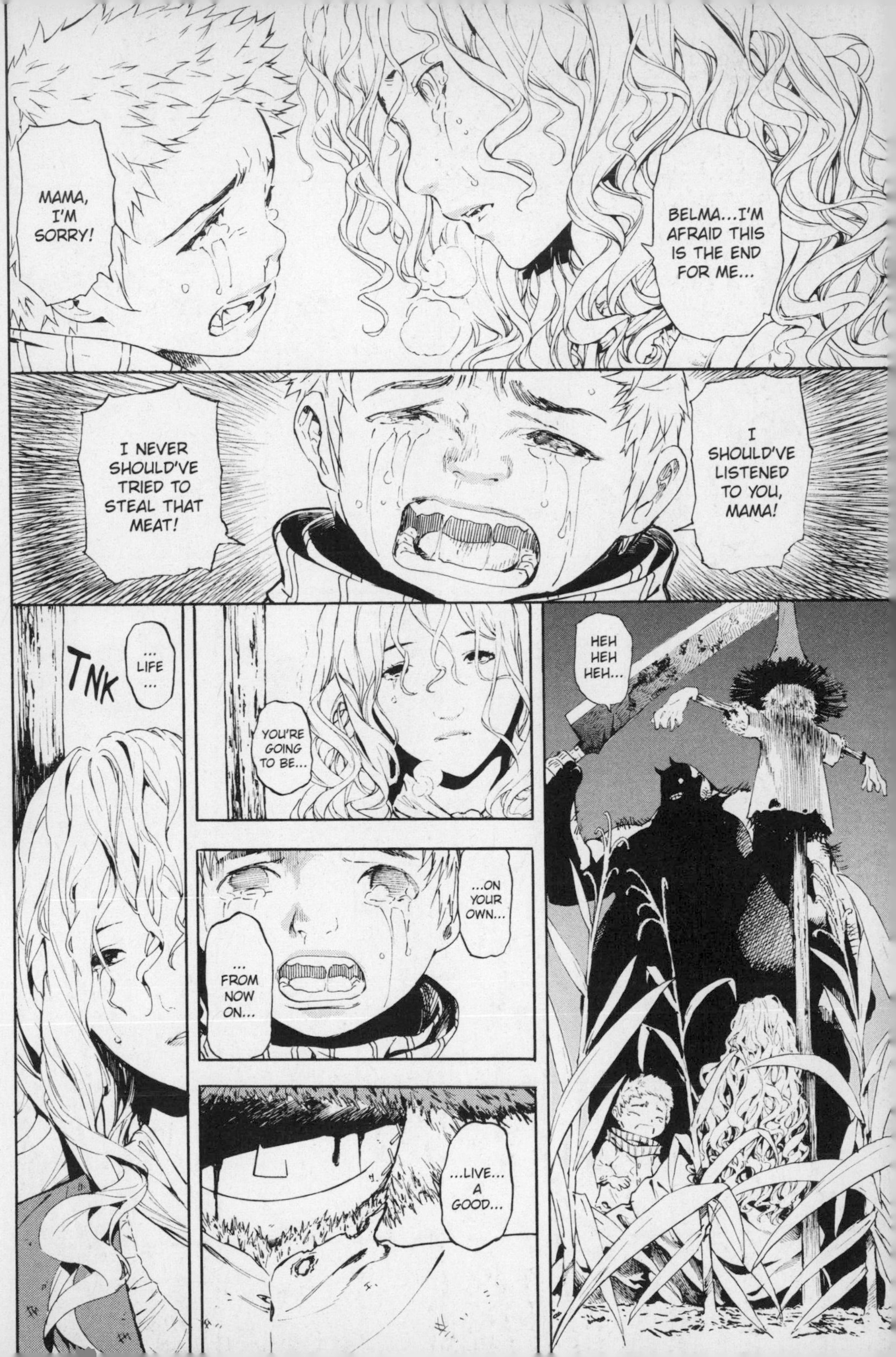
BELMA...I'M AFRAID THIS IS THE END FOR ME...
MAMA, I'M SORRY!
I SHOULD'VE LISTENED TO YOU, MAMA!
I NEVER SHOULD'VE TRIED TO STEAL THAT MEAT!
HEH HEH HEH...
YOU'RE GOING TO BE...
...ON YOUR OWN...
...FROM NOW ON...
...LIVE... A GOOD...
TNK
...LIFE...

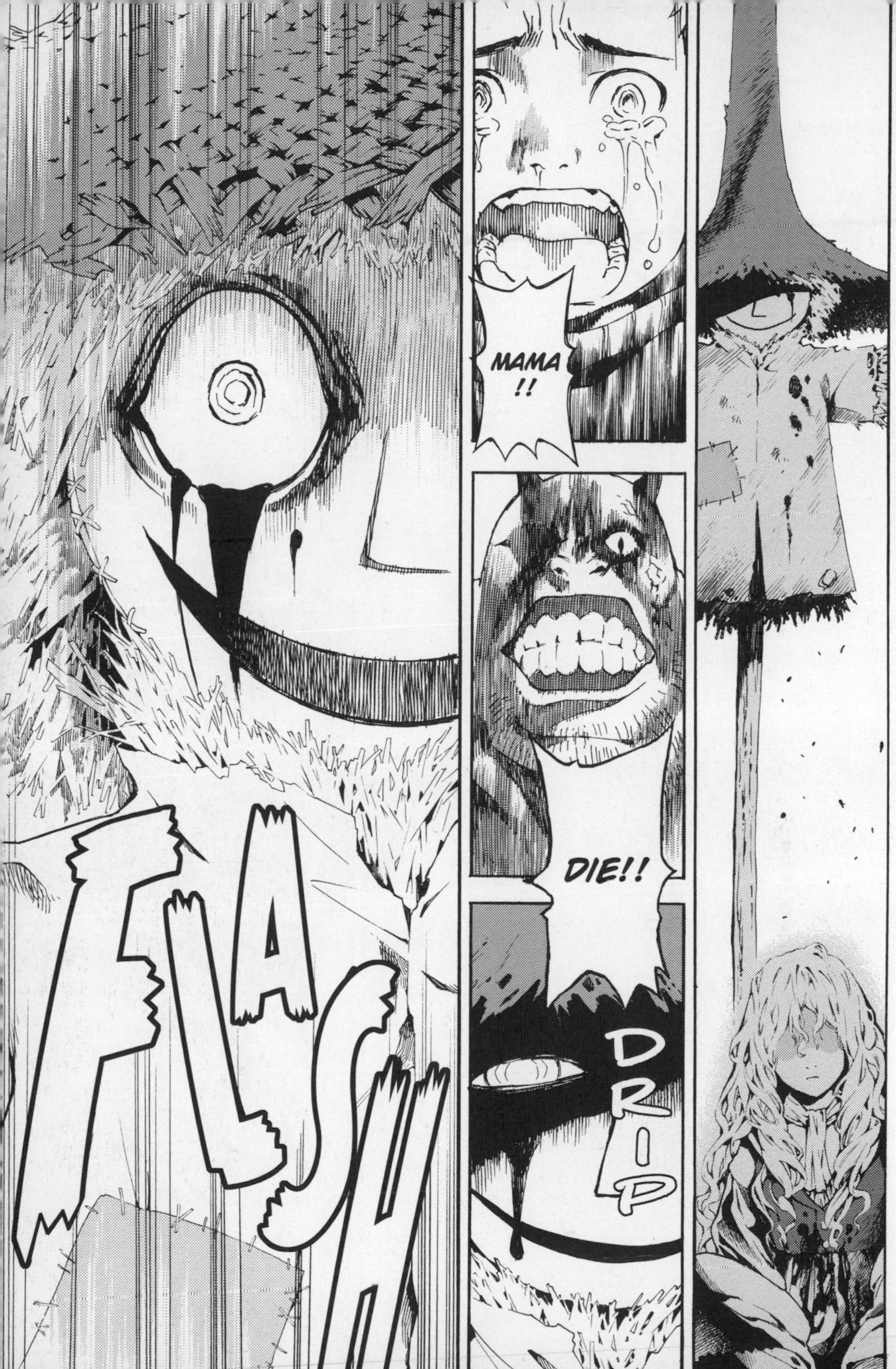
MAMA!!
DIE!!
DRIP
FLASH

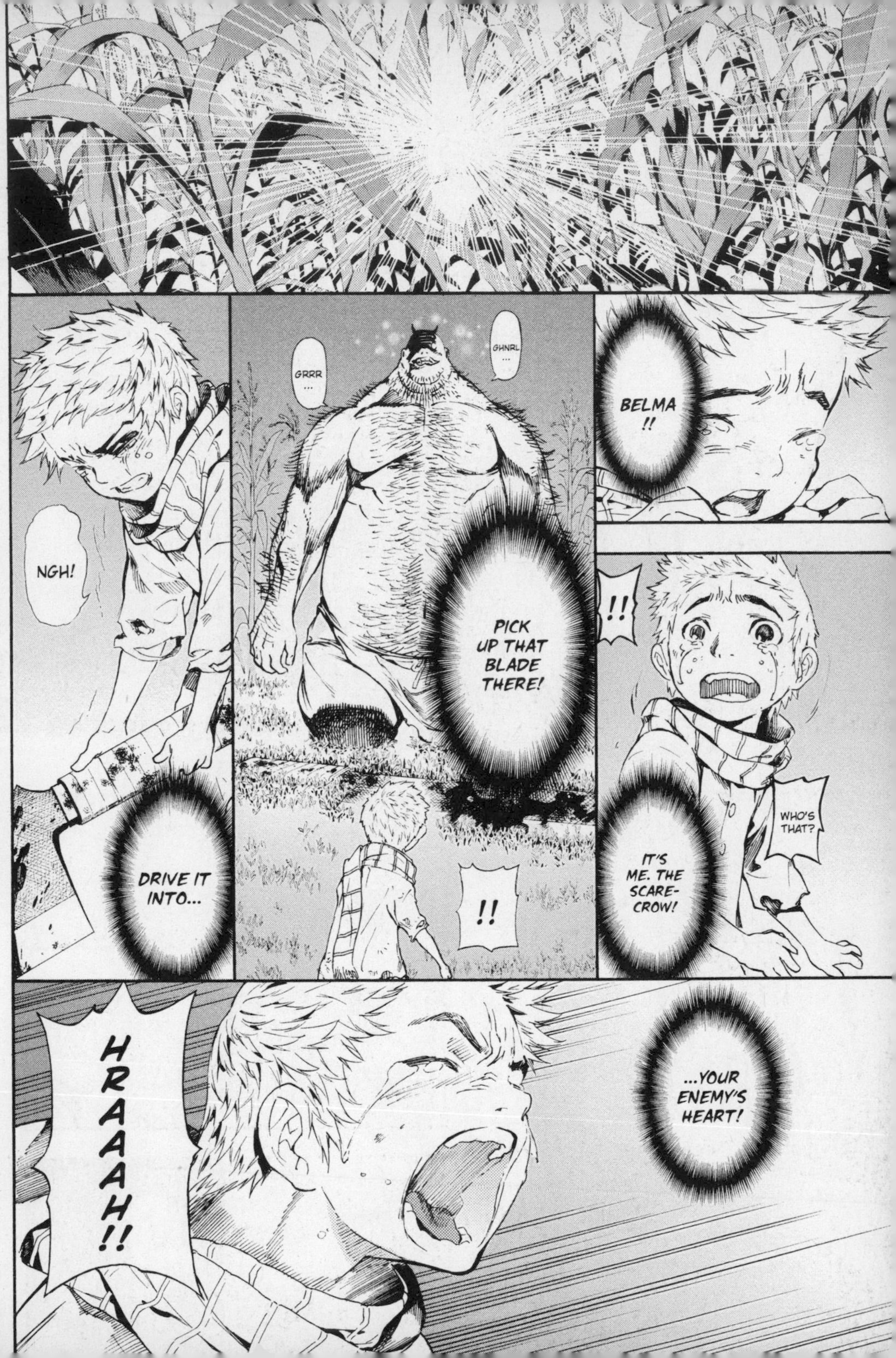
BELMA !!
!!
WHO'S THAT?
IT'S ME. THE SCARE-CROW!
GHNRL ...
GRRR ...
PICK UP THAT BLADE THERE!
!!
NGH!
DRIVE IT INTO...
...YOUR ENEMY'S HEART!
HRAAAAH!!

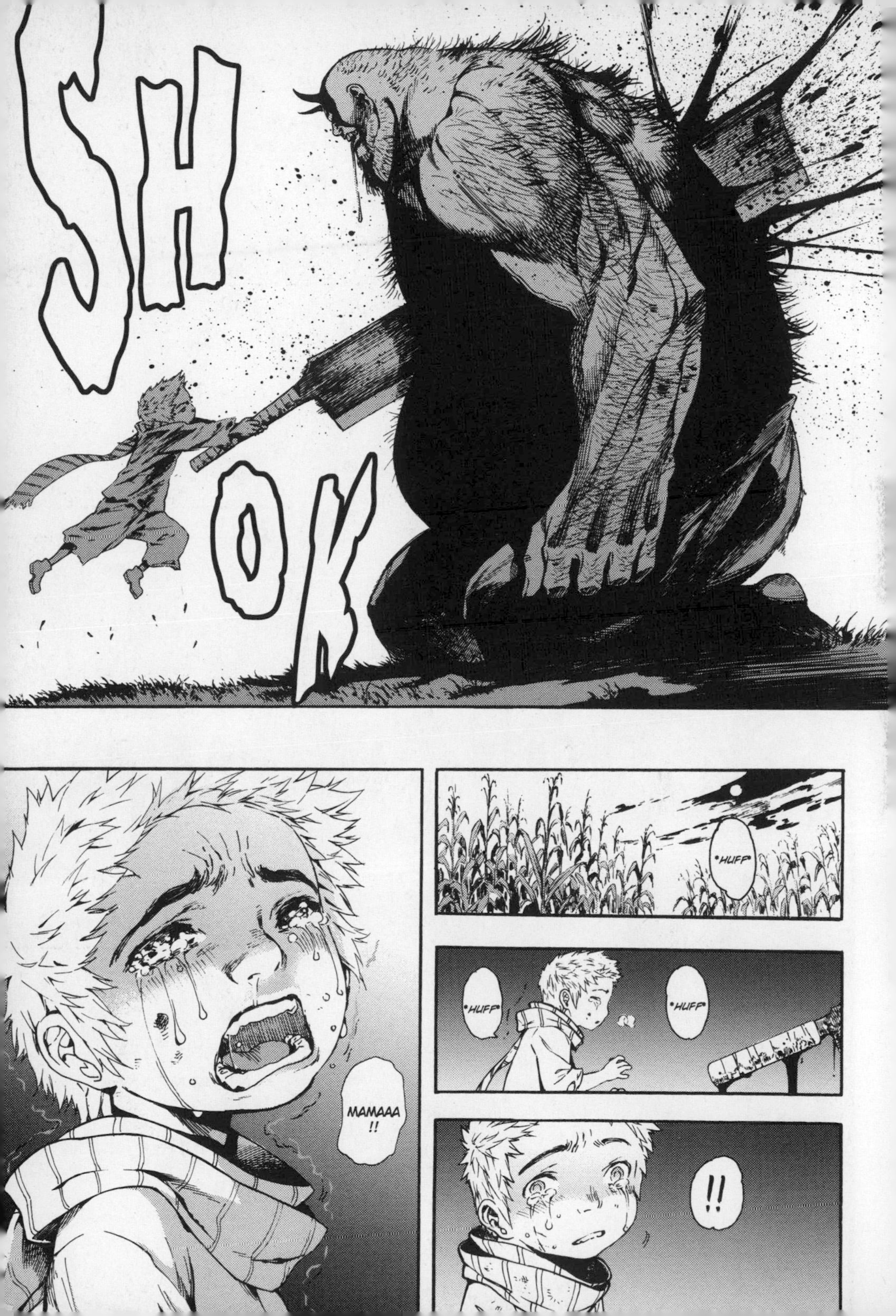
SHOK
HUFF
HUFF
HUFF
!!
MAMAAA !!

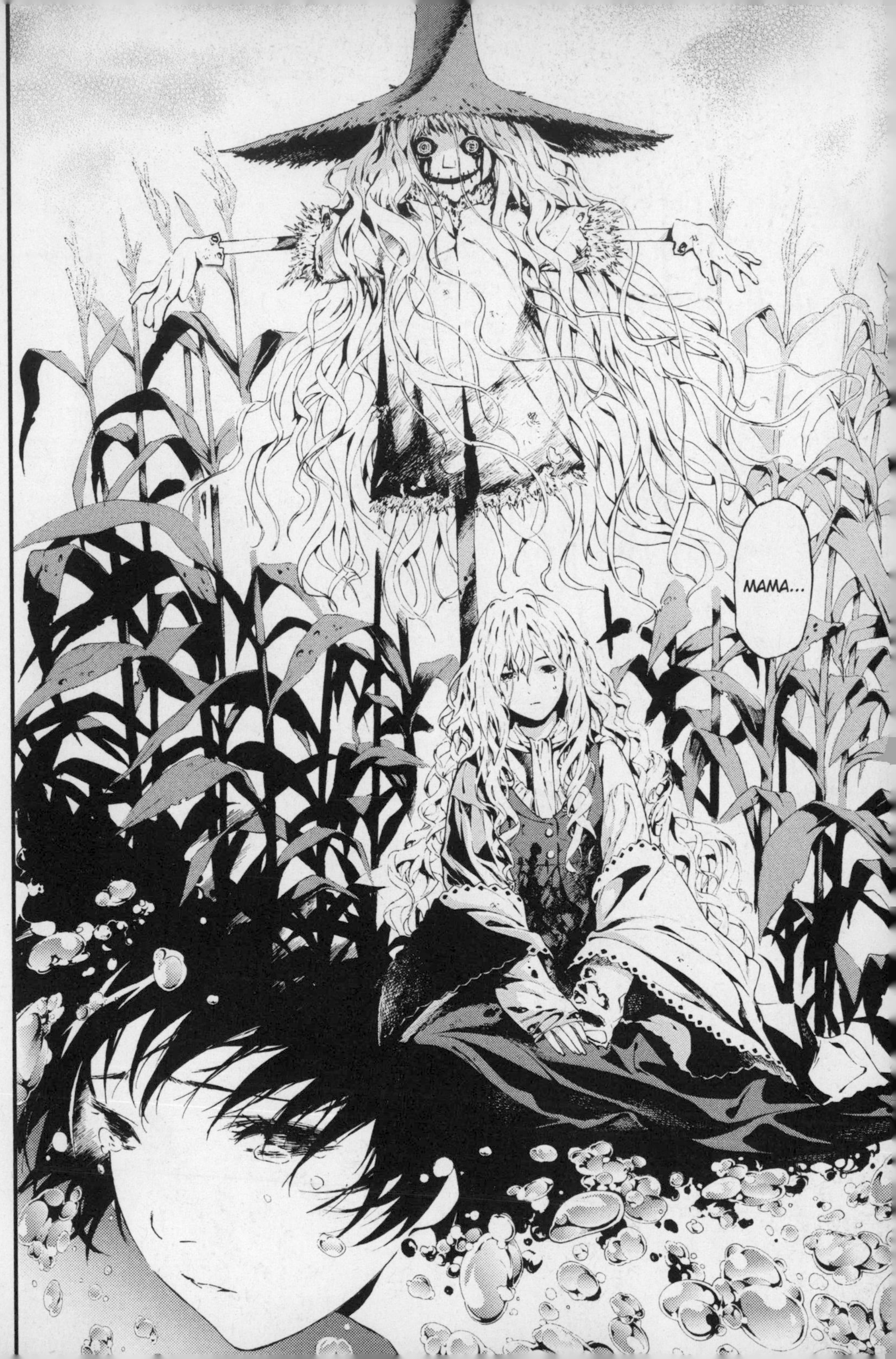
MAMA...

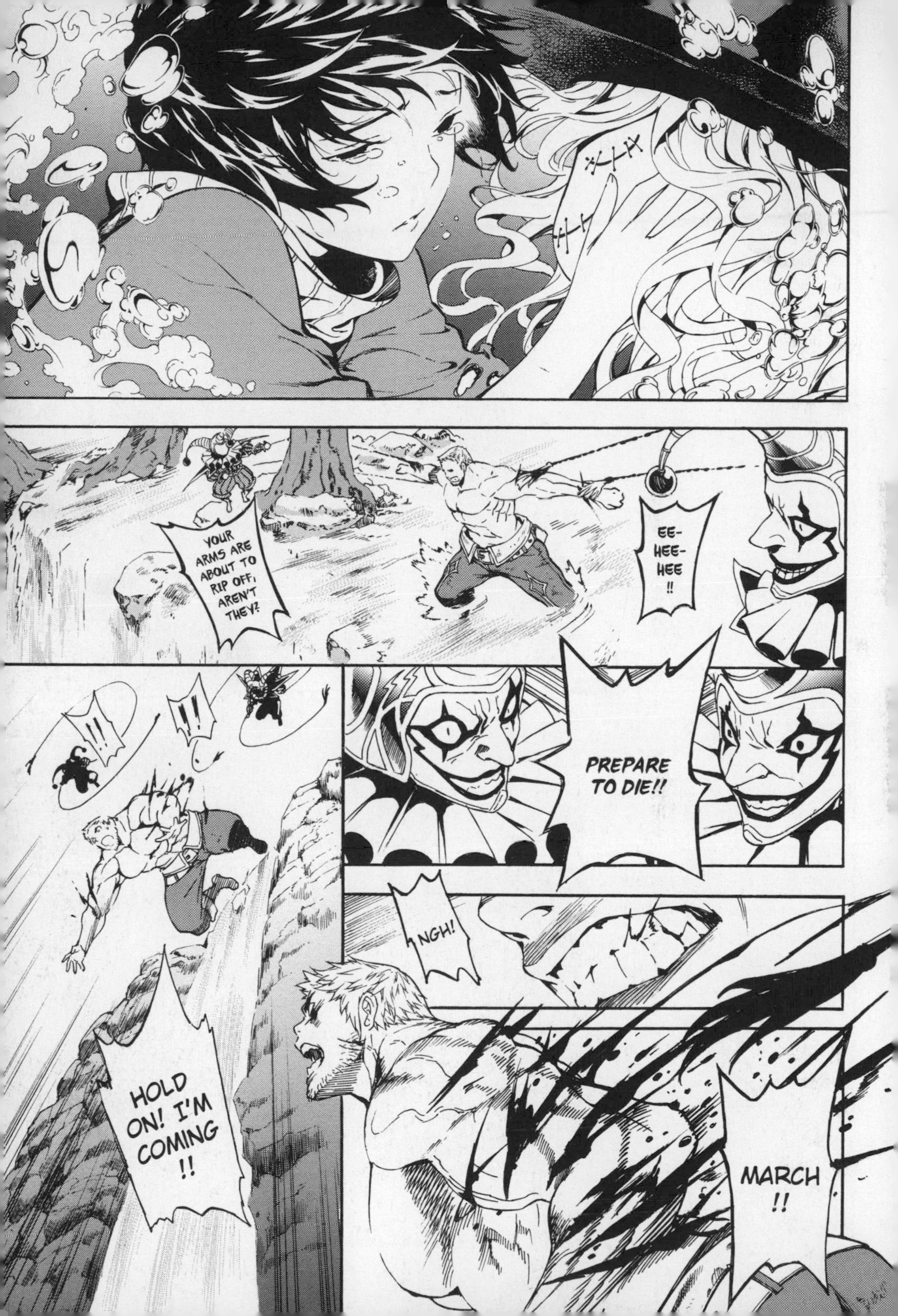
EE-HEE-HEE!!
YOUR ARMS ARE ABOUT TO RIP OFF, AREN'T THEY?
PREPARE TO DIE!!
NGH!
MARCH!!
!!
!!
HOLD ON! I'M COMING!!

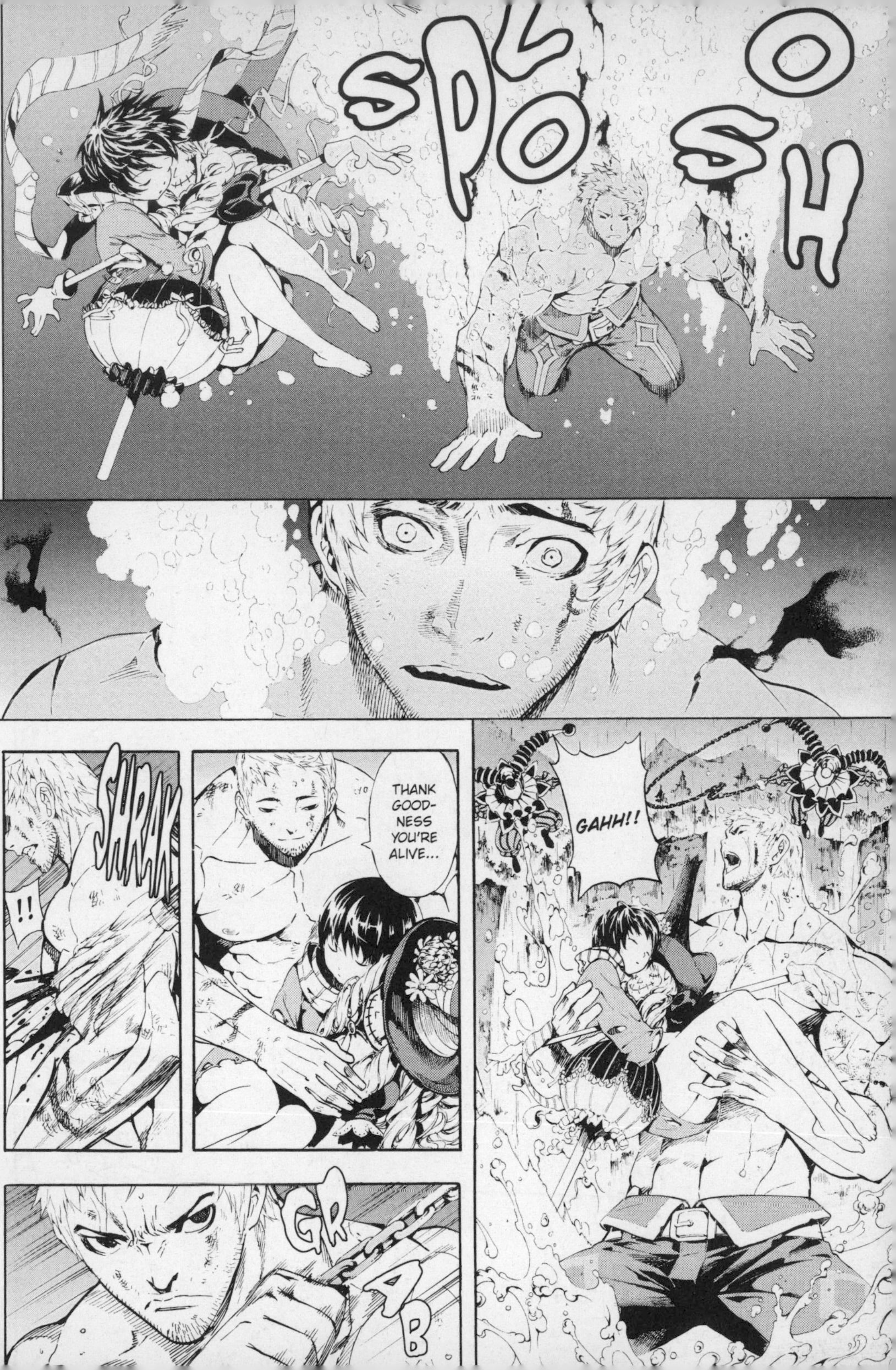
SPLOOSH
GAHH!!
THANK GOODNESS YOU'RE ALIVE...
SHRAK
!!
GRAB

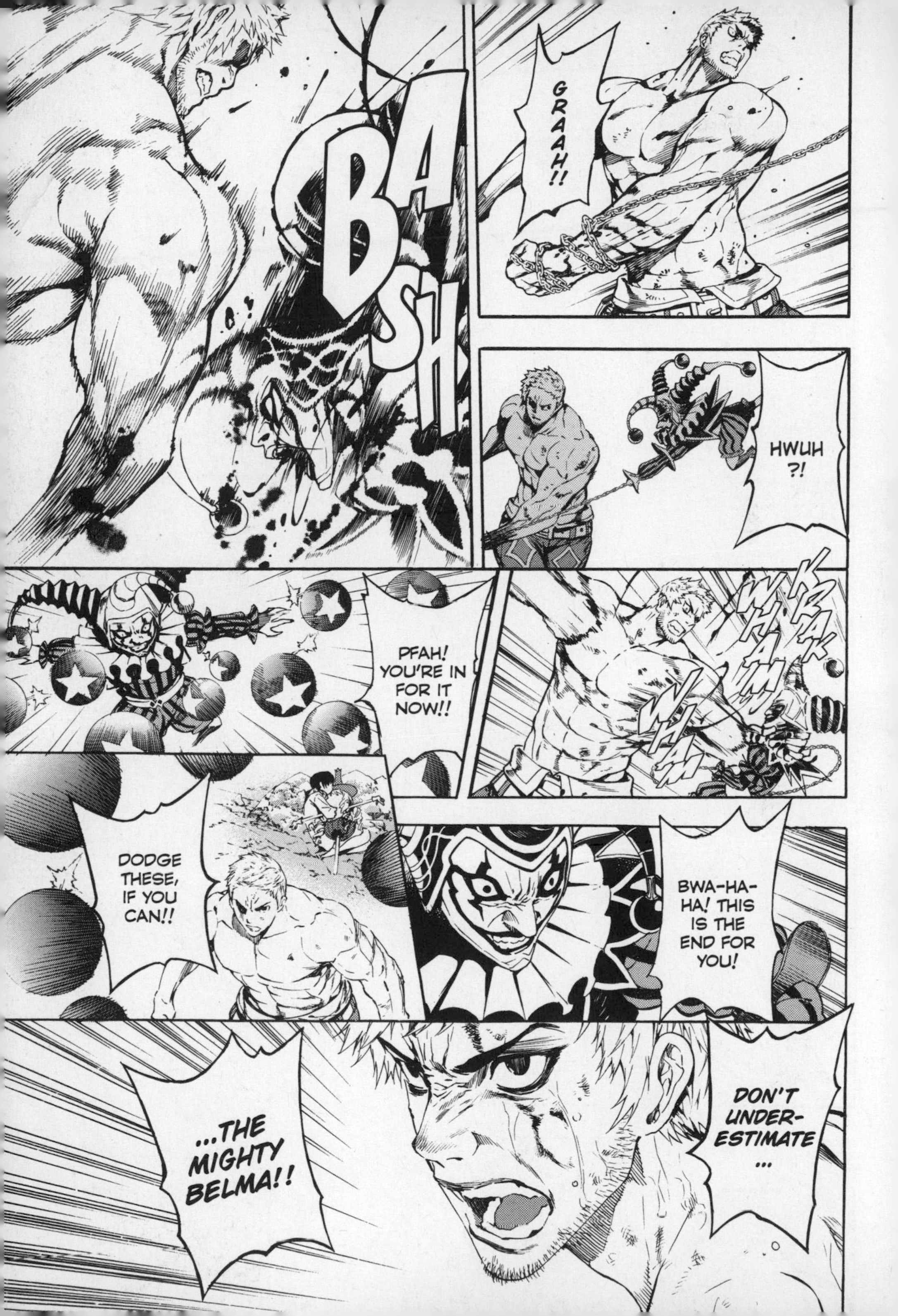
GRAAH!!
HWUH ?!
BASH
KRAK
WHAM
WHAM
PFAH! YOU'RE IN FOR IT NOW!!
BWA-HA-HA! THIS IS THE END FOR YOU!
DODGE THESE, IF YOU CAN!!
DON'T UNDER-ESTIMATE ...
...THE MIGHTY BELMA!!

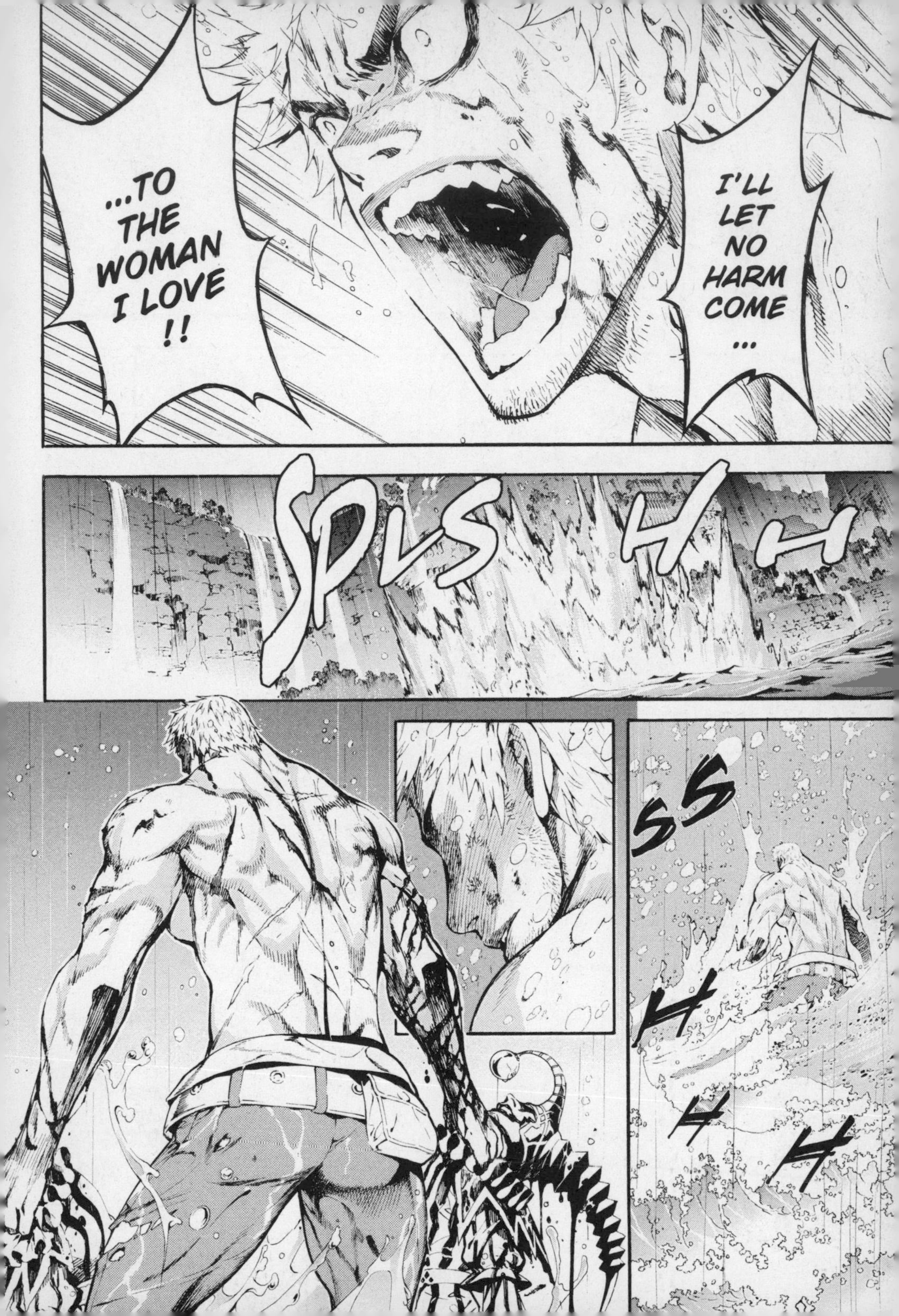
I'LL LET NO HARM COME ...
...TO THE WOMAN I LOVE !!
SPLSHHH
SSHHH

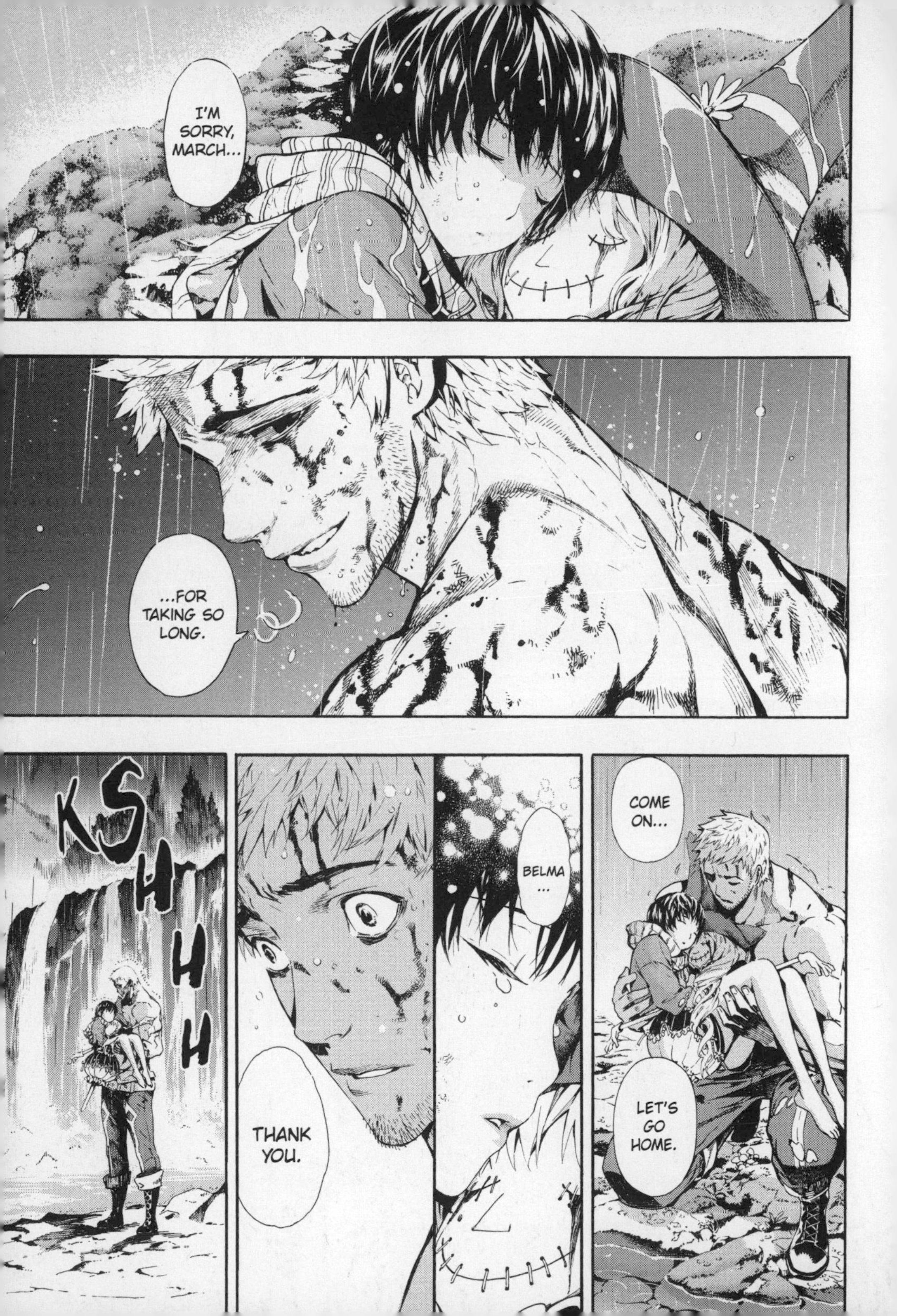
I'M SORRY, MARCH...
...FOR TAKING SO LONG.
COME ON...
LET'S GO HOME.
BELMA...
THANK YOU.
KSHHHHH

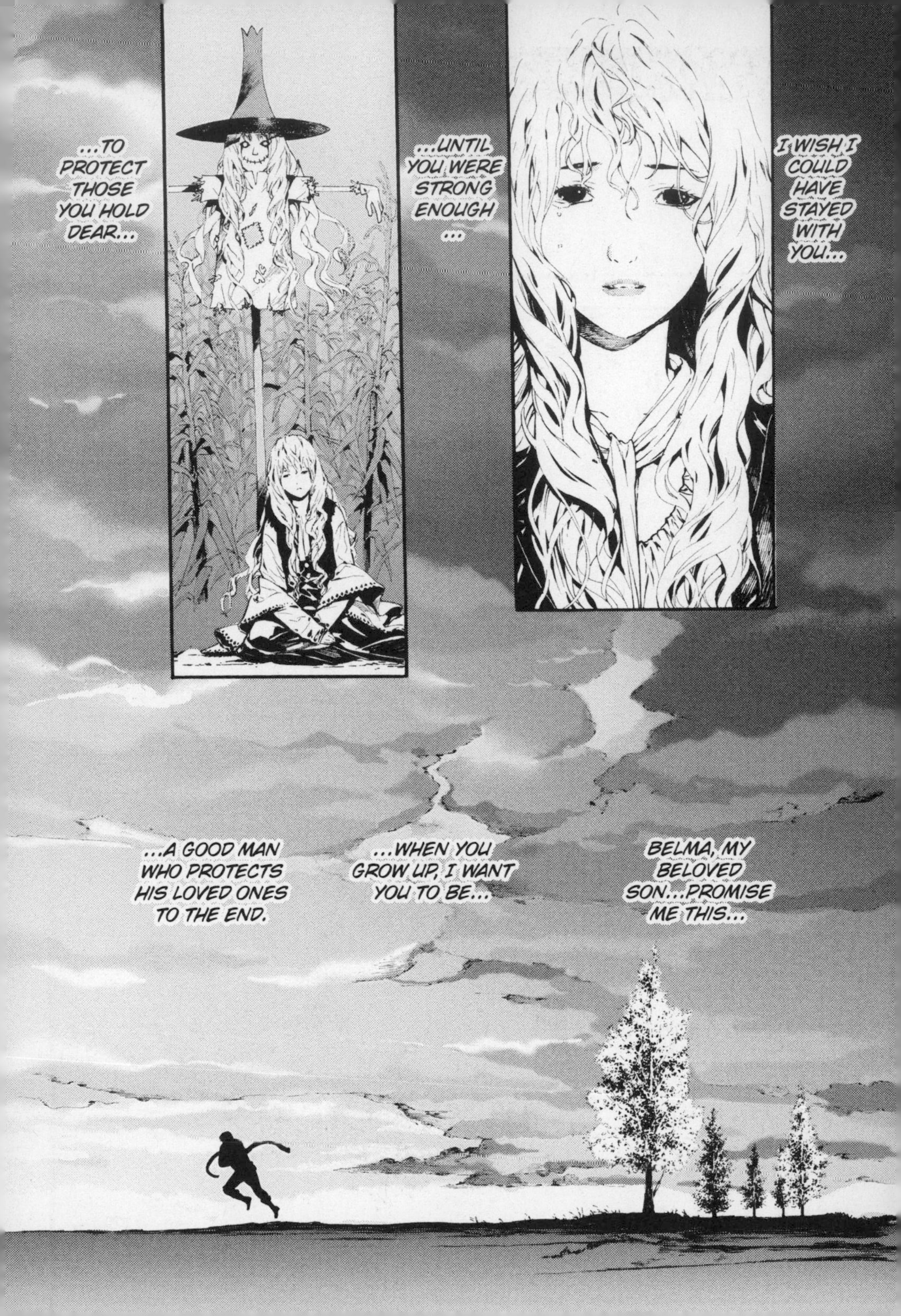
I WISH I COULD HAVE STAYED WITH YOU...
...UNTIL YOU WERE STRONG ENOUGH...
...TO PROTECT THOSE YOU HOLD DEAR...
BELMA, MY BELOVED SON...PROMISE ME THIS...
...WHEN YOU GROW UP, I WANT YOU TO BE...
...A GOOD MAN WHO PROTECTS HIS LOVED ONES TO THE END.

CHAPTER 18: RODIN'S REVENGE

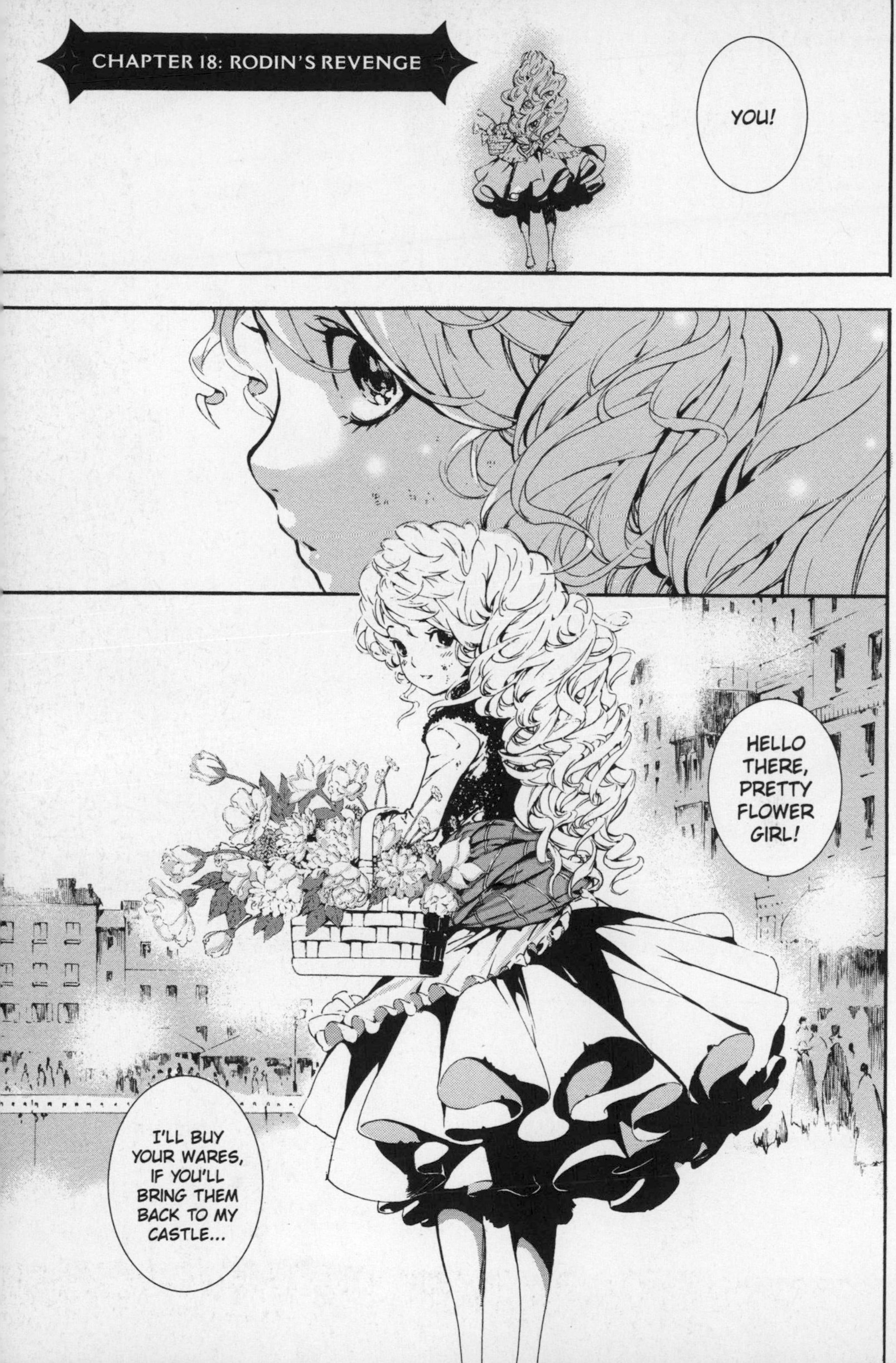
YOU!
HELLO THERE, PRETTY FLOWER GIRL!
I'LL BUY YOUR WARES, IF YOU'LL BRING THEM BACK TO MY CASTLE...

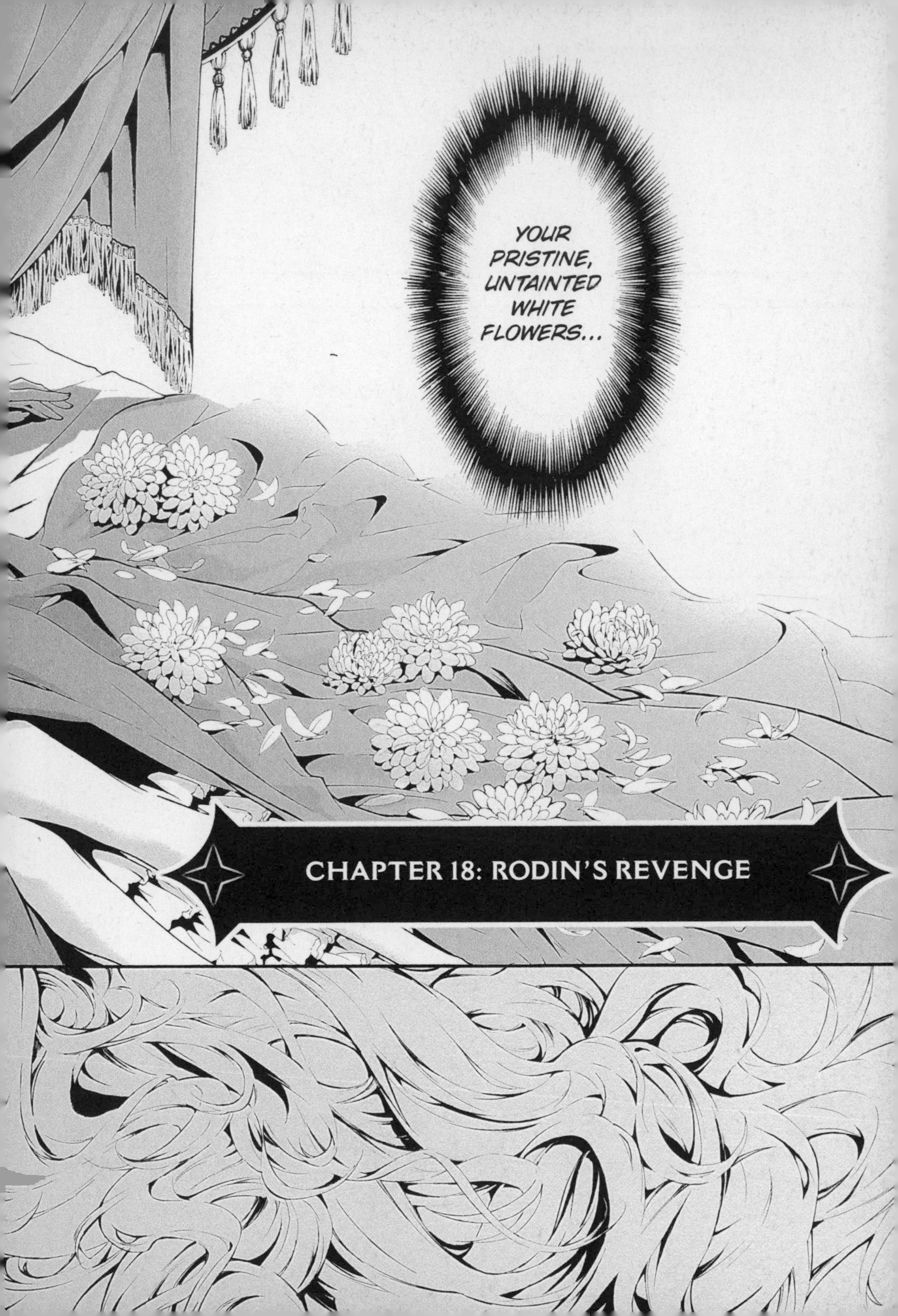
YOUR PRISTINE, UNTAINTED WHITE FLOWERS...
CHAPTER 18: RODIN'S REVENGE

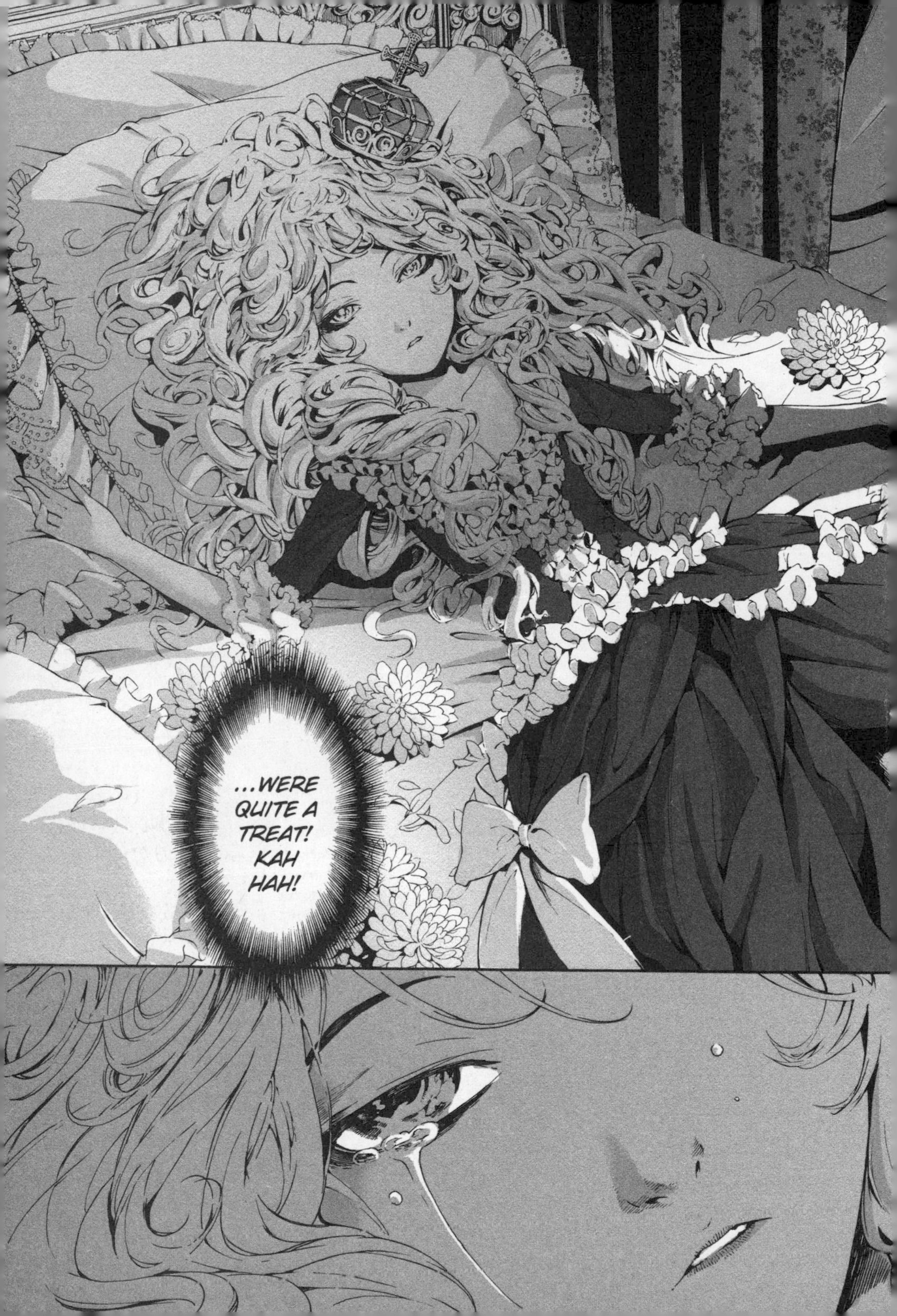
...WERE QUITE A TREAT! KAH HAH!

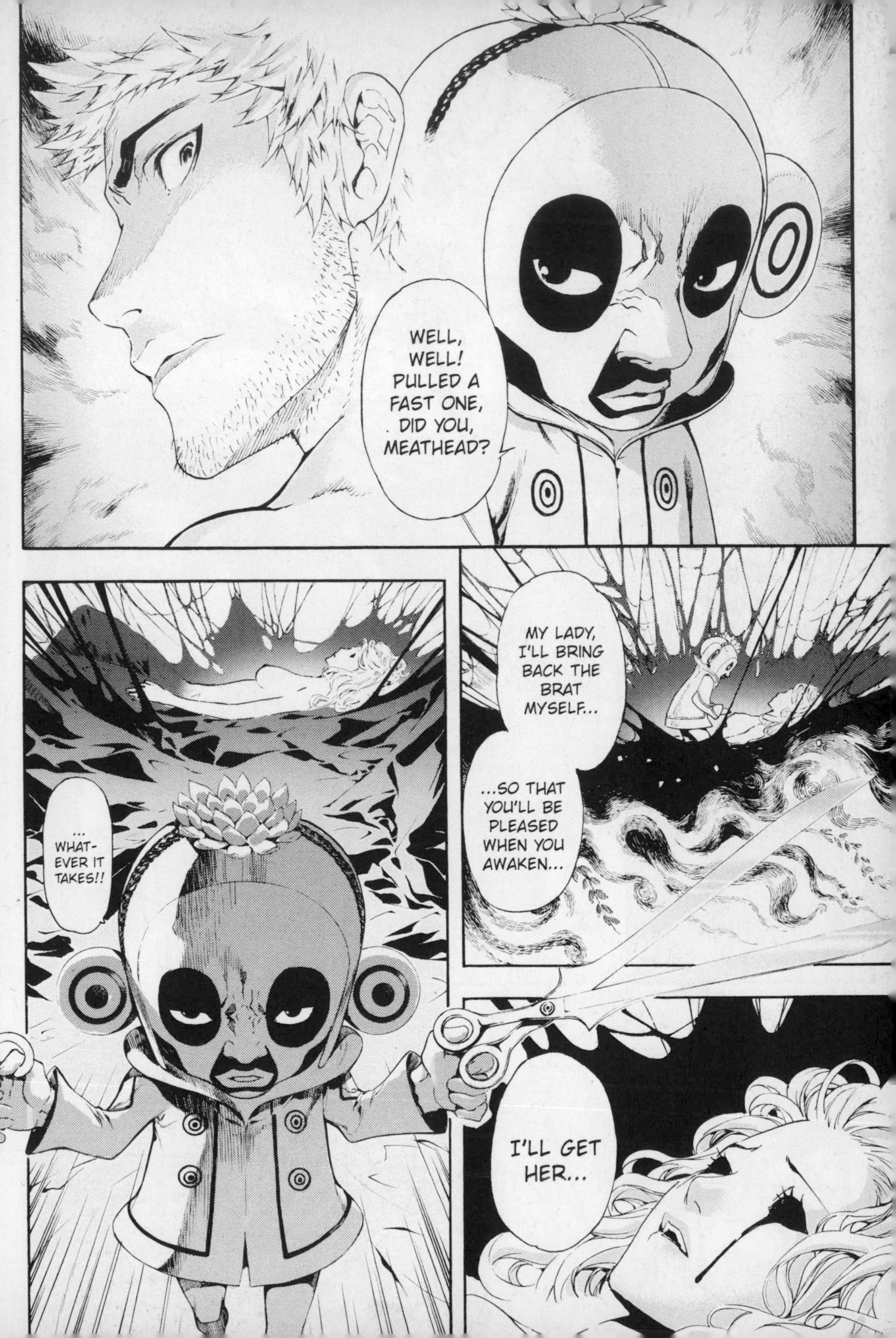
WELL, WELL! PULLED A FAST ONE, DID YOU, MEATHEAD?
MY LADY, I'LL BRING BACK THE BRAT MYSELF...
...SO THAT YOU'LL BE PLEASED WHEN YOU AWAKEN...
I'LL GET HER...
...WHAT-EVER IT TAKES!!

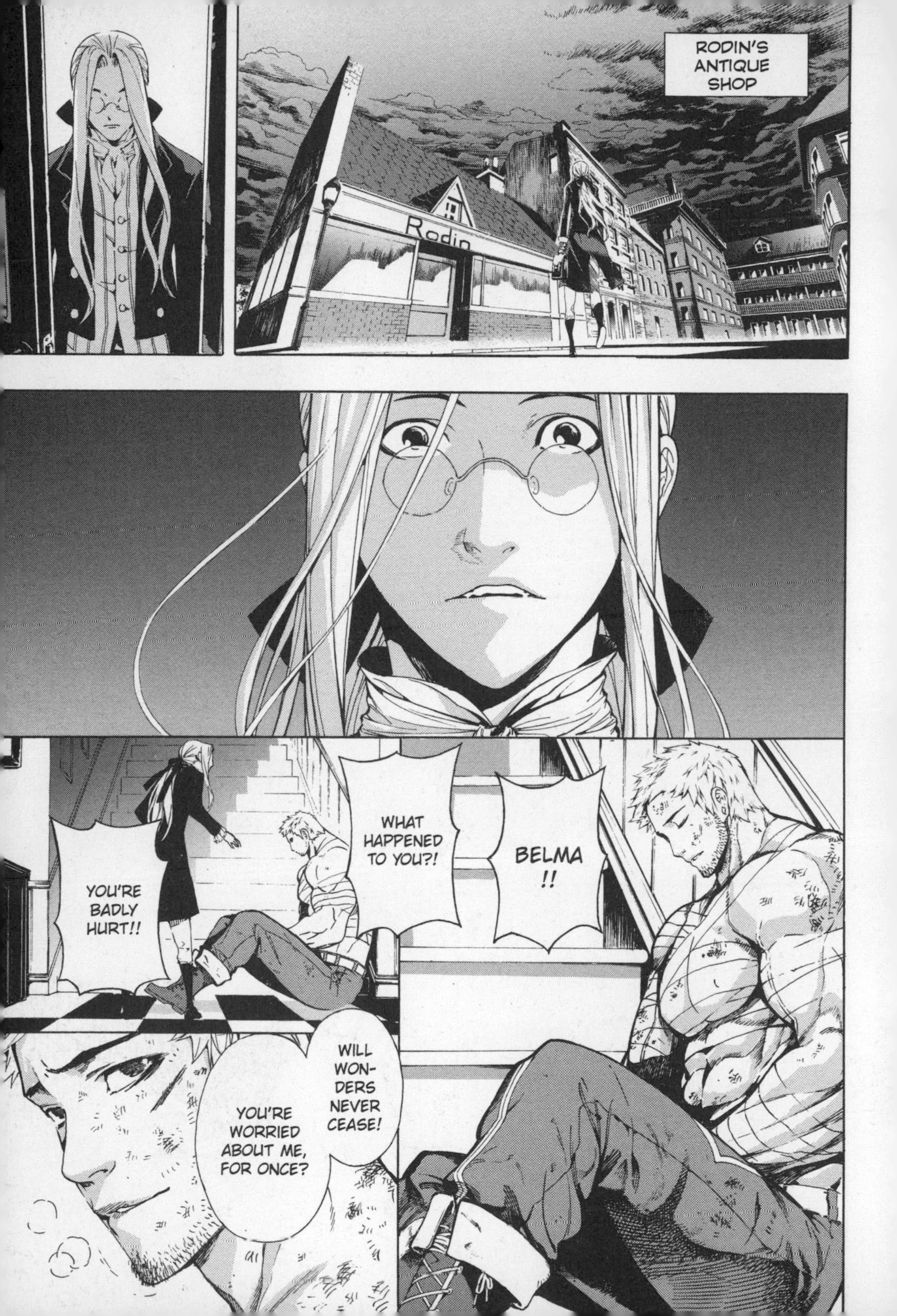
RODIN'S ANTIQUE SHOP
Rodin
BELMA !!
WHAT HAPPENED TO YOU?!
YOU'RE BADLY HURT!!
WILL WONDERS NEVER CEASE!
YOU'RE WORRIED ABOUT ME, FOR ONCE?

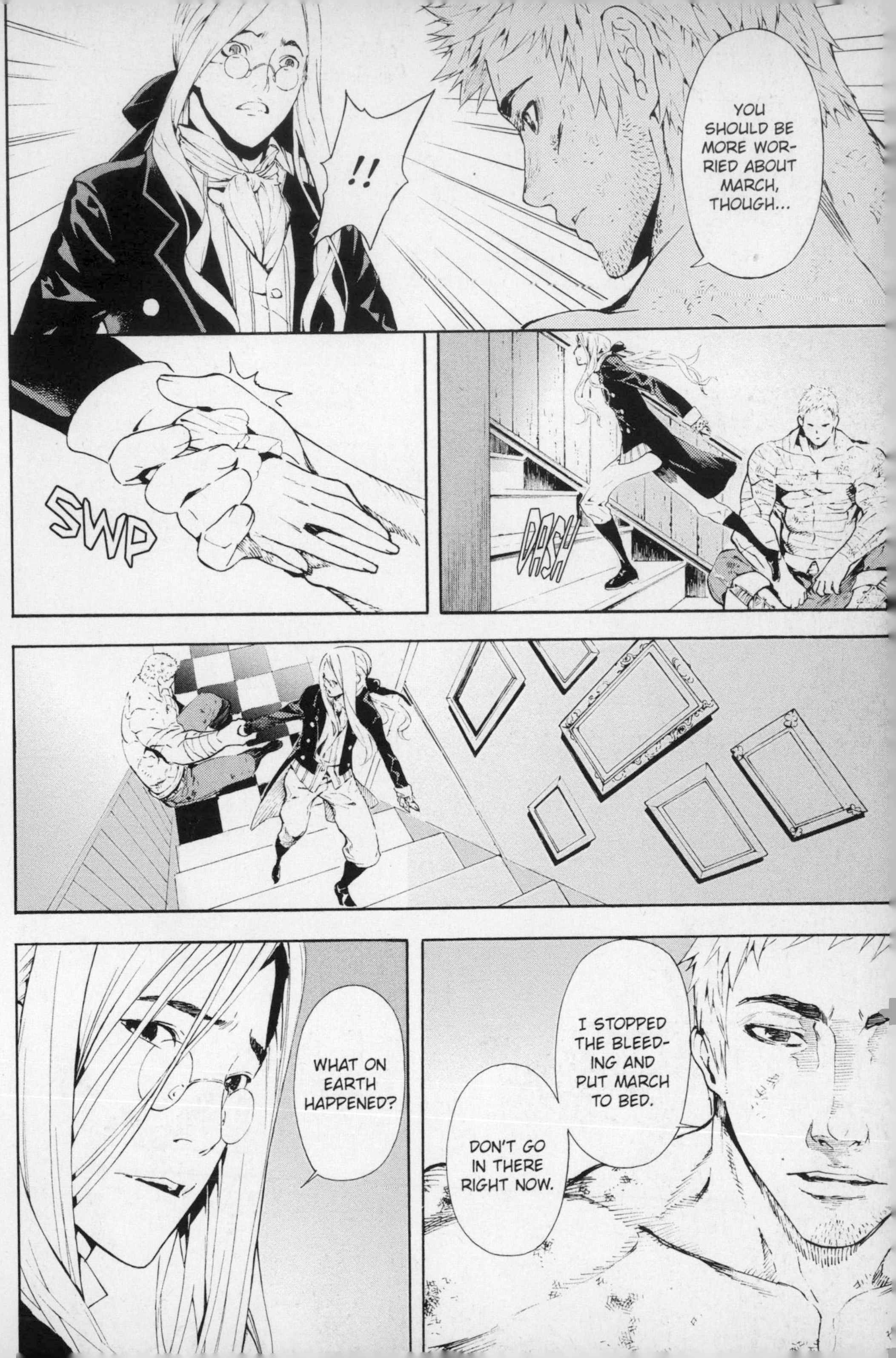
YOU SHOULD BE MORE WORRIED ABOUT MARCH, THOUGH...
!!
DASH
SWP
I STOPPED THE BLEEDING AND PUT MARCH TO BED.
DON'T GO IN THERE RIGHT NOW.
WHAT ON EARTH HAPPENED?

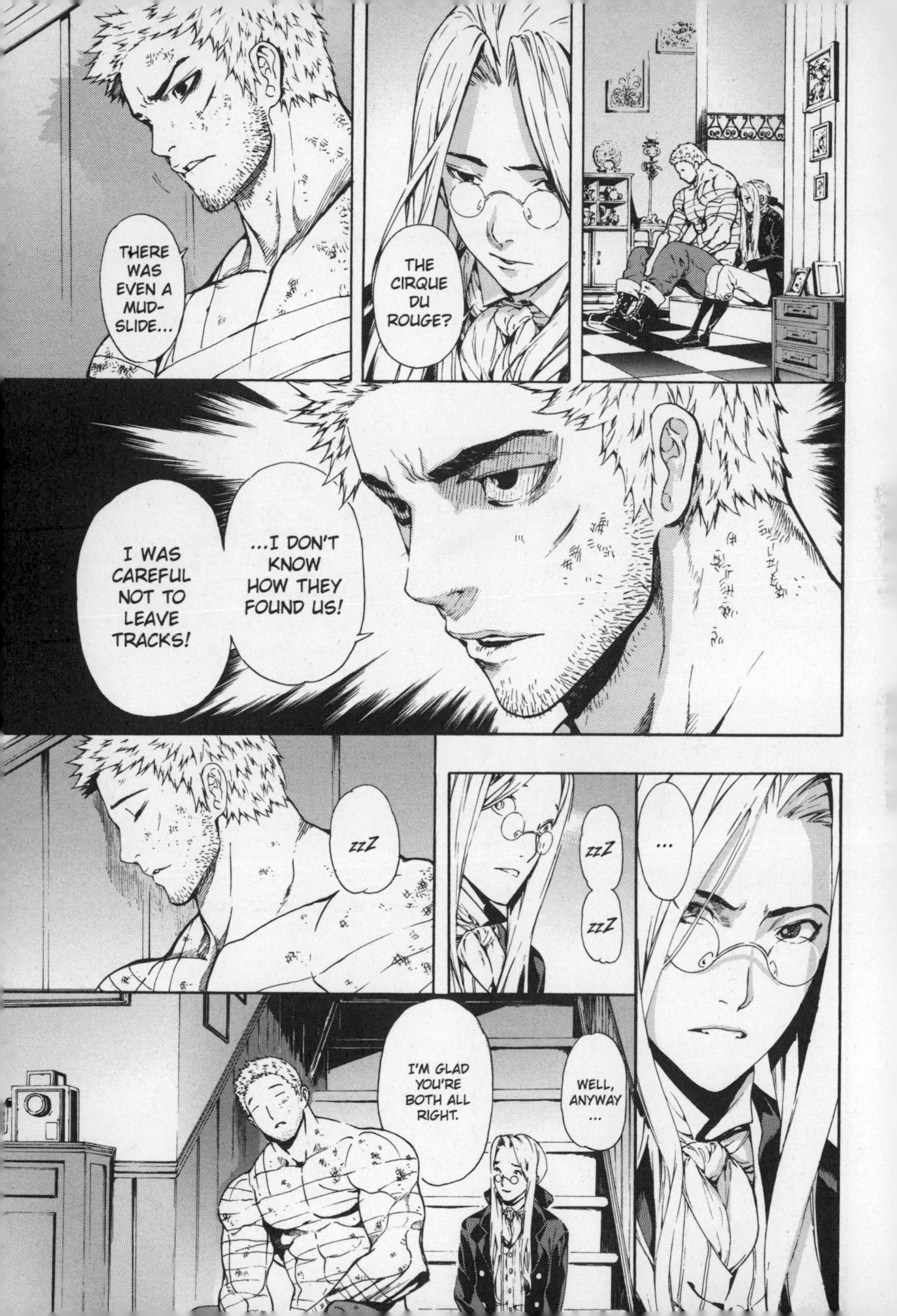
THE CIRQUE DU ROUGE?
THERE WAS EVEN A MUD-SLIDE...
...I DON'T KNOW HOW THEY FOUND US!
I WAS CAREFUL NOT TO LEAVE TRACKS!
...
WELL, ANYWAY ...
zzZ
zzZ
zzZ
I'M GLAD YOU'RE BOTH ALL RIGHT.

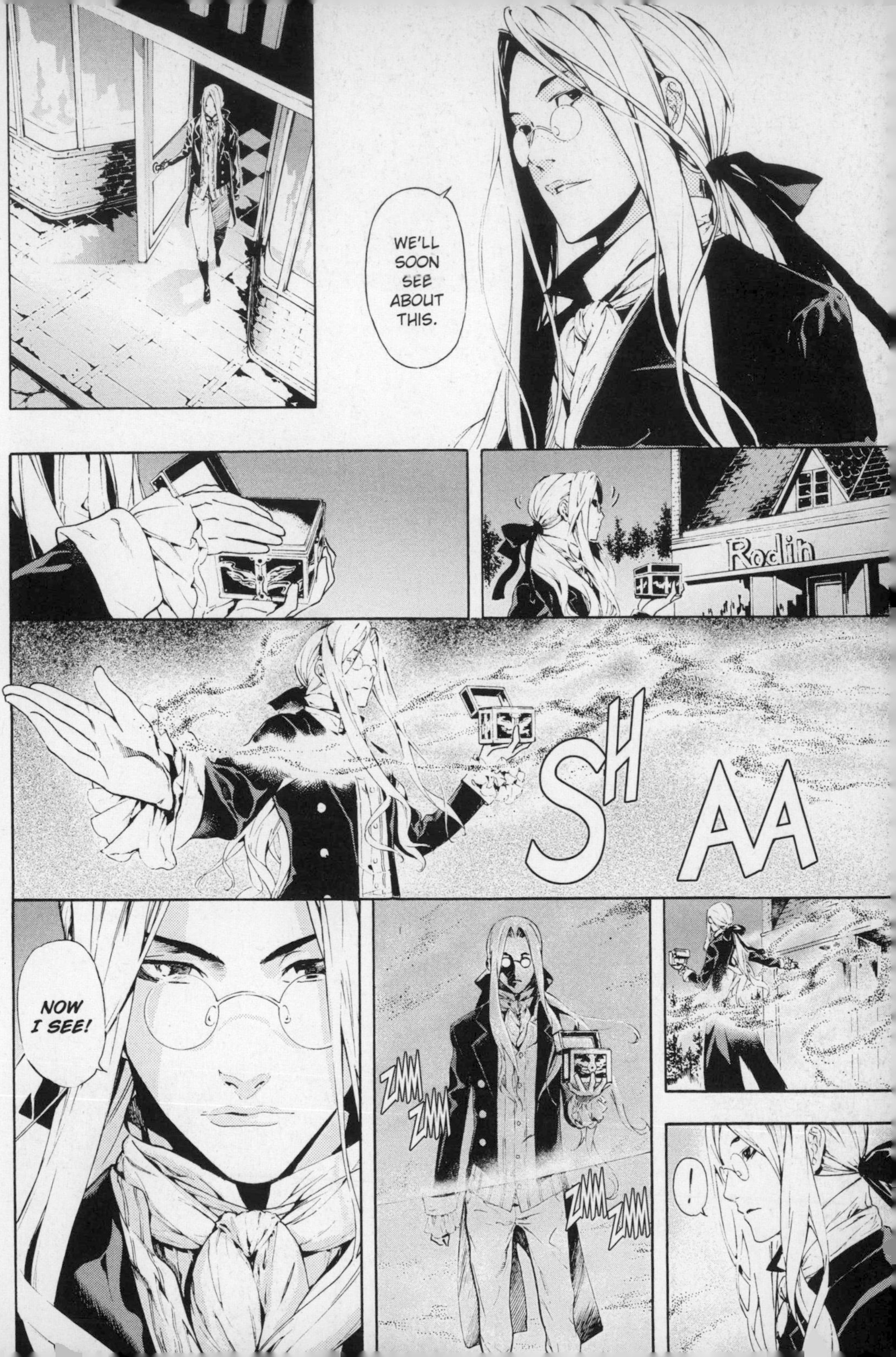
WE'LL SOON SEE ABOUT THIS.
Rodin
SH
AA
!
ZMM
ZMM
ZMM
ZMM
ZMM
NOW I SEE!

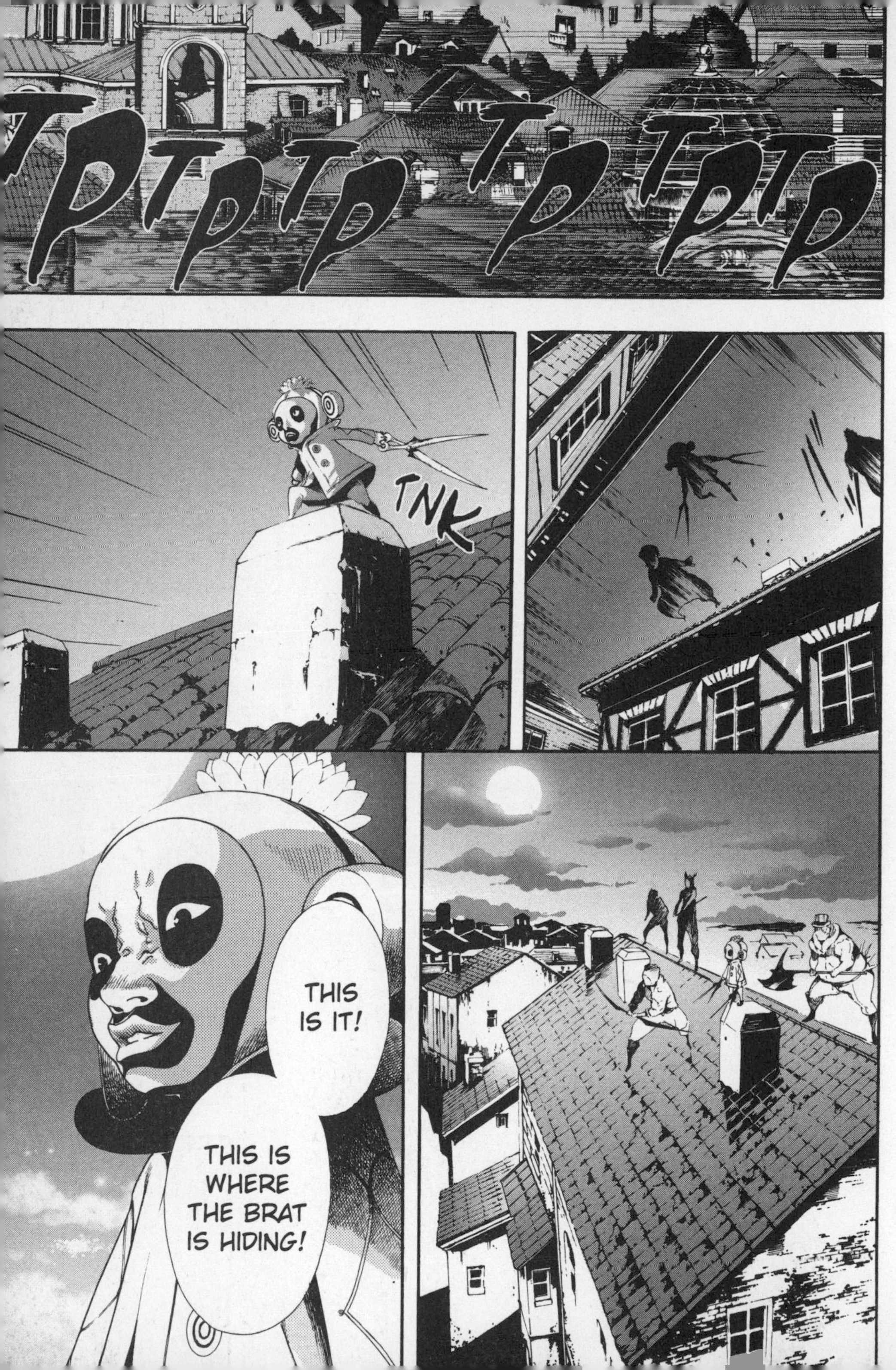
TPTPTP TPTPTP
TNK
THIS IS IT!
THIS IS WHERE THE BRAT IS HIDING!

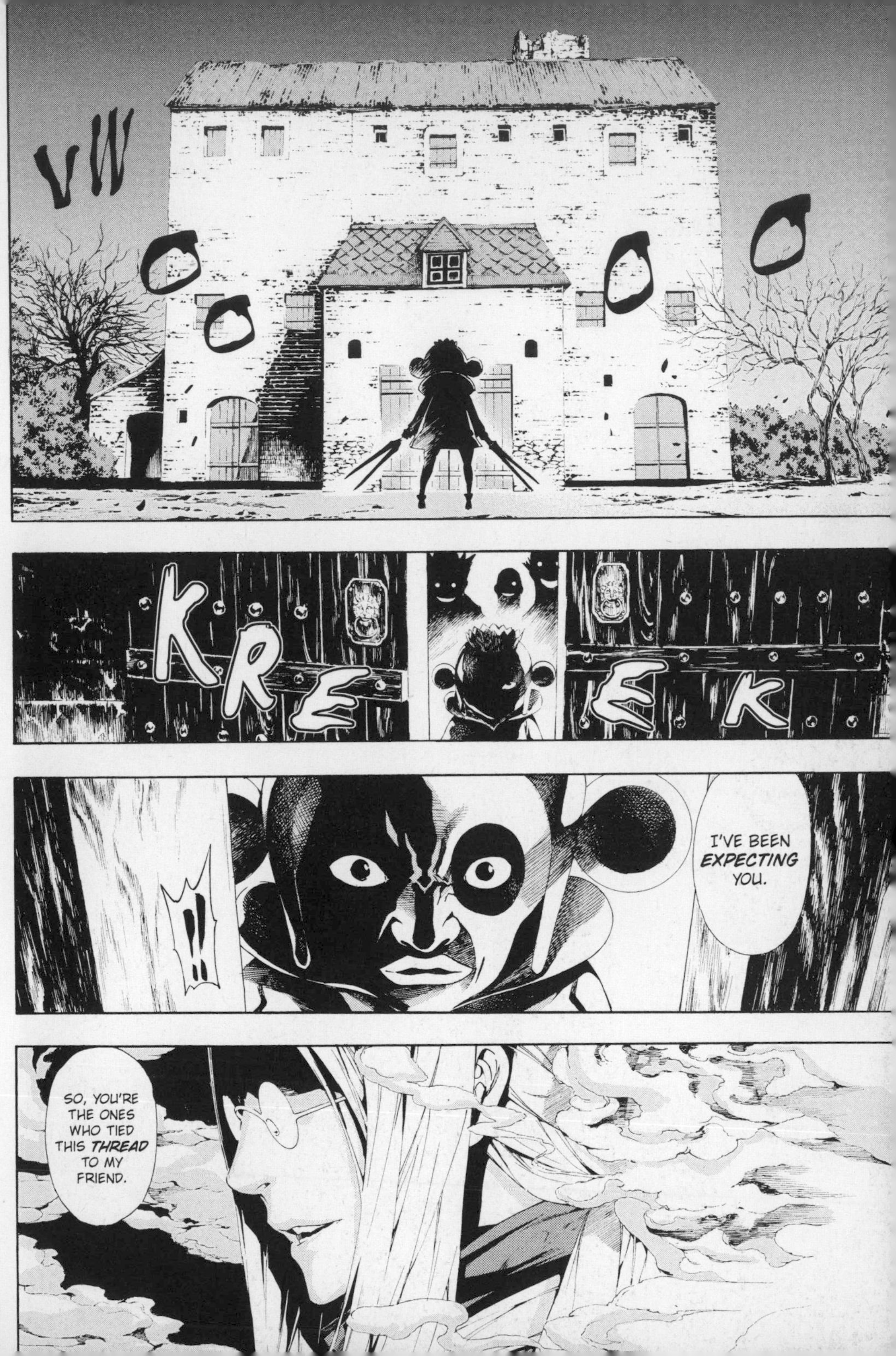
VWOOOO
KREEK
I'VE BEEN *EXPECTING* YOU.
!!
SO, YOU'RE THE ONES WHO TIED THIS *THREAD* TO MY FRIEND.

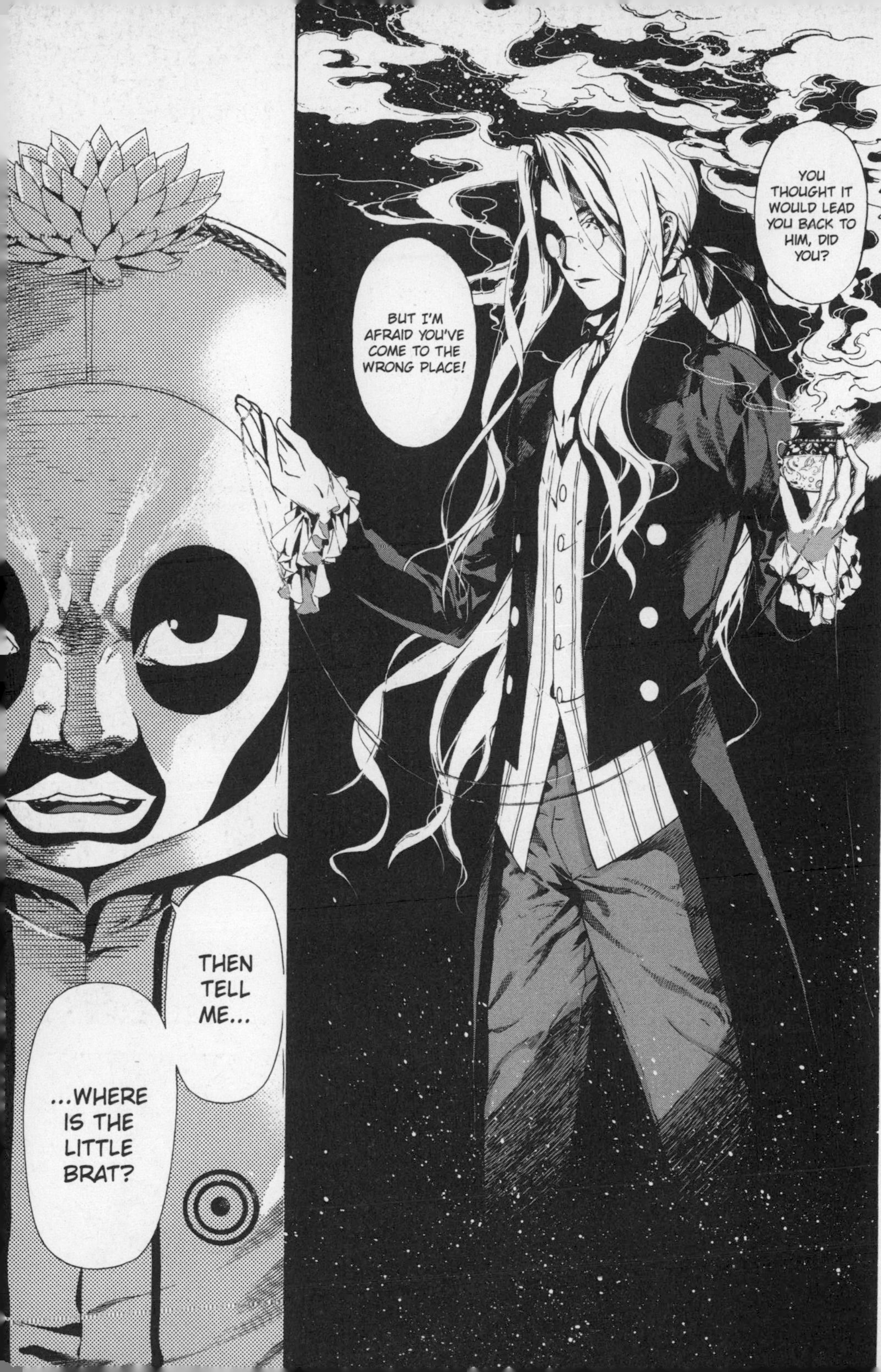
YOU THOUGHT IT WOULD LEAD YOU BACK TO HIM, DID YOU?
BUT I'M AFRAID YOU'VE COME TO THE WRONG PLACE!
THEN TELL ME...
...WHERE IS THE LITTLE BRAT?

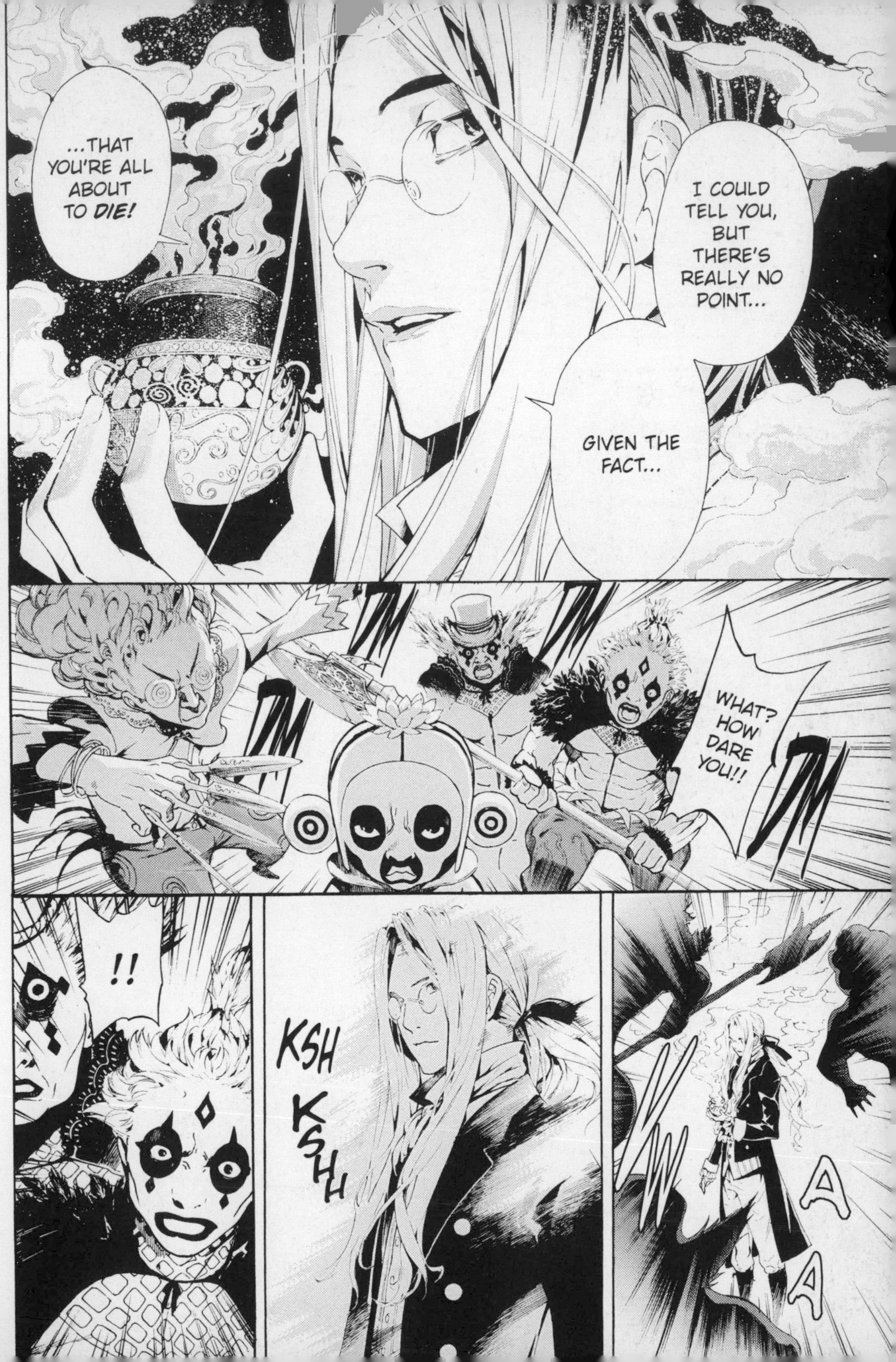
I COULD TELL YOU, BUT THERE'S REALLY NO POINT...
GIVEN THE FACT...
...THAT YOU'RE ALL ABOUT TO DIE!
WHAT? HOW DARE YOU!!
A
A
KSH
KSHH
!!

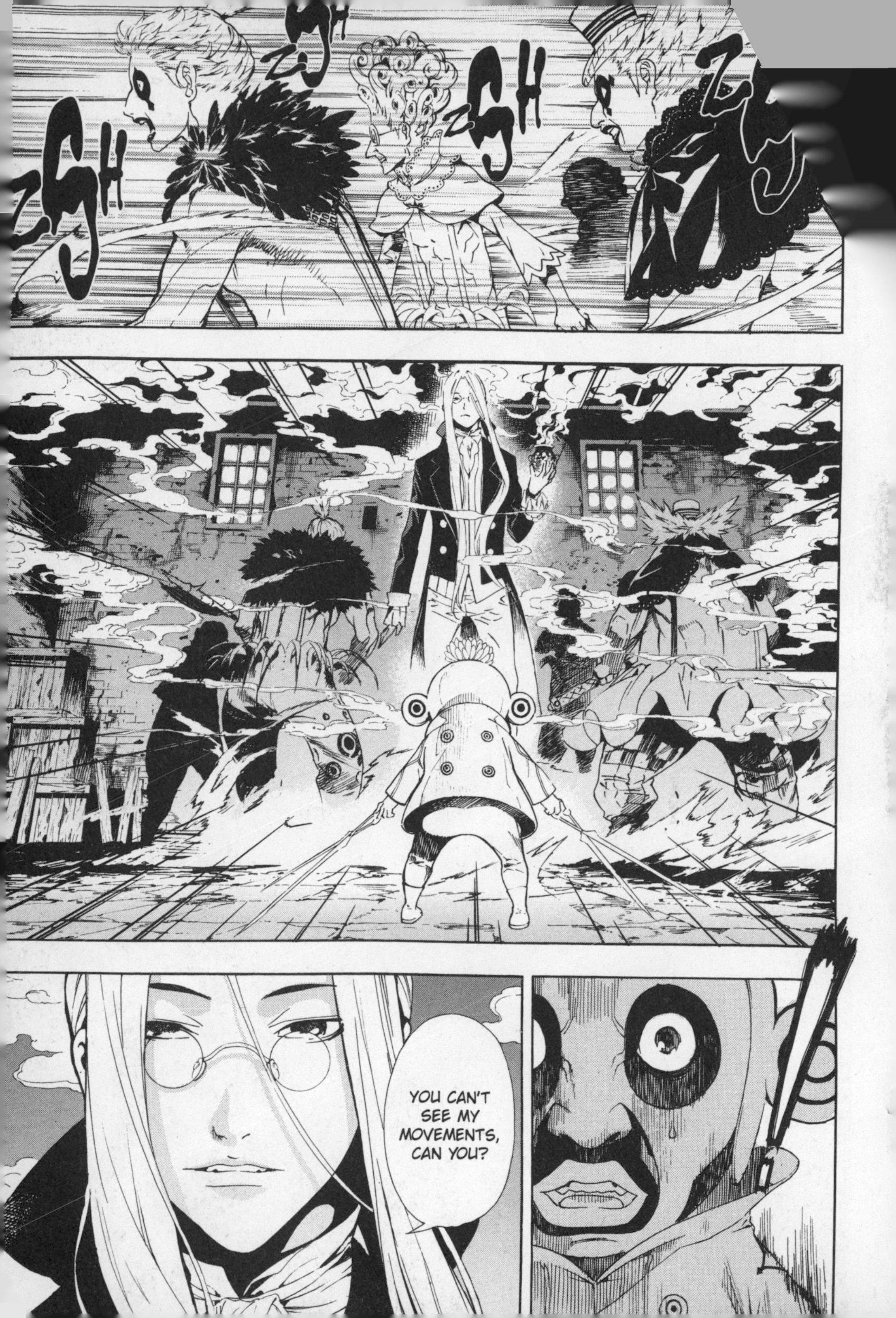
ZGH
ZGH
ZGH
YOU CAN'T SEE MY MOVEMENTS, CAN YOU?

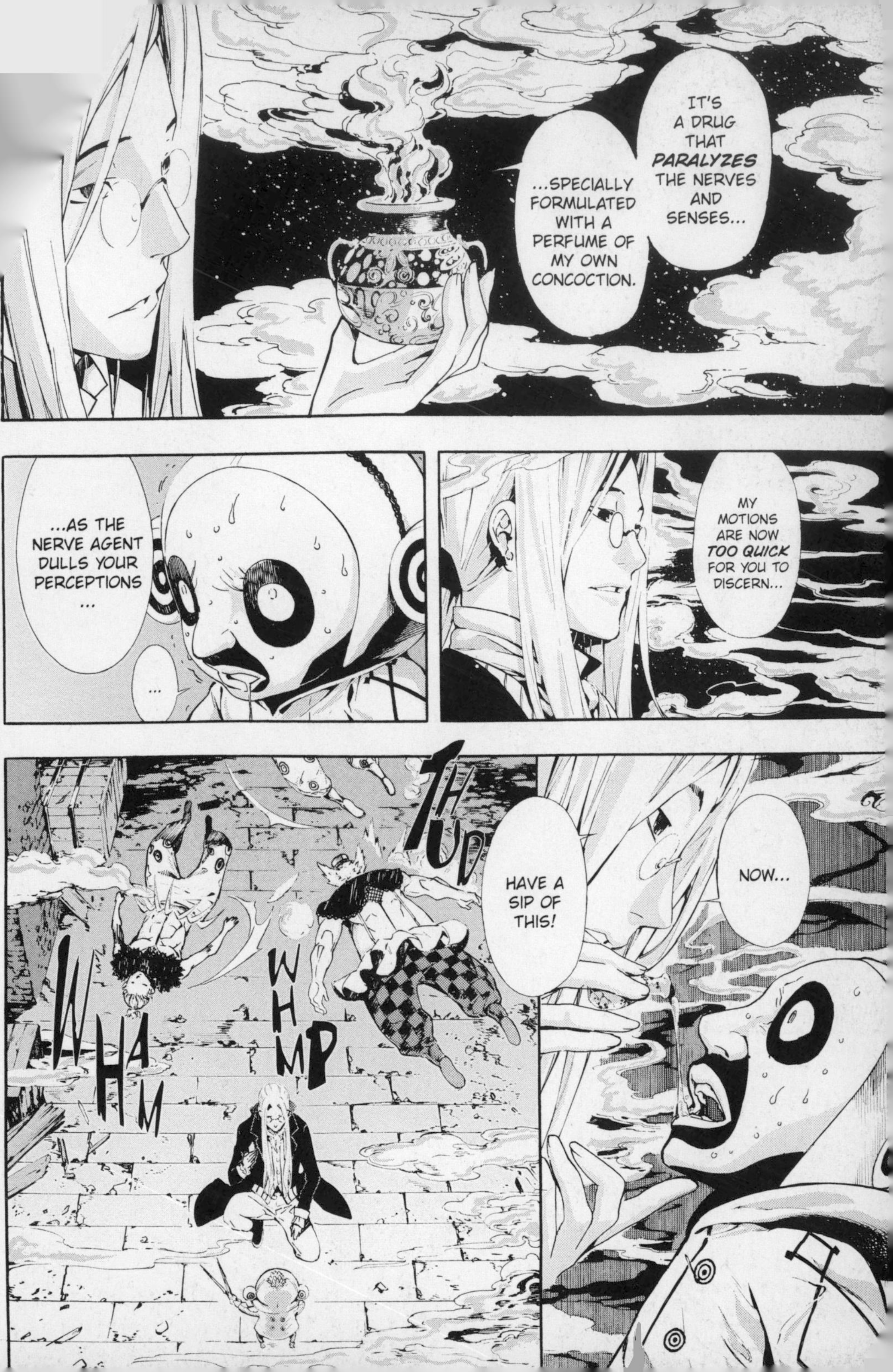
IT'S A DRUG THAT **PARALYZES** THE NERVES AND SENSES...
...SPECIALLY FORMULATED WITH A PERFUME OF MY OWN CONCOCTION.
MY MOTIONS ARE NOW **TOO QUICK** FOR YOU TO DISCERN...
...AS THE NERVE AGENT DULLS YOUR PERCEPTIONS ...
...
NOW...
HAVE A SIP OF THIS!
THUD
WHMP
WHAM

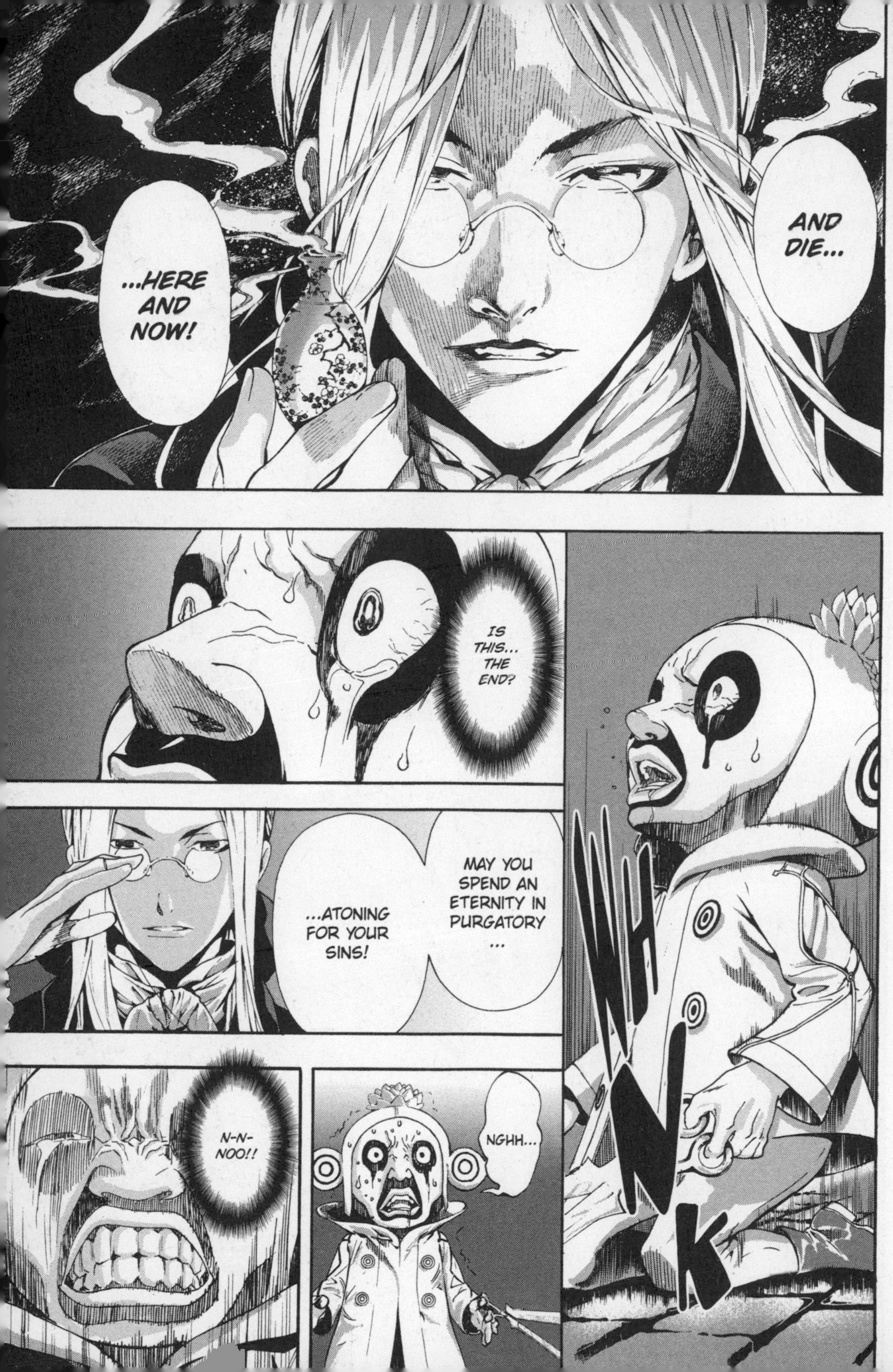
AND DIE...
...HERE AND NOW!
WHNK
IS THIS... THE END?
MAY YOU SPEND AN ETERNITY IN PURGATORY ...
...ATONING FOR YOUR SINS!
NGHH...
N-N-NOO!!

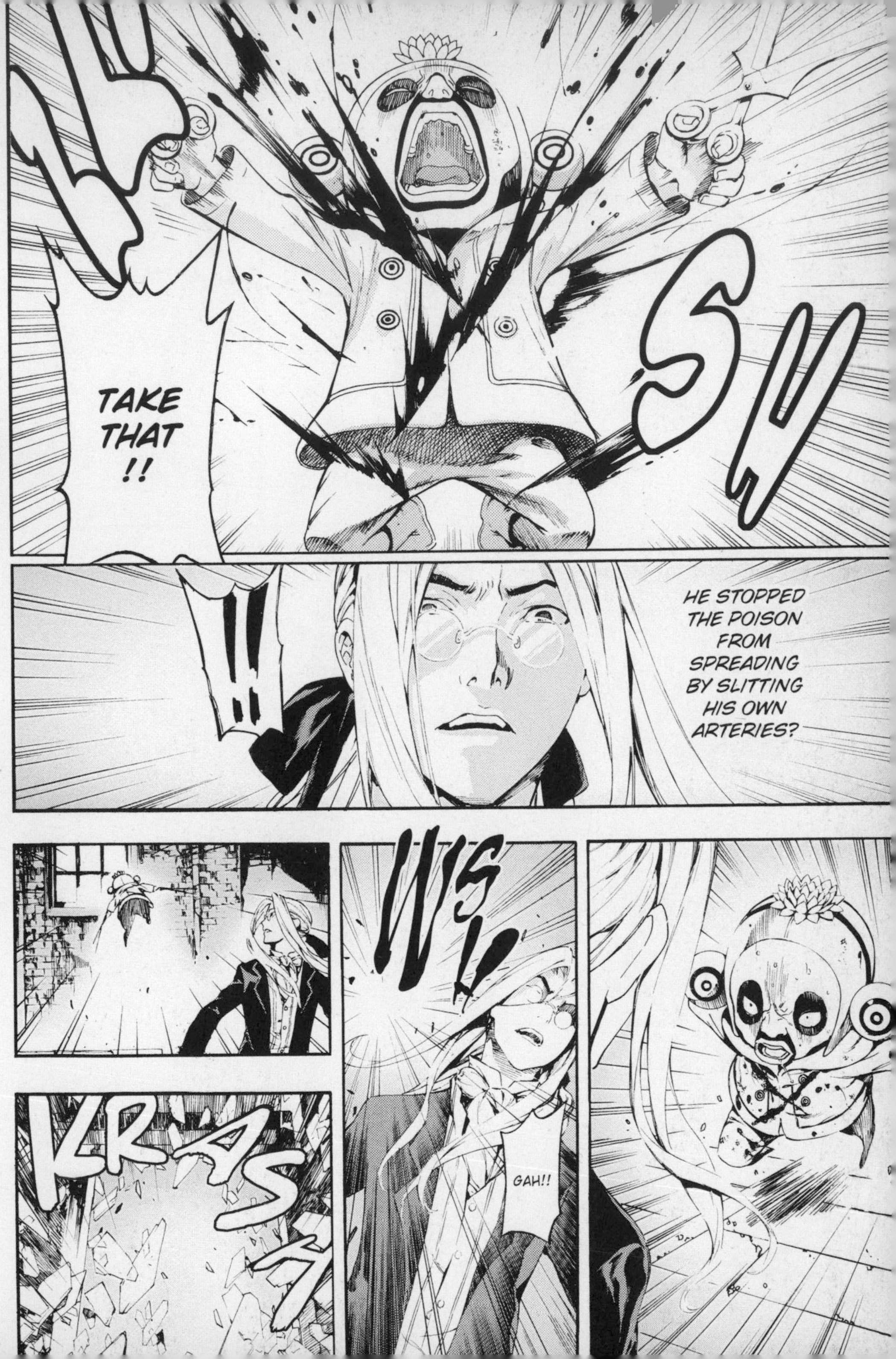
SH
TAKE THAT !!
HE STOPPED THE POISON FROM SPREADING BY SLITTING HIS OWN ARTERIES?
!!
GAH!!
KRASH

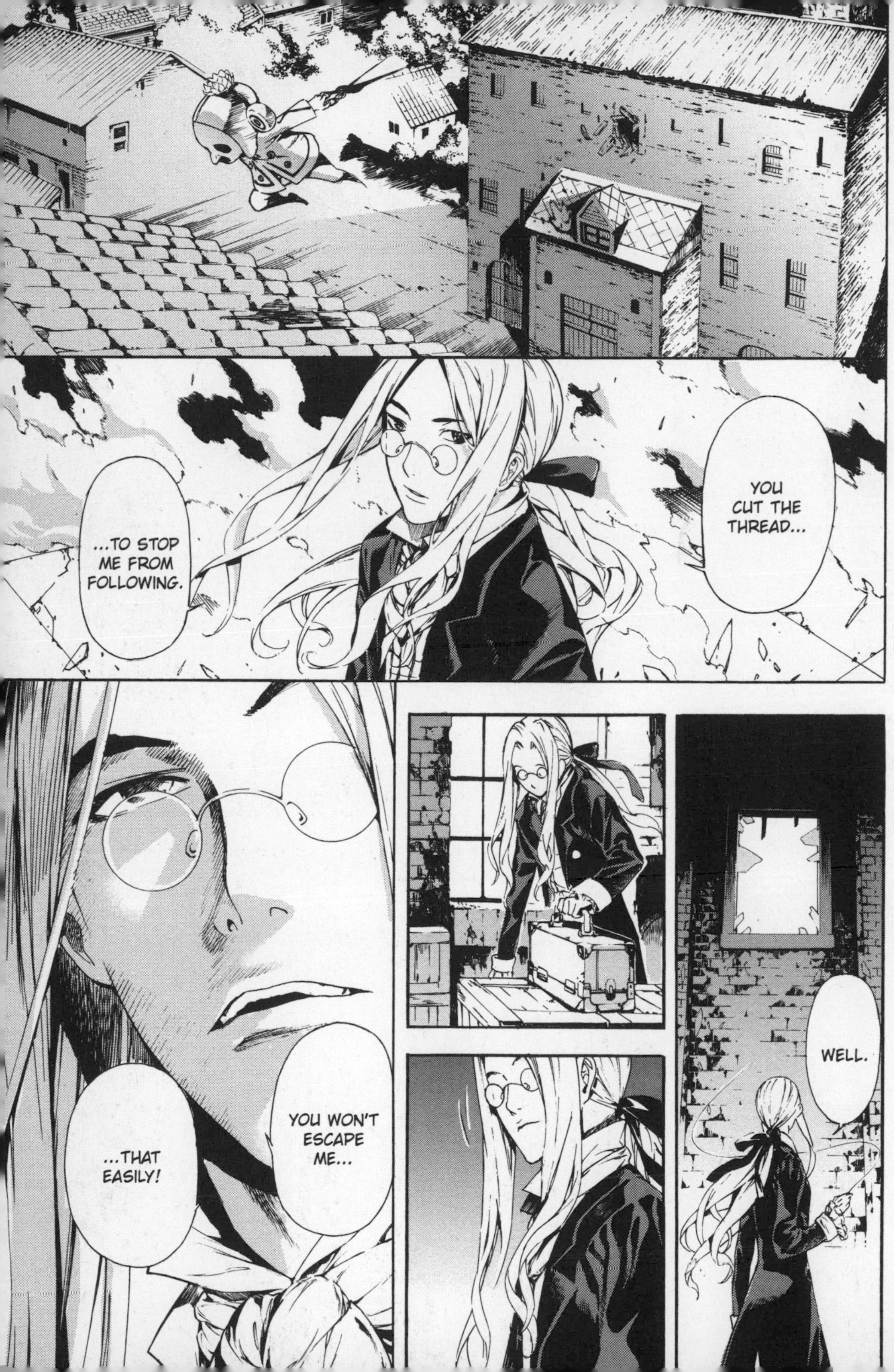
YOU CUT THE THREAD...
...TO STOP ME FROM FOLLOWING.
WELL.
YOU WON'T ESCAPE ME...
...THAT EASILY!

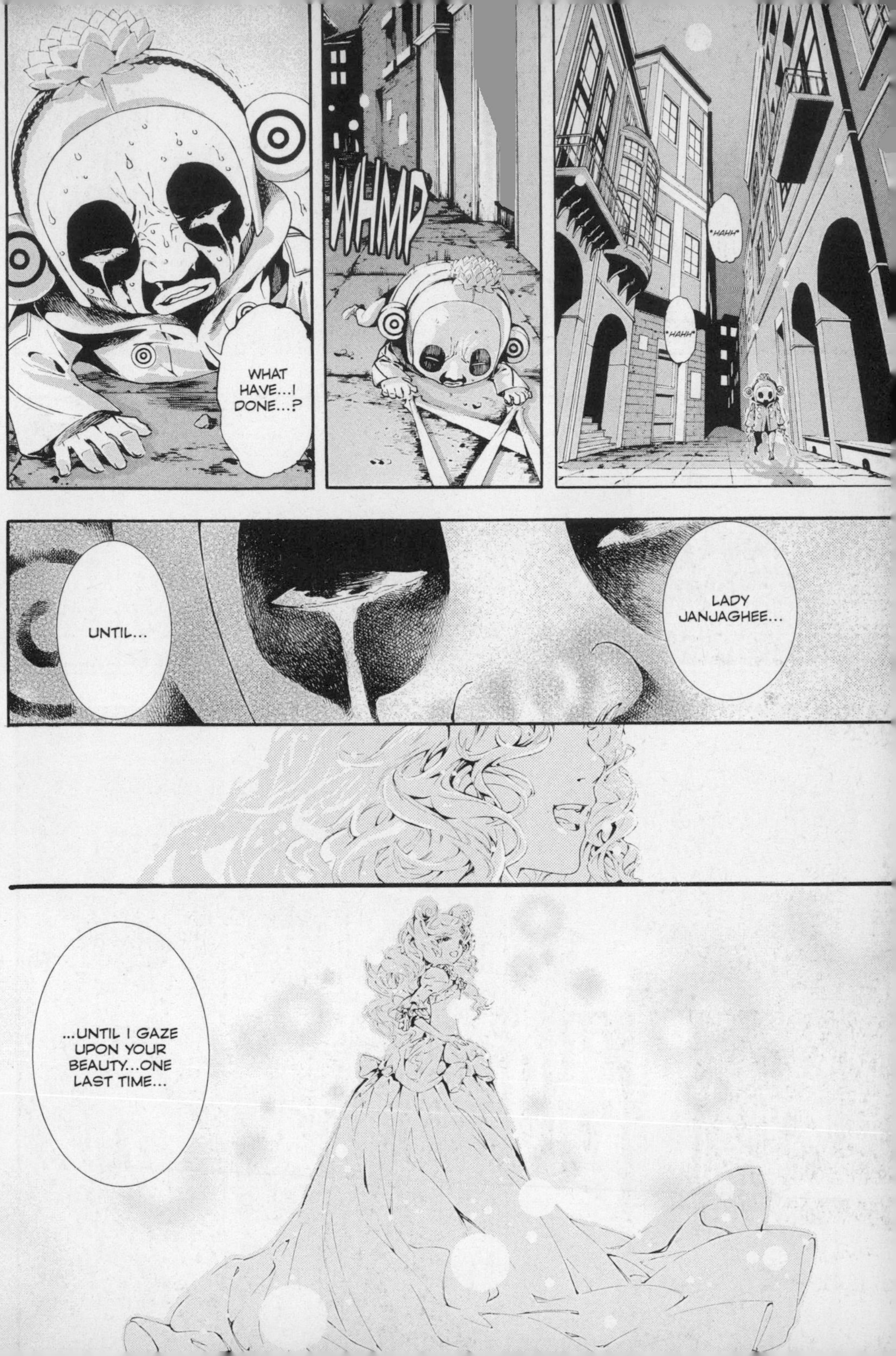
HAHH
HAHH
WHMP
WHAT HAVE...I DONE...?
LADY JANJAGHEE...
UNTIL...
...UNTIL I GAZE UPON YOUR BEAUTY...ONE LAST TIME...

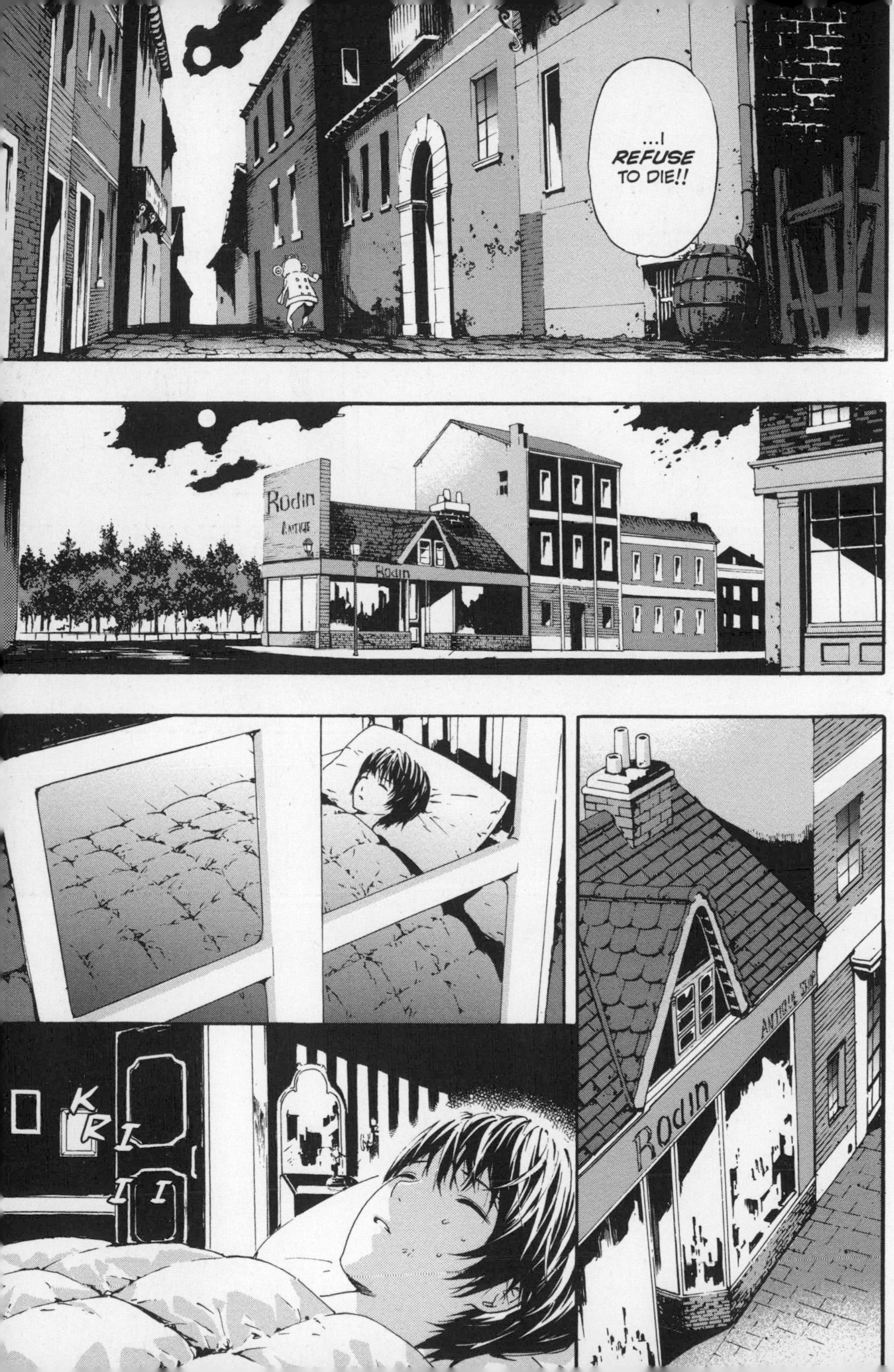
...I REFUSE TO DIE!!
Rodin
ANTIQUE
Rodin
ANTIQUE SHOP
Rodin
KRIII

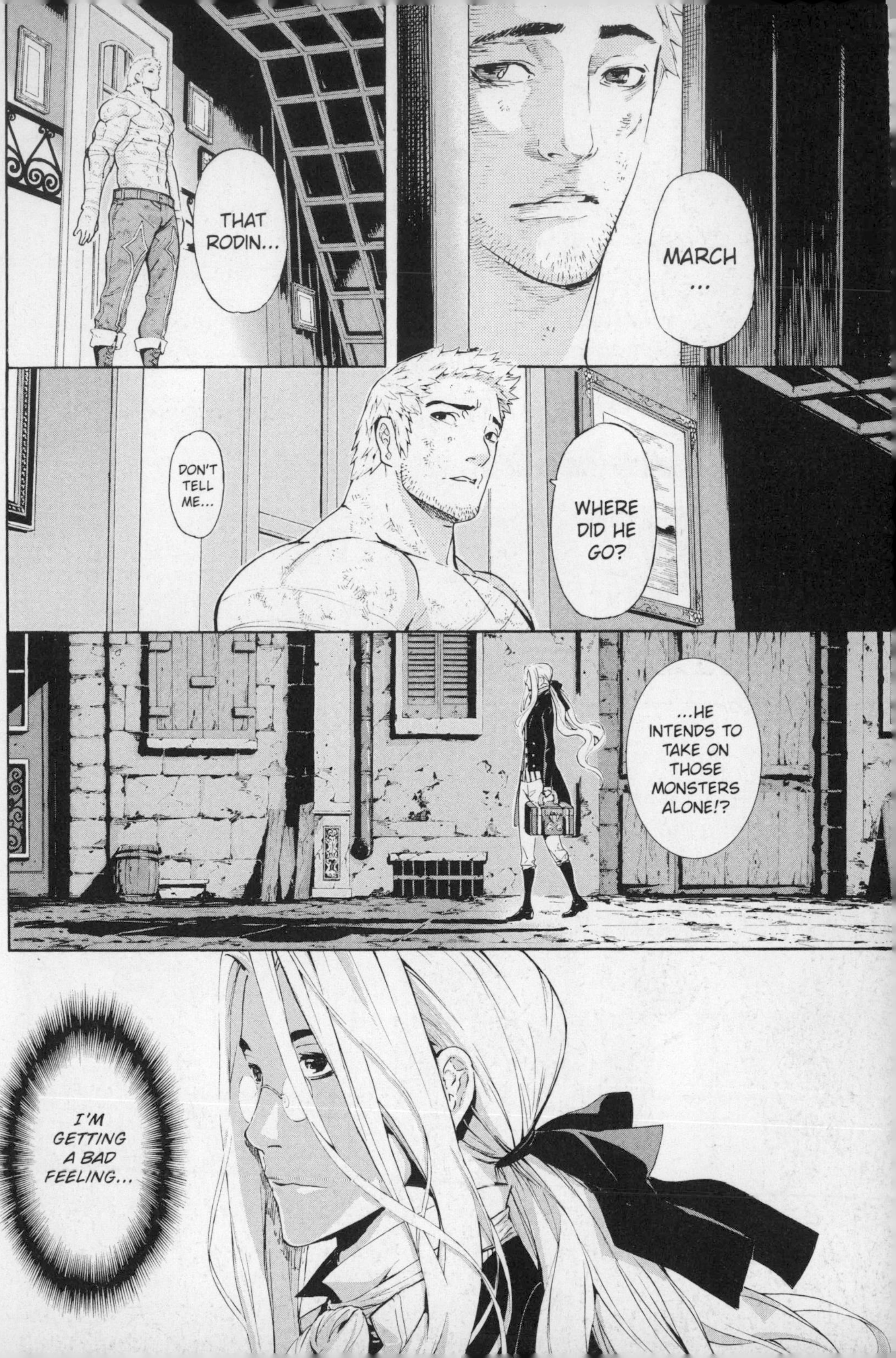
MARCH ...
THAT RODIN...
WHERE DID HE GO?
DON'T TELL ME...
...HE INTENDS TO TAKE ON THOSE MONSTERS ALONE!?
I'M GETTING A BAD FEELING...

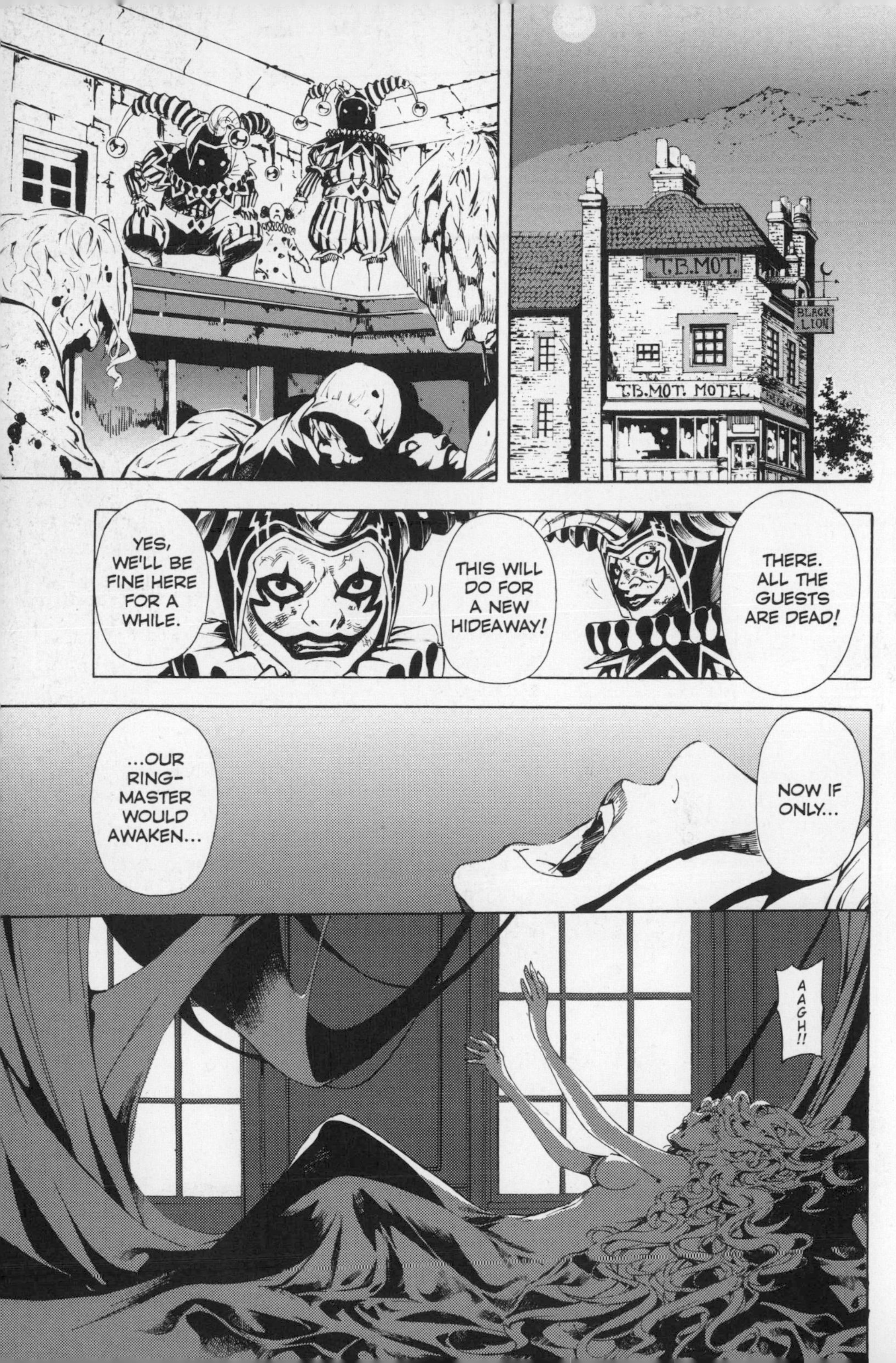
T.B.MOT.
BLACK LION
T.B.MOT. MOTEL
THERE. ALL THE GUESTS ARE DEAD!
THIS WILL DO FOR A NEW HIDEAWAY!
YES, WE'LL BE FINE HERE FOR A WHILE.
NOW IF ONLY...
...OUR RING-MASTER WOULD AWAKEN...
AAGH!!

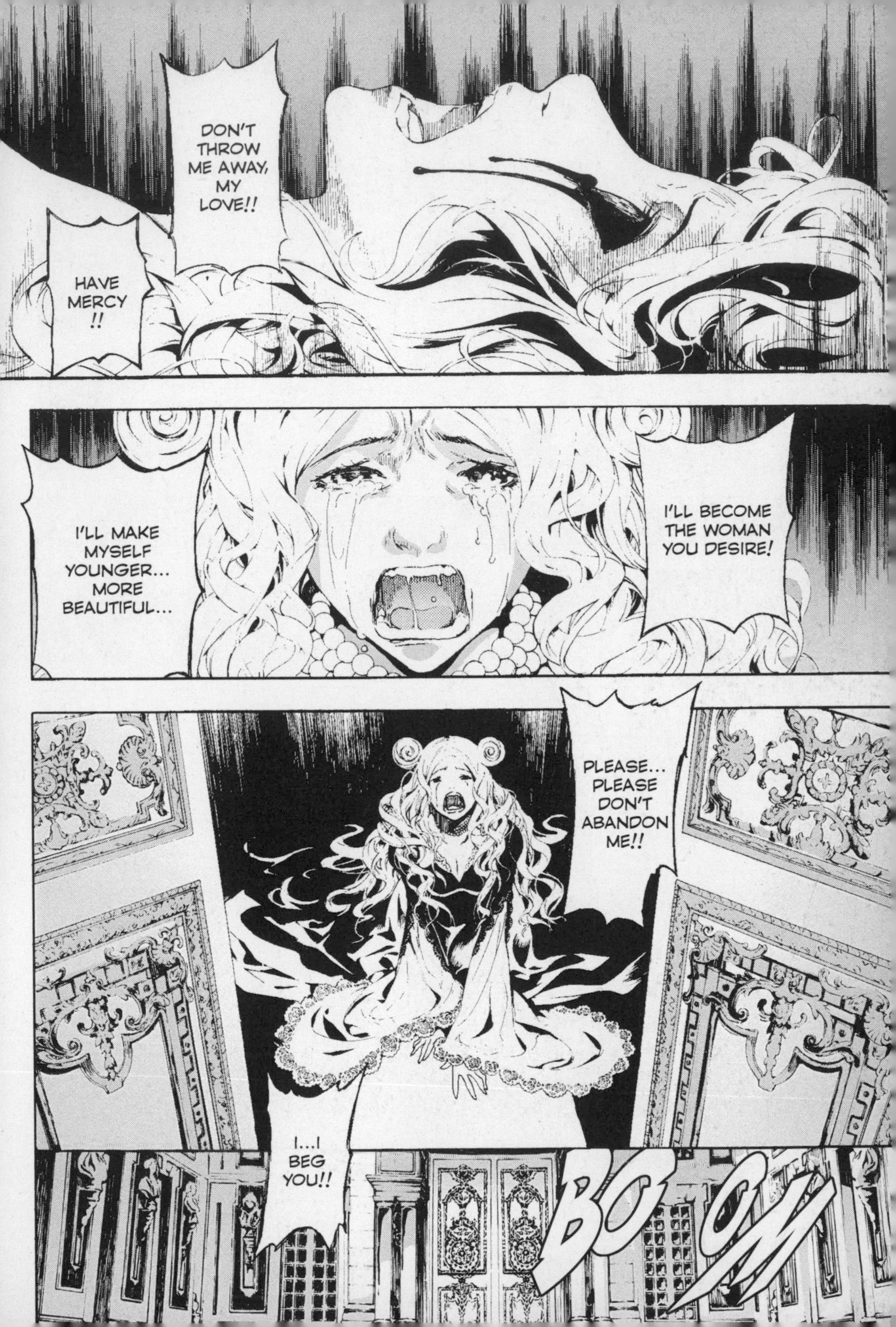
DON'T THROW ME AWAY, MY LOVE!!
HAVE MERCY!!
I'LL BECOME THE WOMAN YOU DESIRE!
I'LL MAKE MYSELF YOUNGER... MORE BEAUTIFUL...
PLEASE... PLEASE DON'T ABANDON ME!!
I...I BEG YOU!!
BOOM

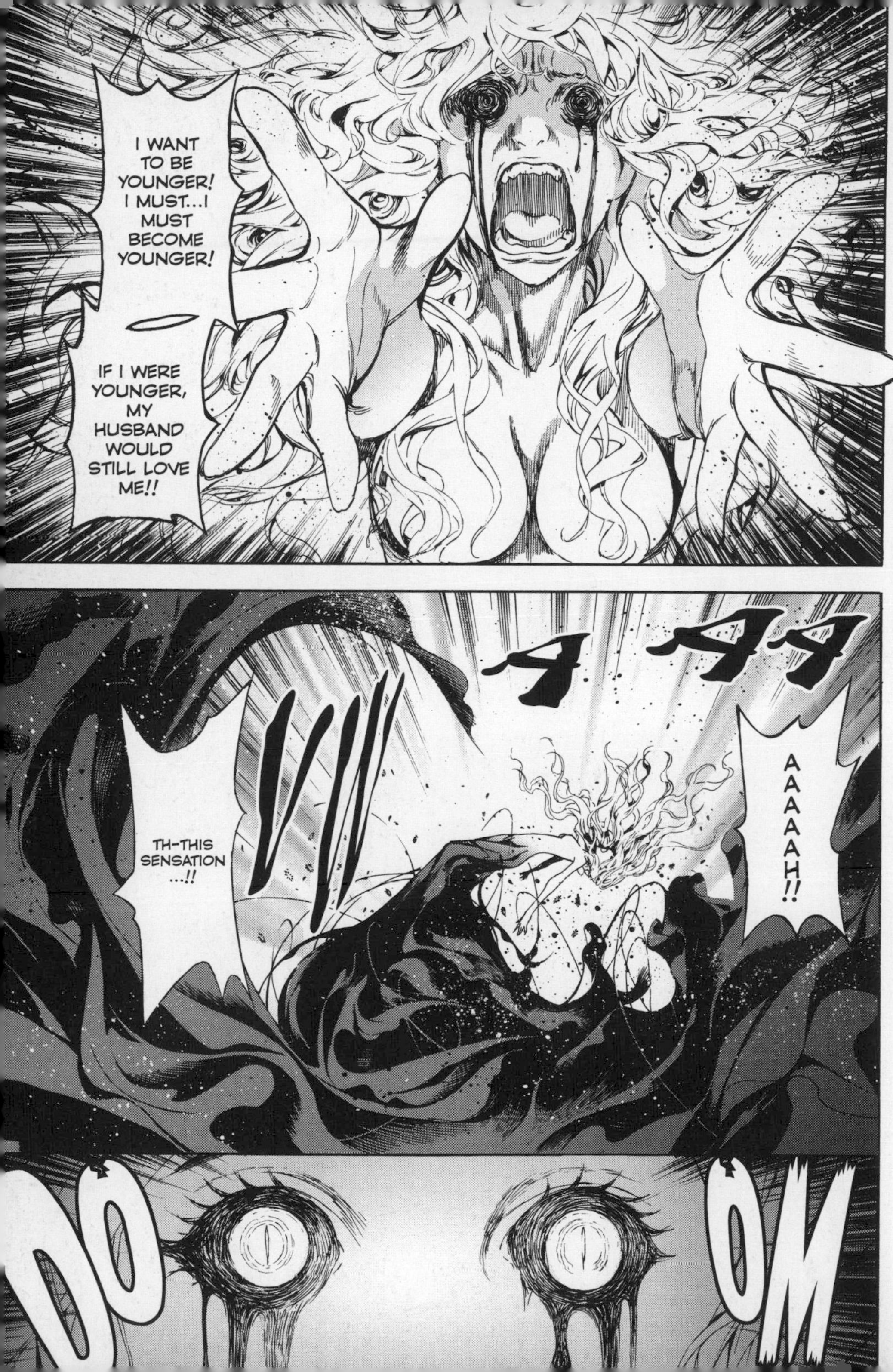
I WANT TO BE YOUNGER! I MUST...I MUST BECOME YOUNGER!
IF I WERE YOUNGER, MY HUSBAND WOULD STILL LOVE ME!!
A AA
AAAAAAH!!
TH-THIS SENSATION ...!!
DOOM

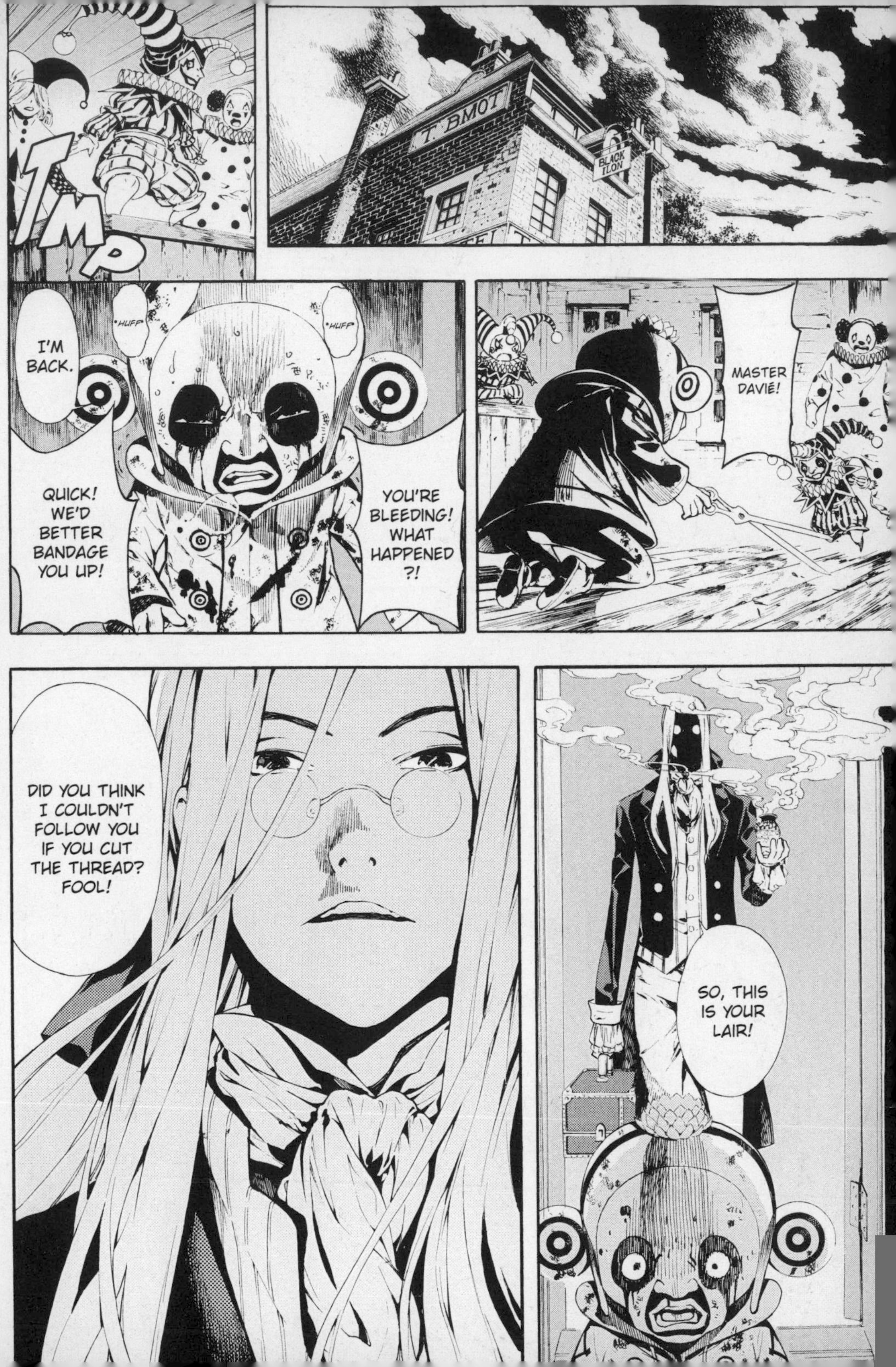
TMP
MASTER DAVIÉ!
HUFF
HUFF
I'M BACK.
YOU'RE BLEEDING! WHAT HAPPENED ?!
QUICK! WE'D BETTER BANDAGE YOU UP!
SO, THIS IS YOUR LAIR!
DID YOU THINK I COULDN'T FOLLOW YOU IF YOU CUT THE THREAD? FOOL!

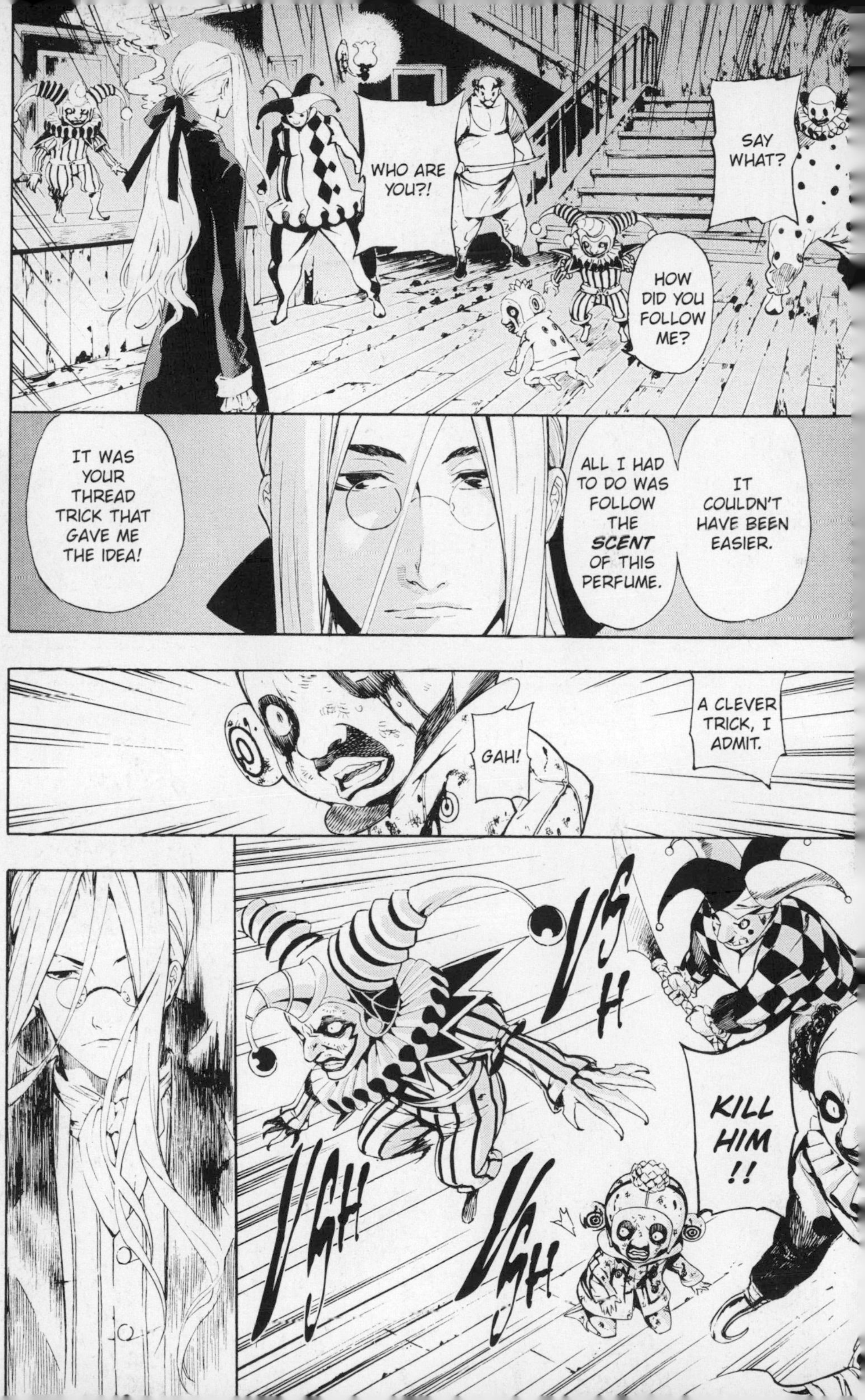
SAY WHAT?
WHO ARE YOU?!
HOW DID YOU FOLLOW ME?
IT COULDN'T HAVE BEEN EASIER.
ALL I HAD TO DO WAS FOLLOW THE SCENT OF THIS PERFUME.
IT WAS YOUR THREAD TRICK THAT GAVE ME THE IDEA!
A CLEVER TRICK, I ADMIT.
GAH!
VSH
KILL HIM!!
VSH
VSH!

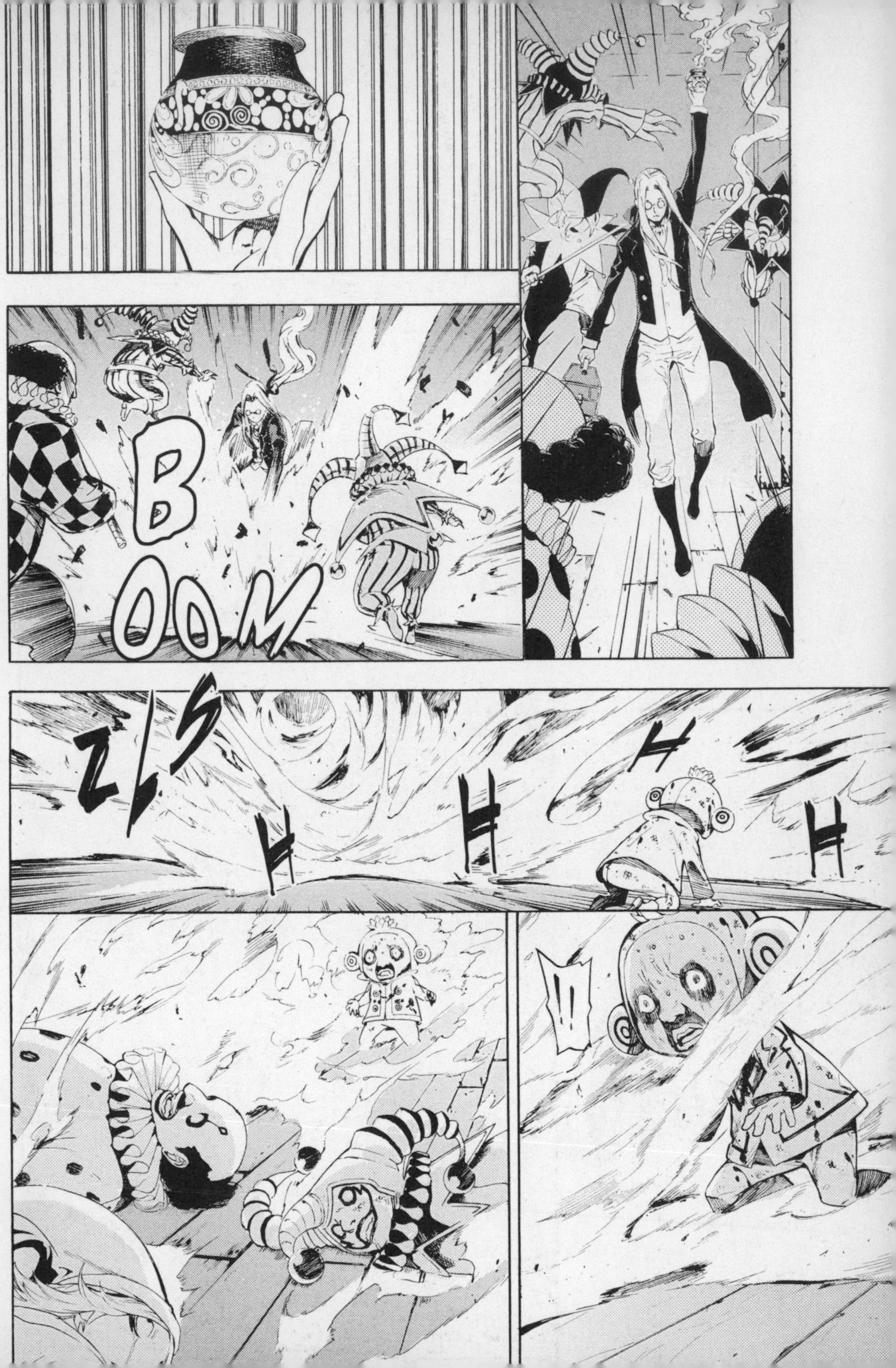
BOOM
ZISHHHH
!!

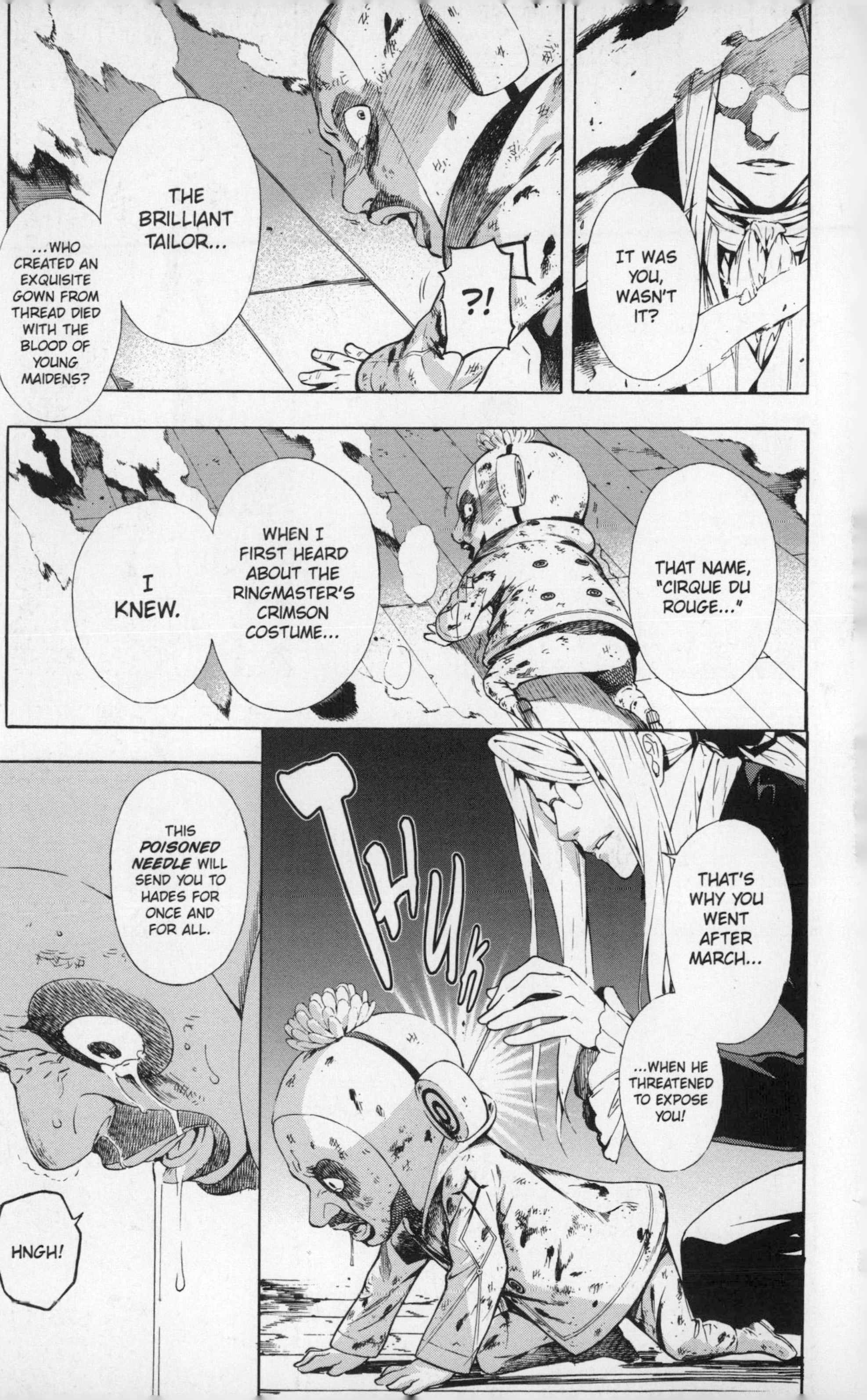
IT WAS YOU, WASN'T IT?
?!
THE BRILLIANT TAILOR...
...WHO CREATED AN EXQUISITE GOWN FROM THREAD DIED WITH THE BLOOD OF YOUNG MAIDENS?
THAT NAME, "CIRQUE DU ROUGE..."
WHEN I FIRST HEARD ABOUT THE RINGMASTER'S CRIMSON COSTUME...
I KNEW.
THAT'S WHY YOU WENT AFTER MARCH...
THUK
...WHEN HE THREATENED TO EXPOSE YOU!
THIS *POISONED NEEDLE* WILL SEND YOU TO HADES FOR ONCE AND FOR ALL.
HNGH!

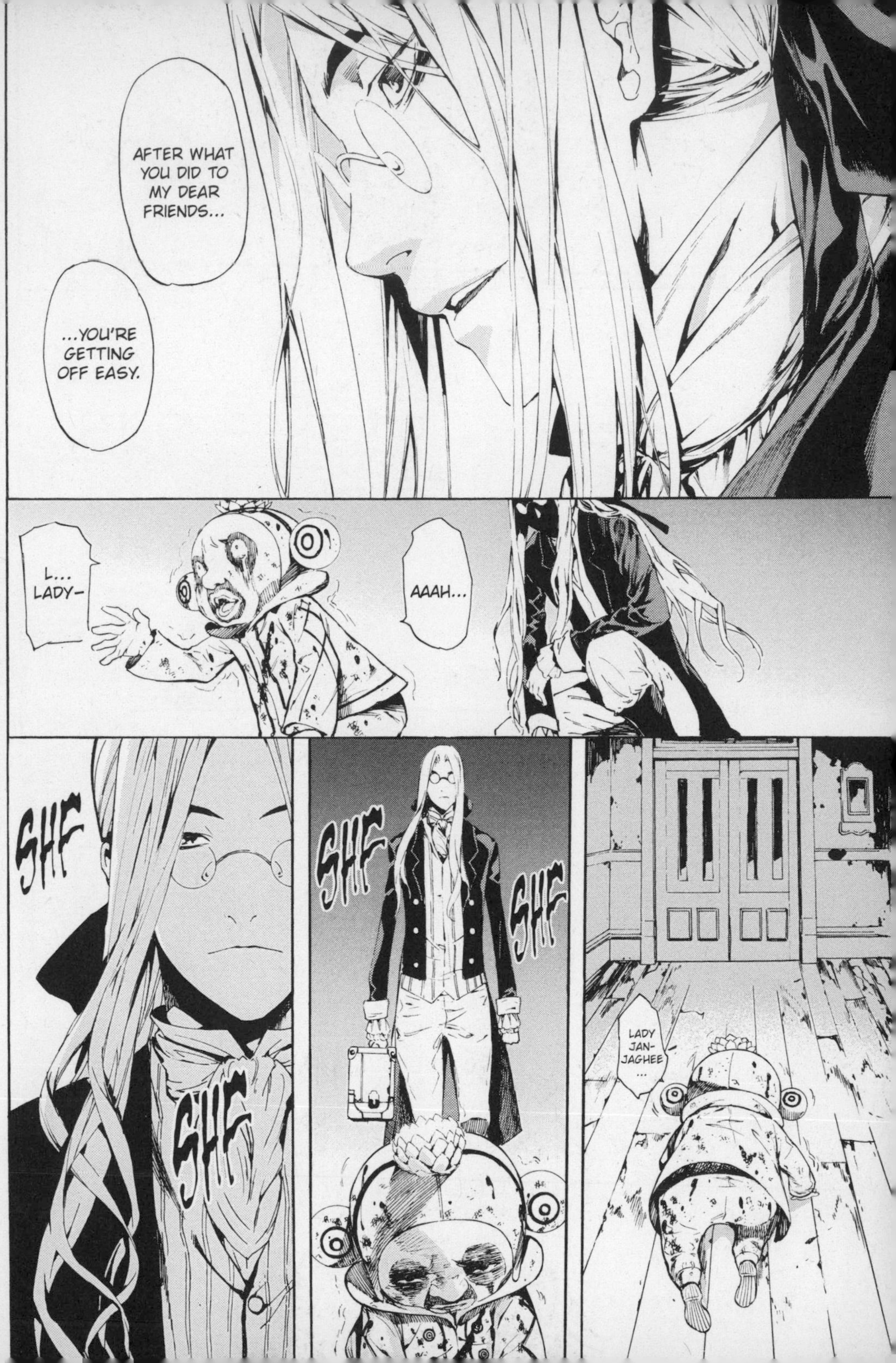
AFTER WHAT YOU DID TO MY DEAR FRIENDS...
...YOU'RE GETTING OFF EASY.
AAAH...
L... LADY-
LADY JAN-JAGHEE...
SHF
SHF
SHF
SHF

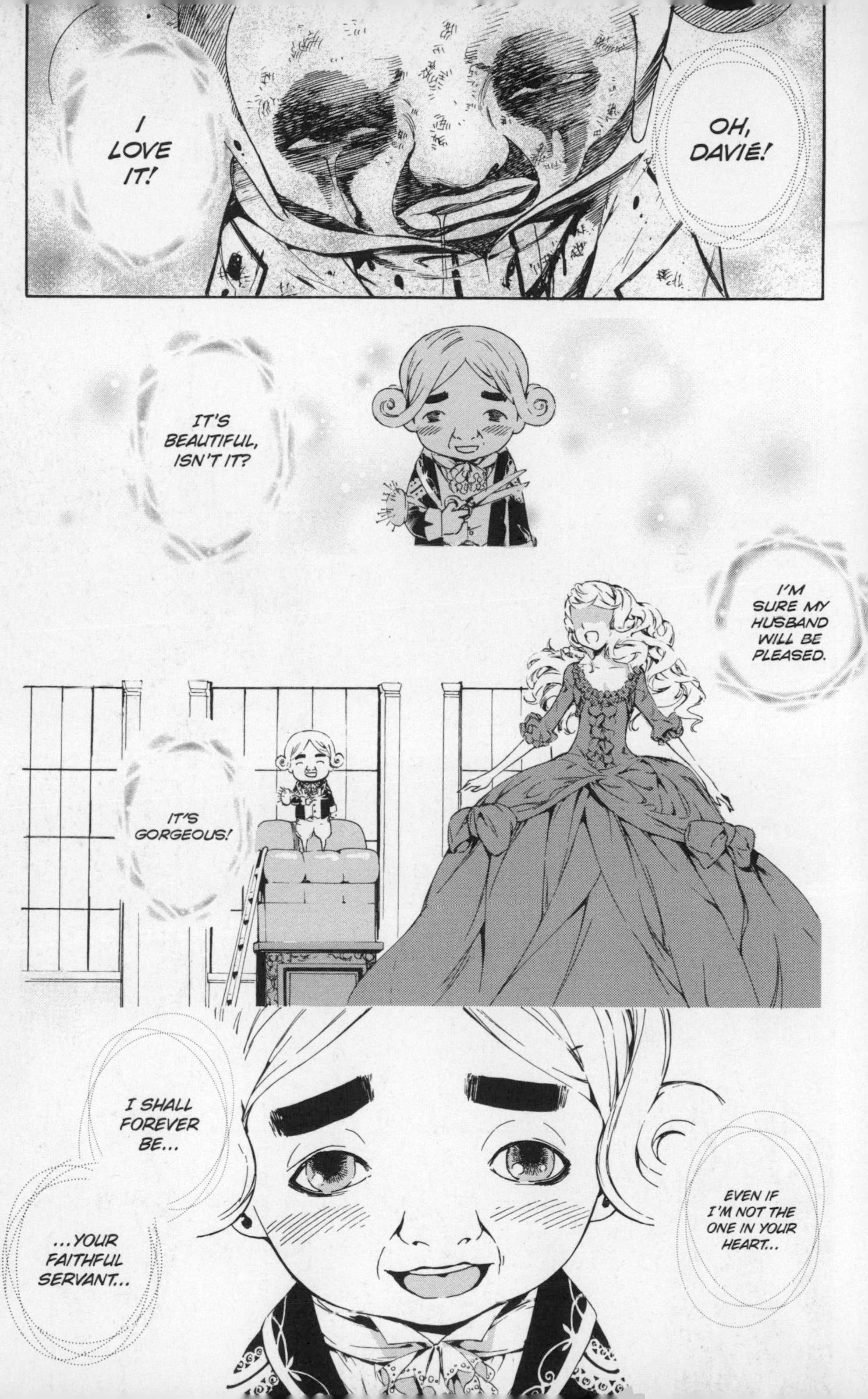
OH, DAVIÉ!
I LOVE IT!
IT'S BEAUTIFUL, ISN'T IT?
I'M SURE MY HUSBAND WILL BE PLEASED.
IT'S GORGEOUS!
EVEN IF I'M NOT THE ONE IN YOUR HEART...
I SHALL FOREVER BE...
...YOUR FAITHFUL SERVANT...

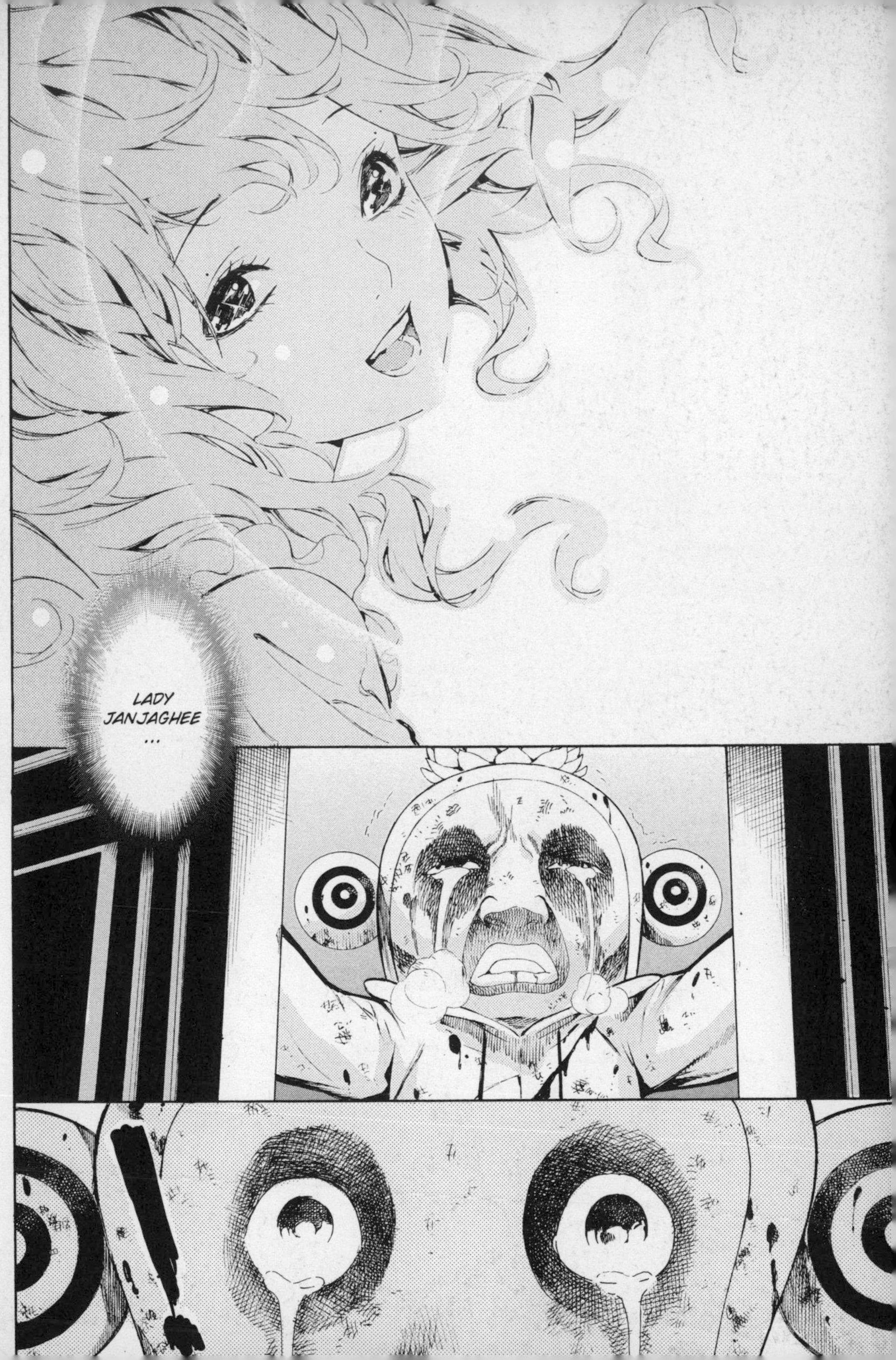
LADY JANJAGHEE ...

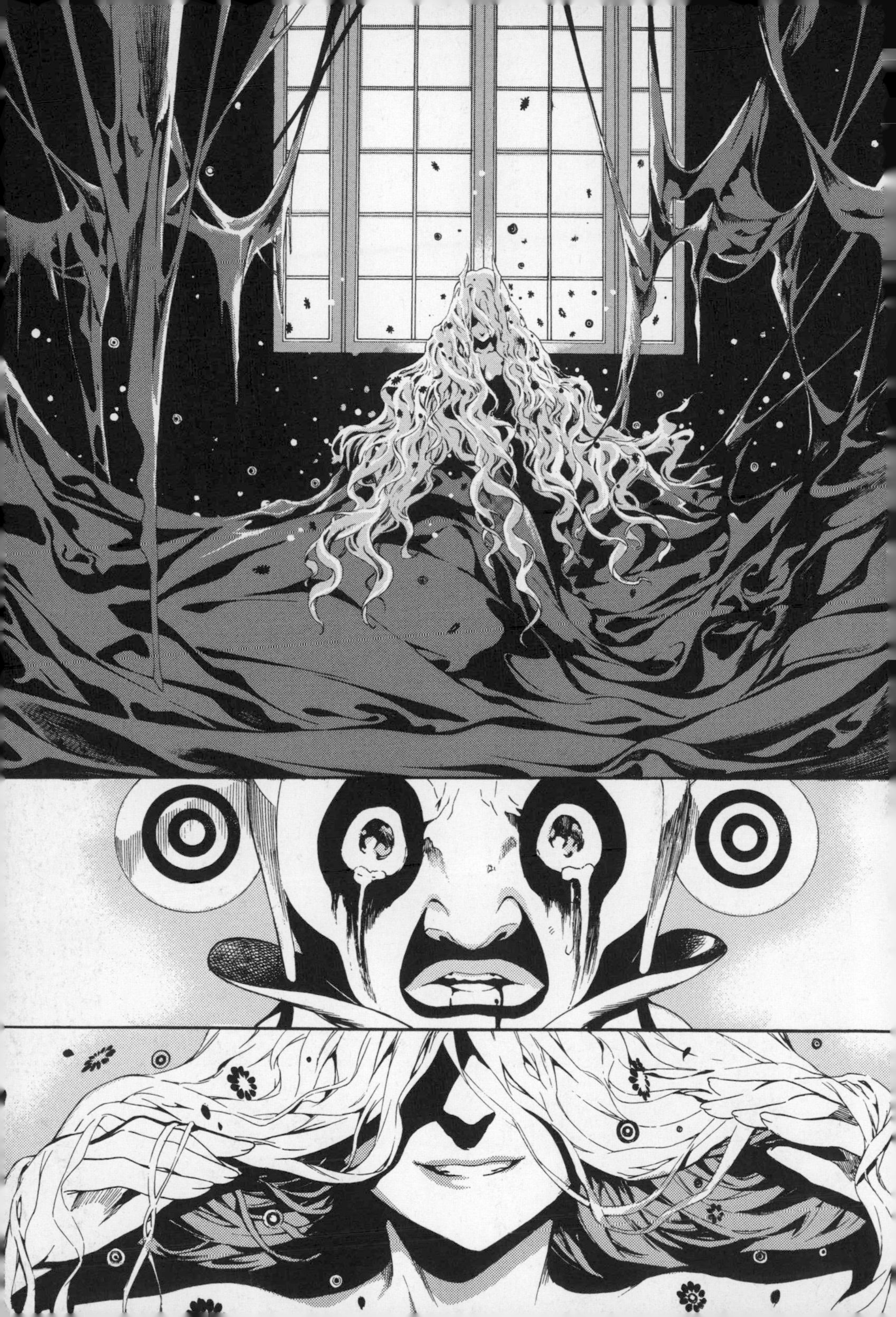

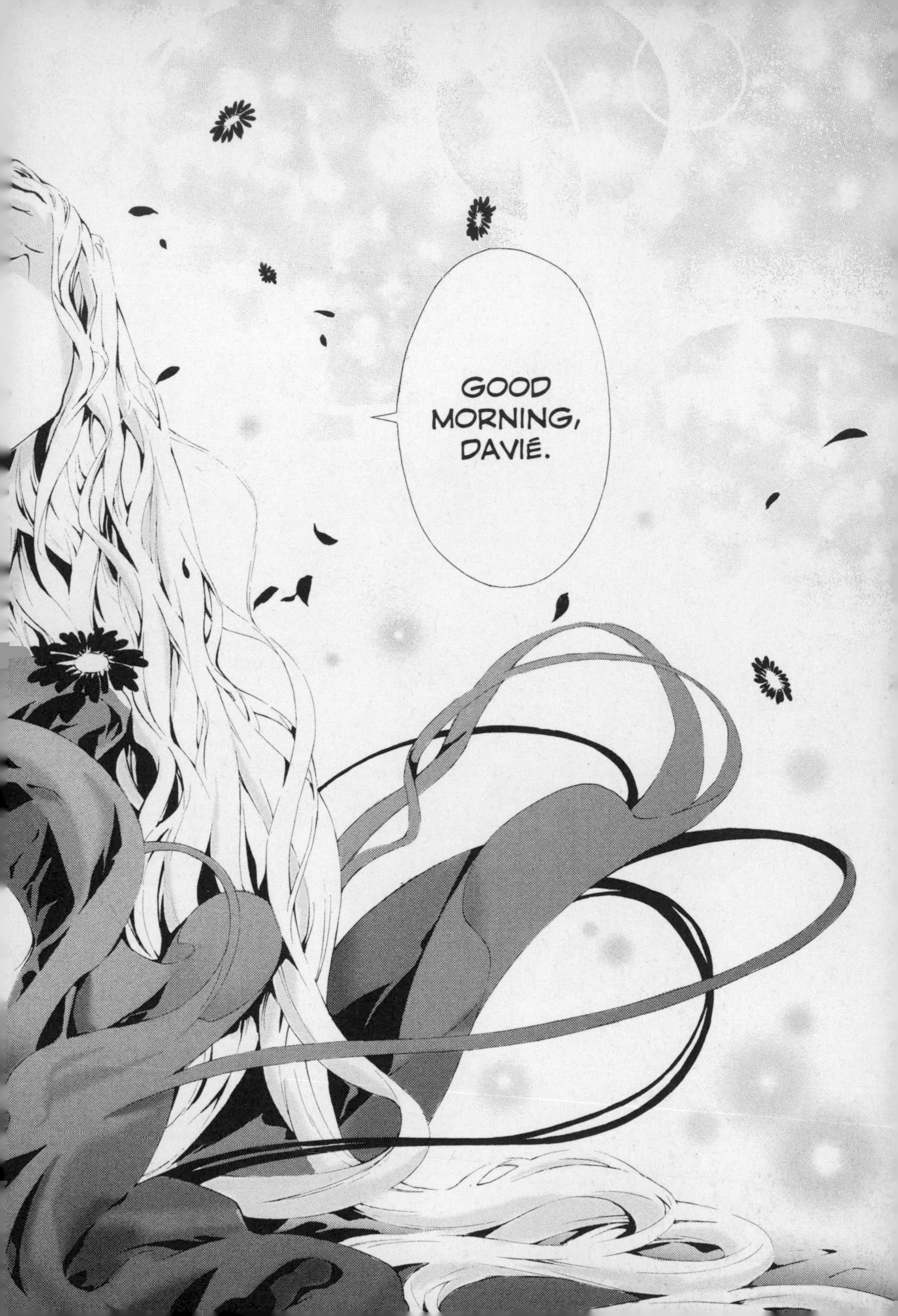
GOOD MORNING, DAVIÉ.

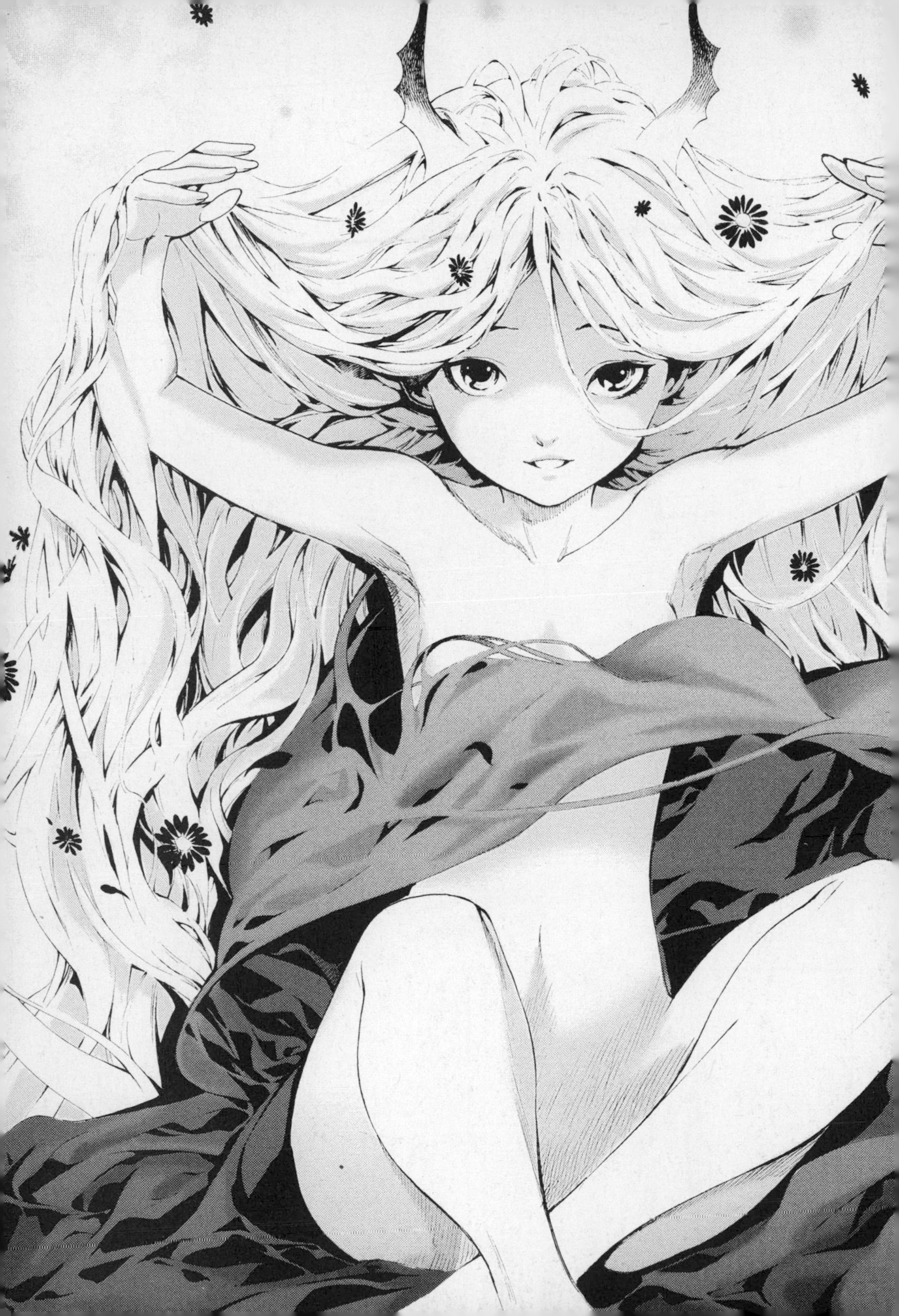

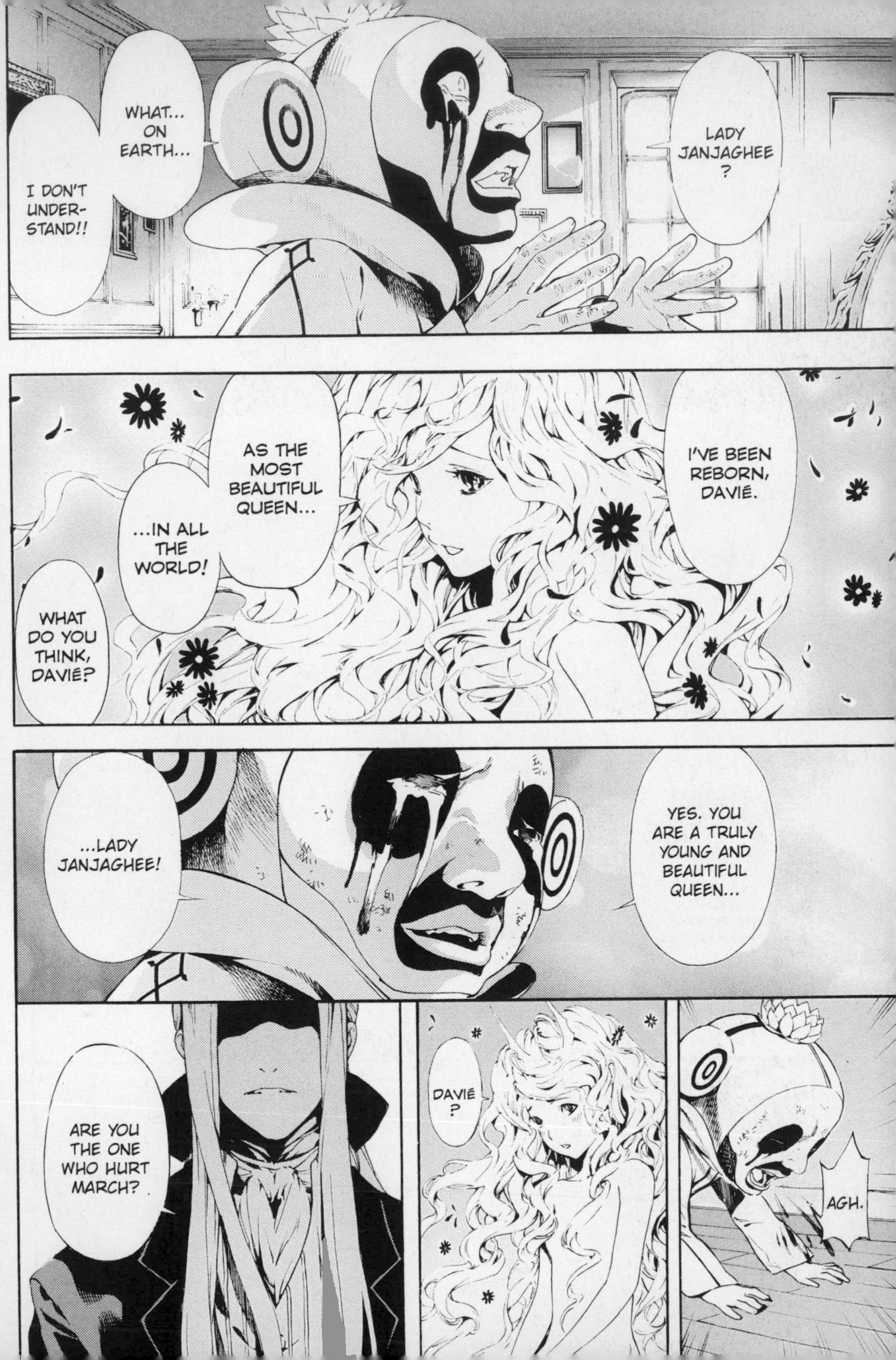
LADY JANJAGHEE ?
WHAT... ON EARTH...
I DON'T UNDER-STAND!!
I'VE BEEN REBORN, DAVIÉ.
AS THE MOST BEAUTIFUL QUEEN...
...IN ALL THE WORLD!
WHAT DO YOU THINK, DAVIÉ?
YES. YOU ARE A TRULY YOUNG AND BEAUTIFUL QUEEN...
...LADY JANJAGHEE!
AGH.
DAVIÉ ?
ARE YOU THE ONE WHO HURT MARCH?

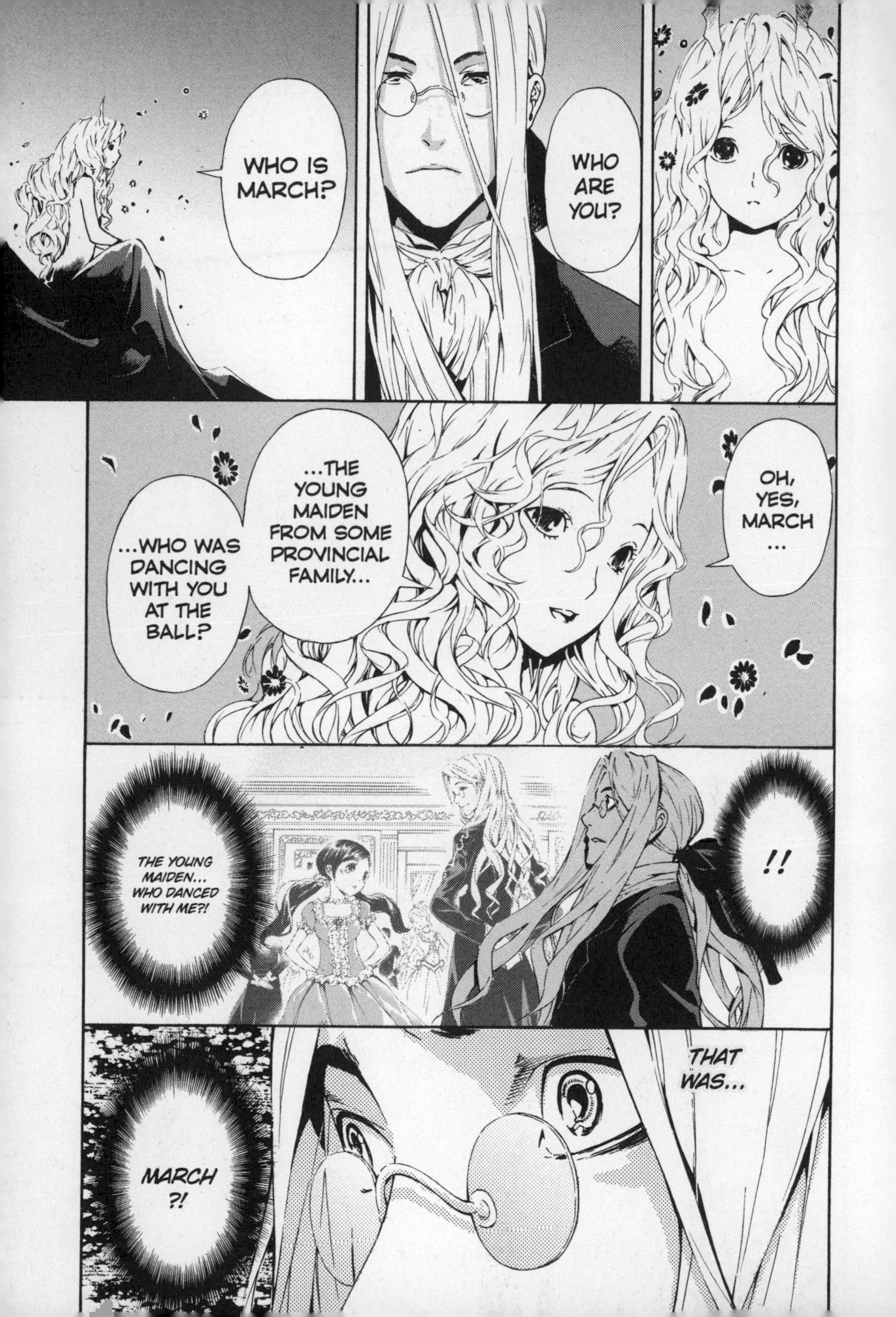
WHO ARE YOU?
WHO IS MARCH?
OH, YES, MARCH...
...THE YOUNG MAIDEN FROM SOME PROVINCIAL FAMILY...
...WHO WAS DANCING WITH YOU AT THE BALL?
!!
THE YOUNG MAIDEN... WHO DANCED WITH ME?!
THAT WAS...
MARCH ?!

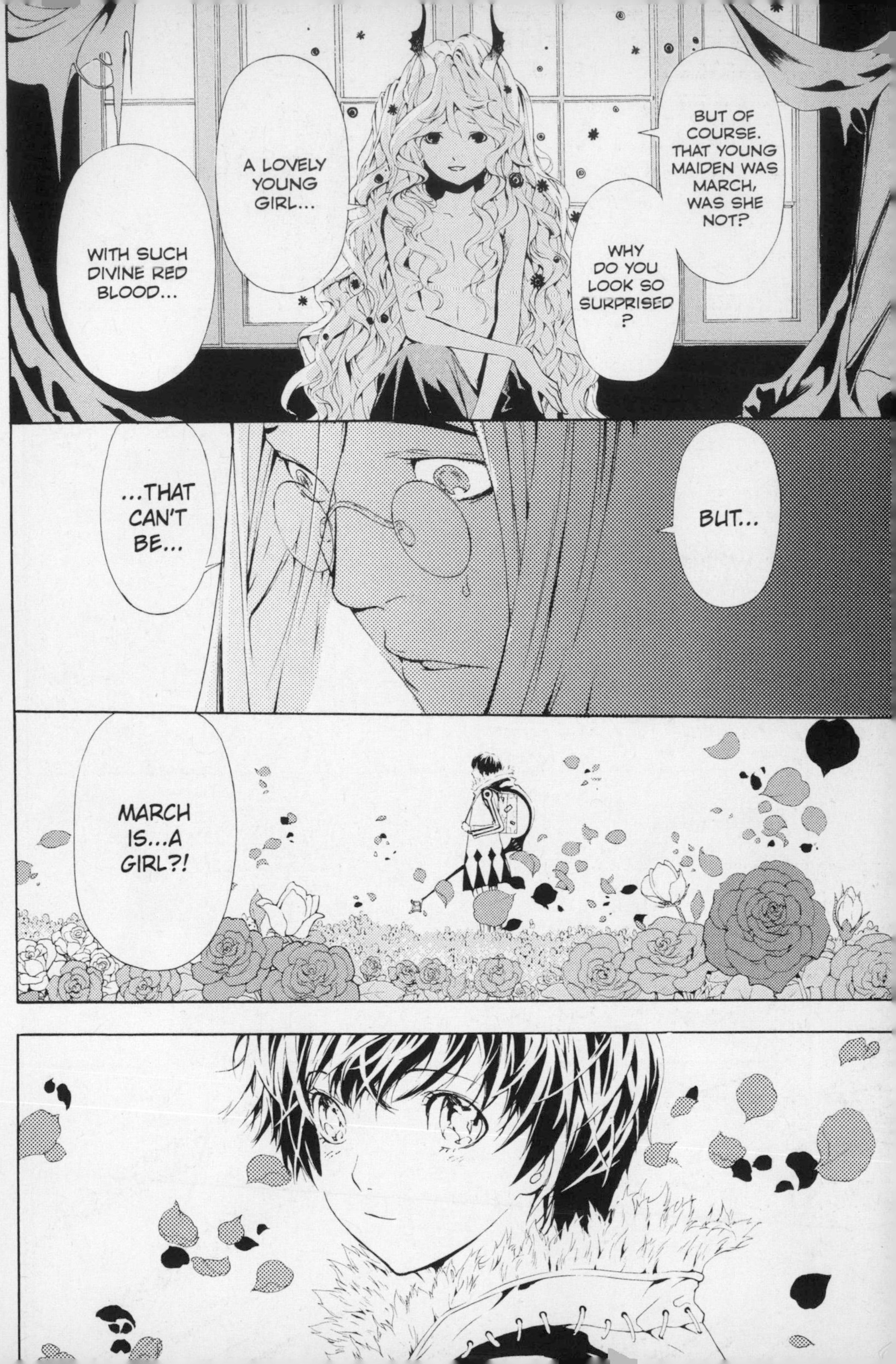
BUT OF COURSE. THAT YOUNG MAIDEN WAS MARCH, WAS SHE NOT?
WHY DO YOU LOOK SO SURPRISED?
A LOVELY YOUNG GIRL...
WITH SUCH DIVINE RED BLOOD...
BUT...
...THAT CAN'T BE...
MARCH IS...A GIRL?!

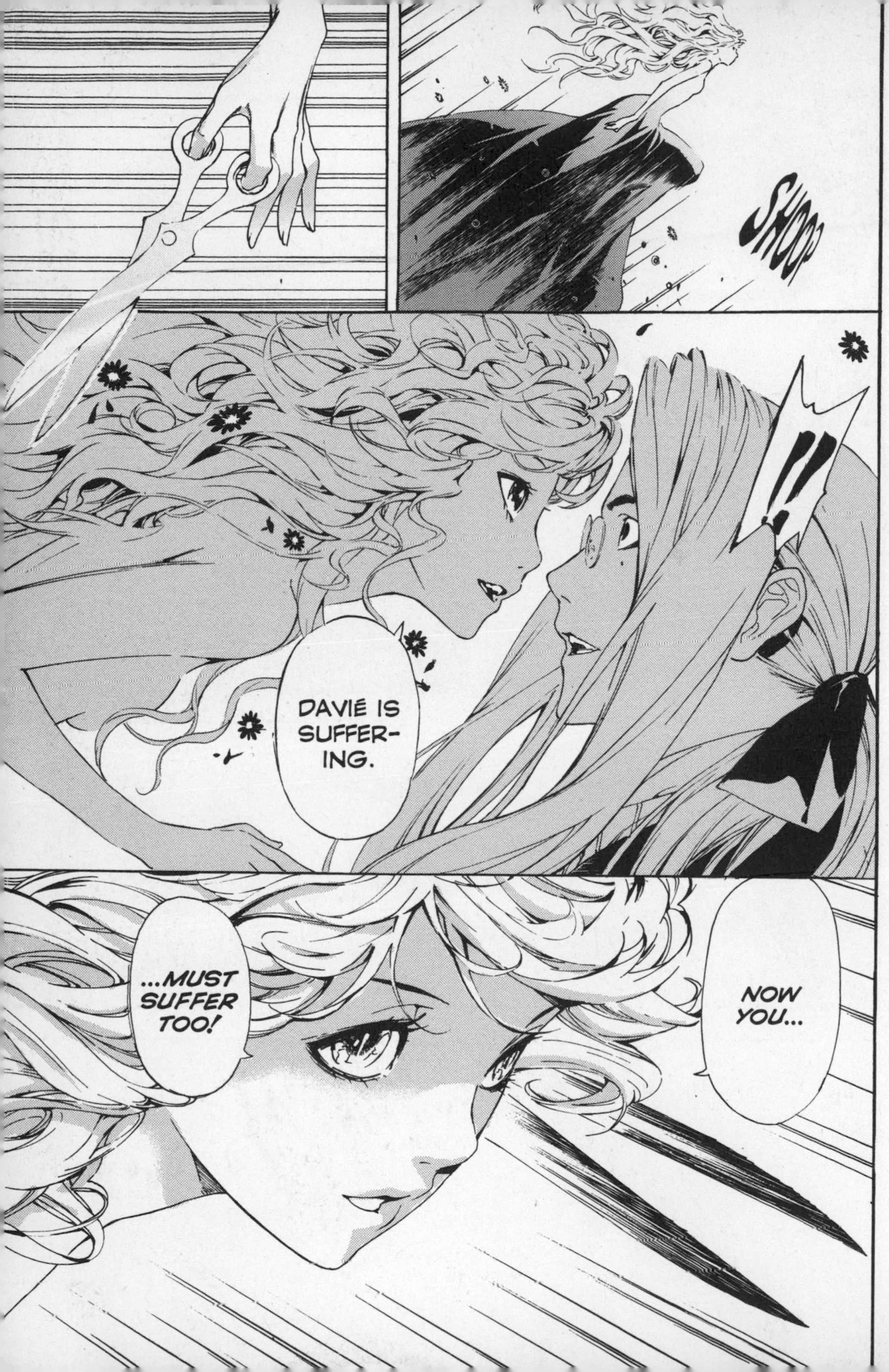
SHOOP
!!
DAVIÉ IS SUFFER-ING.
NOW YOU...
...MUST SUFFER TOO!

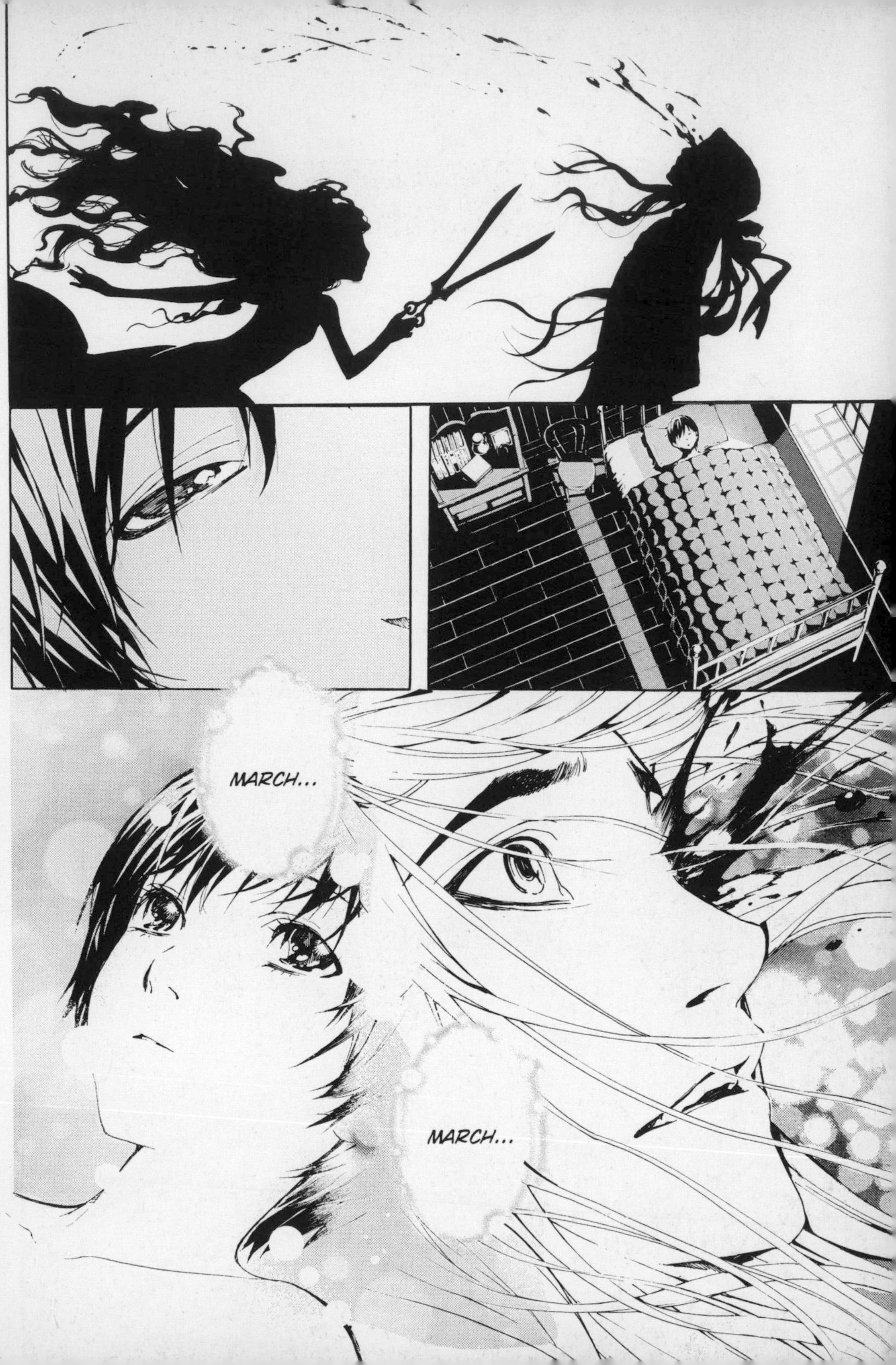
MARCH...
MARCH...

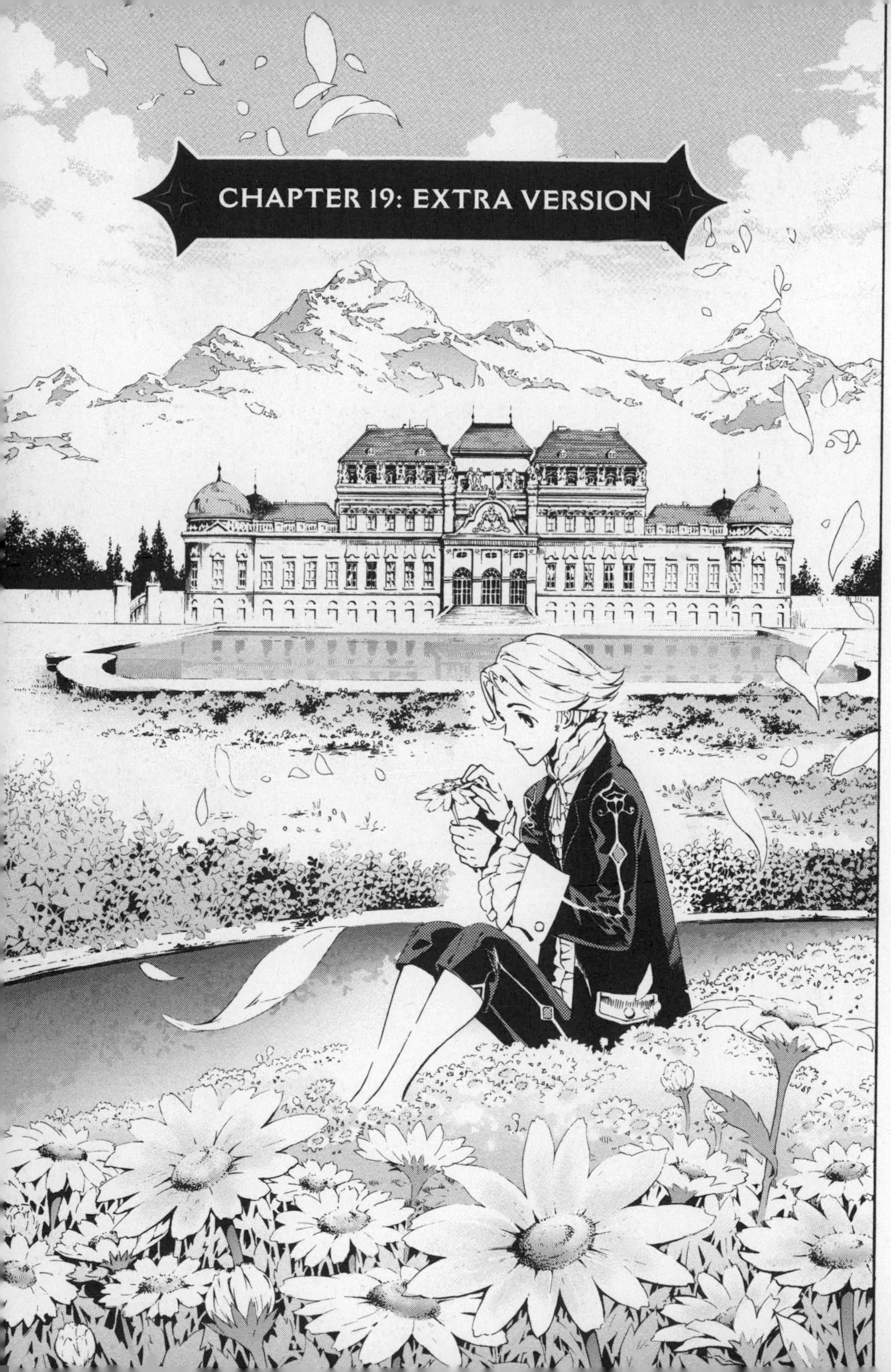
CHAPTER 19: EXTRA VERSION

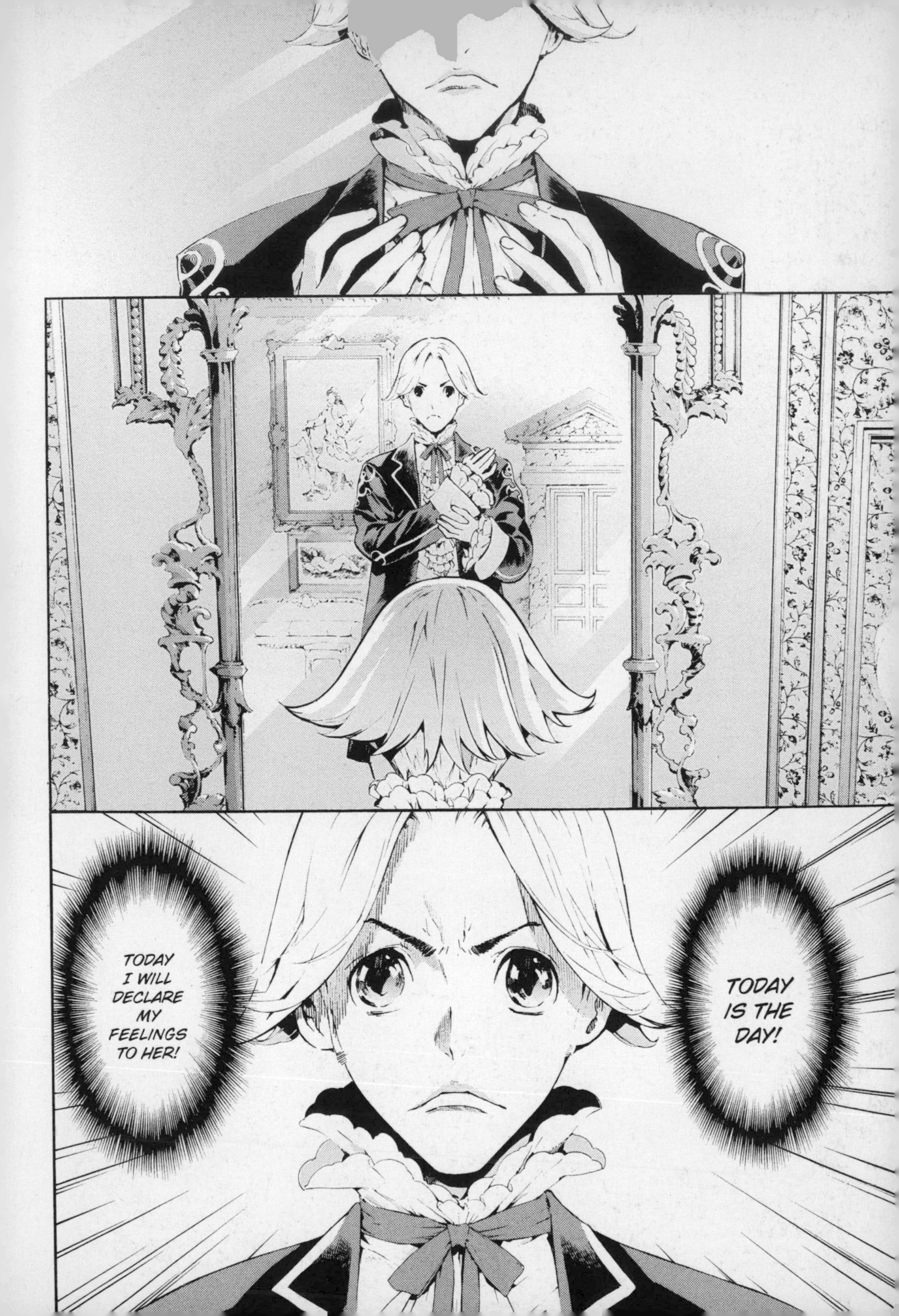
TODAY IS THE DAY!
TODAY I WILL DECLARE MY FEELINGS TO HER!

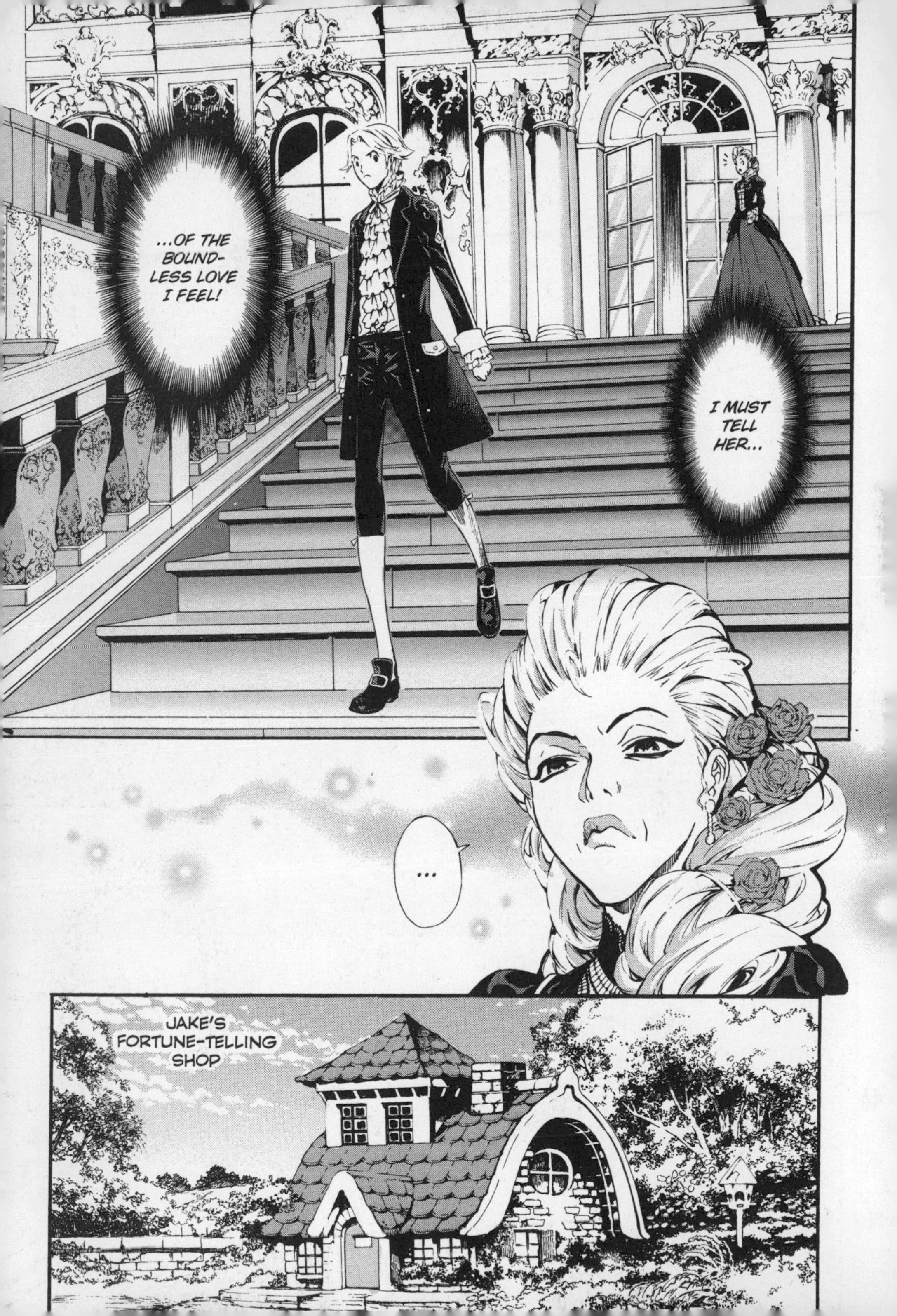
I MUST TELL HER...
...OF THE BOUND-LESS LOVE I FEEL!
...
JAKE'S FORTUNE-TELLING SHOP

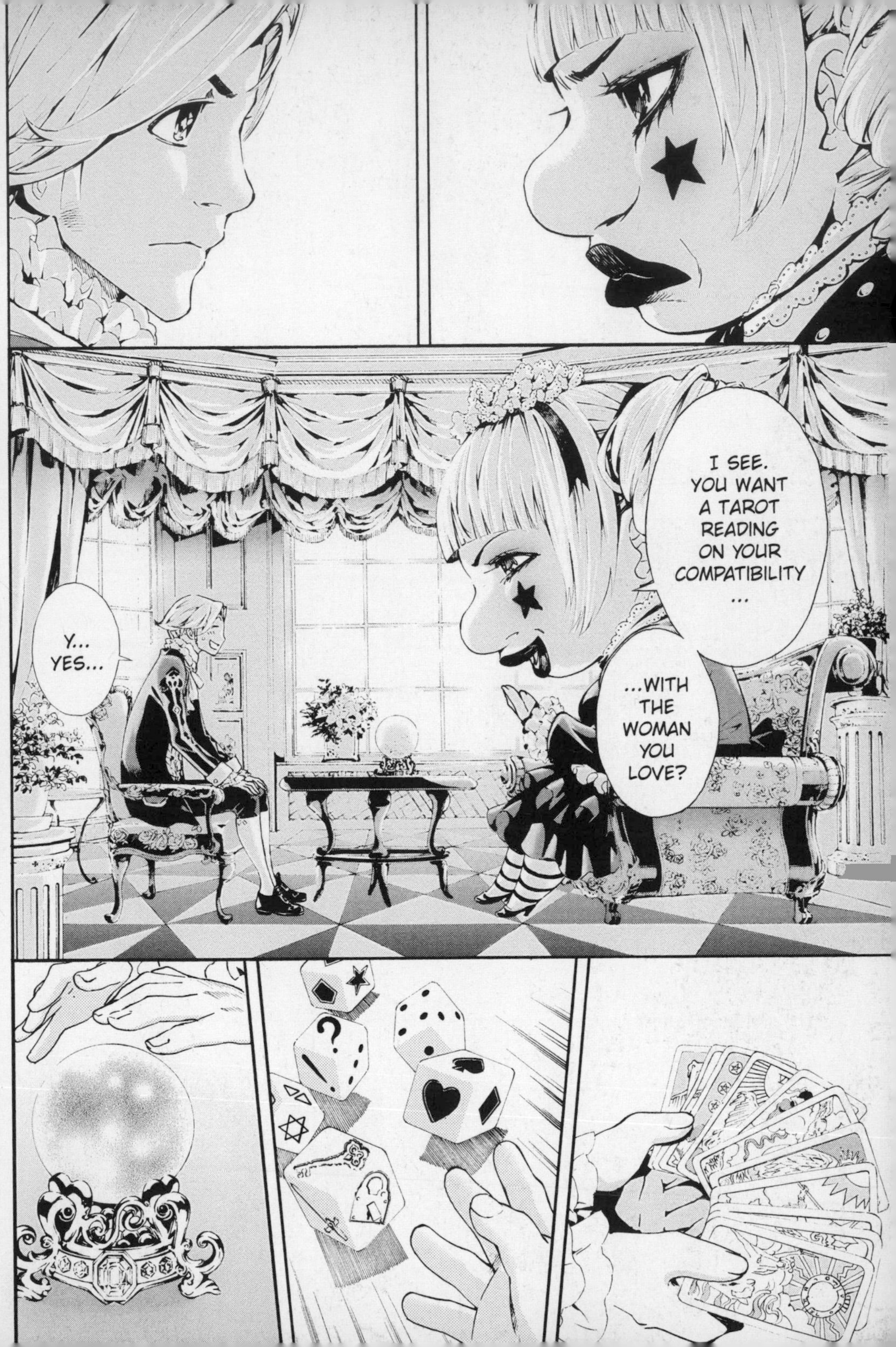
I SEE. YOU WANT A TAROT READING ON YOUR COMPATIBILITY ...
...WITH THE WOMAN YOU LOVE?
Y... YES...

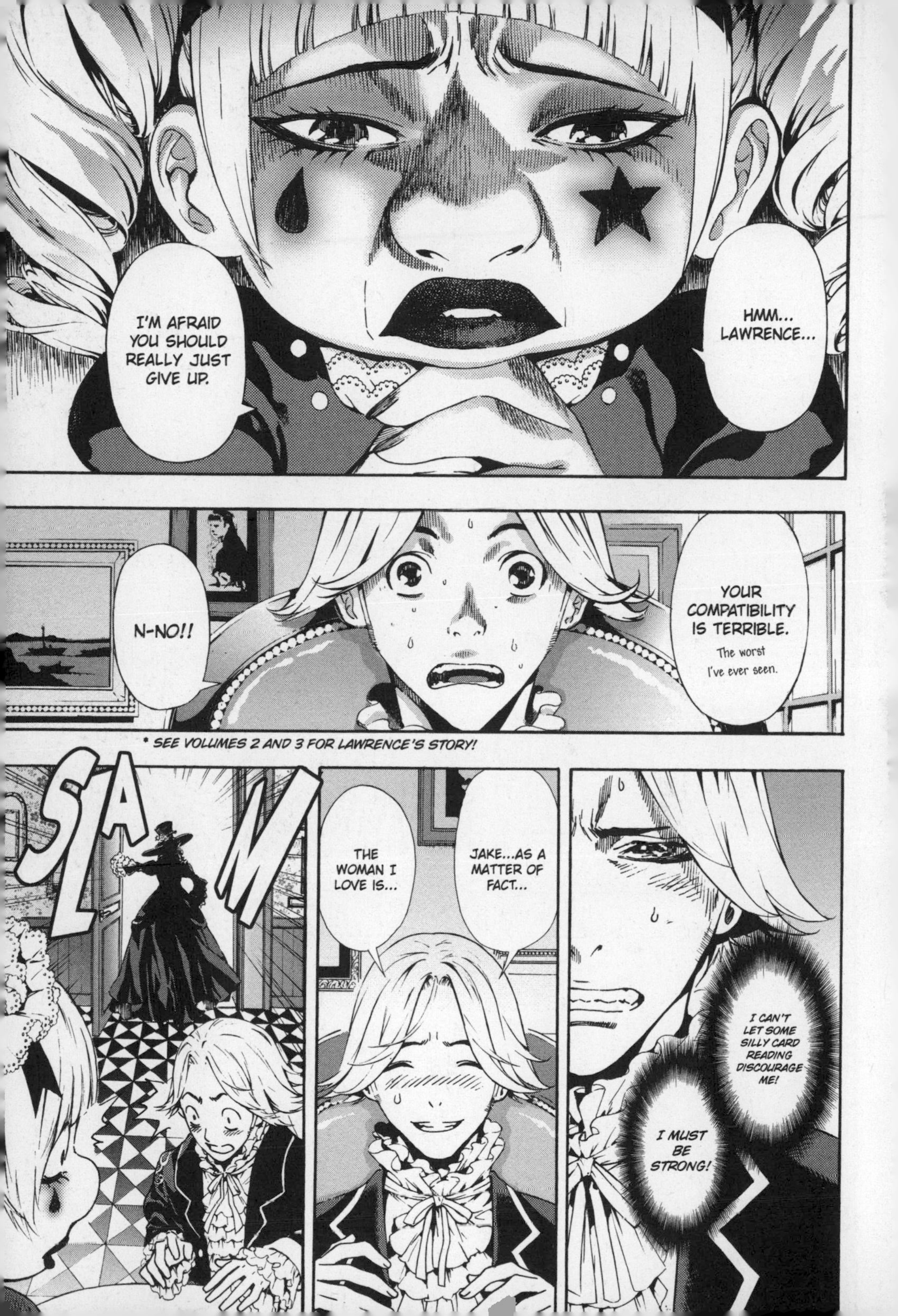
HMM... LAWRENCE...
I'M AFRAID YOU SHOULD REALLY JUST GIVE UP.
YOUR COMPATIBILITY IS TERRIBLE.
The worst I've ever seen.
N-NO!!
* SEE VOLUMES 2 AND 3 FOR LAWRENCE'S STORY!
I CAN'T LET SOME SILLY CARD READING DISCOURAGE ME!
I MUST BE STRONG!
JAKE...AS A MATTER OF FACT...
THE WOMAN I LOVE IS...
SLAM

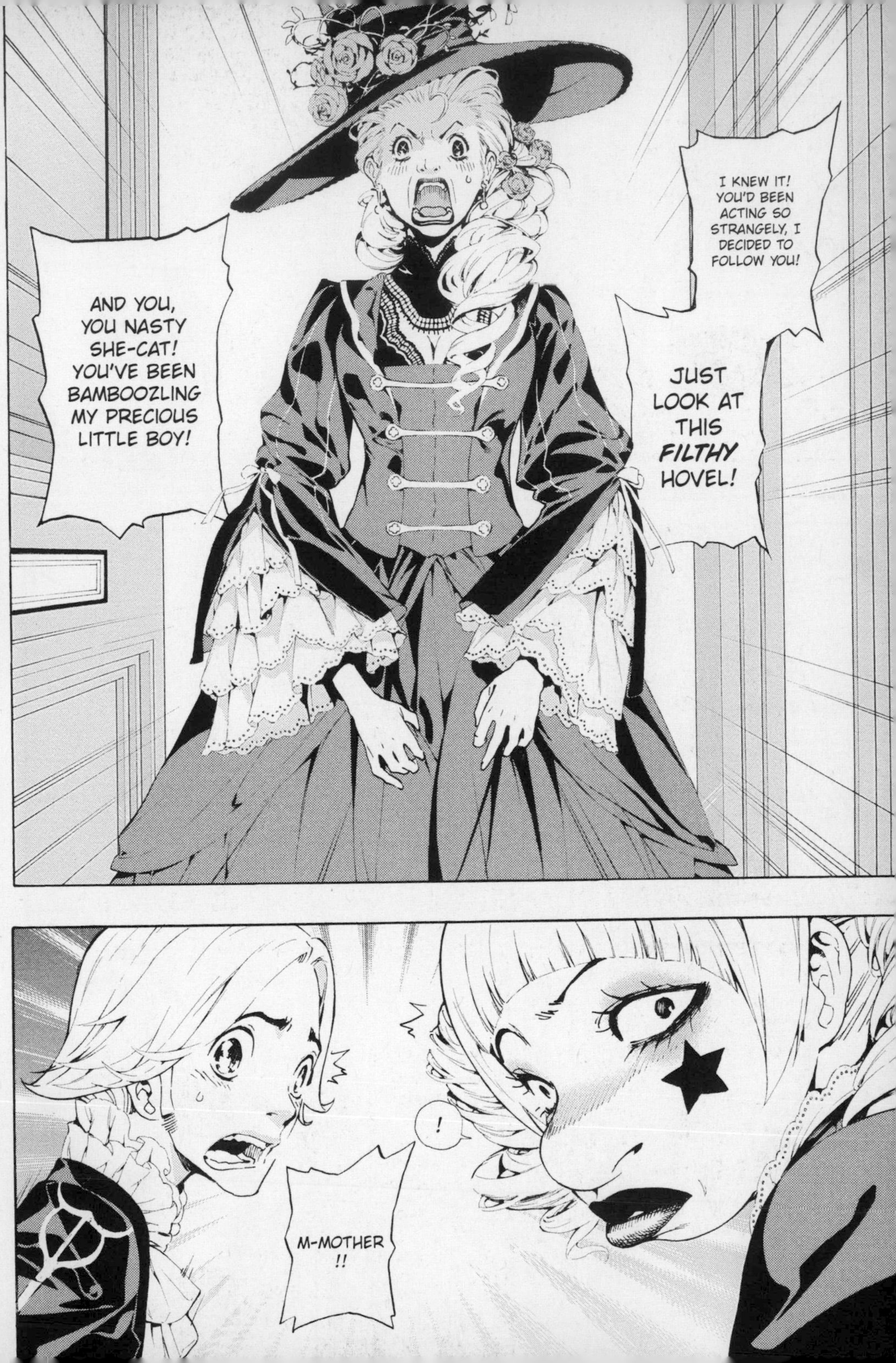
I KNEW IT! YOU'D BEEN ACTING SO STRANGELY, I DECIDED TO FOLLOW YOU!
JUST LOOK AT THIS *FILTHY* HOVEL!
AND YOU, YOU NASTY SHE-CAT! YOU'VE BEEN BAMBOOZLING MY PRECIOUS LITTLE BOY!
!
M-MOTHER !!

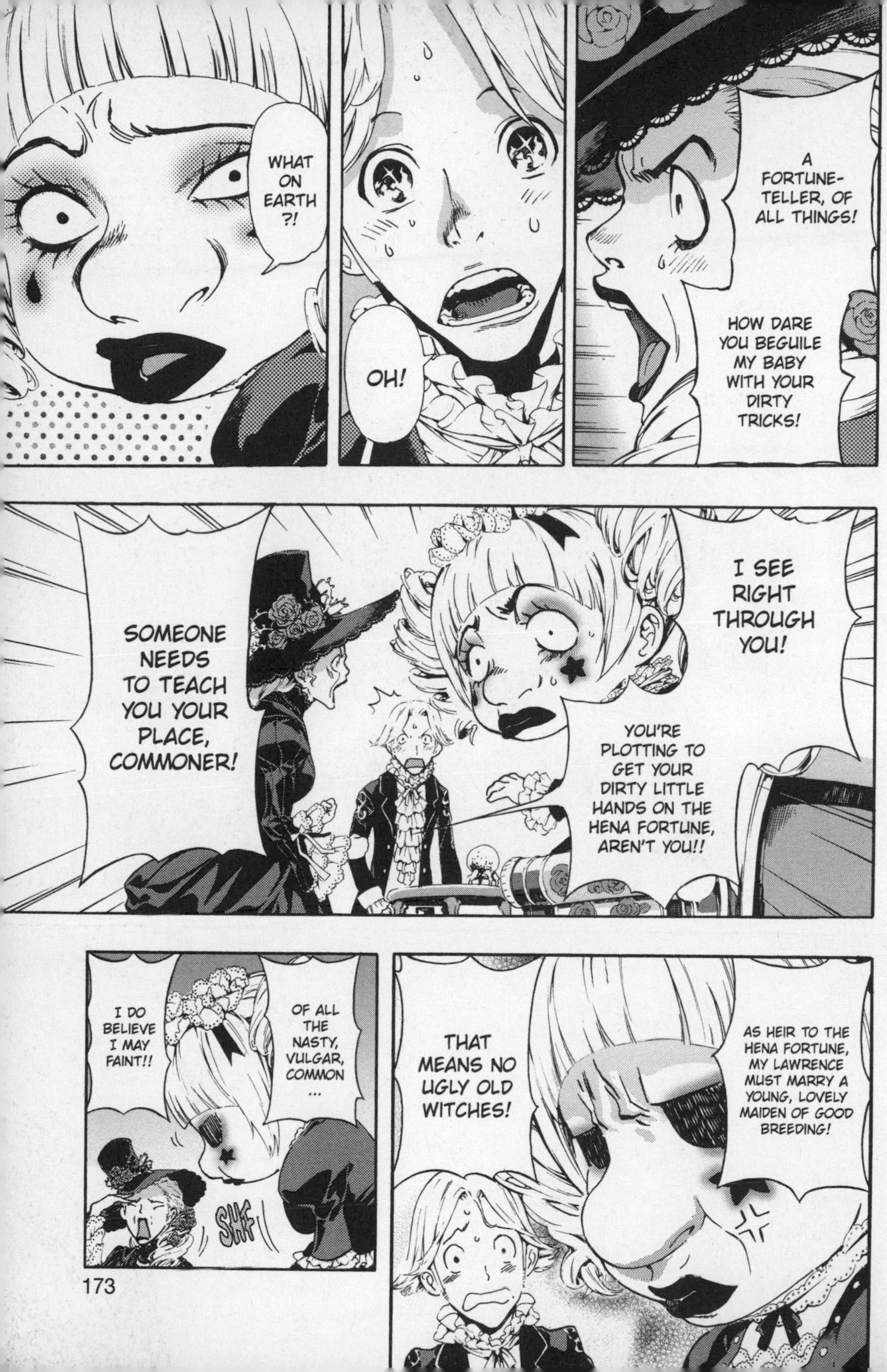
A FORTUNE-TELLER, OF ALL THINGS!
HOW DARE YOU BEGUILE MY BABY WITH YOUR DIRTY TRICKS!
OH!
WHAT ON EARTH ?!
I SEE RIGHT THROUGH YOU!
YOU'RE PLOTTING TO GET YOUR DIRTY LITTLE HANDS ON THE HENA FORTUNE, AREN'T YOU!!
SOMEONE NEEDS TO TEACH YOU YOUR PLACE, COMMONER!
AS HEIR TO THE HENA FORTUNE, MY LAWRENCE MUST MARRY A YOUNG, LOVELY MAIDEN OF GOOD BREEDING!
THAT MEANS NO UGLY OLD WITCHES!
OF ALL THE NASTY, VULGAR, COMMON ...
I DO BELIEVE I MAY FAINT!!
SNIF

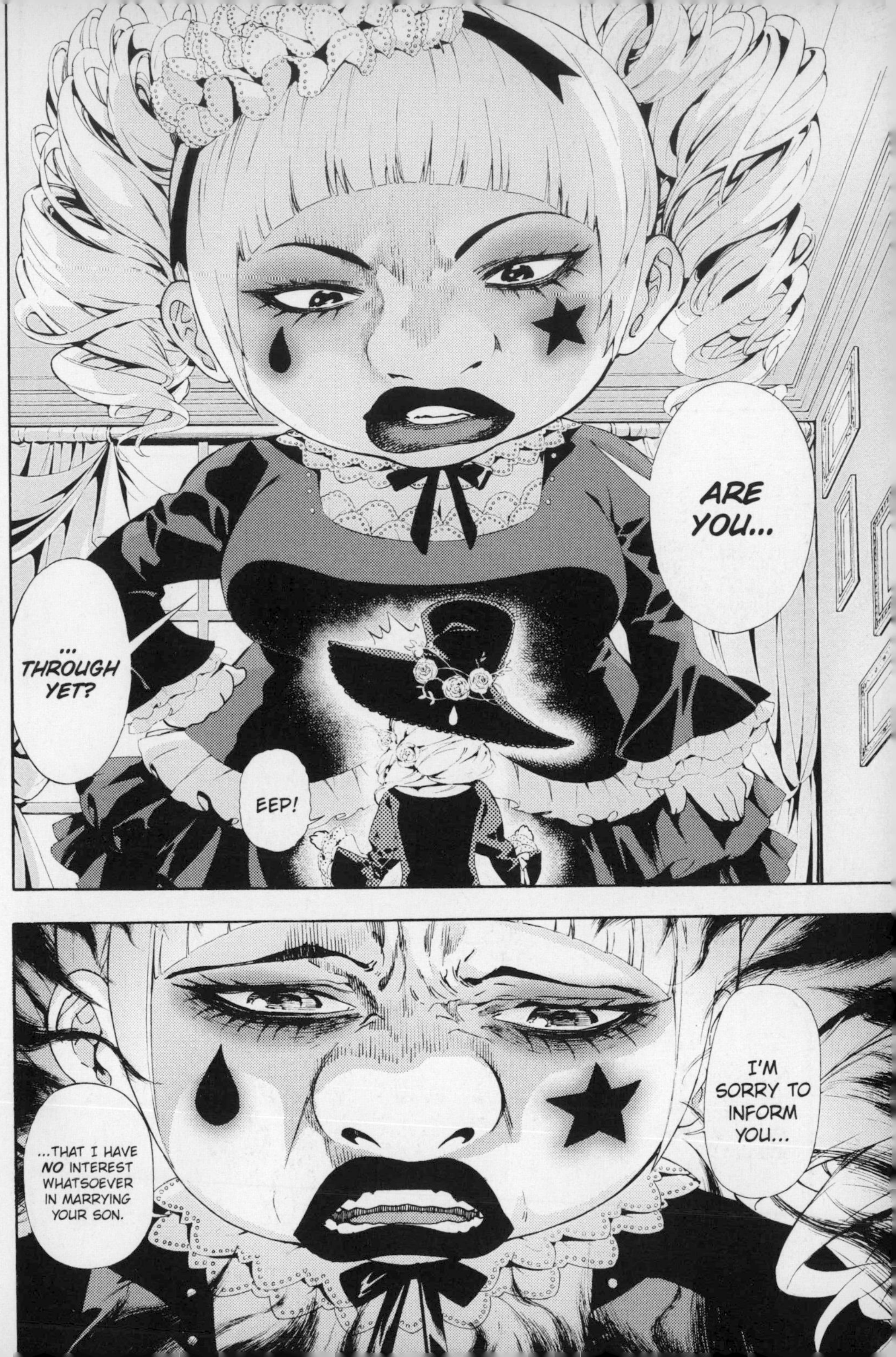
ARE YOU...
... THROUGH YET?
EEP!
I'M SORRY TO INFORM YOU...
...THAT I HAVE ***NO*** INTEREST WHATSOEVER IN MARRYING YOUR SON.

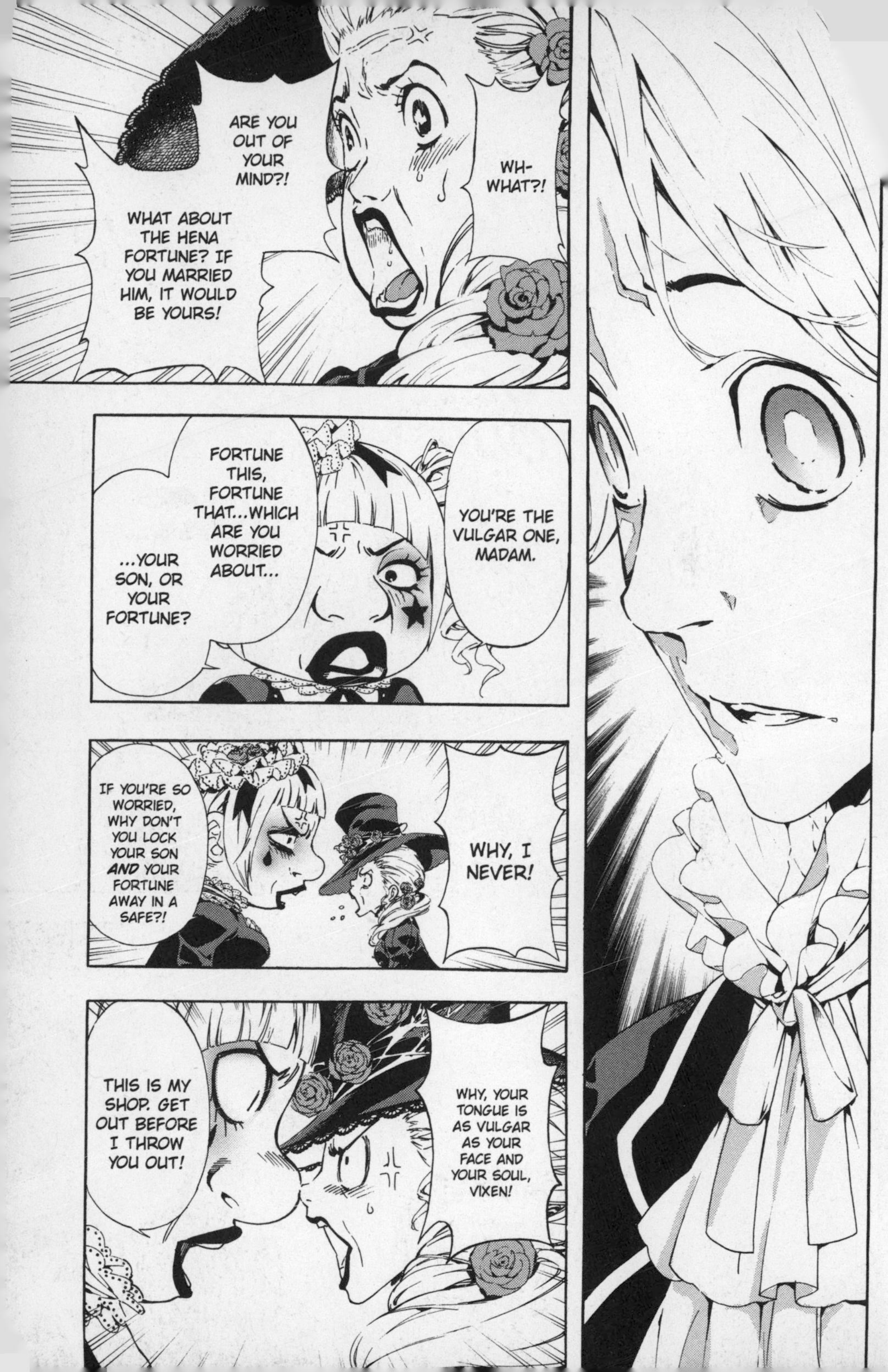
WH-WHAT?!
ARE YOU OUT OF YOUR MIND?!
WHAT ABOUT THE HENA FORTUNE? IF YOU MARRIED HIM, IT WOULD BE YOURS!
YOU'RE THE VULGAR ONE, MADAM.
FORTUNE THIS, FORTUNE THAT...WHICH ARE YOU WORRIED ABOUT...
...YOUR SON, OR YOUR FORTUNE?
WHY, I NEVER!
IF YOU'RE SO WORRIED, WHY DON'T YOU LOCK YOUR SON ***AND*** YOUR FORTUNE AWAY IN A SAFE?!
WHY, YOUR TONGUE IS AS VULGAR AS YOUR FACE AND YOUR SOUL, VIXEN!
THIS IS MY SHOP. GET OUT BEFORE I THROW YOU OUT!

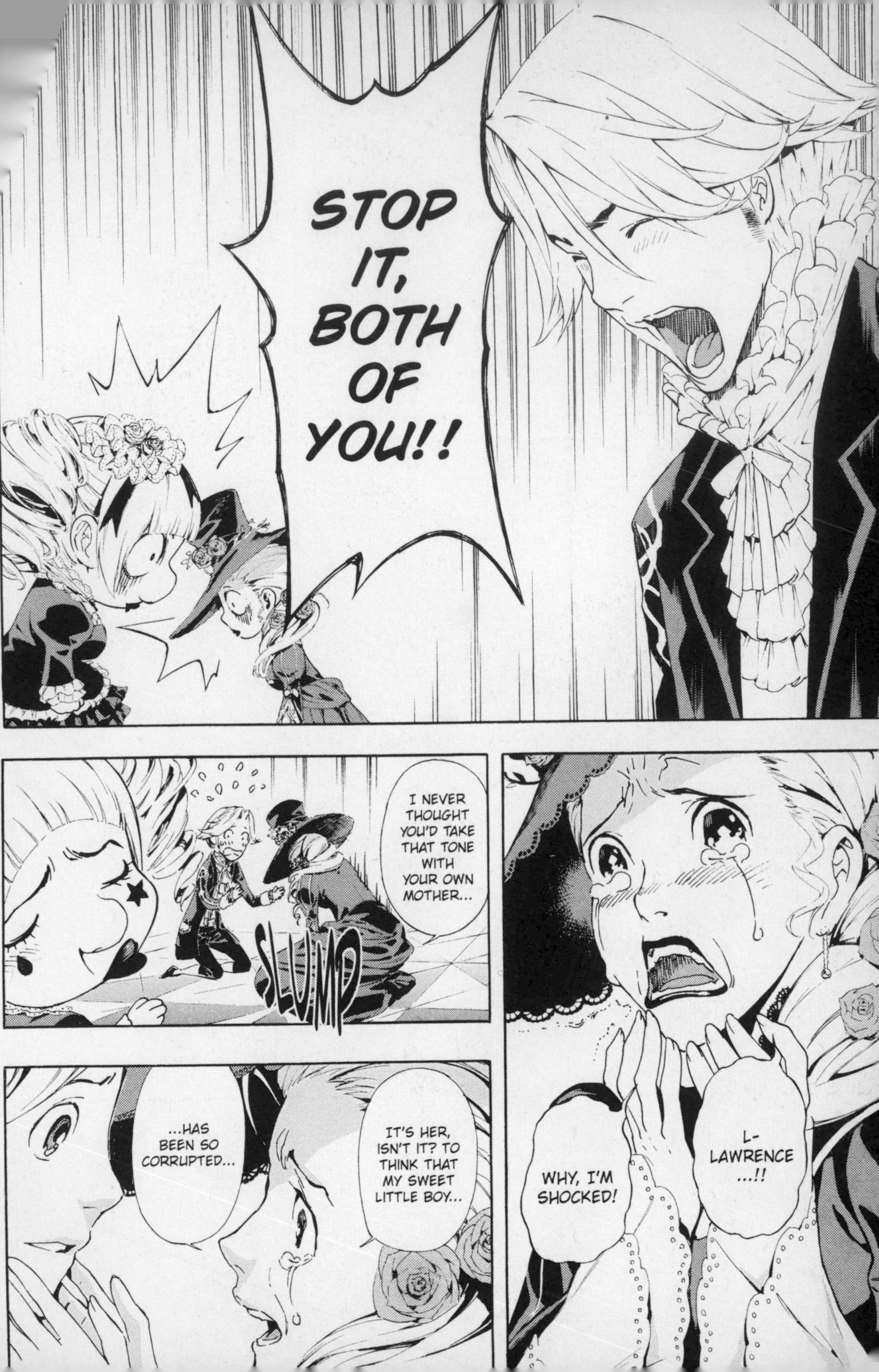
STOP IT, BOTH OF YOU!!
L- LAWRENCE ...!!
WHY, I'M SHOCKED!
I NEVER THOUGHT YOU'D TAKE THAT TONE WITH YOUR OWN MOTHER...
SLUMP
IT'S HER, ISN'T IT? TO THINK THAT MY SWEET LITTLE BOY...
...HAS BEEN SO CORRUPTED...

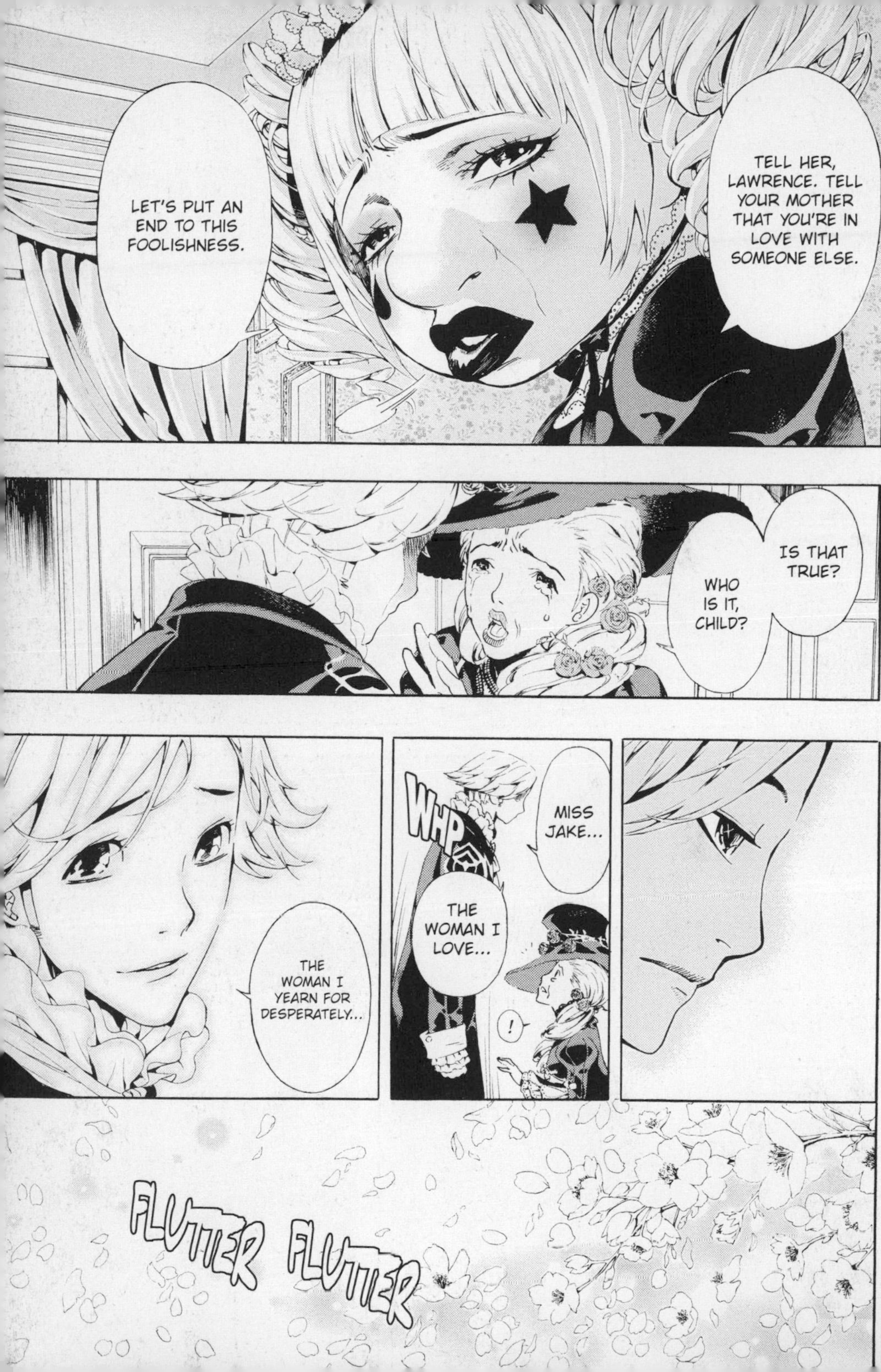
TELL HER, LAWRENCE. TELL YOUR MOTHER THAT YOU'RE IN LOVE WITH SOMEONE ELSE.
LET'S PUT AN END TO THIS FOOLISHNESS.
IS THAT TRUE?
WHO IS IT, CHILD?
MISS JAKE...
WHP
THE WOMAN I LOVE...
!
THE WOMAN I YEARN FOR DESPERATELY...
FLUTTER FLUTTER

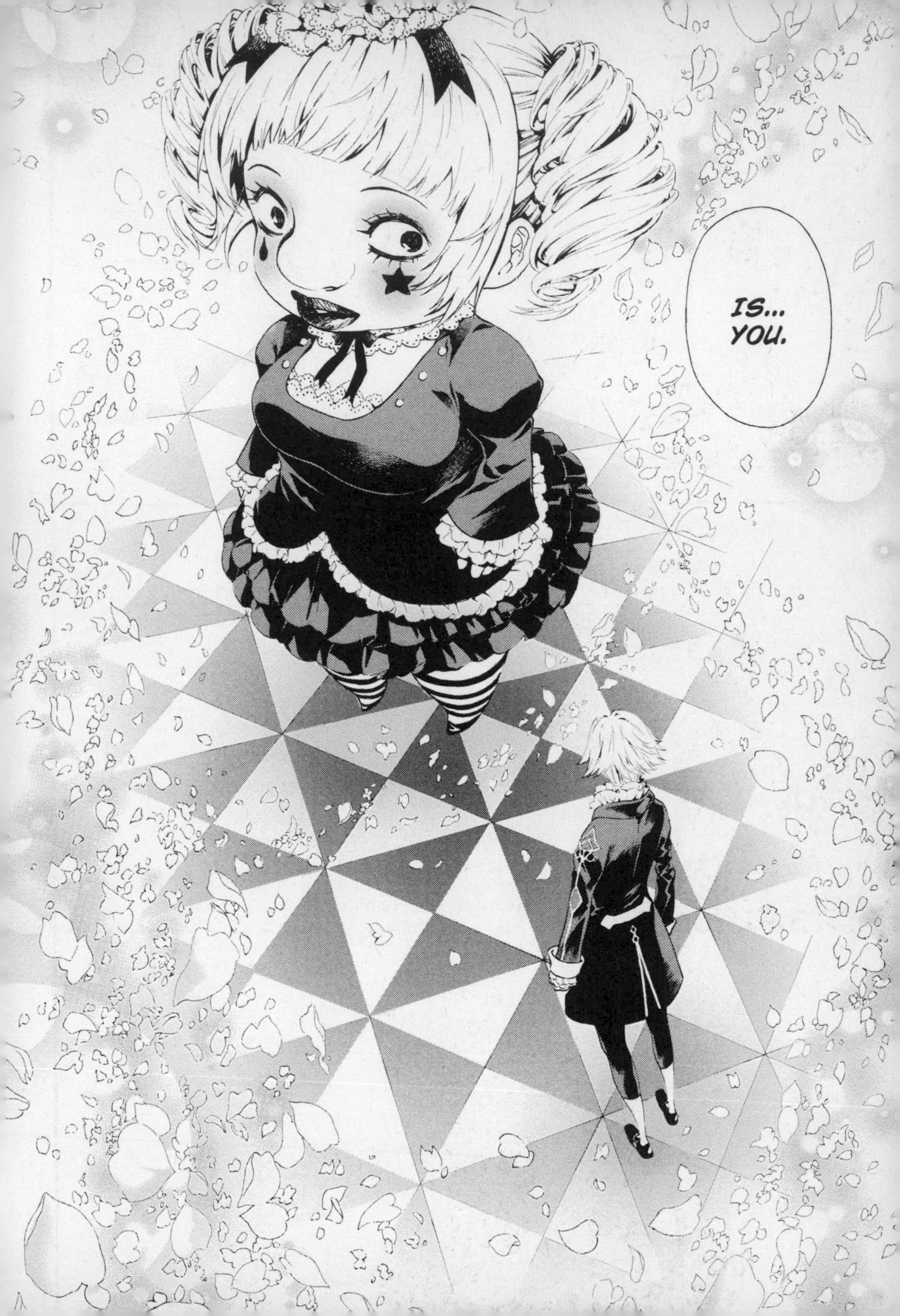
IS... YOU.

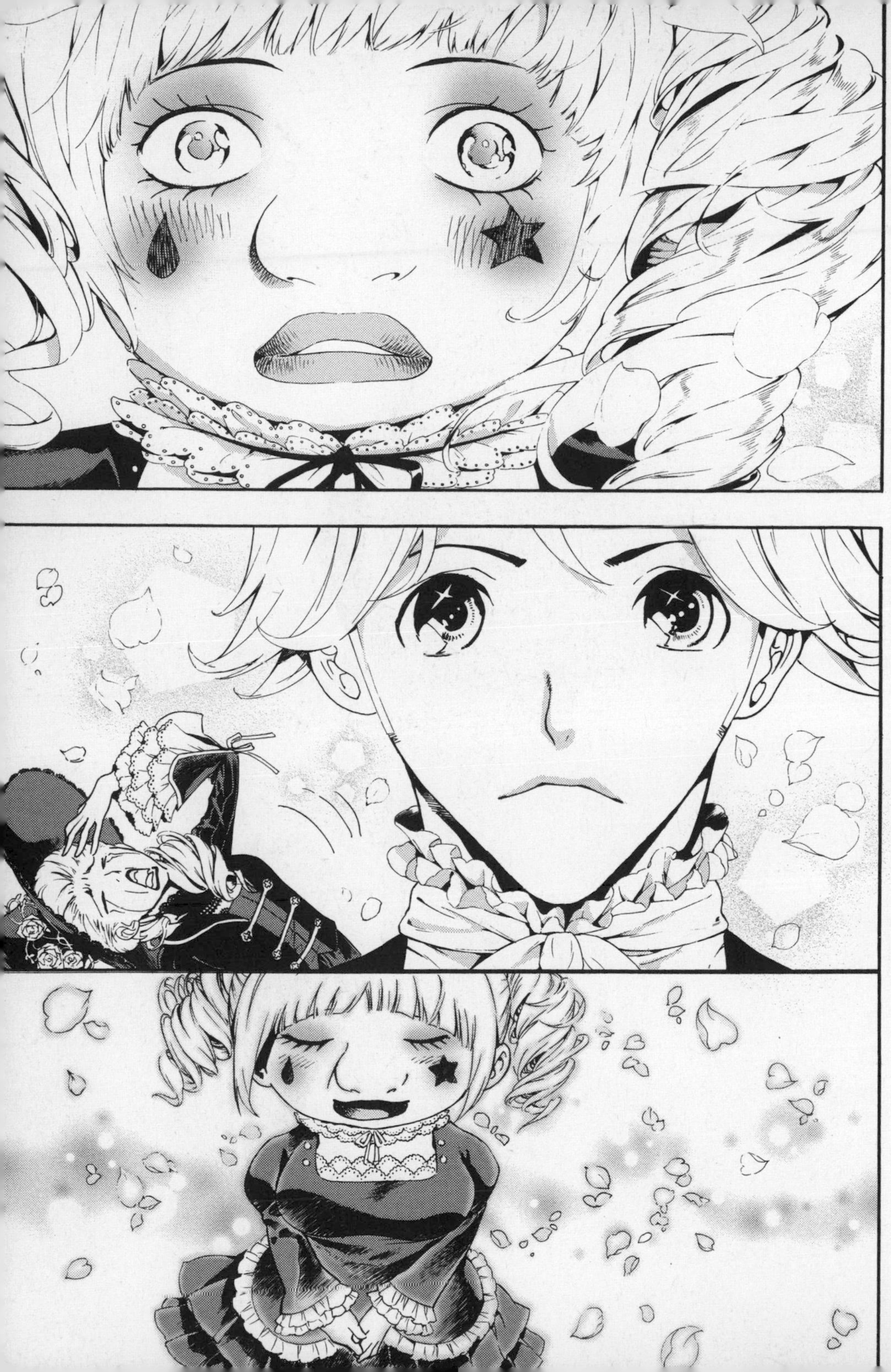

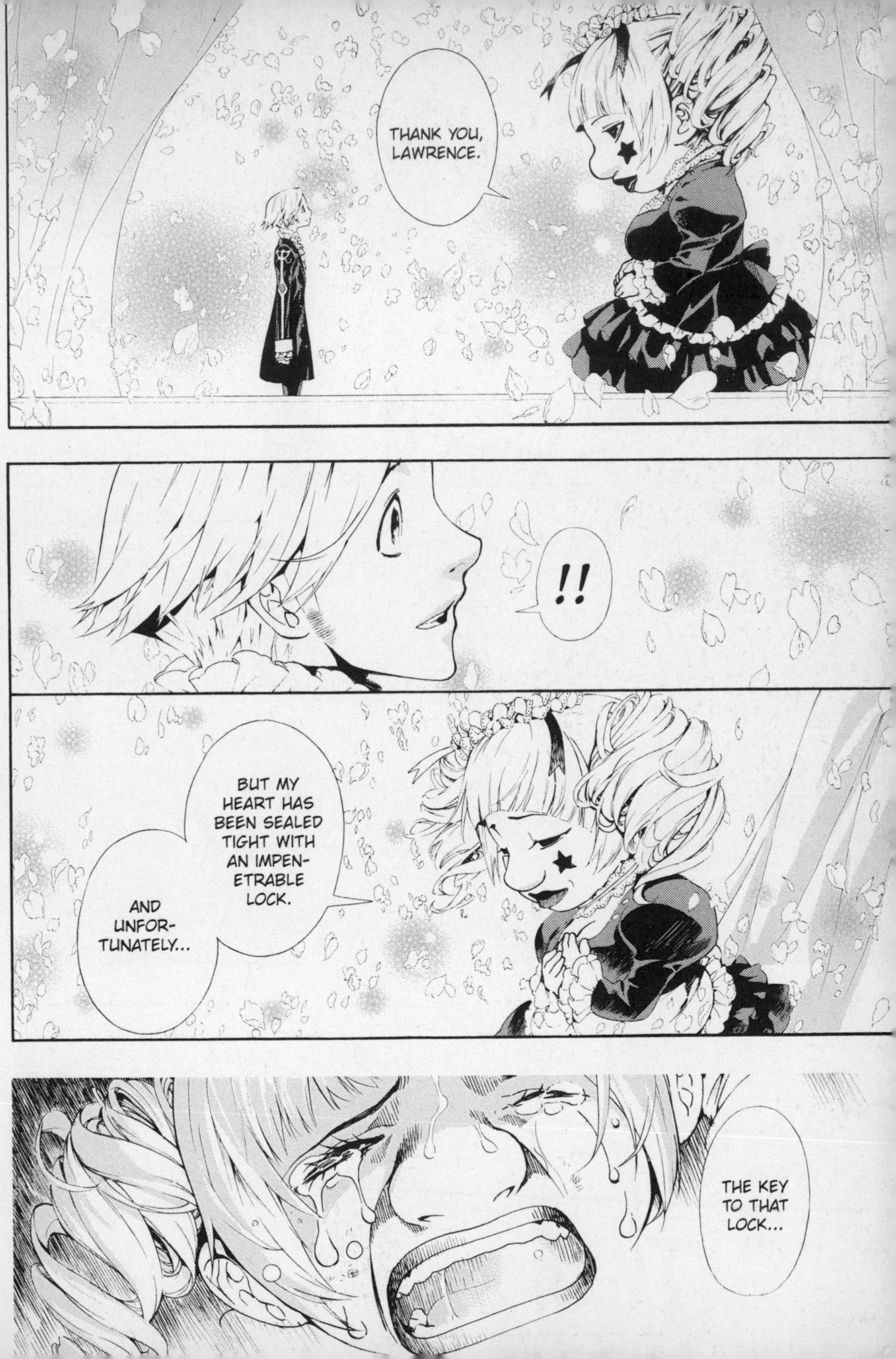
THANK YOU, LAWRENCE.
!!
BUT MY HEART HAS BEEN SEALED TIGHT WITH AN IMPENETRABLE LOCK.
AND UNFORTUNATELY...
THE KEY TO THAT LOCK...

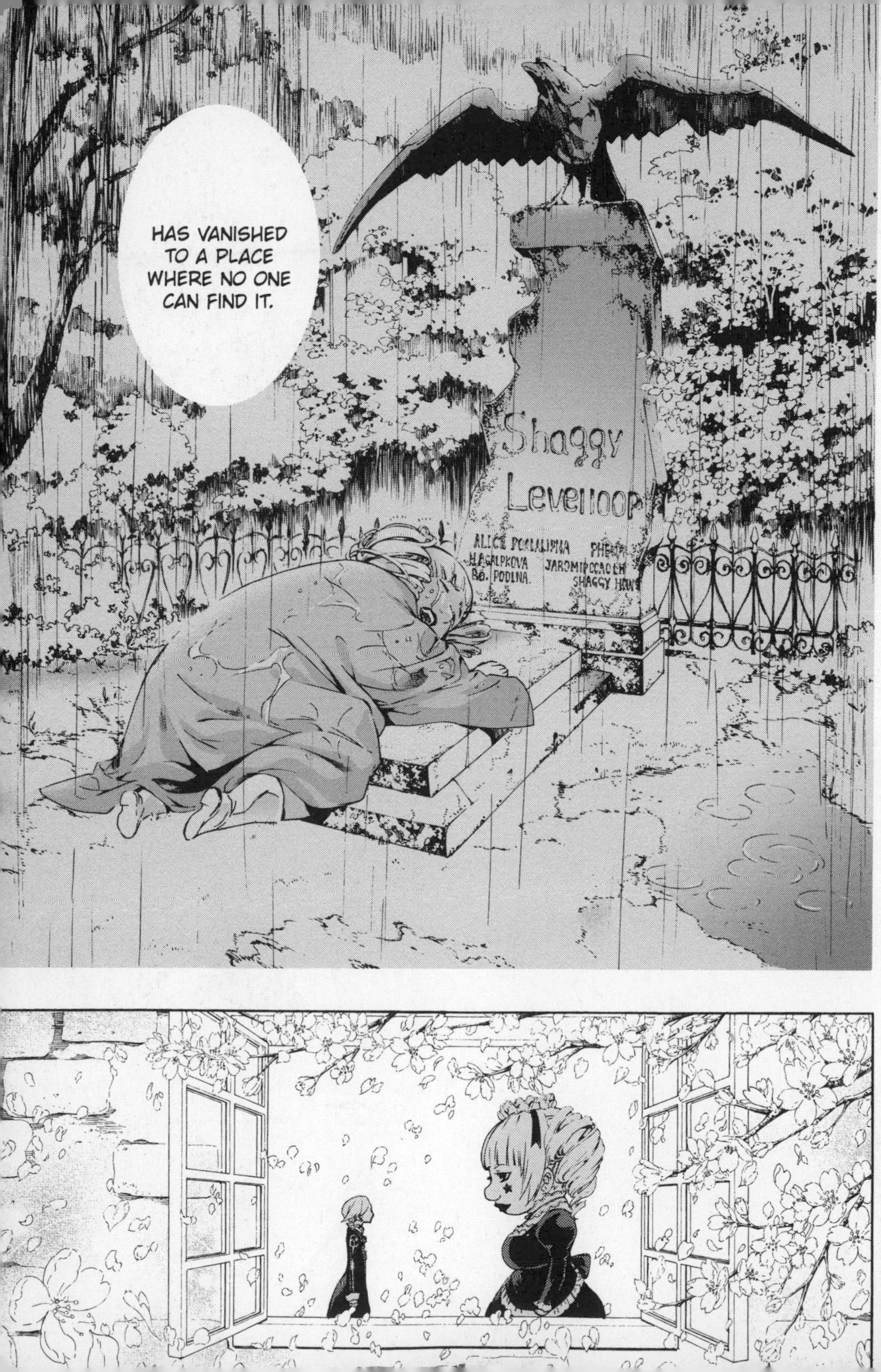
HAS VANISHED TO A PLACE WHERE NO ONE CAN FIND IT.
Shaggy

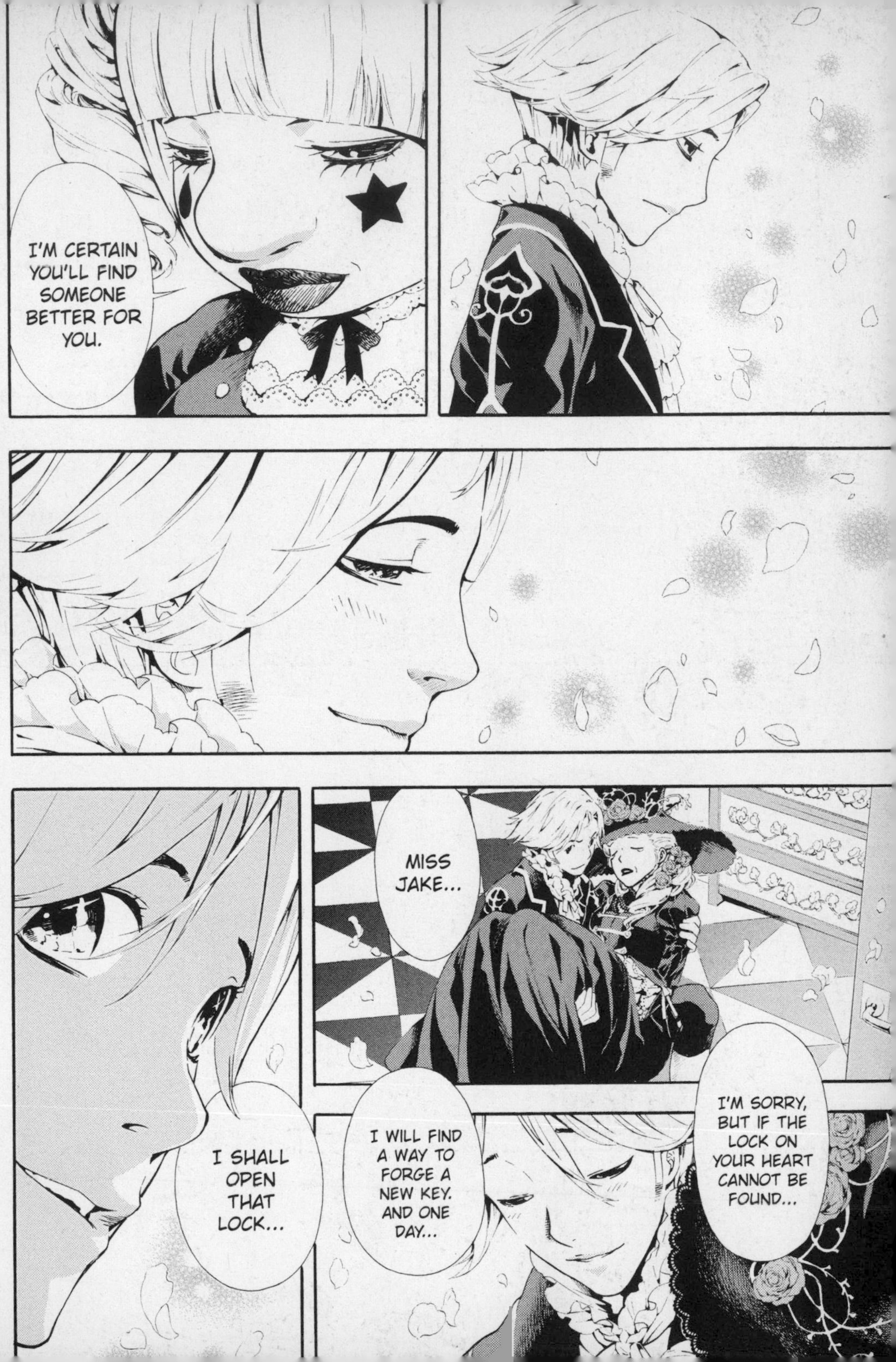
I'M CERTAIN YOU'LL FIND SOMEONE BETTER FOR YOU.
MISS JAKE...
I'M SORRY, BUT IF THE LOCK ON YOUR HEART CANNOT BE FOUND...
I WILL FIND A WAY TO FORGE A NEW KEY. AND ONE DAY...
I SHALL OPEN THAT LOCK...

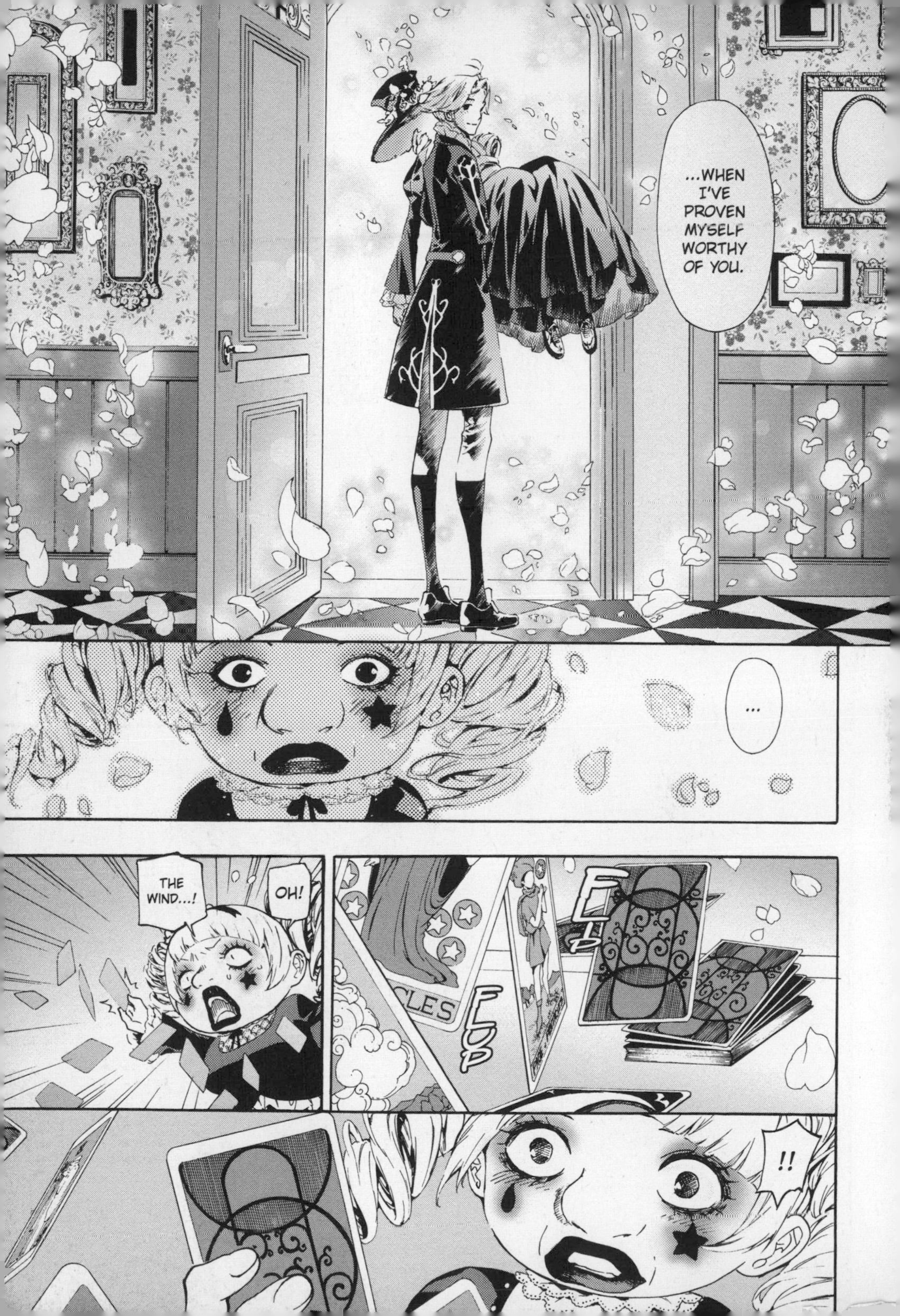
...WHEN I'VE PROVEN MYSELF WORTHY OF YOU.
...
OH!
THE WIND...!
!!

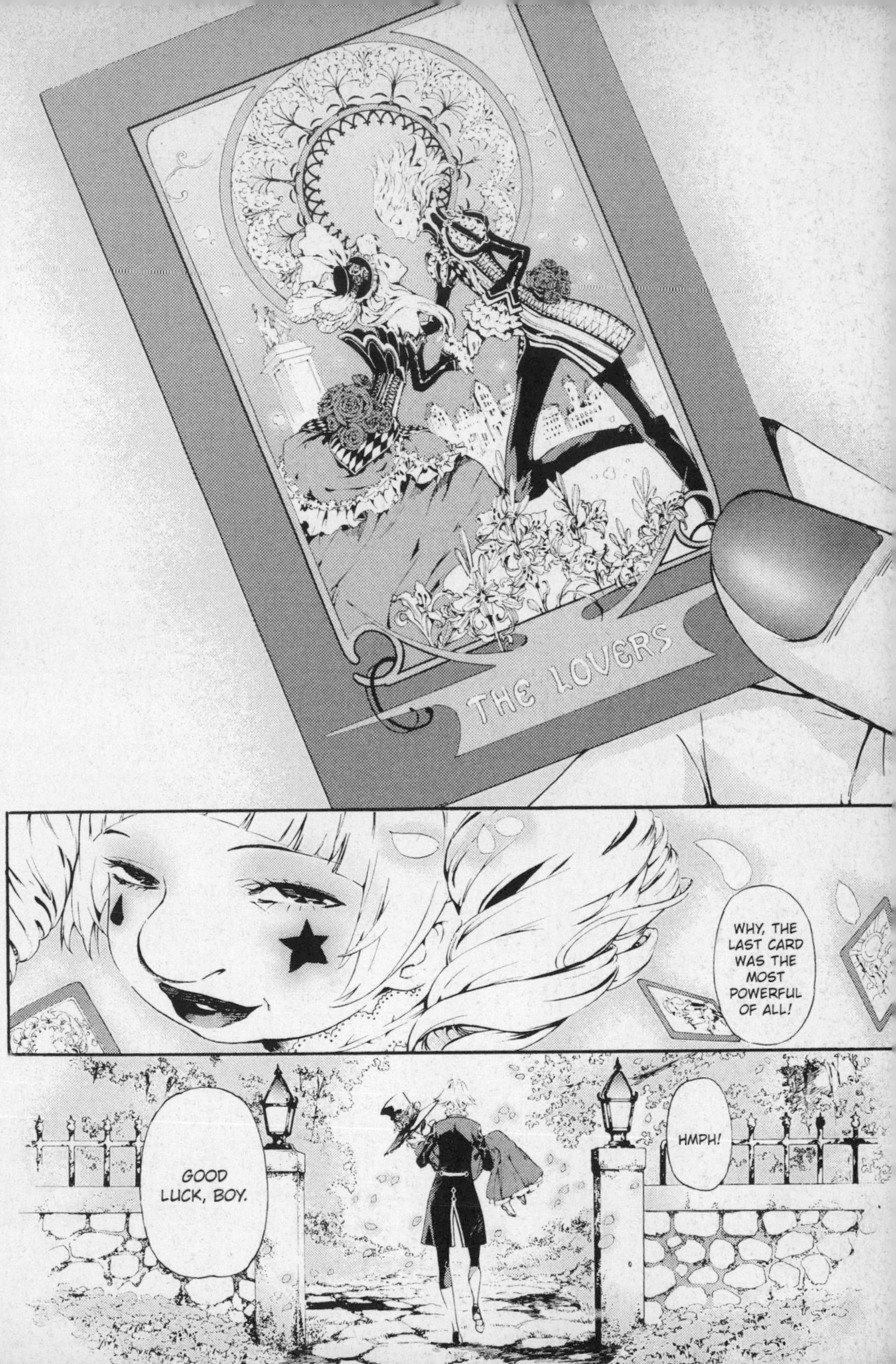
THE LOVERS
WHY, THE LAST CARD WAS THE MOST POWERFUL OF ALL!
HMPH!
GOOD LUCK, BOY.

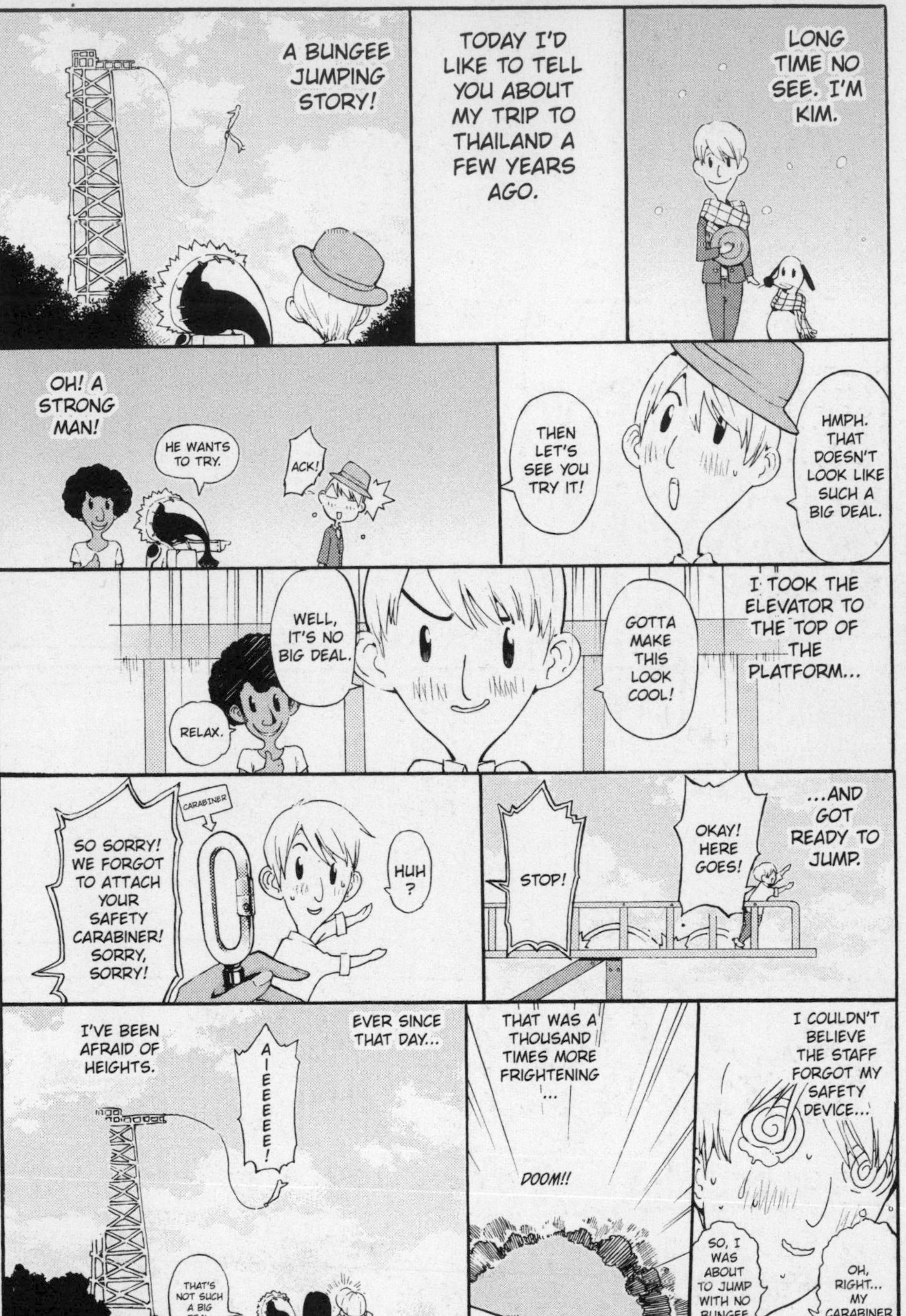
LONG TIME NO SEE. I'M KIM.
TODAY I'D LIKE TO TELL YOU ABOUT MY TRIP TO THAILAND A FEW YEARS AGO.
A BUNGEE JUMPING STORY!
HMPH. THAT DOESN'T LOOK LIKE SUCH A BIG DEAL.
THEN LET'S SEE YOU TRY IT!
OH! A STRONG MAN!
HE WANTS TO TRY.
ACK!
I TOOK THE ELEVATOR TO THE TOP OF THE PLATFORM...
GOTTA MAKE THIS LOOK COOL!
WELL, IT'S NO BIG DEAL.
RELAX.
...AND GOT READY TO JUMP.
OKAY! HERE GOES!
STOP!
HUH?
CARABINER
SO SORRY! WE FORGOT TO ATTACH YOUR SAFETY CARABINER! SORRY, SORRY!
I COULDN'T BELIEVE THE STAFF FORGOT MY SAFETY DEVICE...
OH, RIGHT... MY CARABINER...
SO, I WAS ABOUT TO JUMP WITH NO BUNGEE CORD?!
THAT WAS A THOUSAND TIMES MORE FRIGHTENING...
DOOM!!
EVER SINCE THAT DAY...
I'VE BEEN AFRAID OF HEIGHTS.
AIEEEEE!
THAT'S NOT SUCH A BIG DEAL.

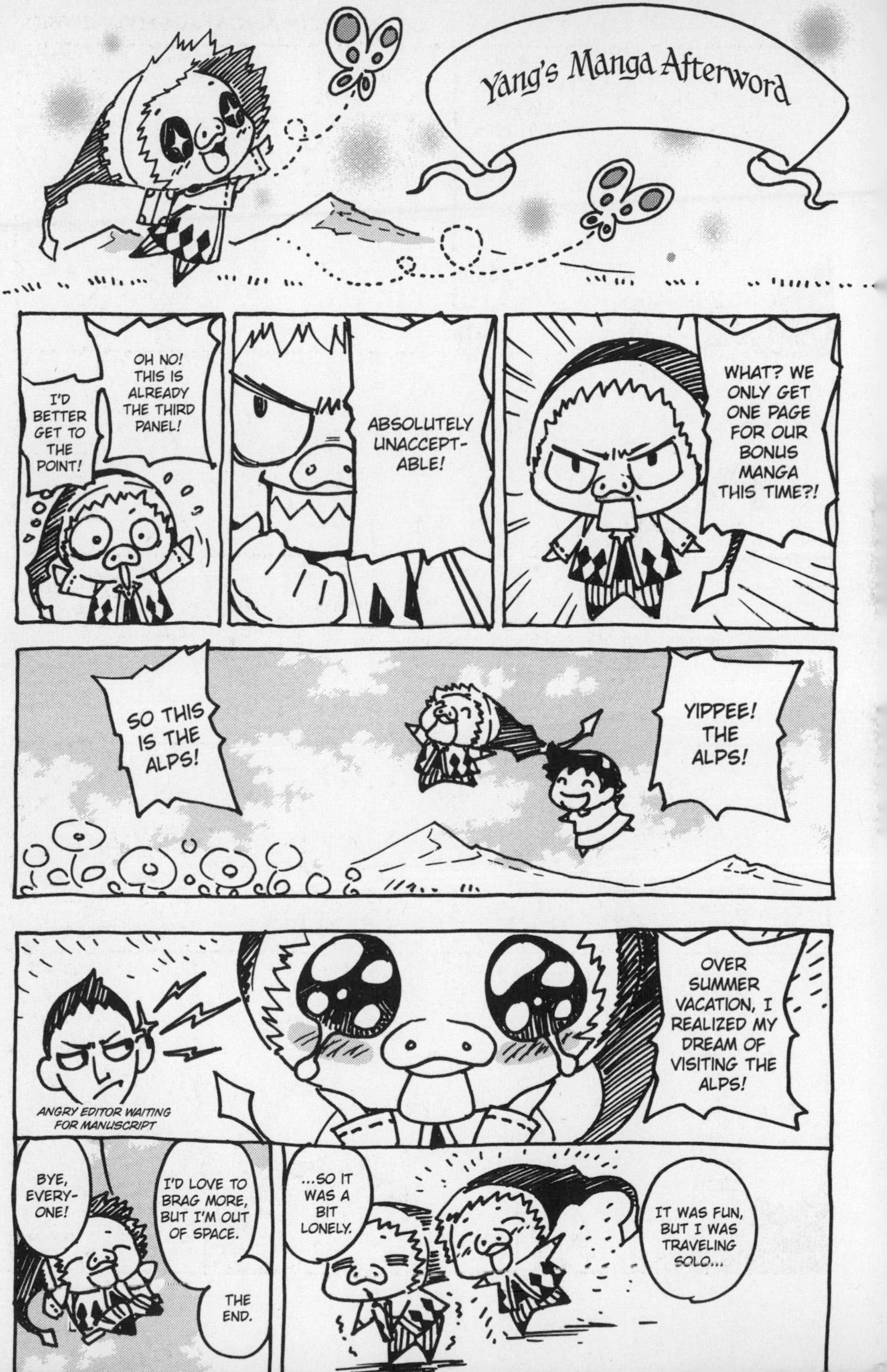
Yang's Manga Afterword
WHAT? WE ONLY GET ONE PAGE FOR OUR BONUS MANGA THIS TIME?!
ABSOLUTELY UNACCEPTABLE!
OH NO! THIS IS ALREADY THE THIRD PANEL!
I'D BETTER GET TO THE POINT!
YIPPEE! THE ALPS!
SO THIS IS THE ALPS!
OVER SUMMER VACATION, I REALIZED MY DREAM OF VISITING THE ALPS!
ANGRY EDITOR WAITING FOR MANUSCRIPT
IT WAS FUN, BUT I WAS TRAVELING SOLO...
...SO IT WAS A BIT LONELY.
I'D LOVE TO BRAG MORE, BUT I'M OUT OF SPACE.
BYE, EVERYONE!
THE END.

YANG KYUNG-IL

Yang kyung-il was born March 26, 1970. His debut work, *Soma Shinhwa Jeongi*, appeared in *Weekly Shonen Champ* in Korea. Notable works include *Zombie Hunter* (original story by Kazumasa Hirai) and *Shin Angyo Onshi* (*Blade of the Phantom Master*, original story by In Wan Youn). Yang also works on *Defense Devil*, currently serialized in *Weekly Shonen Sunday*.

KIM HYUNG-MIN

Kim Hyung-min was born in Jinju, Korea, on December 29, 1978. In 2002 he entered the manga world, and in 2007 he debuted as an original storywriter with *March Story*, published in *Sunday GX*.

MARCH STORY

Volume 4
VIZ Signature Edition

Story by **Kim Hyung-min**
Art by **Yang kyung-il**

© 2008 Kim Hyung-min, Yang kyung-il/Shogakukan
All rights reserved.
Original Japanese edition "MARCH STORY" published by SHOGAKUKAN Inc.

Logo design by Bay Bridge Studio

Translation & English Adaptation / Camellia Nieh
Touch-up Art & Lettering / John Hunt, Primary Graphix
Design / Sam Elzway
Editor / Mike Montesa

Printed in the U.S.A

Published by VIZ Media, LLC
P.O. Box 77010
San Francisco, CA 94107

10 9 8 7 6 5 4 3 2 1
First printing, October 2012

VIZ SIGNATURE

www.viz.com

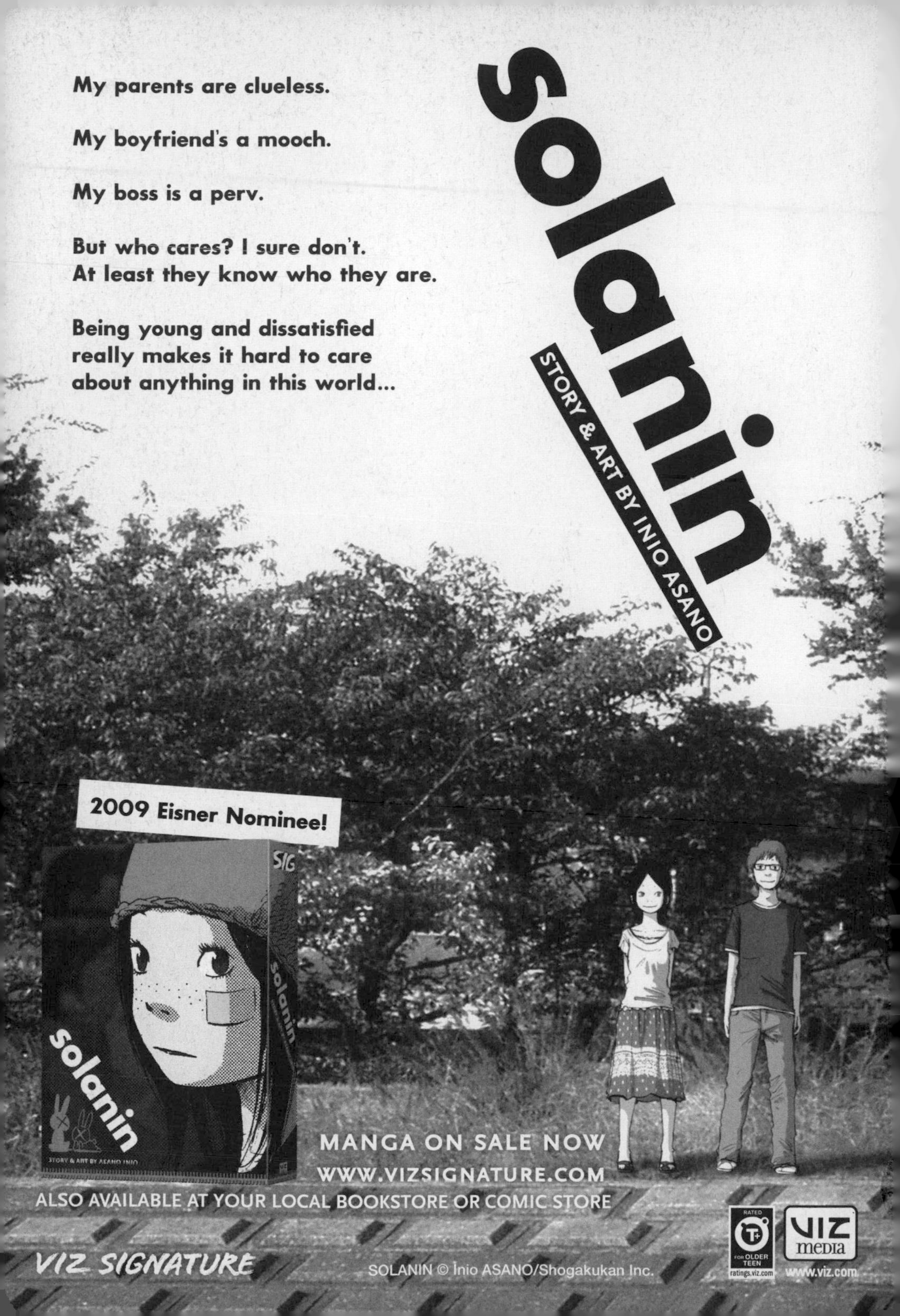
My parents are clueless.
My boyfriend's a mooch.
My boss is a perv.
But who cares? I sure don't.
At least they know who they are.
Being young and dissatisfied really makes it hard to care about anything in this world...
solanin
STORY & ART BY INIO ASANO
2009 Eisner Nominee!
solanin
SIG
solanin
MANGA ON SALE NOW
WWW.VIZSIGNATURE.COM
ALSO AVAILABLE AT YOUR LOCAL BOOKSTORE OR COMIC STORE
RATED T+ FOR OLDER TEEN
ratings.viz.com
VIZ media
www.viz.com
VIZ SIGNATURE
SOLANIN © Inio ASANO/Shogakukan Inc.

Hey! You're Reading in the Wrong Direction!

This is the *end* of this graphic novel!

To properly enjoy this VIZ graphic novel, please turn it around and begin reading from *right to left*. Unlike English, Japanese is read right to left, so Japanese comics are read in reverse order from the way English comics are typically read.

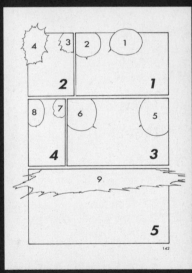

Follow the action this way

This book has been printed in the original Japanese format in order to preserve the orientation of the original artwork. Have fun with it!